STUDIES IN
ICONOLOGY

STUDIES IN
ICONOLOGY

*Humanistic Themes
In the Art of the Renaissance*

BY

ERWIN PANOFSKY

Icon Editions
Harper & Row, Publishers
New York, Evanston, San Francisco, London

This book was originally published in 1939 by Oxford University Press and is here reprinted by arrangement.

First HARPER TORCHBOOK edition published 1962, Benjamin Nelson, editor.

First ICON edition published 1972.

Cover illustration: *The Triumph of Time* by Jacopo Pesellino. (Courtesy of the Isabella Stewart Gardner Museum, Boston, Massachusetts)

STANDARD BOOK NUMBER: 06-430025-0

PREFACE TO THE PAPERBACK EDITION

FACED with the problem of reissuing a book nearly forgotten and entirely out of print, an author finds himself torn between conflicting impulses: either to rewrite the whole thing from beginning to end or not to touch it at all.

Prevented by age and circumstances from adopting the first of these alternatives, yet too much afraid of the Last Judgment to acquiesce in the second, this writer has decided for a compromise. Apart from correcting some palpable errors and misprints, I have left the text unaltered even where it ought to be revised or at least reformulated; but I have tried to encourage the disbelief of the reader by listing a number of books and articles which either appeared after the publication of *Studies in Iconology* or (in two cases) were regrettably overlooked at the time; and by adding, *exigente opportunitate*, a few brief comments of my own. In this way I have both salved my conscience and given, I hope, some help to those who may wish to pursue the subject further.

CHAPTER I (Introductory).

§I: The general validity of the 'iconological' method for the interpretation of Renaissance and Baroque art was challenged by C. Gilbert, 'On Subject and Non-Subject in Renaissance Pictures,' *Art Bulletin*, XXXIV, 1952, p. 202 ss. It is true that 'subject' must not be confused with 'story-telling' and that 'pure' landscape, still-life and genre paintings did exist in the sixteenth century (and achieved tremendous popularity in the seventeenth); but it is equally true that even apparently subjectless productions may convey more than 'meets the eye,' as has been demonstrated, for example, by the recent studies on Velásquez' *Hilanderas* and Vermeer's *Artist in his Studio;** and that, in other cases, an artist's irresolution as to the presentation or even the nature of his theme may reveal a surplus rather than a deficit of interest in subject matter. Only two years ago the classic instance of this kind, Giorgione's *Tempest* (Gilbert, pp. 211-214), was proved susceptible of a fairly convincing or at least debatable interpretation,** and as for the elaborate program underlying Correggio's frescoes in the Camera di San Paolo at Parma, generally supposed to be the product of playful and carefree imagination, I may refer to a recent little book of my own: *The Iconography of Correggio's Camera di San Paolo* (Studies of the Warburg and Courtauld Institutes XXVI) London, 1961.

§II: For the survival and revival of classical mythology in the Middle Ages and the Renaissance, see J. Seznec, *The Survival of the Pagan Gods* (Bollingen Series, XXXVIII, 1953; Harper Torchbook edition, 1961). There is an important review by W. S. Heckscher in *Art Bulletin*, XXXVI, 1954, p. 306 ss. For the mediaeval 'separation between classical motifs invested with a non-classical meaning and classical themes expressed by non-classical figures in a non-classical setting,' cf. E. Panofsky, *Renaissance and Renascences in Western Art*, Stockholm, 1960, particularly pp. 54-103.

p. 20: For the Ottonian Evangelists' portraits and their classical ancestry (Figs. 7-10), cf. W. Weisbach, 'Les Images des Evangélistes dans l'Evangéliaire d'Othon III et leurs rapports avec l'antiquité,' *Gazette des Beaux-Arts*, Series 6, XXI, 1939, p. 131 ss.

p. 23: For more detailed information about the various versions of the

---

* For symbolism in still-life painting, see I. Bergström, *Dutch Still-Life Painting in the Seventeenth Century*, London, n.d. [1956], with interesting Introduction (p. 1 ss.) and exhaustive bibliography (p. 317 ss.).

** E. Battisti, *Rinascimento e Barocco; Saggi*, Rome, 1960, p. 146 ss. For a somewhat analagous case (a composition by Poussin even more drastically altered by the artist than was Giorgione's *Tempest*), see this writer's recent little study, *A Mythological Painting by Poussin in the Nationalmuseum, Stockholm* (Nationalmusei Skriftserie, V, Stockholm, 1960).

Moralized Ovid (French and Latin, in verse and in prose) and the various methods of their illustration, see E. Panofsky, *Renaissance and Renascences in Western Art*, pp. 78-81.

CHAPTER II (The Early History of Man in Two Cycles of Paintings by Piero di Cosimo).

p. 34 ss.: My interpretation of Piero di Cosimo's *Finding of Vulcan* at Hartford (Fig. 17) was attacked by the late R. Langton Douglas (*Piero di Cosimo*, Chicago, 1946, p. 27 ss.), and this attack gave rise to a lively discussion in *Art Bulletin*, XXVIII, 1946, p. 286 ss.; XXIX, 1947, pp. 143 ss., 222 ss., 284.

CHAPTER III (Father Time).

p. 72 s.: For the iconography of Aion, see D. Levi, 'Aion,' *Hesperia*, XIII, 1944, p. 269 ss.

p. 90: The dark-clad figure in the upper left-hand corner of Bronzino's *Exposure of Luxury* (Fig. 66), which I interpreted as a personification of Truth helping Time to lift the veil from the licentious scene, is much more likely to be a personification of Night attempting to obstruct the process of 'unveiling' (personal communication from Professor Walter Friedlaender).

CHAPTER IV (Blind Cupid).

p. 98 (Note carried over from p. 97): Several errors in my description of the Oppian illustrations reproduced in Figs. 93 and 94, caused in part by the unavailability of good photographs of the Marciana manuscript, were corrected in K. Weitzmann's important book, *Greek Mythology in Byzantine Art* (Studies in Manuscript Illumination, IV), Princeton, 1951, p. 123 s.

p. 102 ss.: The iconographical significance of blindness as a symbol of ignorance and other moral and/or intellectual defects has recently

been discussed in an excellent article by W. Déonna, 'La Cécité men-
tale et un motif des stalles de la Cathédrale de St. Pierre à Genève'
(*Zeitschrift für Schweizerische Archäologie und Kunstgeschichte*,
XVIII, 1958, p. 68 ss.).

p. 117: In an article overlooked by me and entitled 'Un Trattato
d'Amore inedito di Fra Guittone d'Arezzo' (*Giornale storico di letteratura Italiana*, CXIX, 1931, p. 49 ss.), F. Egidi demonstrated that
the derogatory description of Love refuted by Francesco Barberino
can be identified: it is a sonnet by Guittone d'Arezzo, where every
detail invested with a positive significance by Barberino bears an
unfavorable, even diabolical implication. While Barberino's optimistic
interpretation is illustrated in the miniature reproduced in Fig. 90,
the frescoes shown in Figs. 88 and 91 would seem directly to reflect
Guittone's poem; it should be remembered, however, that this poem
sums up a tradition which can be traced back to the classics and had
been condensed, and Christianized, in Isidore of Seville's definition of
Love as a 'daemon fornicatonis . . . alatus' (p. 105, Note 31). A versi-
fied and moralized paraphrase of Isidore's description is found among
the poems of Theodulf of Orléans (E. Dümmler, ed., *Poetae Latini
Aevi Carolini*, I, 1881, p. 543 s., No. XLV).

p. 126 s.: The subject of Eros and Anteros has been treated (without
spectacular results) by R. V. Merrill, 'Eros and Anteros' (*Speculum*,
XIX, 1944, p. 265 ss.).

p. 128: The idea of 'Eros *vs.* Anteros' and the related concept of
'Cupid Unblinding Himself' (Fig. 106) seem to have preyed upon
the mind of the Venetian sculptor Nicolò Roccatagliata, nicknamed
'The Master of the Putto.' In one of his charming bronze statuettes
the little putto carries a cock in his left hand (L. Planiszig, *Venezianische Bildhauer der Renaissance*, Vienna, 1921, p. 605, Fig. 669; cf.
our Fig. 98), and in another, which belongs to the same set, he even
wipes his eyes clear (Planiszig, p. 606, Fig. 671).

CHAPTER V (The Neoplatonic Movement in Florence and North Italy).

p. 131 ss.: My brief summary of Marsilio Ficino's system has been justly criticized, in part, in a review by P. O. Kristeller (*Review of Religion*, V, 1940-1941, p.81 ss.); his objections have been taken account of in my more recent *Renaissance and Renascences in Western Art*, p. 182 ss. For more detailed information, cf. Kristeller, *The Philosophy of Marsilio Ficino* (New York, 1943), A. Chastel, *Marsile Ficin et l'art* (Geneva and Lille, 1954); J. C. Nelson, *Renaissance Theory of Love* (New York, 1958).

p. 149, Note 69: For the appearance of a musician in numerous representations of Venus produced by Titian and his followers, see O. Brendel, 'The Interpretation of the Holkham Venus' (*Art Bulletin*, XXVIII, 1946, p. 65 ss.; cf. also the correspondence, *ibid.*, XXIX, 1947, p. 143 ss., 222 s., 284).

p. 150 ss.: As was to be expected, the discussion about the meaning of Titian's *Sacred and Profane Love* (Fig. 108) has been going on since 1939 and will doubtless continue to go on for some time. The literature up to 1948 is conveniently summarized in R. Freyhan, 'The Evolution of the Caritas Figure in the Thirteenth and Fourteenth Centuries' (*Journal of the Warburg and Courtauld Institutes*, XI, 1948, p. 68 ss., particularly p. 85 s.). For the present state of affairs, see E. Wind, *Pagan Mysteries in the Renaissance* (New Haven, 1958, p. 122 ss.); cf. also Guy de Tervarent, *Attributs et symboles dans l'art profane, 1450-1600* (Geneva, 1958-1959, col. 397 s.).

p. 151, lines 5 and 6 from the foot of the page: A number of inaccuracies in the description of the two tapestries in the Musée des Arts Décoratifs (Figs. 116 and 117) has been corrected here on the basis of an excellent article by J. Porcher (originally overlooked): 'Deux Tapisseries à rébus,' *Humanisme et Renaissance*, II, 1934, p. 57 ss.

p. 160 ss.: For Titian's so-called '*Allegory of the Marquis d'Avalos*' (Fig. 118), see Tervarent, *op. cit.*, col. 363 ss.; for Venetian marriage pictures in mythological disguise (such as the painting by Paris Bordone, Fig. 121), see E. Wind, *Bellini's Feast of the Gods* (Cambridge, Mass., 1948, p. 37 s.).

p. 166 ss.: My interpretation of Titian's *Education of Cupid* has been contested by Wind, *Pagan Mysteries in the Renaissance*, p. 76 ss.

CHAPTER VI (The Neoplatonic Movement and Michelangelo).

p. 187 ss.: For Michelangelo's Tomb of Julius II see C. de Tolnay, *Michelangelo*, IV *(The Tomb of Julius II)*, Princeton, 1954, with complete bibliography up to that date; H. von Einem, *Michelangelo*, Stuttgart, 1959, pp. 40 ss., 71 ss., 97 ss., 135 ss.; A. Chastel, *Art et humanisme à Florence au temps de Laurent le Magnifique*, Paris, 1959, p. 459 ss. As for the apes attached to the two *Slaves* in the Louvre, the discrepancy between my and de Tolnay's (p. 98 s.) Neoplatonic interpretation and H. W. Janson's acceptance of Condivi's statement to the effect that the apes symbolize Painting and Sculpture (*Apes and Ape Lore in the Middle Ages and the Renaissance*, Studies of the Warburg Institute, XX, London, 1952, p. 295 ss.) can perhaps be resolved by the assumption that the significance of the *Slaves* (never specifically referred to in the original documents) had undergone a change in Michelangelo's own mind and that this change reflects itself in Condivi's description.

I am, however, still firmly convinced that the first project of the tomb (1505) required a seated and not a recumbent effigy of the Pope (Figs. 131 and 132 of this book as opposed to the reconstruction offered by de Tolnay, Fig. 203, and reproduced, with or without modifications, by Chastel, p. 463, Fig. 9, and von Einem, p. 42, Fig. 6)—only that in my reconstruction the effigy and the two angels supporting it were too large; they have now been reduced to approximately the same scale as the other figures. Both these points—viz., the fact that the effigy showed the Pontiff enthroned but was considerably smaller than I had thought—are demonstrated by a discovery made four years after the publication of *Studies in Iconology:* it has been shown that the blocked-out figure of the Pope, shipped from Carrara to Rome in 1508 and found in Michelangelo's Roman workshop after his death in 1564, was utilized by Nicolas Cordier for a *St. Gregory Enthroned* which can still be seen in S. Gregorio al Cielo (J. Hess, 'Michelangelo and Cordier,' *Burlington Magazine*, LXXXII, 1943, p. 55 ss.). When de Tolnay, p. 15, states that the figure found in Michelangelo's workshop after his death (and, therefore, Cordier's *St. Gregory*) 'must have been' one of the two papal statues (representing Leo X and Clement VII) destined for the Medici Chapel and known to have been quarried and blocked out in 1524, this statement is at variance with the technical and legal circumstances: the marble blocks destined for the Medici tombs were naturally left in Michelangelo's *Florentine* workshop when he left Florence forever in 1534 and were later used for different purposes; whereas the *abbozzo* completed by Cordier was found in Michelangelo's *Roman* workshop.

With reference to the use of the word *bara* in the sense of 'litter' *(una sorte di lettiga)* rather than 'bier,' I am glad to inform those who could not locate the evidence for this usage in the *Vocabulario degli Accademici della Crusca* (de Tolnay, p. 84, Note 7) that the pertinent passages, including one from Machiavelli, can be found in the edition dedicated to Prince Eugene in Vol. I, Venice, 1806, p. 312, and in the current edition (the famous 'Quinta Edizione') in Vol. II, Florence, 1866, p. 57.

p. 199 ss.: For Michelangelo's Medici Chapel, see de Tolnay, *Michelangelo*, III (*The Medici Chapel*), Princeton, 1948, with complete bibliography up to that year; von Einem, *op. cit.*, p. 82 ss. An essentially different, purely dynastic interpretation was proposed by F. Hartt, 'The Meaning of Michelangelo's Medici Chapel' (*Essays in Honor of*

Georg Swarzenski, Chicago, 1957, p. 145 ss.). This interpretation—all the more difficult to accept as it is largely based on the misconstruction of two lines in a poem by Gandolfo Perrino, composed shortly before 1546—will be more fully discussed on another occasion.

p. 211: On account of its whiskers, the animal's head adorning the cash box of Lorenzo of Urbino *(Il Penseroso)* is held by some zoologists to belong to a lynx, and not to a bat (personal communication from Dr. Herbert Friedmann and Professor Edgar Wind). This would not militate against the interpretation here proposed because the sharp-eyed lynx (cf. Cesare Ripa, *Iconologia*, s.v. 'Sensi,' where the lynx is listed as a symbol of the sense of sight) may symbolize parsimoniousness as well as sharp-eyed vigilance (we may remember that the French politely describe a miser as 'un peu regardant'); but it still seems to me and others that the distinctive features of Michelangelo's animal's head, a *mascherone* rather than a naturalistic 'portrait,' suggest a bat rather than a lynx. While it is true that bats have no whiskers, lynxes have sharply pointed ears, comparatively blunt noses and, above all, those large and watchful eyes which are a byword in all languages. The problem has been exhaustively dealt with by O. Cederlöf, 'Fladdermusen', *Symbolister*, I (*Tidskrift för Konstvetenskap*, XXX, Malmö, 1957, p. 89 ss., particularly pp. 99-115).

p. 212 ss.: For the Cavalieri drawings and their relatives (Figs. 158, 159, 162-167), see de Tolnay, *op. cit.*, III, pp. 111 ss., 199 s., 220 s., and V *(The Final Period)*, Princeton, 1960, p. 181 s.; A.E. Popham and J. Wilde, *The Italian Drawings of the XV and XVI Centuries in the Collection of His Majesty the King at Windsor Castle*, London, 1949, p. 265 ss.; von Einem, *op. cit.*, p. 107 ss.; L. Goldscheider, *Michelangelo's Drawings*, London, 1951, Nos. 92-97; L. Dussler, *Die Zeichnungen des Michelangelo, Kritischer Katalog*, Berlin, 1959, Nos. 117,

234, 238, 241, 365, 589, 721. Since an interpretation of *The Dream* (our Fig. 167; cf. also Tervarent, *op. cit.*, col. 263) as Hypnos Aroused by Iris (A. Pigler, 'The Importance of Iconographical Exactitude,' *Art Bulletin*, XXI, 1939, p. 228 ss.) was proved untenable (*ibid.*, p. 402), a certain amount of unanimity as to the meaning of all these compositions seems to have been reached; B.D. Kirschenbaum, Reflections on Michelangelo's Drawings for Cavaliere, *Gazette des Beaux-Arts*, Series 6, XXXVIII, 1951, p. 99 ss. (published as late as November 1960), differs in shades of meaning rather than in substance.

As I learn from A. van de Put, 'Two Drawings of the Fêtes at Binche for Charles V and Philip (II) 1549,' *Journal of the Warburg and Courtauld Institutes*, III, 1939-40, p. 49 ss., particularly p. 52, the erroneous designation of Titian's *Tityus* (Fig. 160) as *Prometheus* can be traced back to Juan C. Calvete de Estrella, writing as early as about 1550, and was duly rejected by P. Beroqui, 'Tiziano en el Museo del Prado,' *Boletín de la Sociedad Española de Excursiones*, XXXIV, 1926, p. 247 ss. Contrary to van de Put, however, Beroqui does not accept but explicitly dissociates himself from the opinion that all the four paintings formerly adorning the '*pieza de las Furias*' in the Palace at Madrid were destroyed in the notorious fire of 1734 and that the two pictures still preserved in the Prado—the *Tityus* and the *Sisyphus*—were mere copies supposedly executed by Alonso Sanchez Coello (d. 1590). This opinion (abandoned, incidentally, also in the fourth edition of the *Klassiker der Kunst* volume, the second edition of which is cited by van de Put) is not supported by the documents in which the *Tityus* and the *Sisyphus*, unlike the *Tantalus* and the *Ixion*, are referred to not as destroyed but only as 'badly damaged' *(maltratado)*. H. Tietze, *Tizian*, Vienna, 1936, I, p. 188, II, p. 298, therefore includes and illustrates the two Prado paintings with the reservation that their present condition makes it impossible to ascertain their status.

The original of Rubens' *Prometheus,* sold by the master himself to Sir Dudley Carleton in 1618 with the remark that the eagle was painted by Frans Snyders, came to light in about 1950 and is now owned by the Philadelphia Museum of Art; see F. Kimball, 'Rubens' *Prometheus,' Burlington Magazine,* XCIV, 1952, p. 67 f. In Fig. 161 a photograph of the splendid original, kindly supplied by Director Henri Marceau, has therefore been substituted for a photograph of the feeble replica which had to be reproduced in 1939.

Appendix

p. 231 s.: As far as Michelangelo's *Victory* (Fig. 173) is concerned, my objections to J. Wilde's hypothesis—according to which the clay model in the Casa Buonarroti (Fig. 172) was made in preparation for the companion piece of this group rather than for the *Hercules Conquering Cacus* on the Piazza della Signoria—were sustained by de Tolnay (*op. cit.,* III, pp. 98 ss., 183 ss.) but were unable to convince Dr. Wilde; see J. Wilde, *Michelangelo's 'Victory'* (The Charlton Lectures on Art Delivered at Kings College in the University of Durham, Newcastle upon Tyne, London, 1954, particularly p. 18 ss.). *Et adhuc sub judice lis est.*

These bibliographical hints do not, of course, aim at completeness. Their chief purpose is to emphasize the fact that *Studies in Iconology* was written more than two decades ago. It must be left to the interested reader to look for contributions here omitted and, above all, to use his own judgment.

ERWIN PANOFSKY

Princeton
January, 1962

PREFACE

THE six *Mary Flexner Lectures** printed in this volume are, in part, not new. The introductory chapter synthesizes the revised content of a methodological article published by the writer in 1932[1] with a study on classical mythology in mediaeval art published in the following year by the writer in collaboration with Dr.F.Saxl;[2] the content of the lecture on Father Time is, in part, identical with that of a chapter in the book Melancholia, likewise composed by the writer and Dr.Saxl;[3] and the lecture on Piero di Cosimo unites two articles recently published in the Journal of the Warburg Institute[4] and in the Worcester Museum Annual.[5]*

An excuse for this may be found in the following considerations: the methodological article has appeared, and the Melancholia will appear, in German, and both may not be easily accessible to English and American readers. The ideas set forth in the study on classical mythology in the Middle Ages are so important for the understanding of the whole series of lectures that it seemed advisable to repeat them here. And the two articles on Piero di Cosimo had to be published, for practical reasons, in two different places, and out of their connection with the other studies.

In a wider sense, Dr.Saxl's share in this little book is even greater. The methods which the writer has tried to apply are based on what he and Dr.Saxl have learned together from the late Professor A.Warburg, and

---

* The lectures were repeated, with kind permission of President M.E.Park of Bryn Mawr College and of the Institute for Advanced Study at Princeton, under the auspices of the Department of Art and Archaeology of Princeton University.
1. *Bibl.*248.
2. *Bibl.*238.
3. *Bibl.*253, second edition of *Bibl.*252, in print.
4. *Bibl.*239.
5. *Bibl.*247.

have endeavoured to practise in many years of personal collaboration. Even after this personal collaboration has come to an end, the writer finds it hard to separate the present from the past, 'nostrasque domos, ut et ante, frequentat.'

The writer wishes to thank: the editors of the Journal of the Warburg Institute *and Director F.H.Taylor of the Worcester Art Museum for permission to reprint the articles on Piero di Cosimo; Messrs. A.E. Austin, Jr., O. Brendel, S.C. Chew, Frhr. H. von Erffa, A.M. Friend, Jr., G. Gerola, H. Gray, T.M. Greene, F.R.B. Godolphin, R. Goldwater, K. Lehmann-Hartleben, H. Janson, R. Offner, A. Panella, K.Th. Parker, J. Rosenberg, M. Schapiro, A. Scharf, O. Strunk, H. Swarzenski, B.L. Ullman, K. Weitzmann, H.E. Wethey, E.T. De Wald, Sir Robert Witt and R. Wittkower, and the Misses M. Bieber, H. Franc, B. da Costa Greene and L.R. Taylor for information, photographs and helpful suggestions; Mrs. Eleanor C. Marquand for her unfailing assistance in botanical matters; Miss Margot Cutter for preparing the index and the bibliography; Messrs. P. Underwood and A.M. Wicks for executing the drawings figs. 131, 132, 136, 137 and the diagram; and Miss M. Scolari for her most helpful participation in the wording of the English text.*

In addition his warmest thanks are due to his friends at Bryn Mawr, both members of the Faculty and students, who by their hospitality and responsiveness have made the delivery of these lectures a pleasure for the lecturer; and to Mr. Bernard Flexner, whose kind and generous interest has made it possible to publish them in their present form.

THE MARY FLEXNER LECTURESHIP

The Mary Flexner Lectureship was established February 17, 1928, at Bryn Mawr College, by Bernard Flexner, in honour of his sister, Mary Flexner, a graduate of the College. An adequate endowment was provided by the gift, the income to be used annually or at longer intervals at the discretion of the Directors of the College as an honorarium to be given to an American or foreign scholar, highly distinguished in the field of the 'Humanities,' using the term 'Humanities' in its broadest connotation. The lecturers have taken up residence at Bryn Mawr for a six weeks' period and besides delivering the series of public lectures have taught graduate and undergraduate students. The object of the Mary Flexner Lectureship is to bring to the College scholars of distinction, who will be a stimulus to the faculty and students, and who will·contribute to the maintenance of those ideals and standards of scholarship which will bring increasing honour to the College. The gift provides that the Mary Flexner Lectures shall be published. The present volume is the seventh in the series.

CONTENTS

LIST OF PLATES AND ILLUSTRATIONS

LIST OF PLATES

LIST OF PLATES

PLATE XIX

33. *Piero di Cosimo, The Myth of Prometheus. Strasburg, Museum*

PLATE XX

34. *Niccolò Soggi (?), Hercules at the Cross Roads. Berlin, Schlossmuseum*

PLATE XXI

35. *Kairos. Classical Relief, Turin, Museum*

PLATE XXII

36. *Phanes. Classical Relief, Modena, Museum*

37. *Girolamo Olgiati, Allegory of Alchemy. Engraving, dated 1569*

PLATE XXIII

38. *Saturn. Pompeian Mural from the Casa dei Dioscuri, Naples, Museo Nazionale*

39. *Saturn. From the Chronograph of 354 (Renaissance copy), Rome, Vatican Library*

40. *Saturn and Jupiter. From Hrabanus Maurus, De Universo, Montecassino, 11th century*

41. *Saturn and Jupiter. From Hrabanus Maurus, De Universo, Rome, Vatican Library, Cod.Pal.lat.291, 15th century*

PLATE LIII

PLATE LIV

PLATE LV

PLATE LXXIX

PLATE LXXX

PLATE LXXXI

PLATE LXXXII

LIST OF PLATES

STUDIES IN
ICONOLOGY

STUDIES IN ICONOLOGY

I. INTRODUCTORY

§ I

ICONOGRAPHY is that branch of the history of art which concerns itself with the subject matter or meaning of works of art, as opposed to their form. Let us, then, try to define the distinction between *subject matter* or *meaning* on the one hand, and *form* on the other.

When an acquaintance greets me on the street by removing his hat, what I see from a *formal* point of view is nothing but the change of certain details within a configuration forming part of the general pattern of colour, lines and volumes which constitutes my world of vision. When I identify, as I automatically do, this configuration as an *object* (gentleman), and the change of detail as an *event* (hat-removing), I have already overstepped the limits of purely *formal* perception and entered a first sphere of *subject matter* or *meaning*. The meaning thus perceived is of an elementary and easily understandable nature, and we shall call it the *factual meaning*; it is apprehended by simply identifying certain visible forms with certain objects known to me from practical experience, and by identifying the change in their relations with certain actions or events.

Now the objects and events thus identified will naturally produce a certain reaction within myself. From the way my acquaintance performs his action I may be able to sense whether he is in a good or bad humour, and whether his feelings towards me are indifferent, friendly or hostile. These psychological nuances will invest the gestures of my acquaintance with a further meaning which we shall call *expressional*. It differs from the *factual* one in that it is apprehended, not by simple identification, but by 'empathy.' To understand it, I need a certain sensitivity, but this sensitivity is still part

3

of my practical experience, that is, of my every-day familiarity with objects and events. Therefore both the *factual* and the *expressional meaning* may be classified together: they constitute the class of *primary* or *natural* meanings.

However, my realization that the lifting of the hat stands for a greeting belongs in an altogether different realm of interpretation. This form of salute is peculiar to the western world and is a residue of mediaeval chivalry: armed men used to remove their helmets to make clear their peaceful intentions and their confidence in the peaceful intentions of others. Neither an Australian bushman nor an ancient Greek could be expected to realize that the lifting of a hat is not only a practical event with certain expressional connotations, but also a sign of politeness. To understand this significance of the gentleman's action I must not only be familiar with the practical world of objects and events, but also with the more-than-practical world of customs and cultural traditions peculiar to a certain civilization. Conversely, my acquaintance could not feel impelled to greet me by removing his hat were he not conscious of the significance of this feat. As for the expressional connotations which accompany his action, he may or may not be conscious of them. Therefore, when I interpret the removal of a hat as a polite greeting, I recognize in it a meaning which may be called *secondary* or *conventional*; it differs from the *primary* or *natural* one in that it is intelligible instead of being sensible, and in that it has been consciously imparted to the practical action by which it is conveyed.

And finally: besides constituting a natural event in space and time, besides naturally indicating moods or feelings, besides conveying a conventional greeting, the action of my acquaintance can reveal to an experienced observer all that goes to make up his 'personality.' This personality is conditioned by his being a man of the twentieth century, by his national, social and educational background, by the previous history of his life and by his present surroundings, but it is also distinguished by an individual manner of viewing things and reacting to the world which, if rationalized, would have

4

to be called a philosophy. In the isolated action of a polite greeting all these factors do not manifest themselves comprehensively, but nevertheless symptomatically. We could not construct a mental portrait of the man on the basis of this single action, but only by co-ordinating a large number of similar observations and by interpreting them in connection with our general information as to the gentleman's period, nationality, class, intellectual traditions and so forth. Yet all the qualities which this mental portrait would show explicitly are implicitly inherent in every single action, so that, conversely, every single action can be interpreted in the light of those qualities.

The meaning thus discovered may be called the *intrinsic meaning* or *content*; it is essential where the two other kinds of meaning, the *primary* or *natural* and the *secondary* or *conventional*, are phenomenal. It may be defined as a unifying principle which underlies and explains both the visible event and its intelligible significance, and which determines even the form in which the visible event takes shape. This *intrinsic meaning* or *content* is, of course, as much above the sphere of conscious volitions as the *expressional* meaning is beneath this sphere.

Transferring the results of this analysis from every-day life to a work of art, we can distinguish in its subject matter or meaning the same three strata:

1—PRIMARY OR NATURAL SUBJECT MATTER, subdivided into FACTUAL and EXPRESSIONAL. It is apprehended by identifying pure *forms*, that is: certain configurations of line and colour, or certain peculiarly shaped lumps of bronze or stone, as representations of natural *objects* such as human beings, animals, plants, houses, tools and so forth; by identifying their mutual relations as *events*; and by perceiving such *expressional* qualities as the mournful character of a pose or gesture, or the homelike and peaceful atmosphere of an interior. The world of pure *forms* thus recognized as carriers of *primary* or *natural meanings* may be called the world of artistic *motifs*. An enumeration of these motifs would be a *pre-iconographical* description of the work of art.

5

2—SECONDARY OR CONVENTIONAL SUBJECT MATTER. It is apprehended by realizing that a male figure with a knife represents St. Bartholomew, that a female figure with a peach in her hand is a personification of Veracity, that a group of figures seated at a dinner table in a certain arrangement and in certain poses represents the Last Supper, or that two figures fighting each other in a certain manner represent the Combat of Vice and Virtue. In doing this we connect artistic *motifs* and combinations of artistic *motifs* (*compositions*) with *themes* or *concepts*. *Motifs* thus recognized as carriers of a *secondary* or *conventional* meaning may be called *images*, and combinations of images are what the ancient theorists of art called '*invenzioni*;' we are wont to call them *stories* and *allegories*.[1] The identification of such *images*, *stories* and *allegories* is the domain of iconography in the narrower sense of the word. In fact, when we loosely speak of '*subject matter* as opposed to *form*' we chiefly mean the sphere of *secondary* or *conventional* subject matter, viz. the world of specific *themes* or *concepts* manifested in *images*, *stories* and *allegories*, as opposed to the sphere of *primary* or *natural subject matter* manifested in artistic *motifs*. 'Formal analysis' in Wölfflin's sense is largely an analysis of motifs and combinations of motifs (compositions); for a formal analysis in the

1. *Images* conveying the idea, not of concrete and individual *persons* or *objects* (such as St. Bartholomew, Venus, Mrs. Jones, or Windsor Castle), but of abstract and general notions such as Faith, Luxury, Wisdom etc., are called either *personifications* or *symbols* (not in the Cassirerian, but in the ordinary sense, e.g. the Cross, or the Tower of Chastity). Thus *allegories*, as opposed to stories, may be defined as combinations of *personifications* and/or *symbols*. There are, of course many intermediary possibilities. A person A. may be portrayed in the guise of the person B. (Bronzino's Andrea Doria as Neptune; Dürer's Lucas Paumgartner as St. George), or in the customary array of a personification (Joshua Reynolds's Mrs. Stanhope as 'Contemplation'); portrayals of concrete and individual *persons*, both human or mythological, may be combined with personifications, as is the case in countless representations of a eulogistic character. A story may convey, in addition, an *allegorical* idea, as is the case with the illustrations of the *Ovide Moralisé*, or may be conceived as the 'prefiguration' of another story, as in the *Biblia Pauperum* or in the *Speculum Humanae Salvationis*. Such *superimposed* meanings either do not enter into the *content* of the work at all, as is the case with the *Ovide Moralisé* illustrations which are visually indistinguishable from non-allegorical miniatures illustrating the same Ovidian subjects; or they cause an ambiguity of *content*, which can, however, be overcome or even turned into an added value if the conflicting ingredients are molten in the heat of a fervent artistic temperament as in Rubens' 'Galerie de Médicis.'

strict sense of the word would even have to avoid such expressions as 'man,' 'horse,' or 'column,' let alone such evaluations as 'the ugly triangle between the legs of Michelangelo's David' or 'the admirable clarification of the joints in a human body.' It is obvious that a correct *iconographical analysis in the narrower sense* presupposes a correct identification of the *motifs*. If the knife that enables us to identify a St. Bartholomew is not a knife but a cork-screw, the figure is not a St. Bartholomew. Furthermore it is important to note that the statement 'this figure is an image of St. Bartholomew' implies the conscious intention of the artist to represent St. Bartholomew, while the expressional qualities of the figure may well be unintentional.

3—INTRINSIC MEANING OR CONTENT. It is apprehended by ascertaining those underlying principles which reveal the basic attitude of a nation, a period, a class, a religious or philosophical persuasion—unconsciously qualified by one personality and condensed into one work. Needless to say, these principles are manifested by, and therefore throw light on, both 'compositional methods' and 'iconographical significance.' In the 14th and 15th centuries for instance (the earliest example can be dated around 1310), the traditional type of the Nativity with the Virgin Mary reclining in bed or on a couch was frequently replaced by a new one which shows the Virgin kneeling before the Child in adoration. From a compositional point of view this change means, roughly speaking, the substitution of a triangular scheme for a rectangular one; from an iconographical point of view in the narrower sense of the term, it means the introduction of a new theme textually formulated by such writers as Pseudo-Bonaventura and St. Bridget. But at the same time it reveals a new emotional attitude peculiar to the later phases of the Middle Ages. A really exhaustive interpretation of the intrinsic meaning or content might even show that the technical procedures characteristic of a certain country, period, or artist, for instance Michelangelo's preference for sculpture in stone

7

instead of in bronze, or the peculiar use of hatchings in his drawings, are symptomatic of the same basic attitude that is discernible in all the other specific qualities of his style. In thus conceiving of pure forms, motifs, images, stories and allegories as manifestations of underlying principles, we interpret all these elements as what Ernst Cassirer has called *'symbolical' values*. As long as we limit ourselves to stating that Leonardo da Vinci's famous fresco shows a group of thirteen men around a dinner table, and that this group of men represents the Last Supper, we deal with the work of art as such, and we interpret its compositional and iconographical features as its own properties or qualifications. But when we try to understand it as a document of Leonardo's personality, or of the civilization of the Italian High Renaissance, or of a peculiar religious attitude, we deal with the work of art as a symptom of something else which expresses itself in a countless variety of other symptoms, and we interpret its compositional and iconographical features as more particularized evidence of this 'something else.' The discovery and interpretation of these *'symbolical' values* (which are generally unknown to the artist himself and may even emphatically differ from what he consciously intended to express) is the object of what we may call *iconography in a deeper sense*: of a method of interpretation which arises as a synthesis rather than as an analysis. And as the correct identification of the *motifs* is the prerequisite of a correct *iconographical analysis in the narrower sense*, the correct analysis of *images, stories* and *allegories* is the prerequisite of a correct *iconographical interpretation in a deeper sense*,—unless we deal with such works of art in which the whole sphere of secondary or conventional subject matter is eliminated, and a direct transition from *motifs* to *content* is striven for, as is the case with European landscape painting, still-life and genre; that is, on the whole, with exceptional phenomena, which mark the later, over-sophisticated phases of a long development.

Now, how do we arrive at a correct *pre-iconographical description*, and at a correct *iconographical analysis in the narrower sense*, with the ultimate goal of penetrating into the *intrinsic meaning or content*?

In the case of a *pre-iconographical description*, which keeps within the limits of the world of *motifs*, the matter seems simple enough. The objects and events whose representation by lines, colours and volumes constitutes the world of *motifs* can be identified, as we have seen, on the basis of our practical experience. Everybody can recognize the shape and behaviour of human beings, animals and plants, and everybody can tell an angry face from a jovial one. It is, of course, possible that in a given case the range of our personal experience is not wide enough, for instance when we find ourselves confronted with the representation of an obsolete or unfamiliar tool, or with the representation of a plant or animal unknown to us. In such cases we have to widen the range of our practical experience by consulting a book or an expert, but we do not leave the sphere of practical experience as such.

Yet even in this sphere we encounter a peculiar problem. Setting aside the fact that the objects, events and expressions depicted in a work of art may be unrecognizable owing to the incompetence or malice aforethought of the artist, it is, on principle, impossible to arrive at a correct pre-iconographical description, or identification of primary subject matter, by indiscriminately applying our practical experience to the work of art. Our practical experience is indispensable, as well as sufficient, as material for a pre-iconographical description, but it does not guarantee its correctness.

A pre-iconographical description of Roger van der Weyden's Three Magi in the Museum of Berlin (*fig.*1) would, of course, have to avoid such terms as 'Magi,' 'Infant Jesus' etc. But it would have to mention that the apparition of a small child is seen in the sky. How do we know that this child is meant to be an apparition? That it is surrounded with a halo of golden rays would not be sufficient proof of this assumption, for similar halos can often be observed in representations of the Nativity where the Infant Jesus is real. That the child in Roger's picture is meant to be an apparition can only be deduced from the additional fact that he hovers in mid-air. But how do we know that he hovers in mid-air? His pose would be no different were he seated on a pillow on the ground; in fact it is highly probable that Roger used for his painting a drawing from life of a child seated on a pillow. The only valid reason for our assumption that the child in the Berlin picture is meant to be an apparition is the fact that he is depicted in space with no visible means of support.

But we can adduce hundreds of representations in which human beings, animals and inanimate objects seem to hang loose in space in violation of the law of gravity, without thereby pretending to be apparitions. For instance, in a miniature in the 'Gospels of Otto III' in the Staats-Bibliothek of Munich, a whole city is represented in the centre of an empty space while the figures taking part in the action stand on solid ground (*fig.* 2).[2] An inexperienced observer may well assume that the town is meant to be suspended in mid-air by some sort of magic. Yet in this case the lack of support does not imply a miraculous invalidation of the laws of nature. The city is the real city of Nain where the resurrection of the youth took place. In a miniature of around 1000 this empty space does not count as a real three-dimensional medium, as it does in a more realistic period, but just as an abstract, unreal background. The curious semicircular shape of what should be the base line of the towers bears witness to the fact that, in the more realistic prototype of our miniature, the town had been situated on a hilly terrain, but was taken over into a representation in which space has ceased to be thought of in terms of perspective realism. The unsupported figure in the van der Weyden picture counts as an apparition, while the floating city in the Ottonian miniature has no miraculous connotation. These contrasting interpretations are suggested to us by the 'realistic' qualities of the painting and the 'unrealistic' qualities of the miniature. But

2. G.Leidinger, *Bibl.*190, PL.36.

that we grasp these qualities in the fraction of a second and almost automatically, must not induce us to believe that we could ever give a correct pre-iconographical description of a work of art without having divined, as it were, its historical '*locus*.' While we believe ourselves to identify the motifs on the basis of our practical experience pure and simple, we really read 'what we see' according to the manner in which *objects* and *events* were expressed by *forms under varying historical conditions*. In doing this, we subject our practical experience to a controlling principle which can be called the *history of style*.[3]

Iconographical analysis, dealing with *images*, *stories* and *allegories* instead of with *motifs*, presupposes, of course, much more than that familiarity with objects and events which we acquire by practical experience. It presupposes a familiarity with specific *themes* or *concepts* as transmitted through literary sources, whether acquired by purposeful reading or by oral tradition. Our Australian bushman would be unable to recognize the subject of a Last Supper; to him, it would only convey the idea of an excited dinner party. To understand the iconographical meaning of the picture he would have to familiarize himself with the content of the Gospels. When it comes to representations of *themes* other than biblical stories or scenes from history and mythology which happen to be known to the average 'educated person,' all of us are Australian bushmen. In such cases we, too, must try to

---

3. To control the interpretation of an individual work of art by a 'history of style' which in turn can only be built up by interpreting individual works, may look like a vicious circle. It is, indeed, a circle, though not a vicious, but a methodical one (cf.E.Wind, *Bibl.*407; *idem*, *Bibl.*408). Whether we deal with historical or natural phenomena, the individual observation assumes the character of a 'fact' only when it can be related to other, analogous observations in such a way that the whole series 'makes sense.' This 'sense' is, therefore, fully capable of being applied, as a control, to the interpretation of a new individual observation within the same range of phenomena. If, however, this new individual observation definitely refuses to be interpreted according to the 'sense' of the series, and if an error proves to be impossible, the 'sense' of the series will have to be re-formulated to include the new individual observation. This *circulus methodicus* applies, of course, not only to the relationship between the interpretation of *motifs* and the history of *style*, but also to the relationship between the interpretation of *images*, *stories* and *allegories* and the history of *types*, and to the relationship between the interpretation of *intrinsic meanings* and the history of *cultural symptoms* in general.

familiarize ourselves with what the authors of those representations had read or otherwise knew. But again, while an acquaintance with specific *themes* and *concepts* transmitted through literary sources is indispensable and sufficient material for an *iconographical analysis*, it does not guarantee its correctness. It is just as impossible for us to give a correct *iconographical analysis* by indiscriminately applying our literary knowledge to the motifs, as it is for us to give a correct *pre-iconographical description* by indiscriminately applying our practical experience to the *forms*.

A picture by the Venetian seventeenth-century painter Francesco Maffei, representing a handsome young woman with a sword in her right hand, and in her left a charger on which rests the head of a beheaded man (*fig.*3), has been published as a portrayal of Salome with the head of John the Baptist.[4] In fact the Bible states that the head of St. John the Baptist was brought to Salome on a charger. But what about the sword? Salome did not decapitate St. John the Baptist with her own hands. Now the Bible tells us about another handsome woman in connection with the decapitation of a man, namely Judith. In this case the situation is exactly reversed. The sword would be correct because Judith beheaded Holofernes with her own hand, but the charger would not agree with the Judith theme because the text explicitly states that the head of Holofernes was put into a sack. Thus we have two literary sources applicable to our picture with equal right and equal inconsistency. If we should interpret it as a portrayal of Salome the text would account for the charger, but not for the sword; if we should interpret it as a portrayal of Judith the text would account for the sword, but not for the charger. We should be entirely at a loss did we depend on the literary sources alone. Fortunately we do not. As we could correct and control our practical experience by inquiring into the manner in which, under varying historical conditions, *objects* and *events* were expressed by *forms*, viz., into the history of *style*, just so can we correct and control our knowledge of literary sources by inquiring into the manner in which, under

4. G.Fiocco, *Bibl.*92, PL.29.

varying historical conditions, specific *themes* or *concepts* were expressed by *objects* and *events*, viz., into the history of *types*.

In the case at hand we shall have to ask whether there were, before Francesco Maffei painted his picture, any unquestionable portrayals of Judith (unquestionable because they would include, for instance, Judith's maid) with unjustified chargers; or any unquestionable portrayals of Salome (unquestionable because they would include, for instance, Salome's parents) with unjustified swords. And lo! while we cannot adduce a single Salome with a sword, we encounter, in Germany and North Italy, several sixteenth-century paintings depicting Judith with a charger;[5] there was a *type* of 'Judith with a charger,' but there was no *type* of 'Salome with a sword.' From this we can safely conclude that Maffei's picture, too, represents Judith, and not, as has been assumed, Salome.

We may further ask why artists felt entitled to transfer the motif of the charger from Salome to Judith, but not the motif of the sword from Judith to Salome. This question can be answered, again by inquiring into the history of *types*, with two reasons. One reason is that the sword was an established and honorific attribute of Judith, of many martyrs, and of such Virtues as Justice, Fortitude etc.; thus it could not be transferred with propriety to a lascivious girl. The other reason is that during the fourteenth and fifteenth centuries the charger with the head of St. John the Baptist had become an isolated devotional image (*Andachtsbild*) especially popular in the northern countries and in North Italy (*fig.4*); it had been singled out from a representation of the Salome story in much the same way as the group of St. John the Evangelist resting on the bosom of the Lord

---

5. One of the North Italian pictures is ascribed to Romanino, and is preserved in the Berlin Museum, where it was formerly listed as 'Salome' in spite of the maid, a sleeping soldier, and the city of Jerusalem in the background (no.155); another is ascribed to Romanino's pupil Francesco Prato da Caravaggio (quoted in the Berlin Catalogue), and a third is by Bernardo Strozzi who was a native of Genoa, but active at Venice about the same time as Francesco Maffei. It is very possible that the type of 'Judith with a charger' originated in Germany. One of the earliest known instances (by an anonymous master of around 1530 related to Hans Baldung Grien) has recently been published by G.Poensgen, *Bibl.*270.

had come to be singled out from the Last Supper, or the Virgin in childbed from the Nativity. The existence of this devotional image established a fixed association between the idea of the head of a beheaded man and the idea of a charger, and thus the motif of a charger could more easily be substituted for the motif of a sack in an image of Judith, than the motif of a sword could have penetrated into an image of Salome.

The interpretation of the *intrinsic meaning or content*, dealing with what we have termed '*symbolical*' *values* instead of with *images, stories* and *allegories*, requires something more than a familiarity with specific *themes* or *concepts* as transmitted through literary sources. When we wish to get hold of those basic principles which underlie the choice and presentation of *motifs*, as well as the production and interpretation of *images, stories* and *allegories*, and which give meaning even to the formal arrangements and technical procedures employed, we cannot hope to find an individual text which would fit those basic principles as John xiii, 21ss. fits the iconography of the Last Supper. To grasp these principles we need a mental faculty com-

OBJECT OF INTERPRETATION	ACT OF INTERPRETATION
I—*Primary* or *natural* subject matter— (A) factual, (B) expressional—, constituting the world of artistic motifs.	*Pre-iconographical description* (and pseudo-formal analysis).
II—*Secondary* or *conventional* subject matter, constituting the world of *images, stories* and *allegories*.	*Iconographical analysis* in the narrower sense of the word.
III—*Intrinsic meaning* or *content*, constituting the world of '*symbolical*' *values*.	*Iconographical interpretation* in a deeper sense (*Iconographical synthesis*).

parable to that of a diagnostician,—a faculty which I cannot describe better than by the rather discredited term *'synthetic intuition,'* and which may be better developed in a talented layman than in an erudite scholar.

However, the more subjective and irrational this source of interpretation (for every intuitive approach will be conditioned by the interpreter's psychology and 'Weltanschauung'), the more necessary the application of those correctives and controls which proved indispensable where only an *iconographical analysis in the narrower sense,* or even a mere *pre-iconographical description* was concerned. When even our practical experience and our knowledge of literary sources may mislead us if indiscriminately applied to works of art, how much more dangerous would it be to trust our intuition pure and simple! Thus, as our practical experience had to be controlled by an insight into the manner in which, under varying historical conditions, *objects* and *events* were expressed by *forms* (history of *style*); and as our knowledge of literary sources had to be controlled by an insight into the manner in which, under varying historical conditions, specific *themes* and

EQUIPMENT FOR INTERPRETATION	CONTROLLING PRINCIPLE OF INTERPRETATION	
Practical experience (familiarity with *objects* and *events*).	History of *style* (insight into the manner in which, under varying historical conditions, *objects* and *events* were expressed by *forms*).	
Knowledge of literary sources (familiarity with specific *themes* and *concepts*).	History of *types* (insight into the manner in which, under varying historical conditions, specific *themes* or *concepts* were expressed by *objects* and *events*).	HISTORY OF TRADITION
Synthetic *intuition* (familiarity with the *essential tendencies of the human mind*), conditioned by personal psychology and *'Weltanschauung.'*	History of *cultural symptoms* or *'symbols'* in general (insight into the manner in which, under varying historical conditions, *essential tendencies of the human mind* were expressed by specific *themes* and *concepts*).	

15

concepts were expressed by *objects* and *events* (history of *types*); just so, or even more so, has our synthetic intuition to be controlled by an insight into the manner in which, under varying historical conditions, the *general and essential tendencies of the human mind* were expressed by specific *themes* and *concepts*. This means what may be called a history of *cultural symptoms*—or *'symbols'* in Ernst Cassirer's sense—in general. The art-historian will have to check what he thinks is the *intrinsic meaning* of the work, or group of works, to which he devotes his attention, against what he thinks is the *intrinsic meaning* of as many other documents of civilization historically related to that work or group of works, as he can master: of documents bearing witness to the political, poetical, religious, philosophical, and social tendencies of the personality, period or country under investigation. Needless to say that, conversely, the historian of political life, poetry, religion, philosophy, and social situations should make an analogous use of works of art. It is in the search for *intrinsic meanings* or *content* that the various humanistic disciplines meet on a common plane instead of serving as handmaidens to each other.

In conclusion: when we wish to express ourselves very strictly (which is of course not always necessary in our normal talk or writing, where the general context throws light on the meaning of our words), we have to distinguish between *three strata of subject matter or meaning*, the lowest of which is commonly confused with form, and the second of which is the special province of iconography in the narrower sense. In whichever stratum we move, our identifications and interpretations will depend on our subjective equipment, and for this very reason will have to be corrected and controlled by an insight into historical processes the sum total of which may be called *tradition*.

I have summarized in a synoptical table what I have tried to make clear thus far. But we must bear in mind that the neatly differentiated categories, which in this synoptical table seem to indicate three independent spheres of meaning, refer in reality to aspects of one phenomenon, namely, the work

16

of art as a whole. So that, in actual work, the methods of approach which here appear as three unrelated operations of research merge with each other into one organic and indivisible process.

§ II

TURNING now from the problems of iconography in general to the problems of Renaissance iconography in particular, we shall naturally be most interested in that phenomenon from which the very name of the Renaissance is derived: the rebirth of classical antiquity.

The earlier Italian writers about the history of art, such as Lorenzo Ghiberti, Leone Battista Alberti and especially Giorgio Vasari, thought that classical art was overthrown at the beginning of the Christian era, and that it did not revive until it served as the foundation of the Renaissance style. The reasons for this overthrow, as those writers saw it, were the invasions of barbarous races and the hostility of early Christian priests and scholars.

In thinking as they did the early writers were both right and wrong. They were wrong in so far as there had not been a complete break of tradition during the Middle Ages. Classical conceptions, literary, philosophical, scientific and artistic, had survived throughout the centuries, particularly after they had been deliberately revived under Charlemagne and his followers. The early writers were, however, right in so far as the general attitude towards antiquity was fundamentally changed when the Renaissance movement set in.

The Middle Ages were by no means blind to the visual values of classical art, and they were deeply interested in the intellectual and poetic values of classical literature. But it is significant that, just at the height of the mediaeval period (thirteenth and fourteenth centuries), classical *motifs* were not used for the representation of classical *themes* while, conversely, classical *themes* were not expressed by classical *motifs*.

For instance, on the façade of St. Mark's in Venice can be seen two large reliefs of equal size, one a Roman work of the third century A.D., the other executed in Venice almost exactly one thousand years later (*figs.5, 6*).[6]

6. Illustrated in *Bibl.*238, p.231.

18

INTRODUCTORY

The *motifs* are so similar that we are forced to suppose that the mediaeval stone-carver deliberately copied the classical work in order to produce a counterpart of it. But while the Roman relief represents Hercules carrying the Erymanthean boar to King Euristheus, the mediaeval master, by substituting billowy drapery for the lion's skin, a dragon for the frightened king, and a stag for the boar, transformed the mythological story into an allegory of salvation. In Italian and French art of the twelfth and thirteenth centuries we find a great number of similar cases; viz., direct and deliberate borrowings of classical motifs while the pagan themes were changed into Christian ones. Suffice it to mention the most famous specimens of this so-called proto-Renaissance movement: the sculptures of St. Gilles and Arles, the celebrated Visitation group at Rheims Cathedral which for a long time was held to be a sixteenth-century work, or Nicolo Pisano's Adoration of the Magi in which the group of the Virgin Mary and the Infant Jesus shows the influence of a Phaedra Sarcophagus still preserved in the Camposanto at Pisa. Even more frequent, however, than such direct copies are instances of a continuous and traditional survival of classical motifs, some of which were used in succession for quite a variety of Christian images.

As a rule such re-interpretations were facilitated or even suggested by a certain iconographical affinity, for instance when the figure of Orpheus was employed for the representation of David, or when the type of Hercules dragging Cerberus out of Hades was used to depict Christ pulling Adam out of Limbo.[7] But there are cases in which the relationship between the classical prototype and its Christian adaptation is a purely compositional one.

On the other hand, when a Gothic illuminator had to illustrate the story of Laocoön, Laocoön becomes a wild and bald old man in contemporary costume who attacks the sacrificial bull with what should be an ax, while the two little boys float around at the bottom of the picture, and the sea snakes appear briskly in a plot of water.[8] Aeneas and Dido are shown as

7. See K.Weitzmann, *Bibl.*395.
8. Cod. Vat. lat. 2761, ill. in *Bibl.*238, p.259.

19

a fashionable mediaeval couple playing chess, or may appear as a group resembling the Prophet Nathan before David, rather than as a classical hero before his paramour (*fig.*12). And Thisbe awaits Pyramus on a Gothic tombstone which bears the inscription 'Hic situs est Ninus rex,' preceded by the usual cross (*fig.*11).[9]

When we ask the reason for this curious separation between classical *motifs* invested with a non-classical meaning, and classical *themes* expressed by non-classical figures in a non-classical setting, the obvious answer seems to lie in the difference between representational and textual tradition. The artists who used the motif of a Hercules for an image of Christ, or the motif of an Atlas for the images of the Evangelists (*figs.*7-10),[10] acted under the

9. Paris, Bibl. Nat., ms. lat. 15158, dated 1289, ill. *Bibl.*238, p.272.
10. C.Tolnay, *Bibl.*356, p.257ss., has made the important discovery that the impressive images of the Evangelists seated on a globe and supporting a heavenly glory (occurring for the first time in cod. Vat. Barb. lat. 711; our *fig.*7), combine the features of Christ in Majesty with those of a Graeco-Roman celestial divinity. However, as Tolnay himself points out, the Evangelists.in cod. Barb. 711 'support *with obvious effort* a mass of clouds which does not in the least look like a spiritual aura but like a material weight consisting of several segments of circles, alternately blue and green, the outline of the whole forming a circle . . . It is a misunderstood representation of *heaven in the form of spheres*' (italics mine). From this we can infer that the classical prototype of these images was not Coelus who holds without effort a billowing drapery (the *Weltenmantel*) but Atlas who labours under the weight of the heavens (cf. G.Thiele, *Bibl.*338, p.19ss., and Daremberg-Saglio, *Bibl.*70, s.v. 'Atlas'). The St. Matthew in cod. Barb. 711 (Tolnay, PL.I, *a*), with his head bowed down under the weight of the sphere and his left hand still placed near his left hip, is particularly reminiscent of the classical type of Atlas, and another striking example of the characteristic Atlas pose applied to an Evangelist is found in clm. 4454, fol.86, v. (ill. in A.Goldschmidt, *Bibl.*118, VOL.II, PL.40). Tolnay (notes 13 and 14) has not failed to notice this similarity and quotes the representations of Atlas and Nimrod in cod. Vat. Pal. lat. 1417, fol.i (ill. in F.Saxl, *Bibl.*299, PL.XX, *fig.*42; our *fig.*8); but he seems to consider the Atlas type as a mere derivative of the Coelus type. Yet even in ancient art the representations of Coelus seem to have developed from those of Atlas, and in Carolingian, Ottonian and Byzantine art (particularly in the Reichenau school) the figure of Atlas, in its genuine classical form, is infinitely more frequent than that of Coelus, both as a personification of cosmological character and as a kind of caryatid. I quote at random: Utrecht Psalter, fol.48v. (E.T.DeWald, *Bibl.*74, PL.LXXVI), fol.54v., (*ibidem*, PL.LXXXV); fol.56, (*ibidem*, PL.LXXXIX); fol.57, (*ibidem*, PL.XCI), our *fig.*9. Aachen, Domschatz, Gospels of Otto II, fol.16 (Terra, in the posture of Atlas, supporting the throne of the Emperor who is here conceived as the ruler of the universe; see P.E. Schramm, *Bibl.*307, pp.82, 191, *fig.*64, our *fig.*10). Copenhagen, Royal Library, cod. 218, fol.25 (M.Mackeprang, *Bibl.*206, PL.LXII). Menologium of Basil II (*Bibl.*289, VOL.II, PL.74).

impression of visual models which they had before their eyes, whether they directly copied a classical monument or imitated a more recent work derived from a classical prototype through a series of intermediary transformations. The artists who represented Medea as a mediaeval princess, or Jupiter as a mediaeval judge, translated into images a mere description found in literary sources.

This is very true, and the textual tradition through which the knowledge of classical themes, particularly of classical mythology, was transmitted to and persisted during the Middle Ages is of the utmost importance, not only for the mediaevalist but also for the student of Renaissance iconography. For even in the Italian Quattrocento, it was from this complex and often very corrupt tradition, rather than from genuine classical sources, that many people drew their notions of classical mythology and related subjects.

Limiting ourselves to classical mythology, the paths of this tradition can be outlined as follows. The later Greek philosophers had already begun to interpret the pagan gods and demi-gods as mere personifications either of natural forces or moral qualities, and some of them had gone so far as to explain them as ordinary human beings subsequently deified. In the last century of the Roman Empire these tendencies greatly increased. While the Christian Fathers endeavoured to prove that the pagan gods were either illusions or malignant demons (thereby transmitting much valuable information about them), the pagan world itself had become so estranged from its divinities that the educated public had to read them up in encyclopaedias,

From an iconographical point of view, too, the Evangelists are comparable to Atlas, rather than to Coelus. Coelus was believed to rule the heavens. Atlas was believed to support them and, in an allegorical sense, to 'know' them; he was held to have been a great astronomer who transmitted the '*scientia coeli*' to Hercules (Servius, *Comm. in Aen.*, VI, 395: later on, e.g., Isidorus, *Etymologiae*, III, 24, 1; Mythographus III, 13, 4, *Bibl.*38, p.248). It was therefore consistent to use the type of Coelus for the representation of God (see Tolnay, PL.I, c), and it was equally consistent to use the type of Atlas for the Evangelists who, like him, 'knew' the heavens but did not rule them. While Hibernus Exul says of Atlas '*Sidera quem coeli cuncta notasse volunt*' (*Monumenta Germaniae, Bibl.*220, VOL.I, p.410), Alcuin thus apostrophizes St. John the Evangelist: '*Scribendo penetras caelum tu, mente, Johannes*' (*ibidem*, p.293).

21

in didactic poems or novels, in special treatises on mythology, and in commentaries on the classic poets. Important among these late antique writings in which the mythological characters were interpreted in an allegorical way, or 'moralized' to use the mediaeval expression, were Martianus Capella's *Nuptiae Mercurii et Philologiae*, Fulgentius' *Mitologiae*, and, above all, Servius' admirable Commentary on Virgil which is three or four times as long as the text and was perhaps more widely read.

During the Middle Ages these writings and others of their kind were thoroughly exploited and further developed. The mythographical information thus survived, and became accessible to mediaeval poets and artists. First, in the Encyclopaedias, the development of which began with such early writers as Bede and Isidorus of Seville, was continued by Hrabanus Maurus (ninth century), and reached a climax in the enormous high-mediaeval works by Vincentius of Beauvais, Brunetto Latini, Bartholomaeus Anglicus, and so forth. Second, in the mediaeval commentaries on classical and late antique texts, especially on Martianus Capella's *Nuptiae*, which had already been annotated by Irish scholars such as Johannes Scotus Erigena and was authoritatively commented upon by Remigius of Auxerre (ninth century).[11] Third, in special treatises on mythology such as the so-called Mythographi I and II, which are still rather early in date and are mainly based on Fulgentius and Servius.[12] The most important work of this kind, the so-called *Mythographus III*, has been tentatively identified with an Englishman, the great scholastic Alexander Neckham (died 1217);[13] his treatise, an impressive survey of whatever information was available around 1200, deserves to be called the conclusive compendium of high mediaeval mythography, and was even used by Petrarch when he described the images of pagan gods in his poem *Africa*.

11. See H.Liebeschütz, *Fulgentius Metaforalis*, Bibl.194, p.15 and p.44ss. Liebeschütz' book is the most important contribution to the history of mythographical traditions during the Middle Ages; cf. also *Bibl.*238, especially p.253ss.
12. Bode, *Bibl.*38, p.1ss.
13. Bode, *ibidem*, p.152ss. As to the question of authorship, see H.Liebeschütz, *Bibl.*194, p.16s. and passim.

22

Between the times of the Mythographus III and Petrarch a further step in the moralization of classical divinities had been taken. (The figures of ancient mythology were not only interpreted in a general moralistic way but were quite definitely related to the Christian faith, so that, for instance Pyramus was interpreted as Christ, Thisbe as the human soul, and the lion as Evil defiling its garments; while Saturn served as an example both in a good and in a bad sense, for the behaviour of clergymen. Instances of this type of writings are the French *Ovide Moralisé*,[14] John Ridewall's *Fulgentius Metaforalis*,[15] Robert Holcott's *Moralitates*, the *Gesta Romanorum* and, above all, the *Moralized Ovid* in Latin, written around 1340 by a French theologian called Petrus Berchorius or Pierre Bersuire who was personally acquainted with Petrarch.[16] His work is preceded by a special chapter on the pagan gods, mainly based on the *Mythographus III*, but enriched by specifically Christian moralizations, and this introduction, with the moralizations cut out for brevity's sake, attained great popularity under the name of *Albricus, Libellus de Imaginibus Deorum*.[17]

A fresh and highly important start was made by Boccaccio. In his *Genealogia Deorum*[18] he not only gave a new survey of the material, greatly enlarged since about 1200, but also tried consciously to revert to the genuine antique sources and carefully collate them with one another. His treatise marks the beginning of a critical or scientific attitude towards classical antiquity, and may be called a forerunner of such truly scholarly Renaissance treatises as the *Historia Deorum Syntagmata* by L.G.Gyraldus who, from his point of view, was fully entitled to look down upon his most popular mediaeval predecessor as a 'proletarian and unreliable writer.'[19]

---

14. Ed. by C. de Boer, *Bibl.*40.
15. Ed. H.Liebeschütz, *Bibl.*38.
16. 'Thomas Walleys' (or Valeys), *Bibl.*386.
17. Cod. Vat. Reg. 1290, ed. H. Liebeschütz, *Bibl.*194, p.117ss. with the complete set of illustrations.
18. *Bibl.*36; many other editions and Italian translation.
19. L.G.Gyraldus, *Bibl.*127, vol.i, col.153: '*Ut scribit Albricus, qui auctor mihi proletarius est, nec fidus satis.*'

It will be noticed that up to Boccaccio's *Genealogia Deorum* the focal point of mediaeval mythography was a region widely remote from direct Mediterranean tradition: Ireland, Northern France and England. This is also true of the Trojan Cycle, the most important epic theme transmitted by classical antiquity to posterity; its first authoritative mediaeval redaction, the *Roman de Troie* which was frequently abridged, summarized and translated into the other vernacular languages, is due to Benoit de Ste. More, a native of Brittany. We are in fact entitled to speak of a proto-humanistic movement; viz., an active interest in classical themes regardless of classical motifs, centred in the northern region of Europe, as opposed to the proto-Renaissance movement; viz., an active interest in classical motifs regardless of classical themes, centred in Provence and Italy. It is a memorable fact which we must bear in mind in order to understand the Renaissance movement proper, that Petrarch, when describing the gods of his Roman ancestors, had to consult a compendium written by an Englishman, and that the Italian illuminators who illustrated Virgil's Aeneid in the fifteenth century had to have recourse to the miniatures in manuscripts of the *Roman de Troie* and its derivatives. For these, being a favourite reading matter of noble laymen, had been amply illustrated long before the Virgil text proper, read by scholars and schoolboys; and had attracted the attention of professional illuminators.[20]

It is indeed easy to see that the artists who from the end of the eleventh century tried to translate into images those proto-humanistic texts could not but depict them in a manner utterly different from classical traditions. One of the earliest instances is among the most striking: a miniature of about 1100, probably executed in the school of Regensburg, depicting the classical divinities according to the descriptions in Remigius' *Commentary on Mar-*

---

20. Between the 'Vergilius Romanus' of the 6th century and the illustrated Virgils of the Quattrocento only two illustrated manuscripts of the Aeneid are known to the writer: Naples, Biblioteca Nazionale, cod. olim Vienna 58 (brought to my attention by Dr. Kurt Weitzmann, to whom I am also indebted for permission to reproduce one miniature in *fig.*12; 10th century) and Cod. Vat. lat. 2761 (cf. R.Förster, *Bibl.*95; 14th century). The illustrations in both manuscripts are unusually crude.

tianus Capella (*fig.*13).[21] Apollo is seen riding in a peasant's cart and holding in his hand a kind of nose-gay with the busts of the Three Graces. Saturn looks like a Romanesque jamb-figure, rather than like the father of the Olympian gods, and the eagle of Jupiter is equipped with a tiny halo like the eagle of St. John the Evangelist or the dove of St. Gregory.

Nevertheless, the contrast between representational and textual tradition alone, important though it is, cannot account for the strange dichotomy of classical *motifs* and classical *themes* characteristic of high mediaeval art. For even when there had been a representational tradition in certain fields of classical imagery, this representational tradition was deliberately relinquished in favour of representations of an entirely non-classical character, as soon as the Middle Ages had achieved a style entirely their own.

Instances of this process are found, first, in classical images incidentally occurring in representations of Christian subjects, such as the pagan idols frequently found in scenes of martyrdom and the like, or the sun and the moon in the Crucifixion. While Carolingian ivories still show the perfectly classical types of the *Quadriga Solis* and the *Biga Lunae*,[22] these classical types are replaced by non-classical ones in Romanesque and Gothic representations. The idols, too, gradually lost their classical appearance in the course of the centuries, although they tended to preserve it longer than other images because they were the symbols par excellence of paganism. Secondly, what is much more important, they appear in the illustrations of such texts as had already been illustrated in late antique times, so that visual models were available to the Carolingian artists: the Comedies of Terence, the texts incorporated into Hrabanus Maurus' *De Universo*, Prudentius' *Psychomachia*, and scientific writings, particularly treatises on astronomy, where mythological images appear both among the constellations (such as Andromeda, Perseus, Cassiopea), and as planets (Saturn, Jupiter, Mars, Sol, Venus, Mercury, Luna).

21. Clm. 14271, ill. in *Bibl.*238, p.260.
22. A.Goldschmidt, *Bibl.*117, VOL.I, PL.XX, no.40, ill. in *Bibl.*238, p.257.

In all these cases we can observe that the classical images were faithfully though often clumsily copied in Carolingian manuscripts and lingered on in their derivatives, but that they were abandoned and replaced by entirely different ones in the thirteenth and fourteenth centuries at the latest.

In the ninth-century illustrations of an astronomical text, such mythological figures as Perseus, Hercules or Mercury are rendered in a perfectly classical fashion, and the same is true of the pagan divinities appearing in Hrabanus Maurus' Encyclopaedia.[23] With all their clumsiness, which is chiefly due to the incompetence of the poor eleventh-century copyist of the lost Carolingian manuscript, the figures in the Hrabanus illustrations are evidently not concocted from mere textual descriptions but are connected with antique prototypes by a representational tradition (*figs.*40, 69).

However, some centuries later these genuine images had fallen into oblivion and were replaced by others—partly newly invented, partly derived from oriental sources—which no modern spectator would ever recognize as classical divinities. Venus is shown as a fashionable young lady playing the lute or smelling a rose, Jupiter as a judge with his gloves in his hand, and Mercury as an old scholar or even as a bishop (*fig.*14).[24] It was not before the Renaissance proper that Jupiter reassumed the appearance of the classical Zeus, and that Mercury reacquired the youthful beauty of the classical Hermes.[25]

All this shows that the separation of classical *themes* from classical *motifs* took place, not only for want of a representational tradition, but even in spite of a representational tradition. Wherever a classical image, that is, a fusion of a classical *theme* with a classical *motif*, had been copied during the Carolingian period of feverish assimilation, this classical image was abandoned as soon as mediaeval civilization had reached its climax, and

23. Cf. A.M.Amelli, *Bibl.*7.
24. Clm. 10268, (14th Cent.), ill. in *Bibl.*238, p.251, and the whole group of other illustrations based on the text by Michael Scotus. For the oriental sources of these new types see *ibidem*, p.239 ss. and F.Saxl, *Bibl.*296, p.151 ss.
25. For the interesting preludes of this reinstatement (resumption of Carolingian and archaic Greek models) see *Bibl.*238, p.247 and 258.

was not reinstated until the Italian Quattrocento. It was the privilege of the Renaissance proper to reintegrate classical *themes* with classical *motifs* after what might be called a zero hour.

For the mediaeval mind, classical antiquity was too far removed and at the same time too strongly present to be conceived as an historical phenomenon. On the one hand an unbroken continuity of tradition was felt in so far as, for example, the German Emperor was considered the direct successor of Caesar and Augustus, while the linguists looked upon Cicero and Donatus as their forefathers, and the mathematicians traced their ancestry back to Euclid. On the other hand, it was felt that an insurmountable gap existed between a pagan civilization and a Christian one.[26] These two tendencies could not as yet be balanced so as to permit a feeling of historical distance. In many minds the classical world assumed a distant, fairy-tale character like the contemporary pagan East, so that Villard de Honnecourt could call a Roman tomb '*la sepouture d'un sarrazin*,' while Alexander the Great and Virgil came to be thought of as oriental magicians. For others, the classical world was the ultimate source of highly appreciated knowledge and time-honoured institutions. But no mediaeval man could see the civilization of antiquity as a phenomenon complete in itself, yet belonging to the past and historically detached from the contemporary world,—as a cultural cosmos to be investigated and, if possible, to be reintegrated, instead of being a world of living wonders or a mine of information. The scholastic philosophers could use the ideas of Aristotle and merge them with their own system, and the mediaeval poets could borrow freely from the classical authors, but no mediaeval mind could think of classical philology. The artists could employ, as we have seen, the motifs of classical reliefs and classical statues, but no mediaeval mind could think of classical archaeology. Just as it was impossi-

26. A similar dualism is characteristic of the mediaeval attitude towards the *aera sub lege*: on the one hand the Synagogue was represented as blind and associated with Night, Death, the devil and impure animals; and on the other hand the Jewish prophets were considered as inspired by the Holy Ghost, and the personages of the Old Testament were venerated as the ancestors of Christ.

ble for the Middle Ages to elaborate the modern system of perspective, which is based on the realization of a fixed distance between the eye and the object and thus enables the artist to build up comprehensive and consistent images of visible things; just as impossible was it for them to evolve the modern idea of history, which is based on the realization of an intellectual distance between the present and the past, and thus enables the scholar to build up comprehensive and consistent concepts of bygone periods.

We can easily see that a period unable and unwilling to realize that classical *motifs* and classical *themes* structurally belonged together, actually avoided preserving the union of these two. Once the Middle Ages had established their own standards of civilization and found their own methods of artistic expression, it became impossible to enjoy or even to understand any phenomenon which had no common denominator with the phenomena of the contemporary world. The high-mediaeval beholder could appreciate a beautiful classical figure when presented to him as a Virgin Mary, and he could appreciate a Thisbe depicted as a girl of the thirteenth century sitting by a Gothic tombstone. But a classical Thisbe sitting by a classical mausoleum would have been an archaeological reconstruction entirely beyond his possibilities of approach. In the thirteenth century even classical script was felt as something utterly 'foreign:' the explanatory inscriptions in the Carolingian *cod. Leydensis Voss. lat.* 79, written in a beautiful *Capitalis Rustica* were copied, for the benefit of less erudite readers, in angular High Gothic script.

However, this failure to realize the intrinsic 'oneness' of classical *themes* and classical *motifs* can be explained, not only by a lack of historical feeling, but also by the emotional disparity between the Christian Middle Ages and pagan Antiquity. Where Hellenic paganism—at least as reflected in classical art—considered man as an integral unity of body and soul, the Jewish-Christian conception of man was based on the idea of the 'clod of earth' forcibly, or even miraculously, united with an immortal soul. From this point of view, the admirable artistic formulae which in Greek and Roman art had expressed organic beauty and animal passions, seemed admissible only when invested with a more-than-organic and more-than-natural meaning; that is, when made subservient to Biblical or theological themes. In secular scenes, on the contrary, these formulae had to be replaced by others, conforming to the mediaeval atmosphere of courtly manners and conventionalized sentiments, so that heathen divinities and heroes mad with love or cruelty appeared as fashionable princes and damsels whose looks and behaviour were in harmony with the canons of mediaeval social life.

In a miniature from a fourteenth-century *Ovide moralisé*, the Rape of Europa is enacted by figures which certainly express little passionate agitation (*fig.*15).[27] Europa, clad in late mediaeval costume, sits on her inoffensive little bull like a young lady taking a morning ride, and her companions, similarly attired, form a quiet little group of spectators. Of course, they are meant to be anguished and to cry out, but they don't, or at least they don't convince us that they do, because the illuminator was neither able nor inclined to visualize animal passions.

A drawing by Dürer, copied from an Italian prototype probably during his first stay in Venice, emphasizes the emotional vitality which was absent in the mediaeval representation (*fig.*16). The literary source of Dürer's Rape of Europa is no longer a prosy text where the bull was compared to Christ, and Europa to the human soul, but the pagan verses of Ovid himself as revived in two delightful stanzas by Angelo Poliziano: 'You can admire Jupiter transformed into a beautiful bull by the power of love. He dashes away with his sweet, terrified load, her beautiful golden hair fluttering in the wind which blows back her gown. With one hand she grasps the horn of the bull, while the other clings to his back. She draws up her feet as if she were afraid of the sea, and thus crouching down with pain and fear, she cries for help in vain. For her sweet companions remain on the flowery shore,

27. Lyons, Bibl. de la Ville, ms. 742, illustrated in *Bibl.*238, p.274.

INTRODUCTORY

each of them crying "Europa, come back." The whole seashore resounds with "Europa, come back," and the bull looks round and kisses her feet.'[28]

Dürer's drawing actually gives life to this sensual description. The crouching position of Europa, her fluttering hair, her clothes blown back by the wind and thus revealing her graceful body, the gestures of her hands, the furtive movement of the bull's head, the seashore scattered with the lamenting companions: all this is faithfully and vividly depicted; and, even more, the beach itself rustles with the life of *aquatici monstriculi*, to speak in the terms of another Quattrocento writer, while satyrs hail the abductor.

This comparison illustrates the fact that the reintegration of classical *themes* with classical *motifs* which seems to be characteristic of the Italian Renaissance as opposed to the numerous sporadic revivals of classical tendencies during the Middle Ages, is not only a humanistic but also a human occurrence. It is a most important element of what Burckhardt and Michelet called 'the discovery both of the world and of man.'

On the other hand, it is self-evident that this reintegration could not be a simple reversion to the classical past. The intervening period had changed the minds of men, so that they could not turn into pagans again; and it had changed their tastes and productive tendencies, so that their art could not

28. F.Lippmann, *Bibl.*196, nr.456, also ill. in *Bibl.*238, p.275. Angelo Poliziano's stanzas (*Giostra* I, 105,106) read as follows:

'Nell'altra in un formoso e bianco tauro
Si vede Giove per amor converso
Portarne il dolce suo ricco tesauro,
E lei volgere il viso al lito perso
In atto paventoso: e i be' crin d'auro
Scherzon nel petto per lo vento avverso:
La veste ondeggia e in drieto fa ritorno:
L'una man tien al dorso, e l'altra al corno.

Le ignude piante a se ristrette accoglie
Quasi temendo il mar che lei non bagne:
Tale atteggiata di paura e doglie
Par chiami in van le sue dolci compagne;
Le qual rimase tra fioretti e foglie
Dolenti 'Europa' ciascheduna piagne
"Europa", sona il lito, "Europa, riedi"-
E'l tor nota, e talor gli bacia i piedi.'

30

simply renew the art of the Greeks and Romans. They had to strive for a new form of expression, stylistically and iconographically different from the classical, as well as from the mediaeval, yet related and indebted to both. To illustrate this process of creative interpenetration will be the aim of the following chapters.

PLATE I

2

I

PLATE II

4

3

PLATE III

6

5

PLATE IV

7

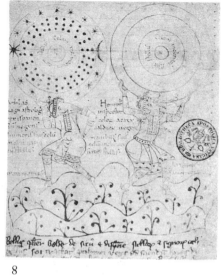

8

9

10

PLATE V

12

11

PLATE VI

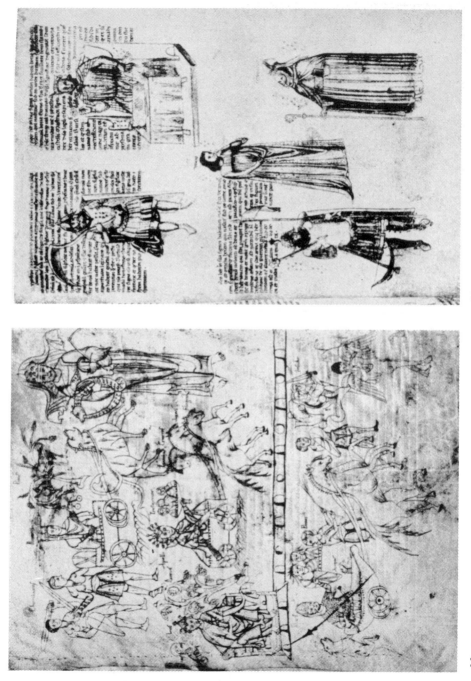

14

13

PLATE VII

15

16

II. THE EARLY HISTORY OF MAN IN TWO CYCLES OF PAINTINGS BY PIERO DI COSIMO

PIERO DI COSIMO (1461-1521) was not a 'great' master, but a most charming and interesting one. Except for a trip to Rome where he participated in the decoration of the Sistine Chapel under his master Cosimo Rosselli, he seems to have spent his whole life in Florence; and, setting aside the influence of Signorelli which is discernible in his earlier works, his style is rooted in the Florentine tradition.

Yet he stands very much alone within the Florentine school of painting. The most imaginative of inventors, he was as an observer a stupendous realist. While his boldly entangled groups of nudes anticipate the tendencies of later Mannerists and made a lasting impression even on Michelangelo, his 'empathic' interest in what may be called the 'souls' of plants and animals, and his delicate sense of luminary and atmospheric values, lend a definitely Northern flavour to his pictures. Unlike most other Florentine painters of his period—particularly Botticelli who may be considered his antipode—he was essentially a painter, not a designer. He felt the tangible epidermis of things, rather than their abstract form, and based his art on colouristic 'valeurs,' rather than on linear patterns. Light profiles set out against a background of dark, gray clouds; fantastic trees reaching far and high into the sky; the dim twilight of impenetrable forests; the bluish haze above tepid waters; and the strong sunlight suffusing open landscapes: these were the phenomena that fascinated him. To capture them, he developed an amazingly flexible technique, sometimes as delicately luminous as that of his Flemish and Venetian contemporaries, sometimes as broad, succulent and somewhat rough as that of seventeenth-century Baroque painters or even nineteenth-century impressionists.

33

All this, however, would not account for the strange lure emanating from Piero's pictures, if their content were not as unusual as their style. It is this content which will be discussed in this chapter.

One of Piero's earliest pictures, acquired in 1932 by the Wadsworth Athenaeum at Hartford, Connecticut, is generally supposed to represent the myth of Hylas and the nymphs *(fig.17)*.[1] To this interpretation there are several objections. According to the mythographical sources,[2] Hylas was the handsome favourite of Hercules, whom he accompanied on the Argonautic expedition. In Mysia in the Propontis, Hercules, Hylas, and, according to some writers, Telamon, left the ship together and ventured into the woods, allegedly because Hercules, owing to his enormous strength, had broken his oar and wanted a tree for a new one. Here they separated, because Hylas had to fetch water for the evening meal. But when he had come to the river Ascanius (or Cius), the naiads fell in love with his beauty and dragged him down to share their crystalline dwelling. He was never seen again, and Hercules strayed through the woods calling for him in vain (from which originated a local rite implying a solemnly pathetic invocation of the lost youth, *'ut litus "Hyla, Hyla" omne sonaret'*).[3]

In an artistic interpretation of this subject, then, we should expect to find the following features, which are indeed characteristic of all the known representations of the Hylas myth:[4] first of all, the presence of a vase or other vessel, which would indicate the purpose of Hylas' errand; secondly, the predominance of water in the scenery; thirdly, an amorous aggressiveness on the part of the naiads; and fourthly, a struggling reluctance on the part of Hylas.

None of these features is present in the Hartford picture. No pitcher or

1. Cf. A.E.Austin, Jr., *Bibl.*16. Also, see R. van Marle, *Bibl.*209, VOL.XIII, p.346, *fig.*237; and L.Venturi, *Bibl.*375, PL.CCXVII, both with further references.
2. Cf. Roscher, *Bibl.*290, s.v. *Hylas.* Cf. also L.G.Gyraldus, *Hercules, Bibl.*127, VOL.I, col.578.
3. Virgil, *Ecl.*VI,44. Hence the Greek phrase τὸν ‵Ὕλαν κραυγάζειν meaning 'to exert oneself in vain' or 'to try the impossible.'
4. Cf. Roscher, *Bibl.*209, s.v. 'Hylas.' See also *Bibl.*151, PL.224.

34

vase is depicted. The scene is laid in a flowery meadow. The stretch of water appearing in the left background is merely a 'landscape-motif' quite unrelated to the main incident. The six maidens show no amorous excitement whatever. They seem to have been suddenly interrupted in the peaceful occupations of gathering flowers and walking with their little dog; so sudden is the interruption that the two on the right have dropped the flowers they were carrying in their billowing draperies. Of these six maidens, the one on the left halts her step with a gesture of surprise, the one on the right looks rather amused in spite of the loss of her flowers, her neighbour points at the boy with an expression of supercilious pity. Finally, the central figure with motherly protectiveness helps the youth to his feet, whereas, were he Hylas, she should be dragging him down.

Here we have, unquestionably, a scene of surprise, kindliness, and hospitality, and not one of tragic passion. The boy, who looks like anything but the favourite of a hero and was very appropriately termed 'a bow-legged youth,'[5] displays a curiously limp and twisted posture. He has obviously met with an accident unexpected enough to cause some alarm, but not serious enough to prevent a certain hilarity. There is only one event in classical mythology which is consistent with this representation: the first misfortune of a god whose very lucklessness, combined with the rare gifts of humorous good nature and inventiveness, made him the most laughable and, at the same time, the most lovable figure of the pagan Pantheon; this is the Fall, or rather the Finding, of Vulcan.

The classical writers are unanimous in stating that Vulcan, or Hephaistos, was 'thrown down from Mount Olympus,' and was not readmitted to the Palace of the Gods before a considerable lapse of time. The tradition varies in certain details; according to some, he was ejected as a child, according to others as a man; still other sources give no definite age. According to some writers, his fall caused his proverbial limp; according to others this limp caused his fall, in so far as his parents were disgusted with the constitutional

5. A.E.Austin, *Bibl.*16, p.6.

stiffness of one of his knees and decided to get rid of him by simply dropping him from Mount Olympus. It is variously told that he found a temporary refuge in the ocean or on the island of Lemnos.[6] Yet the Middle Ages and the Renaissance generally agreed in accepting a uniform version, according to which Vulcan was 'precipitated' from Mount Olympus at a tender age because his mother disliked his deformity, and alighted on the island of Lemnos, where he was hospitably received and carefully brought up by the inhabitants.[7]

This myth is the real subject of Piero di Cosimo's picture. Young Vulcan, characterized by the obvious stiffness of his left knee, has landed right on the meadow where the six maidens had been gathering flowers. Being an immortal, he is unhurt, but slightly dazed and unable to get to his feet. The combined effect of his unexpected apparition, his awkward physique, his dumbfounded expression, and his helpless condition accounts for the various psychological reactions of the maidens: speechless surprise, mild compassion, faint amusement, and, in the main figure, the awakening of motherly instincts.

There is only one thing which does not seem to agree with the Vulcan story. Why is it that the 'inhabitants of Lemnos' are not shown as a group of islanders of both sexes, but are represented exclusively by young girls of nymph-like appearance,—so nymph-like that the Hylas interpretation has remained unchallenged in spite of the fact that Piero's alleged rendering of the Hylas story struck many observers as 'somewhat strange?'[8]

It is not necessary to have recourse to 'artistic licence,' or to the 'painter's lack of classical education;' the nymphs can be accounted for by purely philological methods if we stop to consider the devious paths of post-classical mythography, as outlined in the first chapter.

6. Cf. Roscher, *Bibl*.290, s.v. 'Hephaistos;' Gyraldus, *Bibl*.127, VOL.I, col.413; also H.Freudenthal, *Bibl*.99.
7. Cf. the passages quoted below.
8. A.E.Austin, *Bibl*.16, p.5. Even P.Schubring, *Bibl*.309, p.411, expresses no doubt, although he remarks that the maidens seemed to be land-nymphs, not naiads, and realizes that the central figure helps the boy to get to his feet.

What the early Renaissance knew about classical mythology was, we remember, frequently drawn from post-classical sources. Now, almost everything which these post-classical sources had to say about the youthful experiences of Vulcan is based on Servius' *Commentary on Virgil*. Here we encounter the following lines: '*qui* [viz., Vulcanus] *cum deformis esset et Juno ei minime arrisisset, ab Jove praecipitatus est in insulam Lemnum. Illic nutritus ab Sintiis;*'[9] that is, in English: 'He was precipitated by Jupiter onto the island of Lemnos because he was illshapen and Juno had not smiled at him. There he was brought up by the *Sintii*.' These '*Sintii*' (the Σίντοι or Σίντιες ἄνδρες, as they are called by Homer),[10] do not appear in any other connection in Latin literature, and were thus bound to puzzle the mediaeval scribes, readers, and interpreters. Small wonder that the manuscript or printed copies of the Servius Commentary, as well as the mediaeval treatises based on it, show a great variety of readings, some of which make no sense, while others attempt to make the passage more understandable. One of these interpretative readings is: '*Illic nutritus absintiis*'[11] (or '*absinthio*'),[12] which would mean: 'There he was brought up on wormwood.' Another is, '*Illic nutritus ab simiis,*'[13] which means: 'There he was brought up by apes.' A third, finally, is '*Illic nutritus ab nimphis,*'[14] which means: 'There he was brought up by the nymphs.'

If Piero di Cosimo wished to illustrate this incident in Vulcan's life, he had three choices at his disposal: he could show the god indulging in an extraordinary form of vegetarian diet; or he could submit him to the educational efforts of apes; or he could make him the object of the motherly attentions of nymphs. No one can blame him for having chosen the third alternative.

9. Servius, *Comm. in Verg. Eclog.*, IV, 62.
10. Homer, *Ilias*, I, 594.
11. Servius, *Comm. in Verg.*, *Bibl.*314, fol.7, col.2.
12. Mythographus II, according to the Vatican manuscript adduced by Bode, *Bibl.*38, VOL.II, p.44.
13. Mythographus I, according to the Vatican and Wolfenbüttel manuscripts adduced by Bode, *ibidem*; Servius, *Comm. in Verg.*, *Bibl.*315, fol.18v.
14. Servius, *Comm. in Verg.*, Wolfenbüttel, cod.7.10. Aug.815, adduced by Bode, *ibidem*.

The reading *ab simiis* was, however, accepted by Boccaccio,[15] and this, by the way, accounts for the unexpected presence of apes in the Vulcan fresco in the Palazzo Schifanoia at Ferrara.[16] But Boccaccio was too conscientious and imaginative an author not to attempt an explanation of this extraordinary feature. Apes, he argues, are comparable to humans in that they imitate the behaviour of man just as man imitates the procedures of nature. Now how does man imitate nature? He does it by practising the arts and crafts, for, according to the Aristotelian definition, τέχνη means 'acting as nature acts.' But to practise the arts and crafts man needs fire, and Vulcan is the personification of fire. Consequently, with Boccaccio the tale that Vulcan was found and brought up by apes is an allegorical expression of the fact that men could not use their innate gifts for art and industry before they had discovered fire and had learned to keep it alive. '*Et quoniam homines arte et ingenio suo in multis naturam imitari conantur, et circa actus tales plurimum opportunus est ignis, fictum est simias, id est homines, nutrisse Vulcanum, id est ignem fovisse;*' that is, 'And since man, by his art and genius, endeavours to emulate nature in many ways, and since fire is the most useful thing in such enterprises, it was imagined that apes, viz., men, brought up Vulcan, that is: nurtured fire.'

After this, Boccaccio praises the manifold powers of fire,[17] points out that Vulcan had to be considered, not only as the 'smith of Jupiter' and the 'composer of all sorts of artificial things,' but also as the very founder of human civilization, inasmuch as the 'bringing up of Vulcan,' that is, the purposeful keeping alive of fire, had led to the formation of the first social units, to the invention of speech, and to the erection of buildings. To confirm this Boc-

---

15. Boccaccio, *Genealogia Deorum*, XII, 70.
16. Cf. A.Warburg, *Bibl.*387, vol.II, p.641, where also the 'empty stools' appearing in the Cybele fresco are explained in a similar way: '*Sedes fingantur,*' instead of, '*Sedens fingatur;*' that is, 'Seats should be depicted,' instead of, 'She should be depicted seated.'
17. Boccaccio also quotes a fine enthusiastic passage from Isidorus of Seville: '*Nihil enim paene quod non igne efficiatur . . . igne ferrum gignitur et domatur, igne aurum perficitur, igne cremato lapide cementa et parietes ligantur . . . stricta solvit, soluta restringit, dura mollit, mollia dura reddit.*'

caccio quotes *in extenso* some chapters from Vitruvius which read as follows: 'In the olden days men were born like wild beasts in woods and caves and groves, and kept alive by eating raw food. Somewhere, meanwhile, the close-grown trees, tossed by storms and winds, and rubbing their branches together, caught fire. Terrified by the flames, those who were near the spot fled. When the storm subsided, they drew near, and, since they noticed how pleasant to their bodies was the warmth of the fire, they laid on wood; and thus keeping it alive, they brought up some of their fellows, and, indicating the fire with gestures, they showed them the use which they might make of it. When in this meeting of men sounds were breathed forth with differing intensity, they made customary by daily use these chance syllables. Then, giving names to things more frequently used, they began to speak because of this fortuitous event, and so they held conversation among themselves. Since, therefore, from the discovery of fire a beginning of human association was made, and of union and intercourse; and since many now came together in one place, being endowed by nature with a gift beyond that of the other animals, so that they walked, not looking down, but erect, and saw the magnificence of the universe and the stars, and, moreover, did easily with their fingers whatever they wished; some in that society began to make roofs of leaves, others to dig out caves under the hills; some, imitating the nests and constructions of the swallows, made places, into which they might go, out of mud and twigs. Finding, then, other shelters and inventing new things by their power of thought, they built in time better dwellings.'[18]

By inserting this long passage from Vitruvius into his *Genealogia Deorum*, Boccaccio has lent authority to a doctrine which was not only un-Christian, but positively anti-religious; he feels himself impelled to add, in a facetiously apologetic way, that the eminent Roman writer was obviously ignorant of

18. Vitruvius, *De Architectura Libri decem*, II, 1. I follow the translation given in A.O.Lovejoy and G.Boas, *Bibl.*201, p.375. The Latin text reprinted *ibidem*. Boccaccio's long and correct quotation is evidence of the fact that Vitruvius' manuscripts were available long before Poggio Bracciolini's notorious 'discovery' of 1414 (cf. also J.v.Schlosser, *Bibl.*305, p.219). It is all the more instructive that it took the 'Renaissance spirit' to 'realize' on this inheritance.

the Bible, from which he would have learned that quite another inventor of speech, namely, Adam, had given names to all things,[19] and that Cain had built, not only houses, but a whole city.[20] What the 'eminent Roman writer' taught was nothing but that peculiar brand of Epicurean Evolutionism which had found its conclusive expression in the fifth book of Lucretius' *De Rerum Natura*,[21] and which conceived of humanity, not in terms of divine creation and supervision, but in terms of spontaneous development and progress.

There had been from the very beginning of classical speculation two contrasting opinions about the primeval life of man: The 'soft' or positivistic primitivism as formulated by Hesiod depicted the primitive form of existence as a 'golden age,' in comparison with which the subsequent phases were nothing but successive stages of one prolonged Fall from Grace; whereas the 'hard,' or negativistic, primitivism imagined the primitive form of existence as a truly bestial state, from which mankind had fortunately escaped through technical and intellectual progress.[22]

Both these conceptions were reached by a mental abstraction from civilized life. But while 'soft' primitivism imagines a civilized life cleansed of everything abhorrent and problematic, 'hard' primitivism imagines a civilized life deprived of all comforts and cultural achievements. 'Soft' primi-

19. *Genesis*, II, 19.
20. *Genesis*, IV, 17.
21. *Bibl.*201, p.222.
22. For the expressions 'soft' and 'hard' primitivism, as well as for the problem of primitivistic ideas in general, I must refer my readers to Lovejoy and Boas, *Bibl.*201. It is, of course, true that, particularly in later classical writing, the two contrasting lines of thought frequently intersected one another. Ovid, who, at the beginning of the *Metamorphoses*, revels in the beautiful dream of a Hesiodian 'Aurea Aetas' (I, 89), describes the life of the 'pre-lunar' Arcadians—let alone his own situation in a less civilized environment—with a definite lack of enthusiasm (*Fast.*, II, 289; cf. also *Ars Amat.*, II, 467, quoted in *Bibl.*201, p.373). To Juvenal, as to many others, primitive life meant hardships and coarseness, but also moral superiority (*Sat.*, VI, 1, quoted in *Bibl.*201, p.71); even Lucretius, much as he admired the spontaneous rise of humanity, was not blind to the moral dangers implied by this progress. With him the general evolution assumed the shape of an undulating line: (1) primeval bestiality; (2) rise of a human civilization, with technical achievements, speech, and social life (subdivided into an earlier bronze age and a later iron age); (3) decline of social and moral standards and general anarchy; (4) new rise towards an era of lawfulness.

tivism idealizes the initial condition of the world, and is therefore in harmony with a religious interpretation of human life and destiny, particularly with the various doctrines of Original Sin. 'Hard' primitivism, on the other hand, sought to be realistic in its reconstruction of the initial state of the world, and therefore fitted nicely into the scheme of a rationalistic, or even materialistic, philosophy. This philosophy imagines the rise of humanity as an entirely natural process, exclusively due to the innate gifts of the human race, whose civilization began with the discovery of fire, all ensuing developments being accounted for in a perfectly logical way. First in the sequence of imagined events was a spontaneous forest fire either caused by the friction of wind-tossed trees, as is the opinion of Vitruvius and Pliny,[23] or by lightning, as was assumed by Diodorus Siculus,[24] or by both, as was supposed by Lucretius.[25] Then the courageous approach of one man or a group while others fled; the feeling of comfort caused by the warmth; the decision to bring the fire out of the burning woods and to keep it alive and under control; the gathering of others which necessitated a means of mutual understanding and thus led to the invention of speech; finally, as an ultimate result, the erection of permanent dwellings, the establishment of family life, the domestication of animals, the development of the arts and crafts (where again the observation of natural melting processes suggested the artificial ones),[26] and the institution of social order in general. This is the scheme of things as it was reconstructed by the classical representatives of a philosophy

23. Pliny, *Nat. Hist.*, ii, 111 (107), 1. The Vitruvius Commentator Cesare Cesariano (*Bibl.*379, fol.xxxi) tells of a forest fire in the vicinity of Milan which was caused, in 1480, '*per simile confricatione de venti come narra Vitruuio.*' Cesariano's commentary on the passage in question (fol.xxx ss.) is almost a forerunner of Lovejoy and Boas' *Documentary History of Primitivism*: he adduces, among many others, Hesiod, Virgil (*Aen.*, viii), Ovid (*Metam.*, 1), Juvenal (*Sat.*, vi), Diodorus Siculus, and even Statius' verses on the prelunar Arcadians (*Thebais*, iv, 275, quoted in *Bibl.*201, p.380).
24. Diodorus Siculus, *Bibliotheca*, i, 13, quoted p.43, N.30.
25. Lucretius, *De Rer. Nat.*, v, 1091: '*Fulmen detulit in terram mortalibus ignem . . .*
　　　　Et ramosa tamen cum ventis pulsa vacillans
　　　　Aestuat in ramos incumbens arboris arbor,
　　　　Exprimitur validis extritus viribus ignis . . .
　　　　Quorum utrumque dedisse potest mortalibus ignem.'
26. Lucretius, *De Rer. Nat.*, v, 1241.

of enlightenment, and later was translated into images by the artists of the Renaissance who illustrated either the Vitruvius text or the modern treatises on architecture based on Vitruvius' teachings (*figs.*19-23).[27]

Originally, however, even this wholly materialistic theory had been based on a religious, or at least mythical, conception. Boccaccio was fundamentally right in inserting Vitruvius' Epicurean screed into his chapter on Vulcan, although the Roman author does not mention him or any other mythical character. For long before the cultural importance of fire had been enlarged upon by evolutionistic philosophers, the God of Fire had been praised as the Teacher of Mankind in mythical poetry: 'Sing of Hephaistos, famed for his skill, clear-voiced Muse,' says the Homeric Hymn; 'of him who with bright-eyed Athene taught glorious crafts to men on earth, who aforetime lived in caves like wild beasts.'[28] In Athens Hephaistos and Athene shared a temple, the so-called *Theseion*, as well as the honours of the great *Chalkeia*-Feast, and were considered as the common founders of Hellenic civilization, as the patrons of all good artisans, and as the exponents of what Plato calls φιλοσοφία and φιλοτεχνία.[29] And much as Vitruvius owes to Lucretius, he is no less indebted to a Euhemeristic source which explicitly mentions the name of Hephaistos in connection with the Forest Fire theory: 'When in the mountains a tree was struck by lightning and the nearby woods caught

27. In the first illustrated edition of Vitruvius, *Bibl.*378, the 'discovery of fire' is illustrated, not too convincingly, on fol.13, reprod. in Prince d'Essling, *Bibl.*86, II. Partie, VOL.III, 1, p.214. In the Como edition, *Bibl.*379, fol.xxxi, v., we find a much larger and richer interpretation of this subject (our *fig.*19) which served as a model for the translations *Bibl.*380, fol.15, and *Bibl.*382, fol.lxi (our *fig.*20), where the composition in the Como edition has been improved upon by borrowings from Raphael's Judgment of Paris (Marcantonio Raimondi, engraving B.245) and Dürer's Flight into Egypt, woodcut B.89). A useful bibliography of Vitruvius editions and Italian treatises on architecture is found in G.Lukomski, *Bibl.*203, p.66ss.

28. *Bibl.*201, p.199:

> ''Ηφαιστον κλυτόμητιν ἀείσεο, Μοῦσα λίγεια,
> ''Ος μετ' 'Αθηναίης γλαυκώπιδος ἀγλαὰ ἔργα
> 'Ανθρώπους ἐδίδαξεν ἐπὶ χθονὸς οἳ τὸ πάροσπερ
> ''Αντροις ναιετάασκον ἐν οὔρεσιν, ἠύτε θῆρες.

29. Cf. Roscher, *Bibl.*290, s.v. 'Hephaistos,' V. The Plato passage referred to is found in *Kritias*, 109C (cf. also *Leges*, XI, 120D; *Protagoras*, 321D, and *Kritias*, 112B). The iconography of the Theseion sculptures has been interpreted accordingly in a lecture by Mr.E.C.Olsen.

42

fire, Hephaistos [here conceived as a legendary king of Egypt] enjoyed extremely the warmth in wintertime, and, when the fire went low, he laid on wood. And when he had thus kept the fire going, he convoked the other people to its pleasantness.'[30]

Boccaccio's 'Vitruvian' interpretation of Vulcan throws light on the iconography of a less known, but highly interesting, picture by Piero di Cosimo which was formerly in the collection of Lord Lothian in Dalkeith, Scotland, and has recently been acquired by the National Gallery of Canada, Ottawa (*fig.*18).[31]

In style and general character this painting is evidently very close to the 'Hylas' picture. Both pictures are painted on coarse canvas–'tele' or 'panni,' to quote the expressions used in inventories of the period,–and their dimensions are almost identical. The Hartford picture is 60 x 66.5 inches within the frame, 61.25 x 68.5 inches across the back; the Ottawa picture, 61.5 x 65.5 inches across the back, with a small strip of painted surface sacrificed on either side when the canvas was put on the stretcher.

The inference is that the two paintings belong together.[32] If this is true, and if, on the other hand, the interpretation of the Hartford picture as the 'Finding of Vulcan on Lemnos' is correct, the subject of the other painting,

---

30. This source is transmitted by Diodorus Siculus, *Bibliotheca*, I, 13: Γενομένου γὰρ ἐν τοῖς ὄρεσι κεραυνοβόλου δένδρου καὶ τῆς πλησίον ὕλης καιομένης, προσελθόντα τὸν ῞Ηφαιστον κατὰ τὴν χειμέριον ὥραν ἡσθῆσαι διαφερόντως ἐπὶ τῇ θερμασίᾳ, λήγοντος δὲ τοῦ πυρὸς ἀεὶ τῆς ὕλης ἐπιβάλλειν, καὶ τούτῳ τῷ τρόπῳ διατηροῦντα τὸ πῦρ προκαλεῖσθαι τοὺς ἄλλους ἀνθρώπους πρὸς τὴν ἐξ αὐτοῦ γινομένην εὐχρηστίαν. cf. also *ibidem*, v,74, where Hephaistos is described as teaching mankind all sorts of arts and crafts.
31. The picture had originally been attributed to Signorelli but was vindicated for Piero di Cosimo by A.Venturi, *Bibl.*374, p.69 (with illustration *fig.*39). It is also mentioned by van Marle, *Bibl.*209, VOL.XIII, p.344, but both authorities list it as being in the National Gallery at Edinburgh where it was temporarily exhibited. B.Berenson lists it correctly as being then at Dalkeith, Newbattle Hall, Scotland: *Bibl.*30, p.453, and *Bibl.*31, p.389/390.
32. A.Venturi, *Bibl.*374, p.69, has already pointed out that the 'Edinburgh' painting '*può far riscontro in qualche modo*' to the so-called Hylas picture which was then in the Benson collection. This assumption was endorsed by C.Gamba, *Bibl.*110, who also considers the possibility that the two pictures, together with a series of small-sized panels, may have formed a coherent cycle representing '*il formarsi dell'intelligenza humana*.'

too, would have to be a 'Vulcan story.' This is indeed the case, and the sources adduced in the foregoing paragraphs identify this Vulcan story at first glance. The Ottawa picture shows 'Vulcan as Arch-Craftsman and First Teacher of Human Civilization.'

The tell-tale feature is the scene in the background. Four sturdy labourers erect the frame of a primitive house. They already have some tools such as nails, hammers, and saws, but they still use unsquared tree trunks, and this is exactly what Vitruvius and many of his Renaissance followers tell about the earliest 'technological phase' of human civilization. *'Primumque furcis erectis et virgulis interpositis luto parietes texerunt'* ('And at the beginning they put up rough spars, interwove them with twigs and finished the walls with mud'). The scene looks like a literal translation into images of this description of primitive building, and it is not by accident that the most striking parallels can be found in slightly later woodcuts illustrating the Vitruvius text itself (*figs.22, 23*),[33] and in somewhat earlier drawings illustrating such Renaissance treatises as Filarete's *Trattato di Architettura* (*fig.21*).[34]

With this as a starting point, every element of Piero's composition is easily explained. In the left foreground Vulcan himself can be seen at his anvil. He has the brow of a thinker, the arms and chest of a blacksmith, and the thin, stiff leg which made him the laughing-stock of the Gods. He brandishes his hammer,[35] and it seems that he has just come upon a new invention:

33. Vacat in *Bibl.*378. In *Bibl.*379, fol.xxxii (our *fig.*22). In *Bibl.*380, fol.16, v., our *fig.*23. In *Bibl.*382, fol.lxii. Cf. also the woodcuts in G.A.Rusconi, *Bibl.*292, p.25-28, copied in Polemi's Vitruvius edition, *Bibl.*381, VOL.II, PART I, PL.VIII.
34. Cf. M.Lazzaroni and A.Muñoz, *Bibl.*185, PL.I, *fig.*3 and 4. As to the later use of unsquared trees or roots as a *'motif rustique,'* and as to the Renaissance theory according to which the Gothic style with its elongated pillars, fancy rib-vaults and naturalistic ornamentation was directly derived from the primitive habits of building, cf. E.Panofsky, *Bibl.*240, particularly p.39ss. In classical architecture unsquared spars were, however, used for scaffolding, as can be inferred from the representations of the Tower of Babel in the Encyclopaedia by Hrabanus Maurus (cf. A.M.Amelli, *Bibl.*7, PL.CXIII, and cod. Vat. Pal. lat. 291, fol.193, v.).
35. Cf. 'Thomas Walleys,' *Bibl.*386, fol.19: *'malleum in manu tenens,'* or the *Libellus de Imaginibus Deorum*, ed. Liebeschütz, *Bibl.*194, p.122 (*'maleum in manu tenentis'*) and *fig.*38. The sitting posture of Vulcan—motivated by the weakness of his legs—is not unusual

he is making a horseshoe (another horseshoe has already been finished), and it is evident that the young rider in the centre is keenly interested in this novelty. The kindly old man crouching behind the fire is none other than Aeolus, the God of the Winds,[36] and his presence determines the locale of the scene. In a famous passage Virgil locates the Workshop of Vulcan on one of the islands situated between the coast of Sicily and the island of Lipari, where Aeolus reigned:

> '*Insula Sicanium juxta latus Aeoliamque*
> *Erigitur Liparen fumantibus ardua saxis . . .*'[37]

On the authority of these verses the later mythographers came to imagine a close association between Vulcan and Aeolus, who were finally thought of as something like partners in business. 'The reason why Vulcan was said to have his workshop between Mount Aetna (in Sicily) and Lipari,' Servius says, 'is a natural one, namely, fire and wind, which are both suitable for blacksmith's work. Mount Aetna is a burning mountain (viz., a volcano), and Lipari belongs to the islands ruled by Aeolus,'[38]—a statement which was almost literally repeated by Alexander Neckham,[39] and is also alluded to by Boccaccio.[40] It is only one more step in the same direction when in the *Libellus de Imaginibus Deorum* Aeolus came to be described as working

---

in classical art (cf., e.g., S.Reinach, *Bibl.*276, p.189, or A.Furtwängler, *Bibl.*109, 1896, PL.23, no.2482, PL.32, nos.4266, 4268). It is this type from which derives the '*zum Schmieden sehr wenig geeignete*' posture of Adam in two Byzantine Rosette Caskets (A.Goldschmidt and Kurt Weitzmann, *Bibl.*116, VOL.I, 1930, PL.XLVIII, no.67 e, and PL.XLIX, no.68d, our *fig.25*), where the First Parents are shown as metal-workers, possibly because the caskets were destined to keep jewelry.

36. Cf. Roscher, *Bibl.*290, s.v. 'Aiolos' and Gyraldus, *Bibl.*127, VOL.I, col.188.
37. Virgil, *Aen.*, VIII, 416.
38. Servius, *Comm. in Aen.* VIII, 416: '*Physiologia est, cur Vulcanum in his locis officinam habere fingitur inter Aetnam et Liparen; scilicet propter ignem et ventos, quae apta sunt fabris. "Aeoliam" autem "Liparen" ideo (scil. appellat), quia una est de septem insulis, in quibus Aeolus imperavit.*'
39. Mythogr. III, 10, 5, *Bibl.*38, p.224.
40. Boccaccio, *Genealogia Deorum*, XII, 70.

two actual blacksmith's bellows (*'flabia, instrumenta fabrilia'*),[41] and was illustrated accordingly (*fig.24*).[42]

Thus the figure of Aeolus in Piero di Cosimo's picture becomes fully understandable. The two big objects which he presses with his hands would be difficult to identify without a knowledge of their textual and representational ancestry. As it is, we can recognize them as leather bags which serve the same purpose as the foot-driven bellows in the illustrations of *Libellus de Imaginibus Deorum*. Piero di Cosimo may have substituted an archaic and therefore more dignified device for a modern one by reason of personal taste and inclinations (which we shall shortly analyse). But it is also possible that he had become acquainted with Homer's account of Aeolus sealing the naughty winds into wine skins, or with one of those numerous earlier representations more or less conforming to the Homeric description, as found on classical gems, Byzantine ivory caskets and Romanesque capitals.[43]

The tiny camel emerging from behind a rock with its pack-saddle, and the lovely giraffe which looks on with bashful curiosity (and, incidentally,

---

41. H.Liebeschütz, *Bibl.*194, p.121: *'tenens sub pedibus flabia, instrumenta fabrilia, quasi cum illis insuflans et flata movens.'* According to a Euhemeristic theory transmitted by Servius, Aeolus was really nothing but a good meteorologist who observed the fogs and fumes of his volcanic neighbourhood and was thus able to predict storms and gales (Servius, *Comm. in Aen.*, I, 52; repeated in Mythograph. II, 52, *Bibl.*38, p.92, and Mythograph. III, 4, 10, *Bibl.* 38, p.170). In these texts the storms or gales are called *'flabra'* (*'praedicens futura flabra ventorum imperitis visus est ventos sua potestate retinere'*). The author of the 'Libellus' was apparently unfamiliar with this very poetical word, and, thinking as he did in terms of visual images (cf. *figs.*25, 26), interpreted the word *'flabra'* (or, as he spells it, *'flabia'*) as actual blacksmith's bellows.

42. H.Liebeschütz, *Bibl.*194, PL.XXII, *fig.*36. The figure of Aeolus bears, therefore, a definite resemblance to that of Vulcan himself (*ibidem*, PL.XXIII, *fig.*38).

43. Homer, *Odyss.*, x, 17ss. Of representations I should like to adduce some classical gems showing Odysseus with Aeolus' wine skin (A.Furtwängler, *Bibl.*109, PL.XX, no.20 and PL.XXVII, no.50, also ill. in Daremberg-Saglio, *Bibl.*70, VOL.I, *fig.*156); the Eve in the Byzantine Rosette Caskets; and particularly the personifications of the four Wind Gods in the well-known capital in Vézelay, Ste. Madeleine, ill. in A.Kingsley Porter, *Bibl.*275, VOL.II, PL.31, our *fig.*26 (cf. also the capital in Cluny, ill. in V.Terret, *Bibl.*336, cf. PL.LVI). The Vézelay Wind Gods handle both modern bellows, as in our *fig.*25, and archaic leather skins, as in our *fig.*24. A combination of the wind bag with the more usual wind head can be seen in a representation of 'Aër' in cod. Vind. 12600, fol.30, ill. in H.J.Hermann, *Bibl.*143, p.79, *fig.*36.

46

dates the two Vulcan pictures some time after November 11, 1487),[44] can be accounted for by Piero's 'madly enraptured' interest in the *cose che la natura fà per istranezza*;[45] moreover these motifs determine that precise period in which domestic animals had already been tamed,[46] and wild animals were not yet shy. But we have still to explain the sleeping youth in the foreground and the family group behind him,[47] distinctly Signorellesque in flavour, or even already Michelangelesque. These motives, too, are connected with the character of Vulcan as interpreted in classical literature. In a general way they illustrate the simple happiness of primitive civilization,

44. With a passionate *'animalier'* like Piero who spared no trouble to see strange beasts (cf. the following footnote) and left a whole book of *'disegni d'animali'* (cf. Vasari, *Bibl.*366, VOL.IV, p.138), we may safely assume that he had drawn the giraffe from life, whereas her somewhat mis-shapen baby, carefully keeping step with its mother, seems to be a free invention. Now we learn from Luca Landucci's Diary that a shipment of rare animals presented by the Sultan to the Signoria, which reached Florence on November 11, 1487, included a giraffe: *'Una giraffa molto grande e molto bella e piacevole; com'ella fussi fatta se ne può vedere i molti luoghi in Firenze dipinte. E vissi qui più anni'* (L.Landucci, *Diario, Bibl.*181, p.52, also quoted in this connection by C.Gamba, *Bibl.*110, with the additional information that the poor creature broke its neck at a doorpost before 1492). This giraffe is probably the one which Piero used as a model (it is obviously the same which is mentioned by Schubring under the erroneous date of 1492 in connection with its appearance in a Cassone-panel ascribed to Bartolommeo di Giovanni, *Bibl.*309, no.396, ill. PL.XCIII). A date not too long after 1490 would agree with the style of Piero di Cosimo's Vulcan pictures, which are unanimously acknowledged to belong in his earliest Florentine period and still show a strong influence of Signorelli.
45. Cf. Vasari, *Bibl.*366, VOL.IV, p.134: *'Recavasi spesso a vedere o animali o erbe o qualche cose che la natura fa per istranezza o da caso di molte volte e ne aveva un contento e una satisfazione che lo furava tutto di se stesso.'*
46. Both the vital importance of domestic animals for the development of human civilization and the original friendship between animals and men is permanently emphasized in primitivistic literature. As to the first aspect, suffice it to adduce Ovid, *Fast.*, II, 295:
    'Nullus anhelabat sub adunco vomere taurus. . ,
    Nullus adhuc erat usus equi. Se quisque ferebat.
    Ibat ovis lana corpus amicta sua.'
   As to the friendship motif, cf. *Bibl.*201, p.34, 60, 93ss.
47. Cf. especially the 'Josia' group in the Sistine ceiling. For Signorelli cf. the central figure in the Moses fresco in the Sistine Chapel and the background figures in the Holy Family *tondi* in the Uffizi and in Munich. The ultimate origin of this compact group of crouching figures can be traced back to classical art, where similar groups were used when a comparatively narrow strip had to be filled with figures whose scale was not supposed to be smaller than that of other figures placed in a space of normal proportions. Cf., e.g., the 'Agate de Tibère,' Babelon, *Bibl.*17, PL.I, or such ivories as R.Delbrück, *Bibl.*72, Tafelband, 1929, PL.2.

that is, of a civilization restful and self-sufficient because it had become established on the principle of 'family life.' (The group of father, mother, and child is duplicated on a diminutive scale in the left background of the picture.) But, in addition, the contrast between the sleeping lad and the 'ideal social group' next to him has a specific meaning in connection with Vulcan's personality. For at the very beginning of that famous passage which has already been adduced with reference to the figure of Aeolus, Virgil characterizes Vulcan, the zealous, early-rising workman, in the following terms: 'Then when in mid-career of night, now largely spent, first rest had from his eyes chased drowsy slumber, when she who is forced to make a living by the distaff and the ill-paid loom first stirs the embers and the slumbering fire, adding to her labour-time the hours of night . . . that she may keep pure her husband's home and bring up her little ones, just so and with no less zeal at that time does the Fire-God rise off his downy bed and take his workman's tools.'[48] This unforgettable description is obviously the source of inspiration for the four figures under discussion. Vulcan and his faithful disciples and helpers are already at work 'in mid-career of night, now largely spent' when ordinary people, as represented by the huddled figure in the foreground, are still asleep; only the eager young couple rises from 'drowsy slumber;' the young husband, not yet quite awake, limbers up his stiffened limbs, while the wife attends to her 'little one.' It is the dawn of a new day which, at the same time, symbolizes the dawn of civilization.

---

48. Virgil, *Aen.*, VIII, 407-415:

> 'Inde ubi prima quies medio iam noctis abactae
> Curriculo expulerat somnum, cum femina primum,
> Cui tolerare colo vitam tenuique Minerva
> Impositum, cinerem et sopitos suscitat ignis
> Noctem addens operi, famulasque ad lumina longo,
> Exercet penso, castum ut servare cubile
> Coniugis et possit parvos educere natos:
> Haud secus ignipotens nec tempore segnior illo
> Mollibus e stratis opera ad fabrilia surgit.'

I follow A.H.Bryce, *The Works of Virgil, a literal translation*, 1894, p.375, but have rendered the '*quies*' by 'rest' instead of 'sleep,' and omitted an unwarranted 'worthily' before 'bring up.'

Thus the Ottawa picture demonstrably corresponds to the Hartford painting not only in style and size, but also in iconography.[49] Whether the two
compositions were just companions or belonged to a whole series of 'Vulcan
stories' remains, of course, a matter of surmise. But a strong argument in
favour of the second alternative can be found in the fact that Vasari mentions
a painting by Piero di Cosimo now lost or at least unknown, which showed
'Mars, Venus with her Cupids, and Vulcan.'[50] This painting, depicting, as
it does, a third chapter of the Vulcan epic, may well have been the third
element of one coherent series, the other parts of which Vasari had either not
seen or did not remember, or chose to omit because he could not identify
their subjects.[51]

From a purely iconological point of view, the Ottawa picture may be
compared to the two cassone panels (one in Munich, the other in Stras-

49. I was informed by the previous owner of the Ottawa picture that Dr.A.Scharf, who is
preparing a monograph on Piero di Cosimo, had suggested the legend of Phoroneus, King
of Argos, as a possible subject of the painting. This interpretation is understandable, inasmuch as Pausanias relates what follows: 'They (viz., the people of Argos) attribute the
invention of fire to Phoroneus' (*Periegesis*, II, 19, 5), and: 'Phoroneus . . . first gathered
men together in communities who before lived scattered and solitary; so the city in which
they were first gathered together was called Phoronicum' (*ibidem*, II, 15, 5). It is, however,
evident, and was felt by Pausanias himself, that the local patriots of Argos had simply
transferred the myths of Prometheus and Vulcan to their legendary king who is otherwise only known: either as a legislator (Plato, *Timaeus*, 22, A/B; Eusebius, *Chronic.*, p.29.
Helm; Isidorus, *Etymolog.*, v, i.6; Brunetto Latini, *Tesoro*, I, 17, *Bibl.*184, VOL.I, p.52;
Boccaccio, *Genealog. Deor.*, VII, 23; cf. also the relief at the Campanile at Florence, ill. in
J.v.Schlosser, *Bibl.*304, *fig.6*); or as the founder of the local cult of Hera (Mythographus II,
8, *Bibl.*38, p.77, on the basis of Hyginus, *Fabulae*, 225 and 274). Pausanias is the only
writer to transmit the glorified conception built up by the Argos patriots, and it is highly
improbable that Piero di Cosimo could have become familiar with this version. For
Pausanias was practically unknown in the fifteenth century; the first Greek edition
appeared in Venice, 1516, and the first Latin translation, by Romolo Amaseo, was not
finished and published before 1547, although another one had been begun in 1498 (cf.
C.B.Stark, *Bibl.*321, p.93). In addition, the legend of Phoroneus would not account for as
many details of the Ottawa picture as does the myth of Vulcan, and would be incompatible
with the content of the painting in Hartford.
50. Vasari, *Bibl.*366, VOL.IV, p.139: '*E così un quadro di Marte e Venere con i suoi Amori e
Vulcano, fatto con una grande arte e con una pazienza incredibile.*'
51. It must be remembered that the possessions of Francesco del Pugliese, for whom the pictures were probably painted, had been dispersed when Vasari wrote his '*Vite.*'

49

burg) which represent the myth of Prometheus and Epimetheus (*fig.33*).[52] In both these cases the imagination of the artist is centred around the 'Awakening of Humanity,' and in both cases the stimulus of this awakening is fire. However, the two Prometheus panels are of a much later date; in fact, they seem to belong in the very latest period of Piero's activity, and they differ from the Vulcan compositions in style and execution, as well as in content and atmosphere. Not only do they show a severe suppression of realistic and picturesque details in favour of simplicity and dramatic concentration, but they also describe a phase of human civilization which has definitely surpassed the primitive stage depicted in the Vulcan picture. The technical and social organization of life has already reached high standards, the buildings are no longer constructed with tree trunks and branches, people no longer live in scattered family groups. The 'technological' phase of man's evolution is completed, and the next step to be taken cannot but lead to a craving for mental autonomy which, encroaching on the rights of the gods, spells deification rather than humanization. It presupposes sacrifice and entails punishment. The later mythographers, especially Boccaccio, have always insisted on the fact that, while Vulcan personifies the *ignis elementatus*, that is, the physical fire which enables mankind to solve its practical problems, the torch of Prometheus lighted at the wheels of the sun's chariot ('*rota solis, id est e gremio Dei*'), carries the 'celestial fire' which stands for the 'clarity of knowledge infused into the heart of the ignorant,' and that this very clarity can only be attained at the expense of happiness and peace of mind.[53]

52. The Strasburg panel (our *fig.33*) is illustrated in Schubring, *Bibl.*309, PL.XCVI, no.413 and van Marle, *Bibl.*209, VOL.XIII, *fig.*256; the Munich panel in Schubring, *Bibl.*310, PL.XV, no.412. As to the iconography of both pictures cf. K.Habich, *Bibl.*130, and K.Borinski, *Bibl.*45.
53. According to Boccaccio, *Genealogia Deorum*, XII, 70 the (invisible) *elementum ignis* is personified by Jupiter, whereas Vulcan personifies the *ignis elementatus* which can be divided into the aerial fire (lightning) and the earthly fire. Vulcan's limp would symbolize both the zigzag-shape of lightnings and the wavering-instability of flames (for all this, cf. Remigius' Commentary on Martianus Capella as related by H.Liebeschütz, *Bibl.*194, p.44ss., and Mythographus III, 10, 4, *Bibl.*38, p.223). As to the Prometheus myth, cf. Boccaccio, *ibidem*, IV, 44: '*Hanc demum flammam, id est doctrinae claritatem, immittit pectori lutei*

Thus the Prometheus compositions might be considered a belated post-script to the Vulcan epic, related to it in the abstract rather than concretely. There is, however, another set of small panels by Piero di Cosimo which is connected with the Vulcan pictures not only intellectually but also in style, period, aesthetic attitude, and possibly even in destination. This set consists of: (1) the 'Hunting Scene' and the 'Return from the Hunt,' both in the Metropolitan Museum in New York; (2) the 'Landscape with Animals,' formerly owned by Prince Paul of Yugoslavia, now in the Ashmolean Museum at Oxford (*figs.27-29*).[54]

hominis, id est ignari.' In Piero's Strasburg panel this idea is beautifully expressed by the triumphal gesture of the statue which forms a striking contrast with the tortured position of Prometheus. The punishment of the latter symbolizes the price which mankind has to pay for its intellectual awakening, that is, '*a meditationibus sublimibus anxiari*' (to be tortured by our profound meditation), and to recover only in order to be tortured again. For the fundamental importance of the Prometheus-myth see G.Habich, *Bibl*.130, and K.Borinski, *Bibl*.45; furthermore E.Cassirer, *Bibl*.59, p.100. I should like to mention three significant passages by Marsilio Ficino, the founder of the Neoplatonic movement in the Renaissance: *Quaestiones quinque de mente, Bibl*.90, p.680; *Comment. in Platon. Philebum, ibid.*, p.1232; *Comment. in Platon. Protagoram, ibid.*, p.1298.

54. As to the two panels in the Metropolitan Museum, viz., the *Hunting Scene*, Catal. P.61, 1 (henceforth referred to as 'A') and the *Return from the Hunt*, Catal. P.61,2 (henceforth referred to as 'B'), cf. Schubring, *Bibl*.309, no.383 and 384, ill. PL.XC, and van Marle, *Bibl*.209, VOL.XIII, p.248 and *fig*.169 (with further references). As to the 'Landscape with Animals' formerly owned by the Prince Paul of Yugoslavia (henceforth referred to as 'C'), cf. Schubring, *Bibl*.310, no.932, ill. PL.XVI, and van Marle, *l.c.*, p.346 and *fig*.236 (with further references). The dimensions, partly inaccurate, partly misprinted in Schubring's Corpus, but already corrected in Roger Fry's article, quoted below, are:

A, our *fig*.27, Schubring 383: 28 x 66¼ inches,
B, our *fig*.28, Schubring 384: 28 x 66⅞ inches,
C, our *fig*.29, Schubring 932: 28 x 77⅜ inches.

The uniformity in style and mood, as well as the identity in height, of the three panels, have already been stressed by Roger Fry, Pictures at the Burlington Fine Arts Club, *Bibl*.107. They illustrate a unified iconographical program, and were certainly destined to adorn the walls of a room (cf. also F.J.M. [Mather], *Bibl*.211). Roger Fry ascribed the whole series to Piero di Cosimo and thereby corrected the attribution by Schubring to Bartolommeo di Giovanni. R. van Marle, curiously enough, ascribes A and B to Bartolommeo di Giovanni while assigning C to Piero di Cosimo. Berenson correctly attributes all the panels to Piero di Cosimo (*Bibl*.31, pp.389, 390). To this series of three, Schubring has added a fourth panel (henceforth referred to as 'D'), the 'Battle of Lapiths and Centaurs' in the Ricketts-Shannon Collection, now on loan in the National Gallery in London (*Bibl*.309, no.385 and PL.XC, cf. van Marle, *l.c.*, p.248), our *fig*.30. It is true that this picture was executed—by Piero di Cosimo, of course, cf. again Berenson, *l.c.*—at about the same time as A, B, and C, and that it has the same height (28 x 102 inches). But its icono-

These three panels depict the phase of human history which preceded the technical and social developments brought about by the teachings of Vulcan, in other words, the age of stone in contrast with the age of metal. They all have in common the absence of the achievements emphasized in the Ottawa picture; the details of man's truly primeval existence when he was still ignorant of the uses of fire, are elaborated by Piero with the same archaeological, or rather, palaeontological, conscientiousness which he had bestowed on the rendering of the life under Vulcan.[55] There are no metal tools or weapons; consequently, the tree trunks which serve as masts for the caned boats and

graphy militates against the assumption that it belongs to the same series. In contrast with A, B, and C, it shows the paraphernalia of a higher civilization, especially metal objects and woven materials, and has a definite mythographical content,—so much so that even the curious detail of the use of a burning altar as a missile can be accounted for by Ovid's description of the Centaur Gryneus (*Met.*, XII, 258ss.). D was most probably an independent work like many other contemporary representations of the same subject, for instance Michelangelo's famous relief in the Casa Buonarroti. It should be mentioned in passing that a connection exists between this relief and Piero's Battle of Lapiths and Centaurs. Both compositions show the striking motif of a woman torn between a Lapith and a Centaur, and a reminiscence of the central group in Piero's picture may be seen in the compact groups of crouching panic-stricken figures in the fresco of the Flood (in a remodelled form, similar groups reoccur in the drawings of the thirties), as well as in the Ignudo on the right of Daniel.

Two other pictures mentioned in connection with the panels here under discussion (Schubring, *Bibl.*309, no.386, van Marle, *l.c.*, p.248, both without illustrations or measurements) are owned by Mr. Francis Howard in London (formerly by Mr.A.Meyer in London) and represent the Marriage Feast of Pirithous and Hippodamia (or Deidamia). The author of these pictures (ill. in *Bibl.*65, p.52 and 53) is, however, Bartolommeo di Giovanni; see B.Berenson, *Bibl.*29, 1909, p.98. I am indebted to Dr.A.Scharf, London, for information concerning these pictures. Through a curious coincidence which should warn us against laying too much stress on identical measurements, the two Howard panels have almost exactly the same dimensions (31.5 x 51 inches) as two authentic panels by Piero di Cosimo which were executed for Giovanni (or Guidantonio) Vespucci. For these pictures, which should not be confused with the Francesco del Pugliese series, see p.58ss. and *figs.*31, 32.

55. The two ships appearing in the background of the 'Return from the Hunt' (our *fig.*28) with their boldly curved bow and long ram at the stern are, e.g., very similar to those occurring on archaic Greek vases. Cf., for instance, C.Torr, *Bibl.*359, *fig.*15. The fact that ancient vases were known to and utilized by the Italian Renaissance artists has been rightly emphasized, in connection with Antonio Pollaiuolo, by F.R.Shapley, *Bibl.*317, and can be corroborated by a long and ecstatic description of pottery found in Arezzo (Ristoro d'Arezzo, *De la composizione del mondo*, reprinted in V.Nannucci, *Bibl.*227, VOL.II, p.201; cf.J.v.Schlosser, *Bibl.*305, p.31, and *idem*, *Bibl.*306, p.152).

rafts in the 'Return from the Hunt' are not only unsquared for want of planes, but also untrimmed for want of saws. (Note the protruding branches and rough edges.) There are no woven materials for clothing or comfort; consequently, people go naked, or clad in skins or hides. There are no domesticated animals, no real buildings, and no family life. The ruling principle of this aboriginal state, namely the unfamiliarity of mankind with the use of fire, is conspicuously emphasized by what might be termed the '*leitmotiv*' of the whole series: the forest fire, which can be seen ravaging the woods and frightening away the animals in all three panels;[56] in two of them it even appears repeatedly. The persistent recurrence of this motif cannot be accounted for by mere pictorial fancy. It is, most evidently, an iconographical attribute rather than a whimsical *concetto*, for it is identical with the famous forest fire which had haunted the imaginations of Lucretius, Diodorus Siculus, Pliny, Vitruvius, and Boccaccio. We remember that it appeared regularly in all the illustrations of Vitruvius, and in the Renaissance it was as characteristic of representations of the Stone Age as the tower was of images of St. Barbara.

The '*priscorum hominum vita*,' then, to quote the Como edition of Vitruvius, is the common subject of the three paintings. Within this general program, however, the two pictures in the Metropolitan Museum appear to be more closely connected than either of them is with the Oxford panel, not only in size, but also in content. In the two Metropolitan pictures unbridled passions prevail. As there is no real separation between mankind and animals on the one hand, mankind and half-beasts such as satyrs and centaurs on the other, all these creatures love and mate, or fight and kill, indiscriminately, without paying any attention whatever to their common enemy, the forest fire. Yet even this ultra-primitive world offers two different aspects. In the 'Hunting Scene' (*fig.27*) there is nothing but horror and death, with a ghastly corpse in the foreground: a jungle fight of all against all (for instance,

---

56. The woodcuts in the Como edition (our *fig.19*) and the French translation also show animals frightened out of the woods by the fire.

a lion attacking a bear but at the same time being attacked by a man), a mutual destruction in which Pollaiuolo's heroes, resurrected as a horde of satyrs
and cavemen, fight for their lives with clubs, teeth and the sheer force of
muscular arms,

'*Arma antiqua manus ungues dentesque fuerunt
Et lapides et item silvarum fragmina rami.*'[57]

No women appear in the composition, and no traces of constructive activity
can be discerned.

The 'Return from the Hunt' (*fig.*28) shows the same primeval form of
life in a somewhat friendlier light. The ferocious killing is over. The booty
is brought 'home' on the ingenious boats already described. (Incidentally,
the boars' skulls attached to the masts of the foremost craft are further evidence of Piero's archaeological interests.)[58] One man is shown building a new
raft. And the ladies are not absent here; in fact, some of the groups seem to
realize the wishful dream of many civilized men,[59] an '*Isle de Cythère*' of the
stone age.

In the Oxford panel, one of the earliest real landscape paintings in post-
classical art, the proto-human passions have subsided, and a certain progress
toward civilization is in evidence (*fig.*29). There is a little hut, no matter
how crude, and nearby can be seen some figures busy with primitive vessels
(cf. the woodcut from the Venice Vitruvius edition of 1511). The time has

---

57. Lucretius, *De Rer. Nat.*, v, 1283.
58. As a matter of fact the earliest form of ornamental ship's rams was a bronze boar's head.
Cf. C.Torr, *Bibl.*359, p.64 and *figs.*17, 43; furthermore, Daremberg-Saglio, *Bibl.*70, VOL.IV,
*figs.*5282, 5958. A Renaissance 'archaeologist' might easily have come to the conclusion
that this feature originated from a primitive habit of using real animals' skulls as a protective charm, as was, and is still, the case in rural districts all over the world (for Italy, cf.
L.B.Alberti, *De Architectura*, x, 13, where a horse's skull put up on a pole is recommended
as a protection against caterpillars, which practice has survived up to our own day).
Moreover it was known from Tacitus, *Germania*, 45, that the 'Aestii,' that is, the coast
dwellers of the Baltic Sea, had been in the habit of using boars' images as a 'totem:' '*insigne
superstitionis formas aprorum gestant; id pro armis omnique tutela securum deae cultorem
etiam inter hostes praestat.*'
59. According to the *New Yorker*, *Bibl.*229, Ealine Scroggins and Herman Jarrett married
in a cave while clad in the skins of wild animals.

not come for woven clothes, but the man in the middle plane on the right wears a coarse leather coat instead of uncured skins. The woods are still haunted by the strange creatures which resulted from the promiscuous mating of men and animals, for the sow with the face of a woman and the goat with the face of a man are by no means Bosch-like phantasms: they are meant to bear witness to a very serious theory,—contested, and thereby effectively transmitted, in no less than thirty-five lines of Lucretius.[60] These strange creatures seem peacefully to share the woods and fields with lions, deer, cranes, cows, and an enticing family of bears. Were it not for the admirable refinement of pictorial technique, one would think of Henri Rousseau or of Edward Hicks.[61] But, in truth, what looks like the camaraderie of a 'Peaceable Kingdom' is chiefly due to common fear and common fatigue; for these beasts and half-beasts are not so much peaceful as exhausted by flight and stunned by terror of the forest fire. Man, too, is now aware of this fire, but instead of being frightened he seizes his chance to catch some of the cows and oxen that have fled from the burning woods; their future yoke he carries providently on his shoulder.

The system on which Piero di Cosimo's evolutionistic compositions are based bears some resemblance to the theological division of human history into the era *ante legem*, the era *sub lege*, and the era *sub gratia*. Using the same prepositions, we could speak of an era *ante Vulcanum*, an era *sub*

60. Lucretius, *De Rer. Nat.*, v, 890-924. There is one case in early mediaeval art where, owing to an overconscientious interpretation of Genesis, the half-human monsters (transmitted through the *Physiologus*, Bestiaries and Encyclopaedias) have been included in a representation of the Paradise, from which results, without the artist's knowledge, an effect comparable to that of Piero di Cosimo's 'primitivistic' paintings: the ivory plaque ill. in A.Goldschmidt, *Bibl.*117, vol.I, 1914, PL.LXX, no.158: Adam and Eve's menagerie includes not only centaurs and sirens, but also satyrs with deers' heads and human beings with cows' and dogs' heads.—In the Renaissance a 'realistic' interpretation of such hybrid monsters, called to my attention by Professor M.Schapiro, has been attempted not only by Piero di Cosimo, but also by Cima da Conegliano who, however, tries to explain them ethnologically, rather than palaeontologically: the satyrs in his Procession of Silenus (L.Venturi, *Bibl.*375, PL.CCCX) are of an unmistakably negroid type.—For the influence of Lucretius on Florentine Quattrocento art see A.Warburg, *Bibl.*387, VOL.I, p.41ss., 321 and VOL.II, p.478; furthermore H.Pflaum, *Bibl.*265, p.15ss.

61. Cf. the interesting article by Louisa Dresser, *Bibl.*78, with illustration.

Vulcano, and an era *sub Prometheo*; the analogy of ideas holds good to the extent that in both cases the inaugurator of the third phase is crucified for those whom he was destined to save. Therefore, the 'Vulcan on Lemnos' in Hartford, and the Ottawa picture with 'Vulcan and Aeolus as Teachers of Mankind,' would be an interpretation of the era *sub Vulcano*, while the three little panels in New York and Oxford would interpret the era *ante Vulcanum*. And since it is unanimously acknowledged that the two series were painted at the same time, it would be an attractive hypothesis to think that they also belong together in a more technical sense, that is, that they were planned as a single decorative scheme and all were originally under the same roof. This hypothesis agrees with what we learn from Vasari. According to him, Piero di Cosimo painted for the house of Francesco del Pugliese 'some stories with little figures, disposed around a room.' 'One cannot express,' Vasari continues, 'the diversity of the fantastic things which he enjoyed depicting in these paintings, huts and animals and various costumes and implements, and other fanciful inventions which suited him because they were so fabulous.'[62] It is more than likely, and has been rightly assumed by others,[63] that these fanciful pictures are identical with the three panels in Oxford and New York, which really have no definite meaning in the sense of a mythological 'story.' Moreover Vasari relates that 'after the death of Francesco del Pugliese and his sons these paintings were removed, and I do not know what has become of them,'[64] from which we learn that they were panels, not frescoes. Immediately after this, now, Vasari proceeds to the lost picture with Venus and Vulcan: 'And also a painting of Mars and Venus with her Cupids, and Vulcan;'[65] and though it is not absolutely certain that

---

62. Vasari, *Bibl.*366, VOL.IV, '*Fece parimente in casa di Francesco del Pugliese intorno a una camera diverse storie di figure piccole; nè si può esprimere la diversità delle cose fantastiche che egli in tutte quelle si dilettò dipignere, e di casamenti e d'animali e di abiti e stromenti diversi, ed altre fantasie, che gli sovvennono per essere storie di favole.*'

63. *Bibl.*200, no.225.

64. '*Queste istorie, doppo la morte di Francesco del Pugliese e de' figliuoli, sono state levate, ne sò ove sieno capitate.*'

65. Italian text quoted p.49, N.50.

Vasari's *E così* means to express that this painting was also executed for Francesco del Pugliese, such a conclusion is permissible and has, as a matter of fact, already been drawn by writers who based themselves on nothing but the Vasari text.[66]

Thus there is really good reason to suppose that the three panels in New York and Oxford and the 'Vulcan series' were executed for the same employer; one would like to imagine that the three smaller panels, which could only have been destined for a room of very moderate dimensions, decorated an anteroom which led to a *Salone* adorned with the monumental Vulcan stories, and that the Oxford panel, depicting a transition from unmitigated bestiality to a comparatively human life, was placed above the doorway. If arranged like this, the two series of paintings here discussed would have formed one comprehensive cycle which, in a rich and persuasive manner, would have represented the two earliest phases of human history as described in classical writing, and illustrated in two successive woodcuts in the editions of Vitruvius: 'Vulcanus,' raging in the woods, while man, not yet befriended by him, shares the excitements and fears of animals and hybrid monsters; and 'Vulcanus' again, descending upon the earth in human form and pointing the path towards civilization.

Giovanni Cambi in his *Istorie*[67] speaks of a Francesco di Filippo Pugliese or simply Francesco del Pugliese (*uomo popolano e merchatante e richo*), who was one of the Priori of Florence in 1490-91 (a few years before the probable date of our pictures), and then again in 1497-98. In the troubled year 1513 he was banished from the city for having publicly insulted the name of Lorenzo de Medici the Younger with the Rabelaisian exclamation 'el Mag-

---

66. R. van Marle, *Bibl.*209, VOL.XIII, p.380.

67. Giovanni Cambi, *Bibl.*53, VOL.XXI, pp.58, 125 and VOL.XXII, p.28. The fact that, according to Cambi, Francesco del Pugliese was '*sanza figliuoli d' età 55*' in the year 1513 is corroborated by his will made on February '28, 1502 (1503) in which he leaves his property to his cousins Filippo and Niccolò; cf. H.P.Horne, *Bibl.*148, p.52. Vasari's statement that Francesco del Pugliese's possessions had been dispersed 'after he *and his sons* had died' is therefore obviously erroneous.

57

nifico merda.' If, as is most plausible, this wealthy, plain-spoken democrat was the patron who commissioned the series now in question, it is no wonder that their subject matter revolves around the figure of Vulcan, the only ungentlemanly workman—βάναυσος, to quote from Lucian's *De Sacrificiis*—in the Olympian leisure class. It is even possible that the strikingly individual head of Vulcan in the Ottawa picture portrays Francesco del Pugliese himself, who was about thirty-five when the picture was executed.[68]

However, to account exclusively for the meticulous primitivism of the series just examined by the political persuasions and social standing of Francesco del Pugliese would be absurd. Evidence of Piero di Cosimo's extraordinary preoccupation with the circumstances and emotions of primordial existence is practically ubiquitous in his paintings, regardless of subject, patron, and destination.

That we are faced with a definitely personal trait, with a peculiar consistent interest, constantly on the alert in the artist's mind, is further proved by another series of paintings closely akin to the three panels in New York and Oxford; they, too, were 'disposed around a room' in a patrician palace at Florence. Stylistically, however, they are a little more advanced (there is good reason to believe that they were executed in 1498 or shortly after),

---

68. Signor A. Panella, Soprintendente del R.Archivio di Stato di Firenze, to whom I wish to express my sincerest gratitude, was kind enough to collect the following documentary data concerning Francesco del Pugliese: The family was engaged in the wool and tailoring business. Francesco di Filippo di Francesco del Pugliese—the only Francesco of his generation, which confirms his identity with Piero di Cosimo's patron—was born on May 30, 1458 (*Liber secundus approbationum aetatum*, Serie delle Tratte, 41, CARTA 32 t.). On January 5, 1462 (or 1463 respectively), he was enrolled with the Arte della Lana '*ex persona Filippi sui patris*' (Arte della Lana, 22, CARTA 152). In 1469 he lived in the house of his uncle Piero di Francesco del Pugliese, and his age is then given as ten. In 1480 he is still registered there (Catasto 1001, Campione del Quartiere Santo Spirito, Gonfalone del Drago, a 212), but his age is here given as nineteen, which is an obvious error in view of the two other entries adduced. His first term as 'Priore' began on September 1, 1490, his second term on January 1, 1497. It appears that Giovanni Cambi's statements as to Francesco del Pugliese's age and terms of office are meticulously correct; thus there is no reason to question his story of Francesco's banishment in 1513, although this incident could not be verified by other documents.

and from an iconographical point of view they hold an intermediary position between the Vulcan series and the two Prometheus Cassoni, depicting as they do the contributions of Bacchus to human civilization, particularly the Discovery of Honey.

We find these paintings thus described by Vasari: 'For Giovanni Vespucci who lives opposite to S. Michele della via de'Servi, he executed some bacchanals (*"storie baccanarie"*) which are arrayed around a room. In these he depicted fauns, satyrs, *silvani*, putti and bacchantes so strange that it is a marvel to behold the diversity of shepherds' scrips and costumes, and the variety of caprine features, all with the truest grace and verisimilitude. In one story there is a Silenus riding on a donkey with many children, who support him and give him to drink, and one sees a hilarity true to life, done with great ingenuity.'[69] This lively description has made it possible to identify two of the panels originally constituting the Giovanni Vespucci series which have passed from the Sebright Collection at Beechwood, England, into American museums (*figs.*31, 32).[70]

69. Vasari, *Bibl.*366, VOL.IV, p.141.: *'Lavorò per Giovan Vespucci, che stava dirimpetto a S. Michele della via de'Servi, oggi di Pier Salviati, alcune storie baccanarie che sono intorno a una camera; nelle quali fece sì strani fauni, satiri, silvani, e putti, e baccanti, che è una maraviglia a vedere la diversità de' zaini e delle vesti, e la varietà della cere caprine, con una grazia e imitazione verissima. Evvi in una storia Sileno a cavallo su uno asino con molti fanciulli che lo regge e chi gli dà bere; e si vede una letizia al vivo, fatta con grande ingegno.'* In the current translations the word 'zaino' is rendered by 'bay horse.' But the combination 'zaini e vesti,' as well as the obvious incompatibility of horses with bacchanals proves that Vasari meant not a 'záino,' but a 'zaíno,' that is a pouch or shepherds' scrip, as seen in our *fig.*31; the word is still in use for a knapsack made of fur (in contradistinction to a '*bisaccia*' which may consist of any other material). The motif which seems to have struck Vasari as unusual makes the identification of the two pictures here discussed all the more certain. C.Gamba, *Bibl.*110, suggests that the Vespucci series might have been executed not for Giovanni Vespucci but for his father Guidantonio, who purchased a house on the Via de'Servi in 1498 and had it decorated in the same year by various painters. This date would be in harmony with the stylistic characters of the pictures (unknown to Gamba) which certainly belong into Piero's earlier period, but are apparently somewhat later than the three panels in Oxford and New York.

70. The dimensions of both pictures are 31.25 x 50.25 inches. They were first identified with the Vespucci panels by H.Ulmann, *Bibl.*362, p.129, but this correct identification seems to have been lost in most recent literature, excepting some Vasari editions, such as the German translation *Bibl.*367, p.193, or the new Italian edition (Collezione Salani), *Bibl.*368, p.447s. F.Knapp, *Bibl.*167, p.86s. merely gives a very inaccurate description of the Sebright

One of these panels is (see Fig. 32) unfinished: while the admirable landscape is practically completed, most of the figures are still in the 'underpainting' stage. However, thanks to a text later to be adduced, we can identify the subject. The 'big, deer-like animal,' as it has been called in previous descriptions, is Silenus' donkey who kicks his unfortunate rider while he is falling off. Silenus appears twice more in the composition. On the right his companions help him to his feet again, one of them using a heavy stick as a lever, others uniting their forces in a collective effort. On the left he lies on the ground while his laughing befrienders, including Bacchus and Ariadne, look on and children gather mud in bowls, to smear his face with it (this unusual scene, difficult to understand for a beholder unacquainted with the textual source, is perhaps what Vasari has in mind when he speaks of 'children who give him to drink').

The second panel, (Fig. 31), now owned by the Worcester Art Museum, is admirably preserved. It shows, as leading characters, a rather rustic, broadly smiling Bacchus, characterized by a vine which curls around a small tree-trunk[71] and by a silver cup, and Ariadne, elaborately dressed and bearing a wine-jug of classicizing shape. The god has led his *thiasos* from a peaceful little hill-town down to a meadow dominated in the centre by a gigantic hollow tree. Here the cortège consisting of Silenus and his companions, satyrs of both sexes and varied ages, and a few human females, has separated. Some rest or attend to the little ones, some stray through the woods, but the largest group is intent on making a terrific noise. The purpose of this noise is to cause a swarm of bees to settle on a branch of the hollow tree.

pictures (reprinted, s.v. 'Bartolommeo di Giovanni,' by P.Schubring, *Bibl.*309, nos.391-392). R. van Marle, *Bibl.*209, vol.xiii, p.380, lists the Vespucci panels as 'lost' and ascribes the Sebright pictures to Bartolommeo di Giovanni (*ibid.*, p.248). B.Berenson, *Bibl.*30, and *Bibl.* 31, does not mention them at all, but is reported to have endorsed their attribution to Piero di Cosimo after they had become known to him.

71. The tree-trunk enveloped by a vine is the typical attribute of Bacchus in classical statuary and can perhaps be identified with an elm which is traditionally connected with the vine. Cf. Joachim Camerarius, *Bibl.*54, I, symb. xxiv, with quotation of Catullus, *Carmina*, lxii, 49ss.

Some of the insects have already started to form the characteristic 'grape-like' cluster, thanks to the insistence of three satyrs, two of whom, an adult and a baby, have climbed to a vantage point on the gnarled tree.

The use of noisy instruments to keep swarming bees from straying—a method still practised by bee-keepers throughout the world—has been described by numerous classical poets and naturalists.[72] But it is difficult to see what Bacchus and Ariadne and their votaries have to do with the procedure. The answer lies in a passage from Ovid's *Fasti* (III, 725ss.), which also accounts for the subject of the first picture.[73] Ovid sets out to explain why the rites of the Feast of Bacchus include the offering and eating of sweet cakes called *liba*. The very name of these cakes, he says, is derived from the Latin name of Bacchus, viz. *Liber*, as are the words *libamen* or *libatio* for offerings in general. It was Bacchus who, upon his return from Asia, taught people to light fires on altars and to honour the gods by solemn offerings. That sweet cakes should be offered to Bacchus was most fitting, for he was credited with the discovery of honey: 'Cakes are made for the God because he takes delight in sweet syrups, and because it is said that honey was discovered by Bacchus. Accompanied by satyrs he left the sandy Hebrus and had already reached the Rhodope mountains and the flowery Pangaion [both in Thrace]. The brass-clad hands of his companions clapped. And lo! a young swarm of bees, attracted by the noise, gathers and follows wherever the resounding brass leads them. Liber catches the stragglers and imprisons them in a hollow tree, and gets, as a prize, the honey thus discovered.'[74] His votaries

---

72. Cf. Pauly-Wissowa, *Bibl.*256, vol.v, s.v. 'Biene,' especially col.444ss.
73. It is interesting to note that Ovid's *Fasti* were particularly popular with the Florentine humanists of Piero's time. Angelo Poliziano lectured on them in public and seems to have made them the object of a commentary in Latin verse, and a friend of his, called Michael Verinus, pronounced them '*illius vatis* [viz., Ovid] *liber pulcherrimus*' (cf. A.Warburg, *Bibl.*387, vol.i, p.34).
74. Ovid, *Fasti*, III, 735-744. '*Liba Deo fiunt: Succis quia dulcibus ille*
       Gaudet, et a Baccho mella reperta ferunt.
   Ibat arenoso Satyris comitatus ab Hebro:
    (*Non habet ingratos fabula nostra jocos*)
   Jamque erat at Rhodopen Pangaeaque florida ventum:
    Aeriferae comitum concrepuere manus.

61

enjoy the discovery and of their own accord search the woods for honey-combs. But Silenus, greedy and lazy as he is, drives his donkey near a hollow elm where he hopes to find another bee-hive, and climbs upon the donkey's back. But the branch on which he holds his heavy weight breaks, and the beehive turns out to be a hornets' nest. Thus he is miserably stung on his bald pate, falls from his donkey, gets kicked, wrenches his knee, yells for help and is finally rescued by his companions who laughingly teach him to treat his stings with mud and mire and finally manage to put him on his feet.[75]

This delightful tale explains most of the puzzling features of the two Vespucci panels. It accounts for the combination of the Bacchic cortège with the bee scene, for the prominence of the two hollow trees—one destined to be the home of the first man-controlled swarm of bees, the other harbour-ing the vicious hornets, for the satyrs climbing trees in search of more honey, and for the many misfortunes of Silenus. However, Piero has inter-preted the Ovidian scenario in a highly personal manner.

Even discounting such strikingly individual features as the sentimen-tally expressive donkey later paralleled in seventeenth-century Dutch paint-

Ecce novae coeunt volucres, tinnitibus actae:
  Quaque movent sonitus aera, sequuntur apes.
Colligit errantes, et in arbore claudit inani
  Liber: et inventi praemia mellis habet.'
75. Ovid, *ibid.*, 747-760. 'Ut Satyri levisque senex tetigere saporem:*
  Quaerebant flavos per nemus omne favos.
Audit in exesa stridorem examinis ulmo:
  Adspicit et ceras, dissimulatque senex.
Utque piger pandi tergo residebat aselli;
  Adplicat hunc ulmo corticibusque cavis.
Constitit ipse super ramoso stipite nixus:
  Atque avide trunco condita mella petit.
Millia crabronum coeunt; et vertice nudo
  Spicula defigunt, oraque summa notant.
Ille cadit praeceps, et calce feritur aselli:
  Inclamatque suos, auxiliumque rogat.
Concurrunt Satyri, turgentiaque ora parentis
  Rident. Percusso claudicat ille genu.
Ridet et ipse Deus: limumque inducere monstrat.
  Hic paret monitis, et linit ora luto.'

ings, or the weirdly twisted tree worthy of a German romantic artist,[76] Piero's version differs from all other representations of Bacchic processions in that he does not show the train of the god as a throng of ecstatic votaries but as a fantastic tribe of nomads. Ovid imagines a corybantic procession whose frenzied noise attracts the bees by accident; Piero depicts a group of wanderers some of whom enjoy the halt or go about their business, while others are engaged in purposeful apicultural exertions. Ovid, like all the artists who ever rendered Bacchic rites, imagines the instruments in the *aeriferae comitum manus* as ceremonial cymbals; but Piero's satyrs employ humble household utensils such as pots, pans, ladles, tongs, shovels and graters, and use cudgels, bones, and deer-hoofs for drumsticks. The crouching figure in the right foreground—probably meant to be Pan—smilingly produces three onions from his knapsack (Vasari's *zaino*) where he also keeps his little Pandean pipe. The two women who in any orthodox Bacchanal should be tripping, riotous maenads sedately lead a satyr baby by the hand and carry a big kettle.

Piero's sharp realization of primitive conditions, and his shift from a Dionysian to a pastoral interpretation[77] is more than a good joke, although an element of deliberate parody is unmistakable;[78] it serves to emphasize an

76. Cf., e.g., C.W.Kolbe, ill. in L.Grote, *Bibl*.124, *fig*.13.

77. A similar re-interpretation can be observed in Piero's 'Venus and Mars' (Berlin, Kaiser Friedrich Museum) as compared to Botticelli's rendering of the same subject (National Gallery, London). The subject—a glorification of 'cosmic love' pacifying the universe—can be traced back to Lucretius, *De Rer. Nat.*, I, 31-40 (cf. H.Pflaum, *Bibl*.265, p.20):

> 'Nam tu sola potes tranquilla pace iuvare
> Mortalis, quoniam belli fera moenera Mavors
> Armipotens regit, in gremium qui saepe tuum se
> Reicit aeterno devictus vulnere amoris,
> Atque ita suspiciens tereti cervice reposta
> Pascit amore avidos inhians in te dea visus,
> Eque tuo pendet resupini spiritus ore . . .'

But again an enchantingly primitivistic pastoral has been substituted for a solemnly classicizing allegory.

78. My friend F.Saxl calls my attention to the fact that the Bacchus and Ariadne group travesties classical models like S.Reinach, *Bibl*.277, VOL.II, i, p.129, and that the motif of the onions may allude to the aphrodisiac qualities attributed to that vegetable (Celsus, *De medicina*, II, 32: '*sensus excitant . . . cepa. . . .*').

aspect touched upon but not developed in Ovid's 'jocular tale.' Bacchus, not unlike Vulcan, was a civilizing influence. To the wild, rough, and barren country of Thrace he introduced those values which complement man's purely technical achievements, as represented by Vulcan, and surround the primitive life of shepherds and peasants with a halo of dignity and unsophisticated joy: the simple rituals of pastoral religion, that is the offering of firstlings and spices,[79] and the modest amenities of pastoral life—wine and honey. This evolutionistic aspect of Ovid's apicultural tale was bound to appeal to Piero's imagination, and he has emphasized it further by the device, common in late-mediaeval and Renaissance painting, of dividing the landscape background into two halves of symbolically contrasting character. This '*paysage moralisé*,' as we might call it, is frequent in religious pictures where the '*Aera sub lege*' is contrasted with the '*Aera sub gratia*,' and, more particularly, in the representations of subjects like 'Hercules at the Crossroads' where the antithesis between Virtue and Pleasure is symbolized by the contrast between an easy road winding through beautiful country and a steep, stony path leading up to a forbidding rock. The landscape in this 'Bacchanal' somewhat resembles that of a 'Hercules at the Crossroads' formerly ascribed to Piero, but now mostly attributed to Niccolò Soggi (*fig*.34).[80] The left half whence the *thiasos* unwinds presents a picture of peace and prosperity: the forest has given way to a well-ordered scenery with handsome buildings, lawns and splendid trees above which the sky shines brightly serene. On the right we have a wilderness inhabited by monkeys, lions and a few desperate, mountain-climbing savages; some of the trees are bare and dead, others are running to seed; amid boulders on the uneven ground lies the carcass of an animal surrounded by buzzing flies and wasps, while threatening clouds gather around a terrifying rock as Patinir-like in appearance as the castle on the other side is Bellinesque or even Giorgionesque. However, the symbolical values suggested by this

79. Ovid, *Fasti*, III, 727-732.
80. Cf. E.Panofsky, *Bibl*.243, passim. The Soggi panel ill. *ibidem*, PL.XXXI, *fig*.52, and P. Schubring, *Bibl*.309, no.419.

contrast have been reversed according to the difference between ascetic moralism and hedonistic evolutionism. In representations of Hercules at the Crossroads, the barren and desolate scenery stands for praiseworthy virtues, while the rich and beautiful one stands for reprehensible pleasures. To Piero the same contrast means an antithesis between the merciless hardships of unmitigated wildness and the innocent happiness of a pastoral civilization. Even when illustrating Ovid, he cannot help transforming the poetic vision of an orgiastic cult into a fantastically real picture of primitive life marking a pleasant advance in civilization.

Like Lucretius, Piero conceived of human evolution as a process due to the inborn faculties and talents of the race. It is in order to symbolize these faculties and talents, as well as the universal forces of nature, that his pictures glorify the classical gods and demigods who were not creators like the biblical Jehovah, but embodied and revealed the natural principles indispensable for the 'progress of mankind.' But like Lucretius, Piero was sadly aware of the dangers entailed by this development. He joyfully sympathized with the rise of humanity beyond the bestial hardships of the stone age, but he regretted any step beyond the unsophisticated phase which he would have termed the reign of Vulcan and Dionysos. To him civilization meant a realm of beauty and happiness as long as man kept in close contact with Nature, but a nightmare of oppression, ugliness and distress as soon as man became estranged from her.[81]

An attitude like this, unparalleled as it is in an artist of the early Renaissance, can only be explained on psychological grounds. Fortunately, Piero di Cosimo is better known to us than almost any other artist of his period. Forbidding and fascinating at the same time, his personality lived in everybody's memory to such an extent that Vasari, who was nine when Piero died, was able to immortalize his character by a most convincing psychological portrait.

81. Cf. Lucretius' 'Third period,' referred to p.40, N.22.

We have had occasion to mention Piero's 'mad' love for animals and for the other things that nature produces by 'fancy or accident.' But if he was 'enamoured' of the *sottigliezze della natura*, he correspondingly despised the company of human beings, and especially of his fellow citizens. He hated the various noises of city life and liked to live by himself, though when he condescended to mix with others, he could be full of original witticisms. He was a 'recluse,' a 'friend of solitude,' who derived his greatest pleasure from long, lonely walks: '*quando pensoso da se solo poteva andersene fantasticando e fare suoi castelli in aria.*' He loathed the sound of church bells and the psalmodies of monks; he refused to 'make his peace with God,' although he was 'a good and very zealous man in spite of his bestial life.' Vasari also tells that he disliked normal hot food and lived on hard-boiled eggs which he prepared in advance in large numbers 'in order to save fire.'[82] He would not have his workshop cleaned, nor the plants in his garden trimmed, nor even the fruit picked, because he hated to interfere with nature: '*allegando che le cose d'essa natura bisogna lassarle custodire a lei senza farci altro.*' He was terrified of lightning, the fiery weapon of Vulcan, but he loved to watch a fine downpour.

According to his rationalistic and somewhat snobbish conception of what an artist should be, Vasari calls Piero's manner of living *una vita da uomo piuttosto bestiale che umano*. He describes him as a warning example of mental derangement; as a neurotic with a tendency towards 'animalitarianism'[83] and a fire complex, as we would put it in the language of today. But one of Vasari's expressions furnishes a key to the nature of the man: '*si contentava di veder salvatico ogni cosa, come la sua natura.*' This word *salvatico*, derived from *silva* like our 'savage,' explains in a flash both

82. A psychoanalyst might come to the conclusion that even Piero's aversion to cooked food and his extraordinary habit of preparing '*una cinquantina*' of hard-boiled eggs at a time '*per risparmiar il fuoco*' (van Marle, *Bibl*.209, vol.XIII, p.336, seems to have misunderstood Vasari's meaning, for he states that Piero di Cosimo 'ate about fifty hard-boiled eggs a day') was not only a matter of economy, but also fulfilled an unconscious wish to avoid contact, as far as possible, with the element which both fascinated and terrified him.
83. Cf. A.O.Lovejoy and G.Boas, *Bibl*.201, p.19.

66

Piero's obsession with primitivistic notions and his magic power in bringing them to life by his brush. In his pictures, primitive life is not transfigured in a spirit of Utopian sentimentality, as is the case with the poetic and pictorial evocations of 'Arcadia;'[84] it is reenacted with the utmost realism and concreteness. Piero does not idealize; on the contrary he 'realizes' the first stages of the world to such an extent that the most fantastic of his creatures, such as the animals with human faces, are merely an application of serious evolutionistic theories. The huts of untrimmed logs, the quaintly shaped boats, all the picturesque details that come under the heading of what Vasari calls *casamenti e abiti e strumenti diversi*, are based on archaeological research and paralleled only in scientific illustrations. Piero's world seems fantastic, not because its elements are unreal, but, on the contrary, because the very veracity of his interpretation is convincingly evocative of a time remote from our potential experience. His pictures emanate a pervasive atmosphere of strangeness because they succeed in conjuring up an age older than Christianity, older even than paganism in the historical sense of the word—in fact, older than civilization itself.

Piero di Cosimo might be called an atavistic phenomenon, if we bear in mind that emotional atavisms are quite compatible with the highest degree of aesthetic and intellectual refinement. In his pictures we are faced, not with the polite nostalgia of a civilized man who longs, or pretends to long, for the happiness of a primitive age, but with the subconscious recollection of a primitive who happened to live in a period of sophisticated civilization. While reconstructing the outward appearances of a prehistoric world, Piero seems to have re-experienced the emotions of primeval man, both the creative excitement of the awakening human, and the passions and fears of the caveman and the savage.

84. That is to say: Arcadia in the Virgilian, not in the Ovidian sense. Cf. p.40, and E.Panofsky, *Bibl.*241.

PLATE VIII

17

PLATE IX

PLATE X

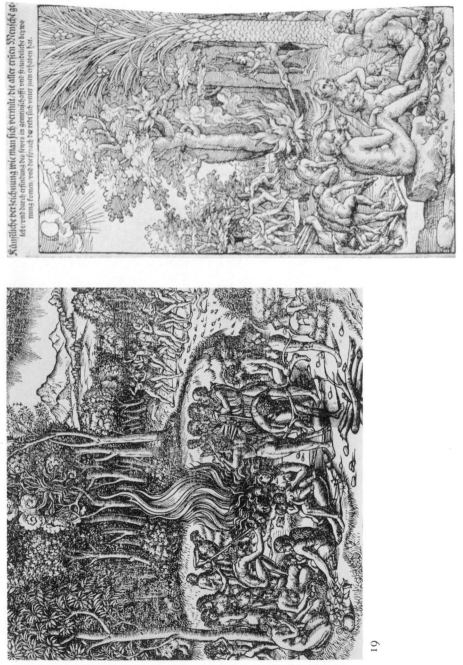

PLATE XI

PLATE XII

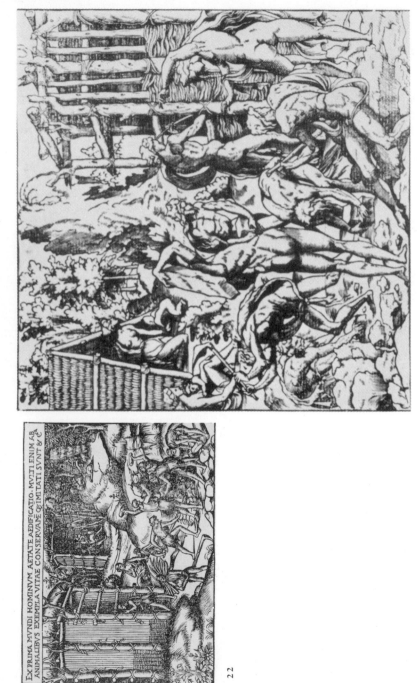

23

22

PLATE XIII

26

24

25

The Cleveland Museum of Art

Ivory Coffret-end

PLATE XIV

27

28

PLATE XV

29 (left half)

29 (right half)

PLATE XVI

PLATE XVII

PLATE XVIII

PLATE XIX

PLATE XX

34

III. FATHER TIME

PIERO DI COSIMO'S secular compositions, based as they are on an almost Darwinian evolutionism and often harking back to a primitive world prior to every historical age, are an extreme and practically unique manifestation of the general tendency to revive the '*sacrosancta vetustas.*' As a rule this tendency confined itself to resuscitating antiquity in the historical sense of the term; Piero himself was, as we have seen, an archaeologist, as well as a primitivist. However,

the reintegration of classical motifs and classical themes is only one aspect of the Renaissance movement in art. Representations of pagan divinities, classical myths or events from Greek and Roman history which, iconographically at least, do not reveal the fact that they were products of a post-mediaeval civilization, exist of course in large numbers. But even larger, and much more dangerous from the viewpoint of orthodox Christianity, was the number of works in which the spirit of the Renaissance did not confine itself to reinstating classical types within the limits of the classical sphere, but aimed at a visual and emotional synthesis between the pagan past and the Christian present. This synthesis was achieved by various methods which could be applied separately and in combination.

The most widely used method might be called the *re-interpretation* of classical images. These images were either invested with a new symbolical content of a secular but definitely non-classical character (witness the in-numerable personifications and allegories evolved during the course of the Renaissance), or they were made subservient to specifically Christian ideas. This again could be done either by way of contrast (for instance, when classi-cal sarcophagi and ruins are shown in a Nativity,[1] or when, in Filippino Lippi's fresco in S.Maria Novella, St. Philip exorcises the dragon in front of a kind of *scaenae frons* teeming with pagan symbolism), or by way of assimilation, as is the case with the Christs repeating the motif of the Apollo Belvedere, and the Virgins modelled upon Venuses or Phaedras. While mediaeval art had appropriated classical motifs without much reflection, the Renaissance tried to justify this practice on theoretical grounds: 'The pagan people attributed the utmost beauty to their heathen God Abblo,' Dürer says, 'thus we shall use him for Christ the Lord who is the most beautiful man, and just as they represented Venus as the most beautiful woman we shall chastely display the same features in the image of the Holy Virgin, mother of God.'[2]

While classical images were thus deliberately reinterpreted, there are many other cases in which the revived classical traditions merged quite naturally, or even automatically, with surviving mediaeval traditions. When a classical character had emerged from the Middle Ages in utterly non-classical disguise (as has been briefly explained in the first chapter), and had been restored to its original appearance by the Renaissance, the final result often showed traces of this process. Some of the mediaeval garments or attri-butes would cling to the remodelled form, and thereby carry over a mediae-val element into the content of the new image.

This resulted in what I would like to call a *'pseudomorphosis:'* certain

1. Cf. A.Warburg, *Bibl.*387, vol.I, p.155s.
2. K.Lange and F.Fuhse, *Bibl.*182, 1893, p.316, also quoted in E.Panofsky and F.Saxl, *Bibl.*238, p.275. It is interesting that such reinterpretations of classical subjects, whether artistic or literary, were later emphatically attacked from opposite sides: The Council of Trent banned the *Moralized Ovid*—not the Ovid text itself—from the point of view of orthodox Catholicism; J.J.Winckelmann ridiculed Pollaiuolo's use of a Diana type for a personifica-tion of Theology from the point of view of puritanical classicism (quotations in E. Panofsky and F.Saxl, *ibidem*).

Renaissance figures became invested with a meaning which, for all their classicizing appearance, had not been present in their classical prototypes, though it had frequently been foreshadowed in classical literature. Owing to its mediaeval antecedents, Renaissance art was often able to translate into images what classical art had deemed inexpressible. In this and in the following chapter I shall endeavour to illustrate typical cases of 'pseudomorphosis' by analysing two reputedly classical characters. Unlike many others of their kind, they managed to withstand the wholesale elimination of humanistic subject matter from late nineteenth-century art and enjoy popularity to this day, so much so that they appear on Valentines and New Year's cards, as well as in comic cartoons and serious advertisements: Father Time and Blind Cupid.

The Father Time seen, for instance, in an advertisement of the Bowery Savings Bank (*text ill.* p.69) is a simple specimen of his kind. Of the attributes which serve to make a personification recognizable he has only the characteristics of old age and a scythe. His ancestors are generally more richly equipped. In Renaissance and Baroque art, Father Time is generally winged and mostly nude. To his most frequent attribute of a scythe or sickle are added, or sometimes substituted, an hourglass, a snake or dragon biting its tail, or the zodiac; and in many cases he walks with crutches.

Some of the features in these more elaborate images can be found in classical or late antique representations of the idea of Time, but none of the peculiar combinations which constitute the type of Father Time in the modern sense can be discovered in ancient art. In it we find, roughly speaking, two main types of conceptions and images. On the one hand, these are representations of Time as 'Kairos;' that is, the brief, decisive moment which marks a turning-point in the life of human beings or in the development of the universe. This concept was illustrated by the figure vulgarly known as Opportunity (*fig.*35). Opportunity was shown as a man (originally nude) in fleeting movement, usually young and never very old, in spite of the fact that Time is sometimes called πολιός (grey-headed) in Greek poetry.[3] He was equipped with wings both at the shoulders and at the heels. His attributes were a pair of scales, originally balanced on the edge of a shaving knife, and, in a somewhat later period, one or two wheels. Moreover his head often showed the proverbial forelock by which bald-headed Opportunity can be seized.[4] It was because of this abstrusely allegorical character that the figure of Kairos or Opportunity appealed to the late antique and mediaeval mind. It survived up to the eleventh century and afterwards tended to merge with the figure of Fortune, this fusion being favoured by the fact that the Latin word for 'Kairos,' viz., *occasio*, is of the same gender as *fortuna*.[5]

On the other hand, the exact opposite of the 'Kairos' idea is represented in ancient art, namely the Iranian concept of Time as 'Aion;' that is, the divine principle of eternal and inexhaustible creativeness. These images are either connected with the cult of Mithra, in which case they show a grim winged

3. See the Diphilos fragment quoted p.74, N.11.
4. Cf. Roscher, *Bibl.*290, s.v. 'Aion,' 'Chronos,' 'Kairos,' 'Kronos,' 'Saturnus.' Also A.Greifenhagen, *Bibl.*122, especially *figs.*2, 3, 5. The famous eleventh-century relief in the Cathedral of Torcello in which the energetic youth who takes Opportunity by the forelock is contrasted with Irresoluteness followed by Repentance is illustrated in Roscher, s.v. 'Kairos,' and in Greifenhagen, *fig.*4. A Coptic allegory of Opportunity is illustrated in J.Strzygowski, *Bibl.*329, *fig.*159. See also G.L.Kittredge, *Bibl.*164. With the attributes slightly changed, the image of Kairos could also be used to represent Time in general, but instances seem to be extremely rare. The only one known to the writer is the famous relief 'The Apotheosis of Homer' where winged Time carries the Iliad and the Odyssey.
5. For the fusion of *Occasio* and *Fortuna* see H.R.Patch, *Bibl.*254, p.115ss.; A.Warburg, *Bibl.*387, vol.I, p.150 and 358; and recently R.Wittkower, *Bibl.*408a (published after this chapter had gone to press). The resulting image of a nude *female* equipped with the attributes of Kairos (forelock, sometimes shaving-knife, etc.), and balanced on a sphere or wheel which often floats in the sea, practically superseded the masculine Kairos in later mediaeval and Renaissance art. It is constantly found wherever emblematic art wished to illustrate the concept of Occasio; cf. particularly Andrea Alciati, *Emblemata*, Emblema CXXI (the epigram being a Latin version of Poseidippos' epigram on the Lysippian Kairos in which this name is rendered by 'Occasio'), or Jacobus Typotius (Typoet, 1540/1601), *Bibl.*361, p.367 with the significant phrase '*fortunam vel occasionem in pila volubili statuens.*' For the immensely influential illustrations of Alciati's *Emblemata*, see H.Green, *Bibl.*121, with facsimile reproductions of the earliest Alciati editions by Steyrer, 1531 (*Occasio* here fol.A 8), Wechel, 1534 (*Occasio* here p.20) and Aldus, 1546 (*Occasio* vacat). In the Lyons edition by Bonhomme, 1551, *Bibl.*4, *Occasio* is found on p.133, and in the Paris edition of 1608—a typical specimen of the comprehensive editions containing the most valuable commentary by Claudius Minos, *recte* Claude Mignault—on p.577, *Bibl.*5. The Roman numerals of the Emblemata refer to the order maintained in practically all the editions after 1574.

figure with a lion's head and lion's claws, tightly enveloped by a huge snake and carrying a key in either hand,[6] or they depict the Orphic divinity commonly known as Phanes, in which case they show a beautiful winged youth surrounded by the zodiac, and equipped with many attributes of cosmic power; he too is encircled by the coils of a snake (*fig.*36).[7]

In none of these ancient representations do we find the hourglass, the scythe or sickle, the crutches, or any signs of a particularly advanced age. In other words, the ancient images of Time are either characterized by symbols of fleeting speed and precarious balance, or by symbols of universal power and infinite fertility, but not by symbols of decay and destruction. How, then, did these most specific attributes of Father Time come to be introduced?

The answer lies in the fact that the Greek expression for time, Chronos, was very similar to the name of Kronos (the Roman Saturn), oldest and most formidable of the gods. A patron of agriculture, he generally carried a sickle. As the senior member of the Greek and Roman Pantheon he was professionally old, and later, when the great classical divinities came to be identified with the planets, Saturn was associated with the highest and slowest of these. When religious worship gradually disintegrated and was finally supplanted by philosophical speculation, the fortuitous similarity between the words Chronos and Kronos was adduced as proof of the actual identity of the two concepts which really had some features in common. According to Plutarch, who happens to be the earliest author to state this identity in writing, Kronos means Time in the same way as Hera means Air and Hephaistos, Fire.[8] The Neoplatonics accepted the identification on metaphysical rather

6. Cf. F.Cumont, *Bibl.*68, vol.i, p.74ss., vol.ii, p.53; also H.Junker, *Bibl.*159, especially p.147.
7. Cf. R.Eisler, *Bibl.*82, p.2, *fig.*28. Also E.Panofsky, *Bibl.*243, p.9, *figs.*8/9. In an engraving by Hieronymus Olgiatus of 1569, repeated in a painting in the possession of Mr.G.W.Younger, London, the Phanes figure is used for an allegory of Alchemy (our *fig.*37). The inscription: '*Hoc monstrum generat, tum perficit ignis et Azoch*' means that time produces raw matter, while fire and mercury perfect it (the united action of fire and quicksilver being believed to transform raw matter into the 'philosopher's stone'). The '*Turba Sophorum*' mentioned in the distich is the title of a famous treatise on alchemy translated from the Arabic and often reprinted in the seventeenth century.
8. Plutarch, *De Iside et Osiride*, 32; *Aetia Romana*, XII, 266 E, F: ὥσπερ ἐνίοι τῶν φιλοσόφων χρόνον οἴονται τὸν Κρόνον εἶναι, τὸ δ' ἀληθὲς εὑρίσκει χρόνος;

than physical grounds. They interpreted Kronos, the father of gods and men,[9] as Νοῦς, the Cosmic Mind (while his son Zeus or Jupiter was likened to its 'emanation,' the Ψυχή or Cosmic Soul) and could easily merge this concept with that of Chronos, the 'father of all things,'[10] the 'wise old builder,' as he had been called.[11] The learned writers of the fourth and fifth centuries A.D. began to provide Kronos-Saturn with new attributes like the snake or dragon biting its tail,[12] which were meant to emphasize his temporal significance. Also, they re-interpreted the original features of his image as symbols of time. His sickle, traditionally explained either as an agricultural implement or as the instrument of castration, came to be interpreted as a symbol of *tempora quae sicut falx in se recurrunt*;[13] and the mythical tale that he had devoured his own children was said to signify that Time, who had already been termed 'sharp-toothed' by Simonides[14] and *edax rerum* by Ovid,[15] devours whatever he has created.[16]

9. *Hymn. Orph.*, XIII, Abel: Μακάρων τε θεῶν πάτερ ἠδὲ καὶ ἀνδρῶν. Aeschylus, *Prometheus*, line 909s: πατρὸς Κρόνου. Cf. also Silius Italicus, *Punica*, XI, 458: 'Saturni . . . patris.'

10. Pindar, *Olymp.*, II, 32 (17), p.13, Schröder.

11. Krates (*Bibl.*168, VOL.I, p.142, fragm.49: Τέκτων σοφός; Diphilos, Kock, *Bibl.*168, VOL.II, p.569, fragm.83: πολιὸς τεχνίτης. Cf. also Chr.A.Lobeck, *Bibl.*197, VOL.I, p.470.

12. See Martianus Capella, *Nupt. Philolog. et Mercur.*, I. 70: '*Verum sator eorum* [viz., Saturn, the father of the gods] *gressibus tardus ac remorator incedit, glaucoque amictu tectus caput. Praetendebat dextra flammivorum quendam draconem caudae quae ultima devorantem, quem credebant anni numerum nomine perdocere.*' If it were true that the dragon biting its tail signifies the Year it would be possible that it originally belonged not to Saturn, but to Janus, as is related by Macrobius, *Saturnal.*, I, 9,12. However, a monster which 'seemed to devour itself' is also connected with the Iranian Aion (cf. H.Junker, *Bibl.*159, p.172, note 90) and in this case its original meaning would have been that of Endlessness or Eternity, as was mostly assumed in later times. Mythographus III, 1, 6, *Bibl.*38, p.155, borrowed the motif (as an attribute of Saturn) from Remigius' Commentary on Martianus Capella and transmitted it to the succeeding tradition.

13. Servius, *In Verg. Georgica*, II, 406, taken over by Mythographus III, 1, 6, *Bibl.*38, p.155.

14. Stobaios, *Eclog. Phys. et Eth.*, I, 8, 22:

"Ότι χρόνος ὀξὺς ὀδόντας
Καὶ πάντα ψήχει καὶ τὰ βιαιότατα.

15. Ovid, *Metam.*, XV, 234.

16. Fulgentius, *Mitol.*, 1, 2, p.18, Helm: '*Filios vero comedisse fertur, quod omne tempus, quodcumque gignat, consumit*' taken over by Mythographus III, 1, 5, *Bibl.*38, p.154.

Thus it is in the iconography of Kronos-Saturn rather than in that of Time proper that we shall have to look for supplementary evidence. But the synthesis which eventually gave rise to the image of Father Time as we know it, did not occur without many vicissitudes. In classical art Kronos or Saturn is a perfectly dignified though somewhat gloomy figure, characterized by a sickle, by a veil over his head (*fig.*38),[17] and, when seated, by a mournful posture with his head resting on his hand.[18] Wings never appear,[19] but neither do staffs nor crutches.

This was changed during the Middle Ages. According to the normal scheme of evolution outlined in the first chapter, the classical image of Saturn was occasionally resurrected both in Carolingian and middle-Byzantine art, but was to survive only for a comparatively brief period. Representations of Saturn more or less literally repeating the classical type best exemplified by the mural from the Casa dei Dioscuri at Pompei are found first, in the copies of a fourth-century calendar known as the *Chronograph of* 354 or the *Filocalus-Calendar* (*fig.*39);[20] second, in the '*planetaria*' appearing in astronomical treatises of both Carolingian and Byzantine origin;[21] third, in eleventh- and twelfth-century manuscripts of St. Gregory's *Homilies*, where incidents of the Saturn myth are shown among other scenes indicative of the immorality of the pagan gods; in the miniature in question he devours the

17. Cf. P.Hermann, *Bibl.*144, PL.122.
18. Cf., for instance, the tomb of Cornutus in the Vatican, ill. in E.Panofsky and F.Saxl, *Bibl.* 253, or the bronze statue in the Museo Gregoriano, ill. in Roscher, *Bibl.*290, s.v. 'Kronos,' *fig.*13. The gesture is even retained when Kronos is shown deceived by the stone; cf. the relief from the Ara Capitolina, W.Helbig, *Bibl.*139, no.511, ill. in Roscher, *Bibl.*290, s.v. 'Kronos,' *fig.*18.
19. The identification of the Mithraic Aion with Kronos-Saturn is late and somewhat doubtful. The fantastic 'Phoenician Kronos' with six wings seen in the coins of Byblos (cf. Roscher, *Bibl.*290, s.v. 'Kronos,' Nachtrag) and illustrated by Cartari, *Bibl.*56, p.19, on the basis of the detailed description in Eusebius' *Praeparatio Evangelica*, 1, 10, 36-39, is certainly a purely Semitic divinity of cherub-like appearance, as is also corroborated by his indigenous name Ἶλος (El).
20. Cf. J.Strzygowski, *Bibl.*328. Contrary to recent theories (C.Nordenfalk, *Bibl.*230), the Renaissance copies which have been preserved would seem to presuppose a Carolingian intermediary.
21. Cf. G.Thiele, *Antike Himmelsbilder*, *Bibl.*337, p.188ss. A better reproduction of the Saturn picture in Cod. Leyd. Voss. lat. 79 will be published in E.Panofsky and F.Saxl, *Bibl.*253.

wrapped-up stone which has been substituted for little Jupiter (*fig.42*).[22] Fourth, in the illustrations of the chapter '*De diis gentilium*' in Hrabanus Maurus' encyclopaedia *De universo* which has come down to us in two independent copies, one executed in Montecassino in 1023 (*fig.40*), the other made in South Germany in the first half of the fifteenth century (*fig.41*); it is interesting to note that in the Montecassino manuscript the classical sickle (faithfully retained in the more recent German copy) has already been replaced by the modern scythe.[23]

During the high Middle Ages, western art abandoned the Carolingian pictures which fell into oblivion till the fifteenth century, and in the meantime were supplanted by thoroughly non-classical types. Owing to the fact that Saturn, like Jupiter, Venus, etc., had been identified with a planet, these new images turn up in the illustrations of both mythographical and astrological texts.

In the capacity of planetarian ruler, Saturn was held to be a peculiarly sinister character; we still use the word 'saturnine' to indicate 'a sluggish, gloomy temperament,' to quote the Oxford Dictionary. Those subject to his power could be mighty and wealthy, but not kindly and generous; they could be wise, but not happy. For men born under Saturn must perforce be melancholy. Even these highly conditional advantages were granted only to a very small minority of Saturn's 'children.' Generally Saturn, coldest, driest,

22. Cf. also H.Omont, *Bibl*.235, PL.CXVIII, 14 (from ms. Coislin 239). For the correct interpretation of the subject and further instances see E.Panofsky and F.Saxl, *Bibl*.253. It is interesting that in the earlier Gregory manuscripts (ninth century) the mythological scenes are either absent, or based on the textual description rather than on a representational tradition. In cod. Ambros. E49/50 Inf., VOL.II, p.752 a very unclassical Saturn is shown splitting the firmament with an ax because a person unfamiliar with pagan mythology could easily misinterpret the Greek text 'Ο ΚΡΟΝΟΣ ΤΟΝ ΟΥ(ΡΑ)ΝΟΝ ΤΕΜΝΟ(Ν) (meaning 'Kronos castrating Uranus') as 'Kronos cutting, or splitting, the sky.' I am indebted to Professor A.M.Friend, Jr. and Dr.K.Weitzmann for having called my attention to the unpublished Gregory manuscripts and for having supplied me with the photograph reproduced in *fig*.42.
23. A.M.Amelli, *Bibl*.7, PL.CVIII. For the South German copy (cod. Vat. Pal. lat. 291), see P.Lehmann, *Bibl*.187, PART II, p.13ss., and E.Panofsky and F.Saxl, *Bibl*.238, p.250. The retention of the sickle in cod. Vat. Pal. lat. 291 corroborates the theory that this copy, in spite of its thoroughly late Gothic style, is iconographically more correct than the Montecassino manuscript.

and slowest of planets, was associated with old age, abject poverty and death.[24] In fact Death, like Saturn, was represented with a scythe or sickle from very early times (*fig.43*).[25] Saturn was held responsible for floods, famines and all other kinds of disasters. Those born under him were classed with the most miserable and undesirable of mortals, such as cripples, misers, beggars, criminals, poor peasants, privy-cleaners, and grave-diggers. It was not until the last quarter of the fifteenth century that the Florentine Neopla-tonists (whose influence on Renaissance art will be touched upon in later chapters) reverted to the Plotinian concept of Saturn, deeming him an exponent and patron of profound philosophical and religious contemplation, and identifying Jupiter with mere practical and rational intelligence.[26] But even this Neoplatonic revival, which was ultimately to result in an identifica-tion of Saturnine melancholy with genius, could not weaken the popular belief that Saturn was the most malignant of the planets.

Astrological imagery—derived in part from Arabic sources—never ceased to emphasize these unfavourable implications. Saturn appears mostly[27] as a morose, sickly old man, more often than not of rustic appearance. His sickle or scythe is frequently replaced by a mattock or spade, even when he is represented as a king enthroned and crowned (*fig.44*),[28] and this spade tends to become transformed into a staff or a crutch indicative of old age and general decrepitude (*fig.48*). As a final result Saturn is shown actually

24. Cf. for instance Mythographus III, 1, 4, *Bibl.*38, p.154: '*Sunt tamen qui asserant eum.* . . . *ab effectu frigidum nuncupari, quod sua videlicet constellatione contraria homines enecet. Mortui enim frigidi sunt. Quod si verum est, non improprie senex fingitur, quoniam senum sit morti semper esse vicinos.*'
25. Death with a sickle occurs as early as in the Uta Gospels clm. 13601 (early XIth century) illustrated in G.Swarzenski, *Bibl.*333, PL.XIII; our *fig.*43. With the scythe, he can be seen in the Gumpert Bible (ante 1195), illustrated in G.Swarzenski, *Bibl.*334, PL.XLI, *fig.*129. Both motifs can be accounted for by *Apocalypse*, XIV, 14-17, and such passages as *Isaiah*, XL, 6-8. As to the iconography of Death in general, cf. recently H.Janson, *Bibl.*155.
26. Cf. below, passim, and E.Panofsky and F.Saxl, *Bibl.*253, passim..
27. As to the Michael Scotus manuscripts and their derivatives (our *fig.*14), where Saturn, owing to an erroneous reading, appears as a warlike, helmeted figure, cf. E.Panofsky and F.Saxl, *Bibl.*238, p.242ss.
28. The Morgan manuscript M.785, from which our *fig.*44 is taken, is derived from Brit. Mus., ms. Sloane 3983, ill. in F.Boll and C.Bezold, *Bibl.*41, PL.XVIII, *figs.*33, 34.

as a cripple with a wooden leg, adumbrating his even more repulsive mutilation (*fig.*49).[29] In miniatures and prints illustrating the influence of the Seven Planets on human character and destiny—a favourite subject of fifteenth- and early sixteenth-century art in Italy, but even more so in the northern countries—the qualities of Saturn's 'children' abundantly reflect the undesirable nature of their 'father:' the pictures show an assembly of poor peasants, lumberjacks, prisoners, cripples, and criminals on the gallows, the only redeeming feature being a monk or hermit, a lowly representative of the *vita contemplativa* (*fig.*48).[30]

In the mythographical illustrations which were evolved exclusively out of textual sources the appearance of Saturn develops from the fantastic into the terrifying and repulsive. In the earliest known specimen, the Regensburg drawing of around 1100 already mentioned (*fig.*13),[31] he wears a big, fluttering veil (illustrating the *caput velatum* or *glauco amictu coopertum*) and carries a sickle, as well as a scythe and, in addition, the dragon biting its tail. The standard type was developed in the fourteenth century when the *Moralized Ovid* and its derivatives began to be illustrated.[32] These pictures usually included supplementary figures connected with the myth of Saturn, which served to dramatize his sinister character and to emphasize his cruelty and destructiveness even more sharply than had been the case in the astrological illustrations. The illuminators did not scruple to depict the hideous process of castration as well as the act of devouring a living child, a scene never shown in classical representations. This cannibalistic image was to become the accepted type in late mediaeval art (*fig.*45)[33] and finally merged

29. Cod. Pal. lat. 1368, fol.i, v., ill. in F.Saxl, *Bibl.*299, PL.XIII. Furthermore cf. O.Behrendsen, *Bibl.*25, PL.XVI (Master J.B., engraving B.11), or H.S.Beham, engraving B.113.
30. F.Lippmann, *Bibl.*195, 1895, PL. C, 1, and E.Panofsky and F.Saxl, *Bibl.*253, passim.
31. See above, p.24s.
32. See the references on p.23ss. In the original French version of the Moralized Ovid, ed. C. de Boer, *Bibl.*40, the description of Saturn is found VOL.I, p.22, line 513ss. Our *fig.*45 after F.Saxl, *Bibl.*299, PL.XVII, *fig.*36.
33. Cf. F.Saxl and E.Panofsky, *Bibl.*253, passim. An exceptional type showing Saturn with a ship or a ship's mast (on account of his long sea-voyage to Latium) is found in some manuscripts of St. Augustine's *Civitas Dei*, ill. in A. de Laborde, *Bibl.*178, VOL.I, p.198s., VOL.II, p.322, 367, 385 and PL.XXIV b, and XXXVII.

with the astrological representations so that at times we find a combination of the castration with the ingestion of the child (*fig.*46),[34] or a combination of the ingestion with the wooden leg motive.[35] In a more or less classicized form both the devouring-scene and the castration continue into high Renaissance (*fig.*47) and Baroque art and even farther; the gruesome Saturn by Goya is known to all, and the castration can still be seen, for instance, in the Villa Lante frescoes ascribed to Giulio Romano.[36]

Such was the state of affairs when the artists began to illustrate Petrarch's *Trionfi*. Chastity, as everybody knows, triumphs over Love, Death over Chastity, Fame over Death, and Time over Fame—to be conquered only by Eternity. Time's outward appearance not having been described by the poet except for his '*andar leggiero dopo la guida sua, che mai non posa,*'[37] the illustrators were at liberty to represent him in whatever shape they liked. Some few scholastic personifications of Time proper had been devised during the Middle Ages, such as a French miniature of around 1400 showing 'Temps' with three heads (to designate the past, the present, and the future), and with four wings, each of which stood for a Season, while each feather symbolized a Month (*fig.*50).[38] But images of this theoretical kind seemed inadequate to express the essence of the mighty, relentless destroyer imagined by Petrarch. Petrarch's Time was not an abstract philosophical principle but a concrete

34. French drawing of around 1420/25, illustrated in E.Panofsky and F.Saxl, *Bibl.*253.
35. Master J.B., engraving B. 11, quoted above, N.29.
36. Cf. J.P.Richter, *Bibl.*282, pl.x, *fig.*1, where, however, the castration of Saturn by Jupiter is erroneously interpreted as that of Uranus by Saturn. The particularly horrifying representation of Saturn devouring a screaming baby is found, e.g., in Jacopo Caraglio's engraving B.24 (our *fig.*47), as well as in the well-known painting by Rubens (Madrid, Prado), whereas Poussin characteristically enough reverts to the classical scheme in which a stone is substituted for the child (cf. our *fig.*67).
37. Petrarca, *Triumphus Temporis*, l.46. The 'guida' is the sun ('*Sol temporis auctor*' as he is called by Macrobius) driving his chariot through space. Curiously enough the illustrators were very reluctant in taking up this motif. Specimens such as the miniature in Paris, Bibl. Nat., ms. Fr. 12424, fol.137, ill. in Prince d'Essling and E.Müntz, *Bibl.*87, p.219, where Time is identified with the Sun, or the woodcut in Petrarch, *Bibl.*262, fol.407 where his winged figure follows in the tracks of the sun's chariot, are rather exceptional.
38. Cf. E.Panofsky, *Bibl.*243, p.4ss., *fig.*5.

alarming power. Small wonder that the illustrators decided to fuse the harmless personification of 'Temps' with the sinister image of Saturn. From the former they took over the wings,[39] from the latter the grim, decrepit appearance, the crutches, and, finally, such strictly Saturnian features as the scythe and the devouring motif. That this new image personified Time was frequently emphasized by an hourglass, which seems to make its first appearance in this new cycle of illustrations, and sometimes by the zodiac, or the dragon biting its tail.

I shall confine myself to adducing five characteristic specimens of Petrarch illustrations: (1) a Venetian woodcut of the late fifteenth century which links up with the mediaeval personifications of 'Temps' by posing the figure in rigid frontality and adorning it with the four wings that used to symbolize the Seasons (fig.52);[40] (2) a cassone panel ascribed to Pesellino in which the wings have been reduced to the normal number of two (fig.54);[41] (3) a cassone panel by Jacopo del Sellaio in which various new and in part unusual attributes have crept in: besides the hourglass, we find a sun-dial and two rats, one black, one white, which symbolize the destruction of life by each day

39. Not all the representations of Time in Petrarch illustrations are winged, but specimens without wings are comparatively rare and mostly exceptional in other respects as well. Cf., e.g., our fig.53. Furthermore see Prince d'Essling and E.Müntz, Bibl.87: a Venetian woodcut of 1488 showing three old men on a chariot drawn by two dragons; one of them is seated and carries a globe, the other is also seated and carries a plaque inscribed 'Tempo,' the third walks on crutches. Or ibidem, p.214 (also E. von Birk, Bibl.35, PL.12 following p.248): a Flemish tapestry where Time, seated on a chariot drawn by two deer, a cock and a raven, is characterized by an hourglass, a crutch and the zodiac. Or ibidem, p.234: a French sixteenth-century miniature, showing Time standing on the ground, characterized by an hourglass. The miniature in Paris, Bibl. Nat., ms. Fr.12424 has already been mentioned.

40. This woodcut is first found in the Petrarch edition Bibl.259, fol.O, 5v., and reappears in several later editions. Cf. Prince d'Essling, Bibl.86, VOL.I, no.79, p.93. A similar four-winged type, perhaps even more closely akin to the mediaeval personification of 'Temps' occurs in a North-Italian miniature of about the same time, illustrated in Prince d'Essling and E.Müntz, Bibl.87, p.167. The three-headed base seen in this miniature symbolizes, of course, the three forms of time, viz., past, present and future (cf. E.Panofsky, Bibl.243, p.2ss.). In the miniature quoted above the Four Seasons appear in person.

41. Prince d'Essling and E.Müntz, Bibl.87, PL. facing p.148, and P.Schubring, Bibl.309, no.267, PL.LX.

and night (*fig.55*);[42] (4) a second Venetian woodcut in which the wings—but not the scythe—have been omitted, while the idea of endless recurrence is brought out by the dragon biting its tail; here as in the other Venetian woodcut the destructive power of Time is manifested by desolate scenery with barren trees and ruinous architecture (*fig.53*);[43] (5) a woodcut from a sixteenth-century edition of Petrarch which, while it shows the winged figure devouring an infant in the late mediaeval, Saturnian tradition, nevertheless illustrates the classicizing tendencies of the high Renaissance by transforming the decrepit old man, in spite of his crutches, into a vigorous nude (*fig.56*).[44]

This, then, is the origin of the figure of Father Time as we know it.[45] Half classical and half mediaeval, half western and half oriental, this figure illustrates both the abstract grandeur of a philosophical principle and the malignant voracity of a destructive demon, and just this rich complexity of the new image accounts for the frequent appearance and varied significance of Father Time in Renaissance and Baroque art.

Sometimes the figure of Father Time is used as a mere device to indicate the lapse of months, years, or centuries, as in Shakespeare's *Winter's Tale*, where Time appears as Chorus before the fifth act, or again in one of

---

42. Prince d'Essling and E.Müntz, *Bibl.*87, PL. facing p.152 and P.Schubring, *Bibl.*309, no.374, PL.LXXXVII. For the motif of the two rats (transmitted to the Western world through the legend of Barlaam and Josaphat) see the references in E.Panofsky, *Bibl.*241, p.233 and *idem, Bibl.*243, p.92.

43. *Petrarch, Bibl.*260, 1508, fol.121v.; cf. Prince d'Essling, *Bibl.*86, no.84, p.98, *fig.* p.101.

44. *Petrarch, Bibl.*261, fol.203. Another instance in which a Petrarch illustrator alludes to the devouring motif is the Madrid tapestry mentioned but not illustrated in Prince d'Essling and E.Müntz, *Bibl.*87, p.218, where Time carries a sickle while strangling an infant and putting his left foot on an hourglass. In the engraving by G.Pencz, ill. *ibidem*, p.262, two infants are shown playing in front of Father Time.

45. It was only on the basis of the conception developed by the Petrarch illustrators that it was possible to reconstruct an image of the 'Phoenician Kronos' as described by Eusebius, and to rediscover the classical Kairos with wings on his shoulders and heels, as he appears in the woodcuts illustrated in F.Saxl, *Bibl.*300, *figs.*2, 4, or in full Lysippian array, as he is described by Ripa, s.v. 'Tempo' (no.4) and illustrated in Greifenhagen, *Bibl.*122, *figs.*19, 20. In other instances a fettered Eros is transformed into a personification of Time (Greifenhagen, *l.c., fig.*13; cf. the fettered Saturn, illustrated in Cartari, *Bibl.*56, p.19). For the combination of Occasio (originally Kairos) with Fortuna see p.72, N.5.

Bernini's projects where he is made to carry an Egyptian obelisk (*fig.58b*),[46] and in innumerable allegories of an antiquarian or historical character.[47] In other and even more numerous cases, however, the figure of Father Time is invested with a deeper and more precise meaning; he may act, generally speaking, either as a Destroyer, or as a Revealer,[48] or as a universal and inexorable power which through a cycle of procreation and destruction causes what may be called a cosmic continuity: 'thou nursest all and murder'st all that are,' to speak in Shakespeare's words.[49]

In the first of these capacities, Time, having appropriated the qualities of the deadly, cannibalistic, scythe-brandishing Saturn, became more and more intimately related to Death, and it was from the image of Time that, about the last years of the fifteenth century, the representations of Death began to borrow the characteristic hourglass,[50] and sometimes even the

46. H.Brauer and R.Wittkower, *Bibl.*48, p.150, PL.113B.
47. Cf., in place of all other instances, Raphael Mengs' wall painting in the Sala dei Papiri in the Vatican, ill. in H.Voss, *Bibl.*384, *fig.*423: Chronos carries on his wings the book into which Clio makes her entries.
48. B.Stevenson, *Bibl.*326, has a fine collection of famous lines on the theme 'Time the Destroyer.'
49. Shakespeare, *Rape of Lucrece*, line 929.
50. Owing to this combination which rapidly became very popular, every timepiece was apt to become associated with the idea of Death and to be provided with inscriptions like '*Una ex illis ultima.*' Ripa, s.v. 'Vita Breve,' quotes a 'Sonetto morale' accompanying an hourglass which his countryman Francesco Copetta had sent to a relative who had lost his brother. The symbolical value of the hourglass or clock is somewhat similar to that of the mirror which during the Middle Ages had been used as an attribute of both Luxury (cf. also the Siren in a Coptic tapestry shown in the loan exhibition '*The Dark Ages*,' *Bibl.*412, no.138) and Death (see such epitaphs as the one in Straubing, Jakobskirche:

> '*Sum speculum vitae Ioannes Gmainer, et rite*
> *Tales vos eritis, fueram quandoque quod estis,*'

In the sixteenth and seventeenth centuries the mirror became an attribute of Time, because, according to Ripa, s.v. 'Tempo,' no.1, '*del tempo solo il presente si vede e ha l'essere, il quale per ancora è tanto breve e incerto che non avanza la falsa imagine dello specchio.*' Inversely the figure of Time was used to draw a curtain from a mirror to reveal the gradual decay of health and beauty (cf. Bernini's drawing for Queen Christina of Sweden, mentioned by H.Brauer and R.Wittkower *Bibl.*48, *l.c.*), and the mirror finally became a typical symbol of transience equally frequent in art ('Vanitas' pictures) and in literature, as is sufficiently evidenced by Shakespeare's Sonnets III and LXXVII, as well as by the magnificent mirror scene in *Richard II.*, IV, 1. Whether the empty roundel carried by Time in the

wings as is the case on Bernini's tomb of Alexander VII.[51] Time in turn could be shown as a procurer of Death whom he provides with victims,[52] or as an iron-toothed demon standing in the midst of ruins (cf. the woodcuts *figs.*52 and 53).[53] This concept of the 'tooth of Time,'[54] in a strange application to archaeology, is rendered very literally and therefore amusingly in the frontispiece of a seventeenth-century publication of *One Hundred Roman Statues Spared by the Envious Tooth of Time*; in it we see Father Time with his scythe and tail-biting snake amidst fragments of architecture and statuary, gnawing away at the Torso Belvedere in exactly the same fashion as old Saturn had been shown devouring his children (*fig.*60).[55]

Time as a Revealer (*fig.*59) is known not only from many proverbs and poetical phrases[56] but also from countless representations of subjects such as Truth revealed or rescued by Time, Virtue vindicated by Time, Innocence justified by Time, and the like.[57] The artistic interpretations of the Time and Truth theme, based on the classical phrase '*veritas filia temporis*,' have been fully discussed in a recent article by Dr.F.Saxl.[58] Thus I shall confine myself to considering one case which deserves some attention because of its seemingly enigmatical character and because of the importance of the artist concerned.

Bernini drawing, H.Brauer and R.Wittkower, *Bibl.*48, PL.113A (our *fig.*58a) was destined to hold a mirror or a clock is a matter of surmise.

51. With emblematic brevity the hourglass itself could be provided with wings. An interesting instance in which the combination of a bird's wing with a bat's wing is used to express the contrast of day and night was brought to my attention by Mr.H.Janson.

52. *Bozzetto* by Bernini, mentioned by H.Brauer and R.Wittkower, *Bibl.*48, p.150, with references to illustrations.

53. Ripa, s.v. 'Tempo,' no.3: '*Huomo vecchio alato il quale tiene un cerchio in mano e sta in mezzo d'una ruina, hà la bocca aperta, mostrando i denti li quali sieno del colore del ferro.*'

54. Cf., p.74. One of the earliest occurrences in modern poetry seems to be in Shakespeare's *Measure for Measure*, V, 1.

55. François Perrier, *Bibl.*258.

56. Cf. B.Stevenson, *Bibl.*326, p.200sss., s.v. 'Time and Truth.'

57. In Otho van Veen's allegory in honour of the Spanish architect Herrera, Time even fulfills the office of separating the hero from Venus (cf. G.Haberditzl, *Bibl.*128, *figs.*39, 40). The same artist has charmingly illustrated an epigram on Time curtailing the wings of Cupid without, however, depriving him of his weapons (Otho Venius, *Bibl.*370, p.237; our *fig.*57).

58. F.Saxl, *Bibl.*300; cf. also G.Bing, *Bibl.*34a.

In the Galleria degli Arazzi at Florence there hangs a tapestry based on a cartoon by Angelo Bronzino, and executed by the Flemish master weaver Giovanni Rost.[59] In this composition, called *L'Innocentia del Bronzino* in an inventory of 1549, Innocence is shown threatened by the powers of evil, symbolized by four wild animals: a dog, a lion, a wolf, and a serpent, which stand for Envy, Fury, Greed, and Perfidy (*fig.61*).[60] Innocence is rescued by Justice, who carries a sword and a pair of scales, and whose gesture is purposely identical to that of Christ rescuing souls from Hell,[61] while winged Time, with an hourglass perched on his shoulder, embraces what a previous writer calls 'a young girl.'[62] But in reality Time is not only embracing, but also unveiling this young girl who thus reveals herself to be a personification of Truth.[63] The composition is therefore a fusion of three interrelated versions of one theme: Truth rescued by Time, Truth unveiled by Time, and Innocence justified after persecution, the third of these subjects being the theme of the famous Calumny of Apelles as described by Lucian.[64]

59. Cf. H.Goebel; *Bibl.*114, PART II, VOL.I, p.382 and PART II, VOL.2, *fig.*380; also M.Tinti, *Bibl.*343, 1920, p.44; and A.McComb, *Bibl.*213, p.25.
60. According to Ripa the wolf means 'Gula,' the lion 'Iracundia,' the dog 'Invidia' (all this s.v. 'Passione dell'Anima'). Furthermore the wolf is a symbol of 'Rapina,' 'Voracità,' 'Peste,' 'Avaritia,' etc., the lion of 'Vendetta,' 'Furore,' 'Fierezza' (s.v. 'Collerico') etc., the serpent of 'Inganno,' 'Furore implacabile,' 'Perfidia' etc.
61. Cf. especially Bronzino's own representation of the subject in his altarpiece of 1552 (Museo di S.Croce, Florence). As shown by Saxl, *Bibl.*300, p.204 and *fig.*4, a transference of the Descent into Limbo scheme to the Time and Truth subject was not uncommon in sixteenth-century art.
62. H.Schulze, *Bibl.*312, p.xxxi.
63. For Time Embracing Truth, see Saxl, *Bibl.*300, *figs.*5, 6, 7; for Time Unveiling Truth, *ibidem*, *figs.*9,11 and many other instances.
64. Cf. R.Foerster, *Bibl.*98; G.Q.Giglioli, *Bibl.*112; and R.Altrocchi, *Bibl.*6. Setting aside the fact that Time does not appear personally in the Calumny pictures, they mostly differ from Bronzino's Innocence composition, first in that the powers of evil are exclusively represented in human form, secondly in that the vindication of the Innocent occurs too late. Truth does not enter the scene before the victim has been dragged away for execution, and Dürer, in his drawing Lippmann 577, makes this particularly clear by introducing a personification of Punishment ('Poena') before Truth. One famous sixteenth-century interpretation of the Calumny theme, however, shares with Bronzino's Innocence composition both the tendency to substitute animals for humans and the introduction of a 'Happy ending.' This is the Calumny by Federico Zuccari (the original, as well as a water-colour sketch rediscovered and published by Giglioli, *l.c.*; a drawing in the Weimar Museum mentioned *ibidem*). Zuccari's composition was also included

This tapestry has a companion piece: the 'Flora' tapestry seemingly executed at a somewhat later date and also preserved in the Galleria degli Arazzi (*fig.62*).[65] In a purely technical sense these two works are unquestionably companion pieces. They have the same dimensions and identical borders. However, the scheme of the 'Flora' tapestry, centred as it is around one predominant figure, does not correspond compositionally with the close-knit network of figures in its counterpart, while iconographically the two conceptions remain irreconcilable. Not only is the idea of a goddess light-heartedly dispensing flowers incompatible with the spirit of an austere moral allegory, but the 'Flora' composition itself can be shown to belong originally to a totally different series of representations. This female figure hovering over, rather than riding on, a ram (and derived, by the way, from Dürer's etching The Abduction on the Unicorn, or, more correctly, The Rape of Proserpine, *fig.63*)[66] should not be called 'Flora,' but Primavera—the differ-

in the later editions of Cartari's *Imagini* (in *Bibl.*56, for instance, p.313) and was divulged by several engravings, the best known of which is that by Cornelis Cort, Le Blan 153, ill. in Förster, *l.c.* Incidentally I should like to mention a pen drawing in the Hamburg Kunst-halle (Inv. 21516), which prepares Cort's engraving and is of some interest in that it shows that the oval medallion in the upper border, now filled with a Triumph of Juno, was originally destined to show the Triumph of Truth carried to heaven by Sol and Luna. In Zuccari's composition, now, the woman usually playing the part of Calumny is replaced by a personification of 'Fraude' according to Dante (*Inferno*, XVII, beginning), viz., by a monster with a human torso and serpents for feet (cf. also Cartari, *Bibl.*56, p.230, with woodcut), and the cast includes two panthers, a wolf and a little freak with a human face, bats' wings and a lion-like body which can be identified as Hypocrisy (cf.F.Saxl, *Bibl.* 300, *fig.*4). Furthermore the victim is saved 'in time,' instead of only being vindicated 'by Time,' through the activity of benevolent powers: the hand of the stupid judge, just trying to unlock the chains of a wicked giant standing for Violence, is stopped by Minerva; and the victim, here identified with the artist himself (cf. Giglioli, *l.c.*; for his ivy wreath see Ripa, s.v. 'Furore poetico' and 'Accademia') is triumphantly led away by Truth and Mercury.

65. H.Göbel, *Bibl.*114, VOL.II, 1, p.382 and VOL.II, 2, *fig.*379; H.Schulze, *Bibl.*312, p.xxxi; A. McComb, *Bibl.*213, p.25; M.Tinti, *Bibl.*343, p.45. This tapestry is said to have been executed in 1553.
66. The subject of Dürer's etching is certainly of a more or less infernal character, more likely than not the Rape of Proserpine. It is significant that the preparatory drawing, Lippmann 817 (Morgan Library), shows an ordinary horse instead of the fabulous monster which combines the features of a horse with those of a goat and a unicorn, and that the rider dashes over a heap of conquered enemies instead of starting for a jump into the void. On the other hand it can be shown that a representation of the Rape of Proserpine with Pluto abducting her on horseback instead of in a chariot was not unusual in late mediaeval art. Cf. Paris, Bibl.Nat.,ms. Fr.1584, fol.144, our *fig.*64.

ence being that Flora is an independent mythological figure while Primavera, Spring, belongs to the cycle of the Four Seasons. Further proof is afforded by the accompanying figures which are not merely 'a ram,' 'a bull,' and 'a couple embracing,' but the zodiacal signs of the three months of Spring: the Ram standing for March, the Bull for April, and the Twins for May. This does not preclude, of course, the fact that Bronzino's composition had a richer meaning than that of a mere 'division of the year associated with a type of weather and a stage of vegetation,' to quote the Oxford Dictionary again; for, according to a belief current over almost two millennia, the four seasons were bound up with such notions as the four ages of man, the four elements, and the four humours, so that Bronzino's Primavera implies, automatically, the notions of youth, air, and the sanguine temperament with all their secondary implications of gaiety and love.[67] It is evident that the so-called 'Flora' tapestry was originally conceived as one of a series of four; its present combination with the Innocence tapestry must have been an afterthought, and not altogether a happy one from an iconographic point of view. The inference is that the 'Flora' tapestry was combined with the Innocence tapestry only because the counterpart which had been planned for the Innocence could not be executed when the weavers got around to it, and this because the cartoon originally executed for the counterpart was no longer available.

As a matter of fact a Bronzino composition perfectly suited to match the Innocence tapestry both in its somewhat crowded arrangement and in its peculiar iconography would be the famous Allegory in the London National Gallery (*fig.66*).[68] This painting, usually placed around 1546, corresponds

67. Whether or not the central group was purposely made to resemble the well-known type of the Venus ἐπιτραγία (cf. R.Hamann, *Bibl.*134 with references) it is difficult to decide, but it seems by no means unlikely in view of Bronzino's archaeological leanings.
68. M.Tinti, *Bibl.*343, *fig.*43; A.McComb, *Bibl.*213, p.70 and PL.21; H.Schulze, *Bibl.*312, p.xxi and PL.XVII. The difference in proportion can either be accounted for by a widening of the original composition in the London panel, or—which is perhaps more probable—by a narrowing of the original composition in the Florence tapestry. It is a well-known fact that the weavers very often changed the dimensions of their cartoons in order to make them fit a given space.

exactly to the cartoon for the Innocence tapestry. Vasari describes it as follows: 'He made a picture of singular beauty which was sent into France to King Francis. In it was a nude Venus with Cupid who kissed her, and Pleasure (*Piacere*) was on one side as well as Jest (*Giuoco*) and other Cupids, and on the other side was Deceit (*Fraude*), Jealousy (*Gelosia*) and other passions of love.'[69]

This description was of course made from memory because the picture had gone to France (whence the use of the past tense instead of the present). Vasari's statement is thus neither complete nor absolutely correct. He omits the figure of Time, again characterized by his wings and hourglass, he covers many details with the summary expression 'and other passions of love,' and finally he lists more figures than actually appear, for he speaks of Jest and Pleasure as well as of other Cupids.[70] Nevertheless Vasari's description is quite good as far as it goes, and even his assertion that Pleasure and Jest were seen 'on one side' while Deceit and Jealousy were placed 'on the other,' unjustified though it is as a description of the compositional structure, can be defended when interpreted as relating to a contrast in meaning. Iconographically the picture does show the pleasures of love 'on the one hand' and its dangers and tortures 'on the other,' in such a way, however, that the pleasures are revealed as futile and fallacious advantages, whereas the dangers and tortures are shown to be great and real evils.

In the main group, Cupid is shown embracing Venus who holds an arrow and an apple. The apple is tendered to the eager boy and the arrow concealed, perhaps implying the idea 'sweet but dangerous.' Furthermore the adolescent age and more than tender gesture of Cupid give quite an ambiguous turn to this presumably harmless embrace of mother and child. This impression is sharpened rather than tempered by the fact that Cupid is shown

69. Vasari, *Bibl.*366, VOL.VII, p.598: '*Fece un quadro di singolare bellezza, che fu mandato in Francia al rè Francesco; dentro il quale era una Venere ignuda con Cupido che la baciava, ed il Piacere da un lato e il Giuoco con altri Amori; e dall' altro la Fraude, la Gelosia ed altre passioni d'amore.*'
70. See p.90, N.79.

as a quasi-sexless being, although the myrtle plant appearing behind him is the classical symbol of love, and the two billing doves at his feet signify 'amorous caresses.'[71] To conclude: the picture shows an image of Luxury rather than an ordinary group of Venus embracing Cupid, and this is corroborated by the fact that Cupid kneels on a pillow, a common symbol of idleness and lechery.[72]

On the left of this exquisitely lascivious group appears the head of an elderly woman madly tearing her hair. For her Vasari's label 'Jealousy' is very acceptable; for, just as Jealousy combines the terrifying aspects of Envy and Despair, so this figure combines the pathos of ancient tragic masks with the gesture of frenzied hair-tearing seen in a Dürer etching known as 'The Desperate Man.'[73] On the right is a putto throwing roses who on his left foot wears an anklet adorned with little bells, an ornament or charm frequently found in classical, particularly Hellenistic art. To him Vasari's terms 'Pleasure' and 'Jest' may be applied with almost equal correctness,[74] and he is certainly intended to establish a contrast with the sinister

71. Ripa, s.v. 'Carezze Amatorie.'
72. It is interesting to note that in Berchorius' *Moralized Ovid* in Latin, still unforgotten in the sixteenth century, the group of Venus and Cupid embracing is explained as follows: '*Cupido matrem osculans significat consanguineos, qui nimis familiariter consanguineos* [should read: *consanguineas*] *osculantur, sic quod inde per appetitum* luxurie *ipse consanguiniee vulneratur* [should read: *vulnerantur*].' See 'Thomas Walleys,' *Bibl.*386, fol. lxxxiiii (commenting upon Ovid., *Met.*, x, 525): '*Namque pharetratus dum dat puer oscula matri . . .*'
    For the symbolic use of the cushion or pillow and its connection with the proverbial '*pluma Sardanapali*' see E.Panofsky, *Bibl.*243, p.97 and *idem*, *Bibl.*251, p.8; furthermore E.Wind, *Bibl.*406. The motif emphasizes the connection between 'lechery' and 'sloth,' and even where Acedia is shown riding a donkey (as is the case, for instance, with the *Eruditorium Penitentiale*, *Bibl.*85, fol.G,1, v., and with all the illustrated manuscripts of Hugo von Trimberg's '*Der Renner*'), she is sometimes provided with a pillow brought to her by a little devil (Cod. Leyd. Voss. G.G.F.4, fol.257, our *fig.*65).
73. With regard to the iconography of this etching (B.70), cf. E.Panofsky and F.Saxl, *Bibl.*253. As to its possible connection with Michelangelo, cf. E.Tietze-Conrat, *Bibl.*342. Bronzino's 'Jealousy' is, however, much closer to Dürer's 'Desperate Man' than to the alleged Michelangelesque prototype of the latter.
74. Such anklets, with or without bells, were worn as amulets, particularly by jesters, dancers and courtesans. Cf. P.Wolters, *Bibl.*410 and 411. Furthermore see Daremberg-Saglio, *Bibl.*70, s.v. 'Tintinnabulum,' particularly p.342, col.2. Bronzino, whose archaeological leanings are well known, might have seen a Graeco-Roman figure of this type, such for

figure of Jealousy. However, his promised pleasures are signalled as futile and treacherous by the ominous presence of two masks, one of a young woman, the other of an elderly and malevolent man.

That masks symbolize worldliness, insincerity and falsehood is too well-known to require further discussion.[75] But the fact that two masks are shown instead of one and that their features indicate a contrast between youth and age, beauty and ugliness, conveys a more specific meaning which links them with the figure emerging from behind the playful Putto. This figure, sometimes described as a Harpy,[76] sometimes, rather inadequately, as a 'girl in a green dress,'[77] is unquestionably identical with what Vasari terms *La Fraude,* or Deceit. Through it Bronzino manages to give a summary of and almost visual commentary upon the qualities of hypocritical falsehood which are described by sixteenth-century iconologists under such headings as *Inganno, Hippocrisia,* and most particularly *Fraude.* According to the dean of these iconologists, Cesare Ripa, *Hippocrisia* has feet like a wolf, half-concealed by her clothes. *Inganno* can be represented as a woman hiding an ugly face beneath a beautiful mask and offering water and fire 'in alternation.' *Fraude,* finally, is endowed with two heads, one young, one old; she holds two hearts in her right hand and a mask in her left, and she has a dragon's tail, as well as griffon's talons instead of human feet.

In Bronzino's figure these features merge into a unity which is, and is meant to be, both attractive and repulsive. His little 'Fraude,' obviously the owner of the two contrasting masks, really looks at first like a charming little 'girl in a green dress.' But the dress cannot fully conceal a scaled, fish-

instance as a charming little bronze in the possession of Professor A.M.Friend, Jr., Princeton, showing a girl dancer with bells sown on her dress and a bell-adorned anklet on her left foot. For the general form and posture of Bronzino's figure see also the little dancer illustrated in Daremberg-Saglio, VOL.IV,2.fig.6055.

75. Ripa mentions the mask as an attribute of 'Bugia,' 'Fraude' and 'Inganno,' and when trodden upon, the mask signifies '*dispregio della fintione*' (s.v. 'Lealtà') and '*Dispregio delle cose mondane*' (s.v. 'Contritione').
76. H.Schulze, *Bibl.*312.
77. A.McComb, *Bibl.*213.

like body, lion's or panther's claws, and the tail of a dragon or serpent. She offers a honeycomb with one hand while she hides a poisonous little animal in the other, and moreover the hand attached to her right arm, that is the hand with the honeycomb, is in reality a left hand, while the hand attached to her left arm is in reality a right one, so that the figure offers sweetness with what seems to be her 'good' hand but is really her 'evil' one, and hides poison in what seems to be her 'evil' hand but is really her 'good' one.[78] We are presented here with the most sophisticated symbol of perverted duplicity ever devised by an artist, yet curiously enough it is a symbol not rapidly seized upon by the modern observer.

Thus the entire group consists of Luxury, surrounded by personifications and symbols of treacherous pleasures and manifest evils;[79] this group, now, is unveiled by Time and Truth. The figure of Time has already been mentioned and it is almost unnecessary to say that the female figure on the left who helps to draw the curtain from the whole spectacle is again none other than Truth, '*Veritas filia Temporis.*' In the Innocence tapestry where the figure of Truth appeared in exactly the same place she revelled in the justification of virtue; here, with a feminine disgust which parallels the masculine wrath of old Chronos, she participates in the exposure of vice. That alluring

78. For the symbolism of the Right and Left Hand in personifications of this kind, see H.R. Patch, *Bibl.*254, p.44.

79. In a less invective fashion—with the Time-Truth motif and the personification of Deceit eliminated, and the relation between Venus and Cupid made more respectable—the main idea of the London Allegory is repeated in Bronzino's picture in Budapest (M.Tinti, *Bibl.*343, fig.32; A.McComb, *Bibl.*213, p.48 and PL.20; H.Schulze, *Bibl.*312, p.V). Venus, holding an arrow, and Cupid, holding an arrow and a bow, are flanked by Jealousy (left) and two Putti making wreaths for each other's hair (right), while beneath them two Satyr-like masks are seen on the ground. In the opinion of the writer, the inaccuracies in Vasari's description of the London picture are due to a confusion of his recollection of the latter with his impression of the Budapest panel. This would account, (1) for the omission of 'Time' and 'Truth,' (2) for the emphasis of a strict symmetry ('*da un lato—e dall'altro*') which is indeed maintained in the Budapest picture, (3) for the mention of 'Giuoco' and 'Piacere,' which error would be explicable by the presence of *two* playful Putti in the Budapest version. Both compositions are, of course, influenced by Michelangelo's Venus (cartoon made for Bartolommeo Bettini, executed in colours by Jacopo Pontormo, the teacher of Bronzino); it shows already the motif of the embrace in combination with that of the masks.

sexual voluptuousness rather than other forms of evil should be selected at this particular date to symbolize vice, is perfectly in harmony with the spirit of the Counter-Reformation.

The reasons for not using the London allegory as companion piece to the Innocence tapestry can only be conjectured. We can infer from Vasari's expression 'a picture of singular beauty' that the London allegory, which is indeed a most haunting work of art, made a great impression on the Florentine court. It is conceivable that the Grand Duke Cosimo was so enthusiastic about the cartoon of this composition that he was unwilling to hand it over to his Flemish weavers and ordered it executed as a painting, so that the design might preserve its firmness and transparency and might be enhanced by the cool lustre of Bronzino's colours. We can readily understand that the Grand Duke chose this picture as a present for his most valued ally.

Originally, however, the cartoon of the London allegory was certainly destined to serve for the companion piece to the Innocence tapestry. Taken together, the two compositions, one showing the Vindication of Innocence, the other the Exposure of Luxury, depict the twofold function of Time the Revealer: 'to unmask falsehood and bring truth to light.'[80]

Time as a universal cosmic principle has been described in poetry from the Orphic Hymns to Edna St. Vincent Millay and Aldous Huxley, in philosophy from Zeno to Einstein and Weyl, and in art from the sculptors and painters of classical antiquity to Salvador Dali. A grandiose conception fusing the image of Time developed by the illustrators of Petrarch with the visions of the Apocalypse is found in Stephen Hawes' *Pastime of Pleasure*: he appears as an aged, bearded man, winged, and his strong body covered with feathers. In his left hand he holds a clock, and in his right a fire to 'brenne the tyme'; he is girt with a sword; in his right wing is the Sun, in his left wing is Mercury, and on his body are seen the other five planets: Saturn 'derkely flamynge' on the top of his head, Jupiter on his forehead, Mars in his mouth, Venus on his breast, and the Moon above his waist (*fig.51*).

80. Shakespeare, *Rape of Lucrece*, line 939ss.

Conscious of his universal power, he refutes the claims of Fame and says:

> 'Do not I tyme/cause nature to augment
> Do not I tyme/cause nature to decay
> Do not I tyme/cause man to be present
> Do not I tyme/take his lyse away
> Do not I tyme/cause dethe take his say
> Do not I tyme/passe his youth and age
> Do not I tyme/euery thynge aswage?'[81]

But no period has been so obsessed with the depth and width, the horror and the sublimity of the concept of time as the Baroque,[81a] the period in which man found himself confronted with the infinite as a quality of the universe instead of as a prerogative of God. Shakespeare alone, leaving all the other Elizabethans apart, has implored, challenged, berated, and conquered Time in more than a dozen sonnets and no less than eleven stanzas of his Rape of Lucrece.[82] He condenses and surpasses the speculations and emotions of many centuries.

In the visual arts a calmer, nearly Cartesian mind, was to create the unsurpassable images of Time as a cosmic power: Nicolas Poussin. When rendering the fateful moment in which Phaethon—the great symbol of man's limitless desires and finite power—asks for the chariot of the Sun, a gift which will spell both his supreme exaltation and his destruction, Poussin substituted the figure of Father Time for the numerous individualized personifications assembled by Ovid whose description he took as a model (*fig.67*). And in his 'Ballo della Vita Humana'—a kind of humanized Wheel of Fortune—the

---

81. Stephen Hawes, *Bibl.*136, p.215ss. I am indebted to Professor Samuel C. Chew for having called my attention both to this interesting passage and to the woodcut appearing in the editions of 1509 and 1517.
81a. The Metropolitan Museum alone has more than half a dozen drawings by G.B.Tiepolo (three of them illustrated in *Bibl.*227 a, no.40, 42, 49) which represent such subjects as Time and Fortune, Time and Truth, Time on a chariot drawn by Dragons, Venus handing over Cupid to Time, etc. The drawing reproduced in our frontispiece (37. 165. 12) represents, in my opinion, Time sending the Future on its way, with the gloomy figure turning its back upon the beholder personifying the past.
82. *Sonnets* XII, XV, XVI, XIX, LV, LX, LXIII, LXIV, LXV, LXXIII, LXXIV, LXXVI, LXXVII. *Rape of Lucrece*, stanzas 133-143 (line 925ss.).

forces which form the inescapable cycle of man's social destiny—Poverty joining hands with Labour, Labour with Wealth, Wealth with Luxury, and Luxury with Poverty again—dance to the lyre of Time while an infant plays with Time's hourglass, and another blows soap-bubbles connoting transience and futility. The whole scene is governed by the imperturbable movement of the Sun driving his chariot through the zodiac (*fig.68*).[83]

The development of the figure of Father Time is instructive in two respects. It evidences the intrusion of mediaeval features into an image which, at first sight, seems to be purely classical in character; and it illustrates the connection between mere 'iconography' and the interpretation of intrinsic or essential meanings.

It is characteristic of classical art that Time was only depicted as either fleeting Opportunity ('Kairos') or creative Eternity ('Aion'). And it is characteristic of Renaissance art that it produced an image of Time the Destroyer by fusing a personification of 'Temps' with the frightening figure of Saturn, and thereby endowed the type of 'Father Time' with a variety of new meanings. Only by destroying spurious values can Time fulfill the office of unveiling Truth. Only as a principle of alteration can he reveal his truly universal power. In this respect even Poussin's renderings of Time differ from the classical ones: he does not suppress the destructive powers of Time in favour of his creativeness, but merges the contrasting functions into a unity. Even with him, the image of Time remains a fusion of the classical Aion with the mediaeval Saturn.

83. With regard to this and some related pictures by Poussin see E.Panofsky, *Bibl.*241, particularly p.241. For the *Ballo della Vita Humana* cf. also the variations on the Wheel of Fortune adduced by Patch, *Bibl.*254, p.171, and, with regard to the origin of the soap-bubbles motif, H.Janson, *Bibl.*155, p.447 (a further article on this motif, by W.Stechow, will appear in the *Art Bulletin*). A rather weak transformation of the 'Ballo' theme is found in J.W.Baumgarten's (?) composition showing the Four Seasons dancing to the pipe of Time, ill. in J.Held, *Bibl.*141, col.361/362.

PLATE XXI

35

PLATE XXII

37

36

PLATE XXIII

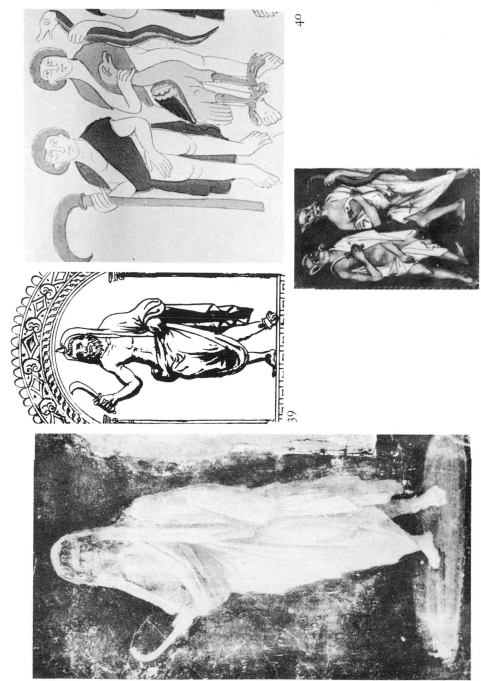

PLATE XXIV

42

44

43

45

PLATE XXV

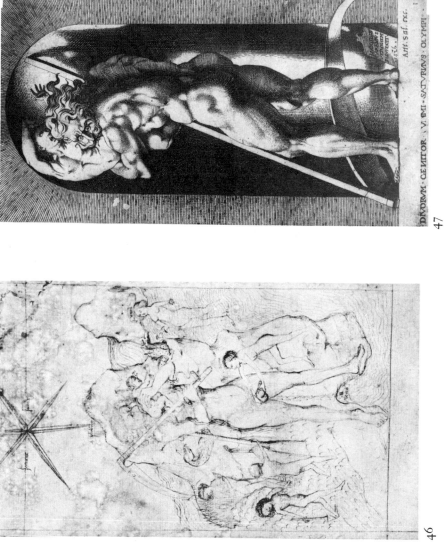

46

47

PLATE XXVI

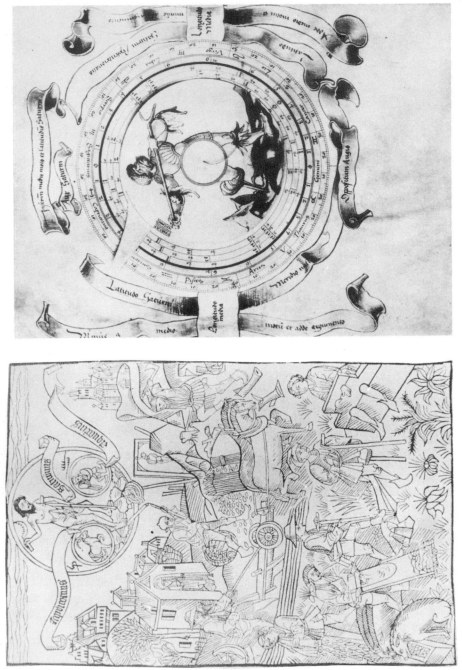

49

48

PLATE XXVII

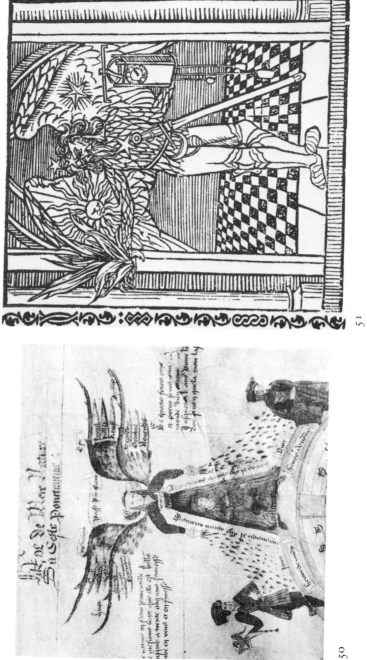

51

50

PLATE XXVIII

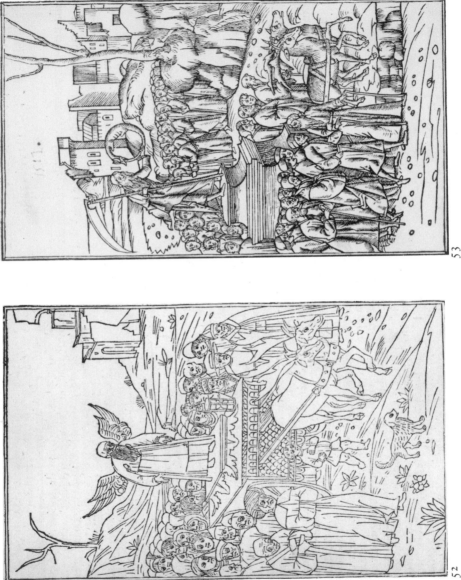

53

52

PLATE XXIX

54

PLATE XXX

55

PLATE XXXI

56

57

PLATE XXXII

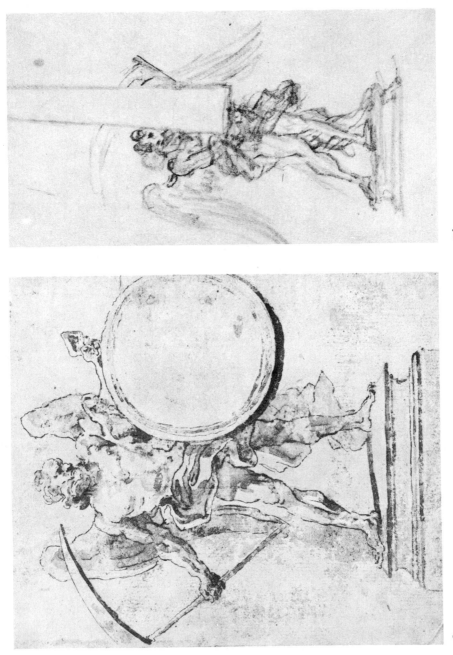

58 b

58 a

PLATE XXXIII

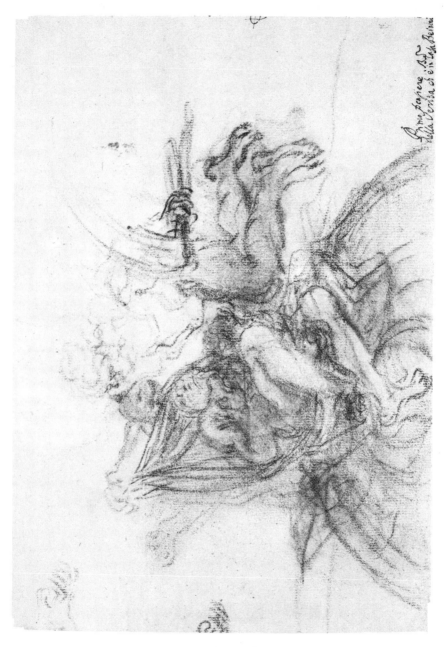

PLATE XXXIV

EIGENTLYKE AFBEELDINGE,
van Hondert der Aldervermaerdste
STATUEN, of ANTIQUE-BEELDEN,
Staande binnen ROMEN.

Afgetekent door den seer wtvermaerde en Constrycken
FRANCISCO PERRIER Burgund.
Nu in Cooper gesneden
door Cornelis van Dalen de Oude, ende de Ionge.

Dienstigh en vermakelyk, voor alle Edellny en Studenten
die tot Romen geweest syn. Ook voor alle oeffenaers
en Liefhebbers der Teicken-Const.
hier is mede by gevoecht onder elck Beeld
syn naam, en waerze staen bin
nen Romen.

PLATE XXXV

PLATE XXXVI

PLATE XXXVII

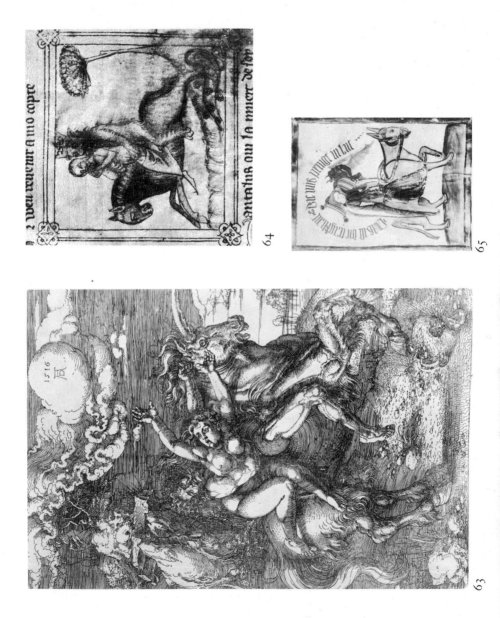

64

65

63

PLATE XXXVIII

PLATE XXXIX

PLATE XL

IV. BLIND CUPID

WHILE the figure of Father Time has proved to be a rather complicated product, due to the fusion of two originally independent elements, the case of Cupid is, on the face of it, a much simpler one. The little winged boy armed with bow and arrow was a very familiar figure in Hellenistic and Roman art. Only this figure was very rarely blind in classical literature, and it was never blind in classical art.

The belief that 'the lover is blinded about what he loves so that he judges wrongly of the just, the good and the honourable,'[1] is of course frequently expressed in classical literature which abounds in such phrases as *caecus*

1. Plato, *Leges*, v, 731e, quoted from B. Jowett, *The Dialogues of Plato*, VOL.V, 1892, p.113. It must be noted that the passage Τυφλοῦται γὰρ περὶ τὸ φιλούμενον ὁ φιλῶν ὥστε τὰ δίκαια καὶ τὰ ἀγαθὰ καὶ τὰ καλὰ κακῶς κρίνει follows the sentence: τὸ δὲ ἀληθείᾳ γε πάντων ἁμαρτημάτων διὰ τὴν σφόδρα ἑαυτοῦ φιλίαν αἴτιον ἑκάστῳ γίγνεται ἑκάστοτε.

amor, caeca libido, caeca cupido, caecus amor sui.[2] But this blindness characterizes love as a psychological emotion, often of a definitely egotistical
nature. When Love is envisaged as a figure, as for instance by Propertius[3]
who describes him in a famous elegy 'as artists depict him,' he appears as a
nude, winged infant, carrying bow and arrows, or a torch, or both. These
are his attributes in Seneca's *Octavia*, in Apuleius' *Golden Ass* and in many
Hellenistic epigrams.[4] Discarding Theocritus' jocular parallel between Eros

2. Cf., for instance, Catullus, *Carmina*, 67,25: '*impia mens caeco flagrabat amore.*' Lucretius,
De Rer. Nat., IV, 1153: '*Nam faciunt homines plerumque cupidine caeci.*' Ovid, *Fasti*, II, 762:
'*et caeco raptus amore fuit.*' Ovid, *Metam.*, III, 620: '*praedae tam caeca cupido est.*' Cicero,
De. invent., I, 2: '*caeca ac temeraria . . . cupiditas.*' Seneca, *Dial.*, I, 6, 1: '*caecam libidinem.*'
Seneca, *ibidem*, VII, 10, 2: '*amorem rerum suarum caecum et improvidum.*' Seneca, *ibidem*,
VII, 14, 2: '*Evenit autem hoc* [viz. the loss of virtue] *nimia intemperantia et amore caecae
rei.*' Seneca, *Epist.*, CIX, 16: '*quos amor sui excaecat.*' Propertius, *Eleg.*, II, 14, 17:
> '*Ante pedes caecis lucebat semita nobis,*
> *Scilicet insano nemo in amore videt.*'
Horace, *Satir.*, I, 3, 39: '*amatorem . . . amicae turpia decipiunt caecum vitia.*' Valerius
Flaccus, *Argonaut.*, VI, 454: '*Quid, si caecus amor saevusque accesserit ignis?*' Gregory of
Nazianzus, *Poemata moralia*, XXIX (*Bibl.*214, VOL.37, col.895/6): '*Tam caeca res est amor et
praepostera.*'

3. Propertius, *Eleg.*, III, 12: '*Quicumque ille fuit, puerum qui pinxit Amorem,*
> *Nonne putas miras hunc habuisse manus?*
> *Hic primum vidit sine sensu vivere amantes*
> *Et levibus curis magna perire bona.*
> *Idem non frustra ventosas addidit alas,*
> *Fecit et humano corde volare deum.*
> *Scilicet alterna quoniam iactamur in unda,*
> *Nostraque non ullis permanet aura locis.*
> *Et merito hamatis manus est armata sagittis,*
> *Et pharetra ex humero Gnosia utroque iacet.*
> *Ante ferit quoniam, tuti quam cernimus hostem,*
> *Nec quisquam ex illo vulnere sanus abit . . .*'

4. Seneca, *Octavia*, I.557ss.: '*Volucrem esse Amorem fingit immitem deum*
> *mortalis error, armat et telis manus*
> *arcuque sacras, instruit saeva face*
> *genitumque credit Venere, Vulcano satum.*'
In reality, love is, according to Seneca, '*vis maga mentis, blandus atque animi calor,*' begotten
by youth, nourished by luxury and leisure. Apuleius, *Metam.*, IV, 30: '*puerum suum pennatum
illum et satis temerarium, qui, malis suis moribus contempta disciplina publica, flammis et
sagittis armatus per alienas domos nocte discurrens . . . committit tanta flagitia.*' Further
instances abound both in Latin and Greek literature (cf., e.g., the epigrams in the *Anthologia
Graeca*, such for instances as *Bibl.*10, VOL.III, p.244, no.440, or VOL.V., p.272, no.196; *ibidem*,
p.276, no.201). For the survival of this conception in Byzantine literature cf. the passage
quoted below.

and Plutus (Wealth) whose 'blindness' was proverbial ever since Hipponax had deplored the unfair distribution of worldy goods,[5] there is only one little Latin poem in which Cupid is described as a blind person, and this poem is of very late date and somewhat dubious authenticity.[6]

The innumerable representations of Cupid in Hellenistic and Roman art agree with the descriptions of Propertius, Seneca and Apuleius. None of them show the motif of a bandage covering the eyes, and wherever modern archaeologists mention a blindfold Cupid of classical origin (Renaissance writers were fully aware of the fact that Cupid was not blind in ancient art), it can be proved that their statements are erroneous.[7] The few Byzantine and Carolingian works of art in which the naked, childlike image of Cupid, like that of many other pagan divinities, was directly revived from classical sources, confirm the fact that the blindfold motif was foreign to Greek and Roman iconography. It is absent from the Byzantine Rosette-caskets (*fig.69*)[8] and the Oppian illustrations (*fig.70*)[9] where Eros appears

5. Theocritus, *Idyll.*, x, 19s. . . . τυφλὸς δ'οὐκ αὐτὸς ὁ πλοῦτος, 'Αλλὰ καὶ ὠφρόντιστος ἔρως.
For the proverbial blindness of Plutus see Roscher, *Bibl.290*, s.v. 'Plutos,' col.2583ss.
6. *Antholog. Lat.*, *Bibl.*11, VOL.I, 2, p.209, no.812:
'*Parce puer, si forte tuas sonus improbus aures . . .*
Sed postquam aurata delegit cuspide telum
Caecus Amor tenuique offendit volnere pectus,
Tum pudor et sacri reverentia pectoris omnem
Labitur in noxam . . .'
7. For Cupid in classical art see Roscher, *Bibl.290*, s.v. 'Eros' and Daremberg-Saglio, *Bibl.70*, VOL.I,2, p.1595, s.v. 'Cupido.' F.Wickhoff's statement that blind Cupids could be seen on monuments such as the well-known Phaedra sarcophagus in Pisa, *Bibl.398*, is an obvious '*lapsus calami.*' E.Müntz, *Bibl.226*, p.48 (and, on his authority, F. von Bezold, *Bibl.33*, p.41) asserts that '*un abbé de St. Étienne de Caën, au XIII* siècle, faisait graver autour d'un Cupidon aux yeux bandés et portant le carquois, l'inscription " ecce mitto angelum meum."* ' However, the seal in question—the '*contre-sceau*' of the Abbot Nicolas of St. Étienne de Caën of 1282—shows, not a blind Cupid but a crowned, winged Victory holding a wreath in her hand; cf. G.Demay, *Bibl.73*, p.iv and p.x, no.64.
8. A.Goldschmidt and K.Weitzmann, *Bibl.*116, vol.I, no.23.
9. Oppian, *Cynegetica*, II, 410ss. For the manuscripts, see A.W-Byvanck, *Bibl.52*. Three illustrated manuscripts are extant: Venice, cod. Marc. Graec. 479 (11th Cent.), Paris, Bibl. Nat., ms. Grec 2736 (15th Cent., the illustrations copied from the former) and Paris, Bibl. Nat., ms. Grec 2737 which is a copy of ms. Grec 2736 executed in 1554 by Ange Vergèce. Our *figs.93* and 94 (the corresponding miniature in the Marcianus illustrated in Charles Diehl, *Bibl.75*, PL.LXXX) show Eros attacking the Olympian Gods. On the left can be seen Athene,

as the great force that rules over the instincts of gods, men and animals, as well as from the Carolingian miniatures found in the manuscripts of Hrabanus Maurus *De Universo* (*fig.*71)[10] and Prudentius' *Psychomachia* where Cupid and his (alleged) brother Jocus (Jest) are represented in flight, following the ignominious downfall of Luxury (*text ill.* p.95 and *fig.*72).[11]

The mediaeval renderings of Cupid not derived from classical models but freely reconstructed on the basis of literary sources conform, of course, to the indications furnished by the texts. Setting aside the epics directly dealing with Homeric or Virgilian subject matter such as the various versions of the Trojan cycle, where Cupid appears as an ordinary member of the classical Pantheon and is described accordingly,[12] these texts can be divided into two main classes. One group 'paraphrases' the image of the little pagan Cupid which still lived in everybody's memory, but, having lost its original signifi-

Venus (?) and two unidentified divinities, on the right Zeus appearing in the sky and Hermes (identified by an inscription) violently arguing with what looks like a Byzantine court official while a lady looks out of a window. This scene may be interpreted either as Hermes, Argos and Io, or preferably, as Hermes, Aglauros and Herse (cf. Ovid, *Metam.*II, 707ss.; a very similar representation of this incident is found in Bartolommeo Montagna's engraving B.18, ill. in A.M.Hind, *Bibl.*146, p.487, no.40). The Christian Saint attacked by a Satyr may be St. Theodora of Alexandria (cf. Cod. Vat. Barb. Graec. 372, fol.195, or London, Brit. Mus., ms. Add. 19352, fol.157). Our *fig.*70 shows Eros pursuing all kinds of animals; a parallel in Byzantine literature is found in Eusthatius Makrembolites, *Bibl.*88, VOL.II, p.63, where Eros is said to use his darts to conquer the men, his torch to conquer the women, his bow to conquer the wild animals, his wings to conquer the birds, and his nudity to conquer the fish:

"Ερως τὸ μειράκιον ὅπλα πῦρ φέρον
Τόξον, πτερῶν, γύμνωσιν ἰχθύων βέλος.

Regarding the fact that Cupid is blind in Paris, ms. Graec. 2737, but not in the two earlier manuscripts, cf. below, p.121s.

10. A.M.Amelli, *Bibl.*7, PL.CXII, mentioned as the only example of the representational tradition of Cupid in mediaeval art in the otherwise very instructive article 'Amor' by L.Freund, *Bibl.*100. For the Hrabanus text, see below.

11. Prudentius, *Psychomachia*, 1,432-439. Cf. R.Stettiner, *Bibl.*325, Tafelband, PL.4 (here only Jocus); 5,1;22,4 (our *fig.*72); 43,2;60,10;98,14;116,4;186,10;197 (the latest manuscript of the group, dated 1289, with Jocus in Gothic costume). The *locus classicus* for the combination of Jocus and Cupid is Horace, *Carmina*, I, 2 where Venus is addressed in the following fashion:

'Sive tu mavis, Ericyna ridens,
Quam locus circumvolat et Cupido . . .'

12. Cf., e.g., Konrad von Würzburg, *Der trojanische Krieg*, *Bibl.*173, p.12, line 964ss.

cance, had come to be interpreted in a metaphorical or allegorical way. The other group builds up a specifically mediaeval concept of exalted love which, when personified, appeared as a visionary figure utterly different from the classical image, but endowed with what may be called emotional actuality. In the first case, we have an interpretative description of Cupid, worked out and transmitted in moralizing mythography; in the second case, we have a metaphysical glorification of Love, evolved in idealistic poetry, however much descriptive detail may have been drawn from classical literature or late-antique and mediaeval scholarship.[13]

Plato's theory of love has left no trace in Greek and Roman poetry. Didactic poets like Lucretius or Oppian glorified love as an all-powerful and omnipresent force, but conceived of this force as a natural, not metaphysical principle, pervading yet not transcending the material universe. In lyrics, on the other hand, love was depicted as the strongest of human emotions, blissful and torturing, life-giving and deadly; but neither Theocritus nor Tibullus, neither Callimachus nor Ovid would have thought of elevating the object of this emotion to a 'supercelestial realm.'

The Platonic creed appealed however to the Islamic East, where it gave rise to the ardent mysticism of Al Ghāzāli and Omar Khayyām, and it was adopted by the Christian Fathers who transformed Plato's theory of love into a theory of divine ἀγάπη or *caritas*, much in the same way as they had turned his epistemology into a logic of the mind of God. The concept of *caritas*, originally limited to the 'love that God hath to us' (I. John iv,16) was subsequently extended to the unselfish love of man to God and to his fellow-beings. But even then *caritas* (*appetitus boni*, or *amor Dei*, or *amor spiritualis*) formed a sharp contrast with the various forms of 'sensual' love which came under the heading of *cupiditas* (*appetitus mali*, or *amor mundi*, or *amor carnalis*).

13. Cf. F.Wickhoff, *Bibl.*398. Furthermore: K.Vossler, *Bibl.*385; P.Rousselot, *Bibl.*291; E. Wechssler, *Bibl.*389 and 390; H.Pflaum, *Bibl.*265, p.1ss.; recently C.S.Lewis, Bibl.193. For Islamic influences see A.R.Nykl, *Bibl.*231.

This contrast was softened, when twelfth-century poetry—probably under oriental influence—sublimated sensual love into what the Troubadours and their followers called 'Amour,' 'Amore,' or 'Minne,' while twelfth-century theology swerved toward emotional mysticism, and religious passions concentrated on the Virgin Mary. The concept of 'sensual love' became spiritualized and, at the same time, imbued with a spirit of woman-worship equally foreign to the pagan West and the Islamic East.

It was on this basis that the thirteenth century was able to achieve a temporary reconciliation of *cupiditas* and *caritas* comparable to the reconciliation of classical and mediaeval principles in High Gothic statuary and Thomistic theology. With the old antithesis still persisting, as it always did, in more conservative ethics and poetry,[14] the genius of a new generation achieved an inextricable fusion between the concrete object of human love and a metaphysical entity of more or less religious character. The *Roman de la Rose* substituted a mystical flower for the real woman; Guido Guinicelli and the other representatives of the 'Dolce stil nuovo' transformed her into an angel; and in Dante's work the supernatural principle personified by Beatrice defies predicability to such an extent that she could be interpreted by the Commentators as The Revelation, Faith, Divine Grace, scholastic Theology, the Church, and finally Platonic Philosophy.

However, this harmony, like all reconciliations of conflicting principles, was not to last. Petrarch rehumanized and resensualized the object of his passion, while, at the same time, idolizing and even deifying it. Contrary to Dante's Beatrice, Petrarch's Laura never ceases to be a real human being and becomes the more desirable as a woman the more she is glorified as an idea, or even treated as a saint sharing the honours of Christ. The theological antithesis between *caritas* and *cupiditas*, temporarily abolished by the 'Dolce stil nuovo' and Dante, reappeared in Petrarch as a psychological tension. Petrarch was great enough to monumentalize this tension. But in his imitators

14. Cf., e.g., the beautiful sonnet by Guittone d'Arezzo: '*Donna del cielo, gloriosa Madre*' (V.Nannucci, *Bibl.*227, VOL.I, p.163), where the poet implores the Virgin Mary to fill him with '*quel divino amore*' that will save him from the '*saette aspre e quadre*' of Cupid.

his influence (which has been termed the 'chronic disease of Italian poetry') was to induce that maudlin and slightly ambiguous attitude—*sinnlich-übersinnlich*, to quote Goethe's Mephistopheles—which is still miscalled 'Platonic love.'[14a]

Most representatives of the 'Dolce stil nuovo' do not attempt any visual description of Love because they identify him with a principle so spiritual and sublime that it transcends by definition the realm of sensual experience. '*E non si può conoscer per lo viso*' as Guido Cavalcanti puts it,[15] or

> '*Ma io dico ch' Amor non ha sustanza,*
> *Ne è cosa corporal ch'abbia figura,*'

to quote an anonymous poet of the same period.[16] Other sources, particularly the authors of allegorical epics of the *Roman de la Rose* type, describe 'il Signor Amore' or 'le Dieu Amour' as a visible figure, or rather as a vision. In these the god is portrayed no longer as an infant, but as a handsome adolescent of princely appearance, often accompanied by a humble servant or by a whole retinue of subsidiary personifications.[17] He remains winged, but is now dressed in resplendent garments, his head encircled by a crown or wreath (*figs.* 73, 74). He is often seated on a throne or shown as the lord of a castle or tower. In other instances he appears in a beautiful garden, preferably on the top of a tree (*fig.* 75), a motif which, I think, can be traced back to Apuleius.[18] He is armed with a torch, or with a torch and a dart, or with two

14a. For the Neoplatonic theory of love developed by Marsilio Ficino and his followers see next chapter.
15. V.Nannucci, *ibidem*, p.290.
16. V.Nannucci, *ibidem*, p.294.
17. Cf. F.Wickhoff, *Bibl.*398, L.Freund, *Bibl.*100; furthermore H.Kohlhaussen, *Bibl.*172, passim, particularly p.39ss.; R.Koechlin, *Bibl.*169; and *idem*, *Bibl.*170, particularly nos.1068,1071, 1076,1077,1080,1092,1094,1098.
18. As for the motif of Love appearing to the author in a tree, which became particularly popular through Guillaume de Machaut's *Dit dou Vergier* (*Bibl.*205), but which occurs already in thirteenth-century French literature, see R.Koechlin, *Bibl.*169. The idea derives from Hellenistic poetry where Cupids are often likened to birds fluttering from branch to branch (cf., e.g., Theocritus, *Idyll.* xv,120ss.:

darts, or with bow and arrows, or, very frequently, with two bows, one of smooth white wood or ivory, the other dark and knotty; each bow has suitable arrows: golden ones to cause love, and black, generally leaden ones, to extinguish it.[19] The beauty of Love is often compared to that of the angels ('*il semble que ce fust uns anges,*' says the *Roman de la Rose*), and Dante goes so far as to characterize 'Amore' in exactly the terms used in the Gospel of St. Mark to describe the Angel revealing the Resurrection of Christ to the Holy Women: '*Che mi parve nella mia camera lungo me sedere un giovane vestito di bianchissime vestimenta.*'[20]

In these poetic descriptions, as well as in the works of art inspired by them,

. . . οἱ δέ τε κῶροι ὑπερπωτῶνται ''Ερωτες,
οἷοι ἀηδονιδῆες ἀεξομένων ἐπὶ δένδρων
πωτῶνται πτερύγων πειρώμενοι, ὄζον ἀπ' ὄζῳ,

or *Antholog. Graeca, Bibl.*10, VOL.III, p.244, no.440), and was often illustrated in painting; the survival of this concept is evidenced by such lines as that in a poem by Guido Guinicelli (V.Nannucci, *Bibl.*227, p.33):

'*Al cor gentil ripara sempre amore*
Siccome augello in selva alla verdura,'

or even in Carmen's *Ah, l'amore è strano augello.* But as far as the *Dit dou Vergier* is concerned, the *locus classicus* seems to be Apuleius, *Metam.* v, 24: '*Nec deus amator humi iacentem* [viz., Psychen] *deserens involavit proximam cupressum deque eius alto cacumine sic eam graviter commotus adfatur.*'

19. Cf. particularly the *Roman de la Rose*, line 865ss. (*Bibl.*288, VOL.II, p.45; for illustrated manuscripts see A.Kuhn, *Bibl.*176) and its numerous imitations, such for instance as the *Echecs Amoureux* (E.Sieper, *Bibl.*318) or John Lydgate's *Reson and Sensuallyte* which is a translation of the *Echecs Amoureux* (*Bibl.*204). E.Langlois, *Bibl.*288, p.303, and Sieper, *Bibl.*204, VOL.II, p.123 give a number of other instances. The source of the concept is, of course, Ovid, *Metam.* I, 467ss., where Cupid has one golden and one leaden arrow. The Middle Ages not only increased the number of the arrows from 2 to 10 or more, and endowed them with specific symbolical meanings (the golden arrows standing for 'Biautez, Simplesse, Franchise, Compaignie, Biaus Semblanz,' the leaden ones for 'Orgiauz, Vilainie, Honte, Deseperance, Noviaus Pensers'), but also invented a special bow for each kind of arrows. Boccaccio, *Amorosa Visione*, v, reverts to Ovid's classical simplicity:

'*In man teneva una saetta d'oro,*
Di piombo un'altra . . .'

20. *Vita Nuova*, XII, quoted by F.Wickhoff, *Bibl.*398. The parallel from *St. Mark's Gospels*, also quoted by Wickhoff, reads: '*viderunt juvenem sedentem in dextris coopertum stola candida*' (XVI, 5). The humble little angel of love appearing in Dante's *Ballata per una ghirlandetta* must, however, not be confounded with the pagan '*puer alatus:*' he is, of course, subsidiary to the monumental 'Amore' appearing in the *Vita Nuova*, and therefore a mere '*angiolel d'amore umile,*' but he remains an angel, and Dante certainly does not imagine him nude and equipped with the classical attributes.

'Amour,' 'Amore,' 'Frouwe Amour,' 'Venus Cupido' or Love however designated,[21] is never blind, and could not be blind in view of the Platonic belief that the noblest of emotions enters the human soul by the noblest of the senses. Statements to this effect are very frequent in high mediaeval poetry: *'E'l suo cominciamento è per vedere,'*[22] or: *'E gli occhi in prima generan l'Amore,'*[23] or: *'Vien da veduta forma che s'intende.'*[24] A sixteenth-century commentator of Petrarch remarks in speaking about the image of Love, that it would be objectionable if the organ by which love comes into existence and pleases, viz., the eyes, were blind instead of beautiful 'for the principle of love is none other than beauty, and the beautiful is luminous to behold.'[25]

In the fourteenth-century derivatives of the *Roman de la Rose*, however, an interesting phenomenon may be observed. While in the original the clearsightedness of Love is taken for granted, some of the later poets go out of their way to insist on this fact, and make it very clear that, in their opinion, Cupid is not blind. John Lydgate's translation of the *Echecs Amoureux*, for instance, has the following lines:

> 'Though somme seyn, in special,
> That he seeth ryght nothing at al,
> But is as blinde as stok or stone . . .
> I espyed by his chere
> That his sight was ryghte clere.'[26]

And Chaucer says:

> 'And al be men seyn that blind is he,
> Al-gate me thoughte he mighte wel y-see.'[27]

21. For the fusion of Cupid and 'Fraw Venus Minne' cf. H.Kohlhaussen, *Bibl.*172.
22. Ser Pace, Nannucci, *Bibl.*227, p.293.
23. Jacopo da Lentino, Nannucci, *ibidem.*
24. Guido Cavalcanti, Nannucci, *ibidem.* p.287. Cf. also such Troubadours as Uc Brunet, F. Diez, *Bibl.*76, 1883, p.122.
25. Petrarch, *Bibl.*262, fol.184: *'Ne si conviene, che quella parte onde amor nasce et piace, cioè la vista, non bella ma cieca sia, non altro essendo d'amore principio che la bellezza, ma il bello, come vuol inferire, è luminoso in vista.'*
26. J.Lydgate, *Bibl.*204, line 5379ss. As to the parallel passage in the *Echecs Amoureux* cf. E.Sieper, *Bibl.*318.
27. Chaucer, *The legend of good women,* line 169s.

Similarly, Petrarch in his 118th Sonnet, describes 'Amore' as follows:

> '*Cieco non già, ma faretrato il veggo,*
> *Nudo, se non quanto vergogna il vela;*
> *Garzon con l'ali, non pinto ma vivo . . .*'[28]

Protestations like these presuppose, of course, the existence of a belief that Cupid *was* blind, and of pictures which thus represented him. The development of this conception can be observed in that other group of textual sources which we have classified as 'moralizing mythography.'

Propertius' Elegy, already mentioned,[29] not only describes the image of Cupid but also gives an allegorical explanation of his characteristic aspects: The childlike appearance symbolizes the 'senseless' behaviour of lovers, the wings indicate the volatile instability of amorous emotions, and the arrows the incurable wounds inflicted upon the human soul by love. Thus it appears that Roman poetry—and rhetoric—had already worked out a moralizing interpretation of the image of Cupid which was distinctly pessimistic from the start, for love was conceived as a dangerous and painful experience which reduced the mind to a state of inconsistency and childishness. In mythographical writing this damaging interpretation not only persisted but also developed, and attained an importance which is frequently overlooked by the historians of 'poetic Love.'

The late antique authors who transmitted mythographical material to the Middle Ages proceeded on exactly the same lines as Propertius. As for the mediaeval writers, while their attention was still focussed on the little nude idol of pagan memory, their disapproval of its significance was sharpened by their theological outlook and led them to multiply Love's more unpleasant traits. Servius in his Commentary on Vergil still transmits Propertius' 'moralization' without any notable changes.[30] Isidorus of Seville and Hrabanus

28. Petrarch, *Canzoniere*, Sonn. CXVIII, '*Non d'atra e tempestosa onda marina . . .*'
29. See above, p.96.
30. Servius, *In Vergil. Aen.* 1, 663: '*Nam quia turpitudinis est stulta cupiditas, puer pingitur, ut inter quas curam Clymenen narrabat inanem, id est amorem, item quia imperfectus est in amantibus sermo sicut in puero . . . Alatus autem ideo est, quia amantibus nec levius nec mutabilius invenitur . . . sagittas vero ideo gestare dicitur, quia et ipsae incertae velocesque sunt.*'

Maurus add an explanation of the torch '*quia inflammat*,'[31] and the Mythographus II feels obliged to account for the nakedness of Cupid in the same way as Fulgentius had accounted for the nakedness of Cupid's mother Venus: 'the turpitude of love is always manifest and never hidden.'[32] The Mythographus III (that is, perhaps, Alexander Neckham) summarizes the whole content of this tradition, adds several humanistic details such as the motif of the two arrows, and furnishes alternative explanations of certain characteristic features.[33]

Now, the immediate followers of Alexander Neckham take the decisive step of adding blindness to the other attributes of Cupid. In Thomasin von Zerclaere's didactic poem entitled *Der Wälsche Gast* (around 1215), Love says: 'I am blind and I make blind,'[34] and except for Petrarch's deliberately classicizing descriptions[35] and a few other special cases, there is hardly a

31. Hrabanus Maurus, *De Universo*, xv, 6 (Migne, *Patrolog. Lat.*, VOL.III, col.432): '*Cupidinem vocatum ferunt propter amorem. Est enim daemon fornicationis, qui ideo alatus pingitur, quia nihil amantibus levius, nihil mutabilius invenitur. Puer pingitur, quia stultus est et irrationalis amor. Sagittam et facem tenere fingitur, quia amor cor vulnerat, facem, quia inflammat.*' The passage is literally copied from Isidorus of Seville, *Etymologiae*, VIII, 9, 80.
32. Mythographus II, 35, *Bibl.*38, p.86, '*Qui pharetratus, nudus, cum face, pennatus, puer depingitur. Pharetratus ideo, quia sicut sagittae corpus, ita mentem vulnerat amor. Nudus, quia amoris turpitudo semper manifesta est et nusquam occulta. Cum face autem, quia turpis amor cum calore et fervore quodam accenditur. Pennatus, quia amor cito pertransit et amantibus nec levius aliquid nec mutabilius invenitur. Puer autem fingitur, quia sicut pueris per imperitiam facundia, sic quoque nimium amantibus per voluptatem deficit.*' Cf. Fulgentius, *Mitologiae*, II, 1.p.40 Helm: '*Hanc* [viz., *Venerem*] *etiam nudam pingunt, sive quod nudos sibi adfectatos dimittat, sive quod libidinis crimen numquam celatum sit, sive quod numquam nisi nudis conveniat.*' Statements to this effect remained, of course, typical in later 'moralizations' of Venus, as well as Cupid; cf., e.g., Mythographus III, 11, 1, *Bibl.*38, p.228, or 'Th.Walleys,' *Bibl.*386, fol.viii: '*dicitur esse nuda propter ipsius indecentiam inevitabilem.*'
33. Mythographus III, 11, 18, *Bibl.*38, p.239: '*Pingitur autem Amor puer, quia turpitudinis est stulta cupiditas, et quia imperfectus est in amantibus, sicut in pueris, sermo . . . Alatus, quia amantibus non levius aliquid nec mutabilius. Sagittas fert, quae et ipsae incertae sunt et veloces; sive, ut vult Remigius, quia conscientia criminis perpetrati stimulet mentem. Aurea autem sagitta amorem mittit, plumbea tollit . . . Ideo nudus, quia turpitudo a nudis peragitur; vel quia in ea turpitudine nihil est secretum.*'
34. Cf. A. von Oechelhäuser, *Bibl.*232, p.25, no.19, also ill. in H.Kohlhaussen, *Bibl.*172, p.40.
35. Cf., in addition to *Sonnet* CXVIII, *Africa*, III, line 215ss. (*Bibl.*263), and *Trionfi*, Triumphus Amoris, line 23ss.:

description of the 'pagan' Cupid later than the 'Mythographus III' which does not insist upon his blindness, however literally the earlier tradition may be followed in other respects. This is true of the original French version of the *Moralized Ovid*,[36] of the *Tesoretto* by Brunetto Latini,[37] Dante's master, of Berchorius' introduction to the *Moralized Ovid* in Latin,[38] of the *Libellus De Imaginibus Deorum* which has been mentioned as an abridgement

> '*Sopr'un carro di fuoco un garzon crudo*
> *Con arco in mano e con saetti a'fianchi,*
> *Contra le qual non val elmo nè scudo:*
> *Sopra l'omeri avea sol due grand' ali*
> *Di color mille, e tutto l'altro ignudo.*'

36. *Ovide Moralisé* I, line 668ss., ed.C.de Boer, Bibl.40, VOL.I, p.75:
> '*Venus tient et porte un brandon*
> *Et Cupido l'arc et la floiche . . .*
> *Jocus et Cupido sont point*
> *Au pointures nu, sans veue,*
> *Quar fole amours et jex desnue*
> *Les musars de robe et d'avoir,*
> *D'entendement et de savoir,*
> *D'amor et de bones vertus.*
> *Pour ce sont il paint avugle,*
> *Qu'amours et jex mains folz avugle.*'

For the combination of '*jex*' with '*amours*' and Venus see p.98.

37. B.Latini, *Tesoretto*, line 2256ss., Bibl.183, p.375:
> '*E'n una gran charriera*
> *Io vidi dritto stante*
> *Ignudo un fresco fante,*
> *Ch'auea l'archo e li strali*
> *E auea penne ed ali.*
> *Ma neente uedea . . .*'

38. 'Th.Walleys,' Bibl.386, fol.viii, v.: '*Vel dic quod Cupido filius Veneris est amor carnalis filius voluptatis: qui alatus pingitur pro eo quod amor subito volare sepe videtur. Constat enim quod homo quandoque subito et sine deliberatione amore alicuius persone inflamatur: et ideo amor iste alatus et volatilis dici potest. Cecus autem iste deus pingitur quia quo se ingerat aduertere non videtur: quia amor ita solet se ponere in pauperem sicut in diuitem in turpem sicut in pulchrum: in religiosum sicut in laicum. Cecus autem aliter dici potest: quia per ipsum etiam homines excecari videntur. Nihil enim est cecius homine inflammato amore alicuius persone vel alicuius rei. Unde dicit Seneca quod amor iudicium nescit. Breviter igitur voluerunt poete duos deos depingere cecos scilicet cupidinem et fortunam: quia scilicet cupido et amor (sicut dictum est) ita cecus est quod aliquando nititur in impossibile sicut patuit in Narcisso qui umbram propriam usque ad mortem amauit. Sicut etiam quotidie videmus quod una utilis persona amabit nobilissimam vel econtrario. Fortuna etiam ac si ceca esset, quandoque subito promouet indignos et deprimit dignos. Roma. II. Cecitas ex parte contigit in israel.*'

of the Berchorius treatise,[39] of Boccaccio's *Genealogia Deorum* (where Cupid is described as blindfold instead of just blind, and with griffons' talons for feet),[40] as well as of the little anonymous poems explaining the popular pictures of *Amor Carnalis*[41] or *Amor Mundanus.*[42]

The allegorical interpretations of this newly acquired handicap are as unflattering as possible. Cupid is nude and blind because he 'deprives men of their garments, their possessions, their good sense and their wisdom.' He is blind 'because he does not mind where he turns, inasmuch as love descends

39. Cod. Vat. Reg.1290, fol.2, cf. H.Liebeschütz, *Bibl.*194, PL.XVIII and p.118: '*Huic* [viz. Veneri] *et Cupido, filius suus alatus et cecus, assistebat, qui sagita et arcu, quos tenebat, Appolinem sagitaverat . . .*'

40. Boccaccio, *Genealogia Deorum*, IX,4: '*Hunc puerum fingunt, ut aetatem suscipientium passionem hanc et mores designent . . . Alatus praeterea dicitur, ut passionati instabilitas demonstretur . . . Arcum atque sagittas ideo ferre fingitur, ut insipientium repentina captivitas ostendatur . . . Has aureas esse dicunt et plumbeas, ut per aureas dilectionem sumamus . . . Per plumbeas autem odium volunt . . . Fax autem illi superaddita ostendit animorum incendia . . . Oculos autem illi fascia tegunt, ut advertamus amantes ignorare quo tendant, nulla eorum esse iudicia, nullae rerum distinctiones, sed sola passione duci. Pedes autem gryphis illi ideo apponunt, ut declaretur, quoniam tenacissima sit passio, nec facile inerti impressa ocio solvitur.*' For the griffons' talons, see below, p.120.

41. Heitz, *Bibl.*137, VOL.59, 1925, no.14 (partially reproduced by L.Freund, *Bibl.*100, col.645 and in our *fig.*84). *Amor Carnalis* is represented as a nude, winged, blindfold woman, equipped with bow and arrows, an ointment jar at her feet. Beneath her can be seen a skull, a sword and the jaws of Hell, inscribed '*Finis amoris.*' St. Gregory, St. Jerome, St. Augustine (twice), Aristotle, 'Philosophus' [Plato ?], St. Bernard, St. Ambrose, Moses and the 'Experiencia Jurisconsultorum' warn against her, as does the auther, saying '*Dein salb ist falsch vnd vngerecht, das klag ich armer knecht.*' The main inscription reads:
   '*Die lieb ist nacket vnd plint vnd plos.*
   Des kumbt manger man von treu [should read '*iret*'] *wegen*
      in der helle schos.
   Sie hat zween flugel die sein vnstill.
   Sie ist zu allen zeitten wo sie will.
   Sie kann salben vnd verwunden,
   Wo sie woll zu stunden.
   Ire wort sind listig vnd behend.
   Gar pitter ist der snoden lieb end.'

42. Cod. Casanatensis 1404, fol.2v., ill. in F.Saxl, *Bibl.*295, PL.XXVI, *fig.*45:
   '*Amor mundanus cernit omnia lumine ceco.*
   Disce, quid sit amor. Amor est insania mentis,
   Dulce malum, mala dulcedo, gratissimus error.'

L.G.Gyraldus, *Bibl.*127, VOL.I, col.409 quotes a little mediaeval rhyme in the style of those occurring in John Ridewall's *Fulgentius Metaforalis*:
   '*Caecus et alatus,*
   Nudus, puer et pharetratus.'

upon the poor as well as the rich, the ugly as well as the handsome. He is also called blind because people are blinded by him, for nothing is blinder than a man influenced by love for a person or a thing.' Or: 'Painters cover his eyes with a bandage to emphasize the fact that people in love do not know where they drive, being without judgment or discrimination and guided by mere passion.'[43]

Considerations like these were also eagerly exploited by the writers of sonnets and other shorter poems, ranging from Federico dell'Amba (around 1290), whose Cupid

> '*Spoglia i cor di libertà regnante,*
> *E fascia gli occhi della providenza,*'[44]

and who in another poem likens him to a Devil rather than to an Angel ('*L'Amore del Diavol tien semblanza*'),[45] to a host of Renaissance and even Baroque poets who untiringly paraphrase the traditional 'moralization.'

These two differing currents of opinion account for the insistence with which some of the 'idealistic' fourteenth-century poets emphasize the fact that the Love God's 'sight was ryghte clere.' Contrasting as they do uplift-

---

43. Sometimes the foolishness of love symbolized by the bandage is expressed even more directly, as is the case, e.g., with John Ridewall's image of *Amor fatuus*, ill. in H.Liebeschütz. *Bibl.*194, p.53, PL.XI, fig.15. It is the '*imago pueri nudi, in cuius capite erat scriptum "Ego sum ignorans et nichil scio."* ' He carries a sword and a torch; a scroll running across his forehead is inscribed '*Qui me diligit, insipiens est.*'

44. V.Nannucci, *Bibl.*227, VOL.I, p.365:
> '*Se Amor, da cui procede bene e male,*
> *Fusse visibil cosa per natura,*
> *Sarebbe senza fallo appunto tale*
> *Com'el si mostra nella dipintura:*
> *Garzone col turcassio alla cintura,*
> *Saettando, cieco, nudo e ricco d'ale.*
> *Dall'ale sembra angelica figura,*
> *Ma chi l'assaggia, egli è guerrier mortale,*
> *Che spoglia i cor di libertà regnante,*
> *E fascia gli occhi della providenza*
> *Saettando disianza perigliosa . . .*'

Cf. also idem, V.Nannucci, *ibidem*, p.367: '*Amore acciecca il cor più cognoscente.*'

45. V.Nannucci, *ibidem*, p.366.

ing spiritual love with debasing sensual passion, they act, so to speak, as witnesses in a law-suit of *Bright-eyed 'Amore,'* extolled in philosophical poetry, *vs. Blind Cupid*, invented and stigmatized by moralizing mythographers.[46]

To the modern beholder the bandage over Cupid's eyes means, if anything, a playful allusion to the irrational and often somewhat puzzling character of amorous sensations and selections. According to the standards of traditional iconography, however, the blindness of Cupid puts him definitely on the wrong side of the moral world. Whether the expression *caecus* is interpreted as 'unable to see' (blind in the narrower sense, physically or mentally) or as 'incapable of being seen' (hidden, secret, invisible) or as 'preventing the eye or mind from seeing' (dark, lightless, black): blindness 'conveys to us only something negative and nothing positive, and by the blind man we generally understand the sinner,' to speak in the words of a mediaeval moralist.[47] Blindness is therefore always associated with evil, excepting the blindness of Homer, which served supposedly to keep his mind unvitiated by sensual appetites, and the blindness of Justice which was meant to assure her impartiality. Both these interpretations however are foreign to classical as well as to mediaeval thought; the figure of blindfold Justice in particular is a humanistic concoction of very recent origin.[48]

46. Even Petrarch has referred to Cupid as *Caecus deus* but only when describing the disastrous affair of Sophonisba with Masinissa and Syphax: *Africa*, v, line 119, *Bibl.*263, p.106.
47. Petrus Berchorius, *Bibl.*27, s.v. 'Cecus, Cecitas:' *'Nota quod cecitas est privatio visus, unde cecitas dicit mihi proprie aliquid negativum et nihil positivum . . . Nota igitur generaliter per cecum intelligitur peccator.'*
48. According to classical tradition blindness was inflicted upon Homer (and Stesichoros) as a punishment for 'slandering' Helen of Troy (cf., e.g., Plato, *Phaidros*, 243 a). It is only in Suidas, *Lexikon* (*Bibl.*330, VOL.III, p.252), that it was reinterpreted in a positive sense. The blindness of Justice has been conclusively dealt with by E. von Mueller, *Bibl.*225, and it appears that this idea is based on an 'Egyptian' allegory transmitted by Plutarch and Diodorus Siculus in which the chief justice was shown eyeless in order to illustrate his impartiality, while his colleagues had no hands with which to take bribes. This questionable concept did not appeal to classical antiquity which, on the contrary, imagined Justice with piercing and awe-inspiring eyes (A.Gellius, *Noctes Atticae*, XIV,4). The 'Egyptian' conception did not come to life before its rediscovery by sixteenth-century humanists. Justice with eyes bandaged occurs for the first time around 1530: in Sebastian

In the Middle Ages we find, therefore, an established association of Day (ruled by the Sun) with Life and the New Testament, and of Night (ruled by the Moon) with Death and the Old Testament. These connections are emphasized in numerous representations of the Crucifixion where the various symbols of good, including a personification of the Church, appear on the right hand of Christ while the symbols of evil, including a personification of the Synagogue, are on His left. The most comprehensive version of this arrangement is found in the Uta Gospels (early eleventh century). Here the personification of the Church is paired with a personification of Life while the inscription *Pia gratia surgit in ortu*, introduces the idea of dawn; on the other hand the personification of the Synagogue is coupled with a personification of Death, and the inscription *Lex tenet in occasum*, brings in the idea of nightfall.[49] In this case the Synagogue (*fig.*78) is not yet blindfold. The fact that she plunges into darkness is only indicated by making the upper part of her head, including her eyes, disappear behind the frame in the same way as the setting sun vanishes behind the horizon. Around the same time, however, or even a little earlier, blindness had come to be denoted by a new symbol: the bandage. This attribute belongs in the same class as other specifically mediaeval motifs such as the Wheel of Fortune,[49a] the mirror of Prudence or the ladder of Philosophy, which differ from the attributes of classical personifications in that they give visible form to a metaphor, instead of indicating a function. The bandage made its appearance in a miniature of about 975, where Night—*caeca nox* as she is constantly called in classical

Brant's *Narrenschiff* (1494, Latin translation 1497) the fool still bandages the eyes of Justice in order to defeat her true purpose. In Cesare Ripa's *Iconologia*, 'Giustizia' is the only personification in which the '*occhi bendati*' bear a favourable implication—in contrast with 'Ambitione,' 'Cupido,' 'Cupidità,' 'Errore,' 'Favore,' 'Ira,' 'Ignoranza' and 'Impeto'—but even here the motif is limited to representations of Wordly Justice, whereas Divine Justice has '*occhi miri*,' for which reason in some later publications dealing with '*utrumque ius*' Justice is shown with two heads, one blindfold, the other seeing.

49. Cf. G.Swarzenski, *Bibl.*333, PL.XIII.
49a. Cf. the pertinent remarks in H.R.Patch, *Bibl.*254, p.176ss. How foreign the idea of the bandage was to classical Antiquity, is illustrated by the fact that Apuleius calls Blind Fortune '*exoculata*' (*Metam.*, VII,2).

literature—is represented as a blindfold woman (*fig.76*)[50] And in view of the interrelations mentioned above we can easily see how the new motif came to be transferred first to the 'benighted' Synagogue (*fig.79*),[51] then with a further expansion of the concept, to such personifications as Infidelity,[52] and, at about the same time, to Death.

The blindfold Synagogue (often described by the phrase *Vetus testamentum velatum, novum testamentum revelatum*) was commonly connected with the verse in Jeremiah: 'The crown is fallen from our heads, woe unto us that we have sinned, for this our heart is faint, for these things our eyes are dim.'[53] She is found as early as the middle of the twelfth century and was soon to become a standard figure in mediaeval art and literature, so much so that a fifteenth-century copyist of the Uta Gospels automatically replaced the figure merely 'plunging into darkness' by a blindfold one.[53a] Blindfold Death appears somewhat later: possibly the earliest and certainly the most impressive representations are found in the interrelated Apocalyptic cycles on the west façades of Notre Dame de Paris, Amiens and Reims, where a grim, blindfold female (*la Mort*) is shown in the act of disem-

50. Berlin, Staatsbibl., cod. theol. lat. fol.192, ill. in Adolph Goldschmidt, *Bibl*.118, VOL.II, PL.107. The type from which this bandaged figure might have been derived is reflected by a miniature in Verdun, Bibl. de la Ville, ms.1, fol.17 (our *fig.77*) which shows Night—also as a bust in a roundel analogously placed within the general composition—covering her face with a veil. A dark veil, dark colours, and a dark halo or mandorla are the normal characteristics of Night in mediaeval art. But in an archivault of Chartres Cathedral she is characterized as a blind person by the fact that Day leads her by the hand and by her well-observed facial expression (E.Houvet, *Bibl*.149, VOL.II, PL.22, our *fig.80*). This illustrates the classicizing spirit frequently noticeable in the French sculpture of this period.
51. Cf. particularly P.Weber, *Bibl*.388, p.70,74,76,90,112. Our *fig.79* illustrates an especially interesting type from Verdun, Bibl. de la Ville, ms.119. The two Verdun manuscripts were brought to my attention by Dr.Hanns Swarzenski, to whom I am also indebted for permission to reproduce his photographs.
52. E.Houvet, *Bibl*.149, VOL.I, pl.86.
53. Lamentations v, 16,17. The blindness of the Synagogue is sometimes expressed by a veil or kerchief, as is the case with a miniature in the Antiphonarium of St. Peter (G.Swarzenski, *Bibl*.334, p.112, PL.CI, *fig*.341). In this miniature the reminiscence of the Jeremiah verses is evidenced by the fact that the hand of the figure is placed on her heart.
53a. Clm. 8201, dated 1415, ill. in P.Weber, *Bibl*.388, p.66. The Synagogue also wears the Jewish hat which had been added to her attire in connection with the rising tide of anti-Semitism, and the figure of Death quoted p.77, N.25 has been replaced by a skeleton.

bowelling her victim (*fig.*81).[54] But the bandage motif frequently persisted even when Death had come to be represented as a mere skeleton. Shakespeare's John of Gaunt still revels in the emotional possibilities of the idea of Blindfold Death when he bewails the banishment of his son:

'My oil-dried lamp and time-bewasted light
Shall be extinct with age and endless night.
My inch of taper will be burnt and done,
And blindfold Death not let me see my son.'[55]

Thus Blind Cupid started his career in rather terrifying company: he belonged to Night, Synagogue, Infidelity, Death and Fortune (the classical *caeca Fortuna*) who—we do not know exactly when—had also joined the group of blindfold personifications.[56] Within this group, he was especially associated with Fortune and Death, because these three were blind both in an intransitive and in a transitive sense. They were blind, not only as personifications of an unenlightened state of mind, or of a lightless form of existence, but also as personifications of an active force behaving like an eyeless person: they would hit or miss at random, utterly regardless of age, social position and individual merit.[57] A French fifteenth-century poet by the name of Pierre Michault condensed these notions into a remarkable poem called

54. The Paris relief is illustrated in Viollet-le-Duc, *Bibl.*377, VOL.VIII, 1866, p.158, *fig.*20. For Amiens see Georges Durand, *Bibl.*79, PL.XXXVIII, 4. For Reims: P.Vitry, *Bibl.*383, VOL.I, PL.LXXXII.
55. *Richard II.*, I, 3. The word, 'blindfold' is used by Shakespeare only in this passage and in *Venus and Adonis*, I. 554 ('blindfold Fury'). Cupid—apart from the famous phrase 'blind bow-boy' in *Romeo and Juliet*, II, 4—is called blind in *Much Ado*, I, 1; *Lear*, IV, 6; *Two Gentlemen of Verona*, IV, 4 ('blinded God'); *Tempest*, IV, 1 ('blind boy'); *Sonnet* CXXXVII ('blind fool Love'); and *Midsummer Night's Dream*, I, 1 (see p.123, N.74). 'Blind Fortune' occurs in *Merchant of Venice*, II, 1 and *Coriolanus*, IV, 6. 'Blind concealing Night' in *Rape of Lucrece*, line 675.
56. Cf. J.B.Carter, *Bibl.*57, p.38, and, more specifically, H.R.Patch, *Bibl.*255, p.191ss. As to illustrations, see *idem, Bibl.*254, especially p.12 and 44, PL.3,4,9. Cf. also A.Doren, *Bibl.*77. The phrase '*caeca Mors*' does not seem to occur in classical writing.
57. In addition Cupid was known to spell death in a spiritual sense. Ridewall's picture of *Amor fatuus*, mentioned p.107, N.42, bears the inscription 'MORS DE ME CRESCIT.'

La Danse aux Aveugles in which Love, Fortune and Death are described as the three great blind powers which make mankind dance to the tune of their wanton, but irrevocable decrees:

> '*Amour, Fortune et Mort, aveugles et bandés,*
> *Font danser les humains chacun par accordance.*' (*fig.*82)[58]

This image of Blind Cupid—or 'mythographical Cupid' as we might call him to distinguish him from 'poetic Love'—developed in different fashions according to historical conditions.

German art, possibly owing to the fact that the words 'Liebe' and 'Minne' are both of feminine gender, shows a strong tendency to personify Blind Cupid by a nude female figure. This is already the case with the illustrations of the *Wälscher Gast* where 'blind and blinding' Love is represented as a naked woman, eyes open or closed according to the conscientiousness of the illuminators, but not as yet bandaged. She shoots an arrow into the eye of the 'loving' or 'foolish' man while the 'wise man' is immune against her weapons (*fig.*85).[59] In Germany, the figure of a nude woman was retained—

---

58. For this poem and its illustrations cf. A. de Laborde, *Bibl.*177, for in this illustrative cycle Death is usually made to ride a '*boeuf chevauchant moult lent,*' to quote a passage of around 1340. See also P. de Keyser (unfortunately unacquainted with Laborde's study), *Bibl.*163, particularly p.57ss. The illustrations of Michaut's poem seem to account not only for several isolated pictures and images of Death riding an ox, but also for the fact that the chariot of Death in representations of Petrarch's Trionfi is almost invariably drawn by two black oxen. This motif is not mentioned in the Petrarch text but had become so popular that Ripa, s.v. 'Carro della Morte,' does not hesitate to attribute it to the poet himself, as he also does the hourglass and crutches of Time.

59. A. von Oechelhäuser, *Bibl.*232. The illustrated manuscripts which have come down to us are all of the fourteenth century or later, but it is a safe assumption that their pictures reflect prototypes devised when the poem was written, that is around 1215. An amusing combination of the German 'Blind Venus' with the international 'Blind Cupid' is found in *Tricinia. Kurtzweilige teutsche Lieder zu dreyen Stimmen, nach Art der Neapolitanen oder Welschen Villanellen*, Nürnberg, 1576.

> '*Venus, du und dein Kind,*
> *seid alle beide blind*
> *und pflegt auch zu verblenden.*'

(quoted in A.Schering, *Bibl.*302, no.139; I am indebted to Mr. Oliver Strunk for the reference).

with or without the bandage—in countless late-mediaeval representations of purely sensual love (*fig.*84).[60]

In France and Flanders, on the other hand, the influence of the pictorial tradition formed under the spell of the *Roman de la Rose* and similar poems was so strong that the 'mythographical Cupid' found in the illustrations of the *Ovide Moralisé* and their derivatives, though blindfold, tended to retain the princely garments and mature appearance of the 'Dieu Amour;' and this despite the fact that the very texts to which the blindfold images belong, explicitly demand a nude and childlike figure—an instructive example of the stubbornness with which established representational traditions can assert themselves against the claim of written words (*figs.*86, 87).[61]

It was in the Italian Trecento and Quattrocento that the process of what we have called 'pseudomorphosis' was to be completed. Here Cupid, his sex unchanged, shrank in size, was deprived of his garments and thus developed into the popular *garzone* or *putto* of Renaissance and Baroque art, who—except for his newly acquired blindness—resumed the appearance of the classical *puer alatus*.

However, even in Italy this evolution was not a simple process. For a while no basic distinction was made between the image of a blindfold nude as required by the mythographical texts, and that hybrid French type where the bandage appeared in combination with the courtly apparel of the 'Dieu Amour;'[62] and the typical Cupid of the Renaissance as exemplified by Piero

60. The woodcut of *Amor Carnalis* (see p.107, N.41). Some other nude but not blindfold figures occurring in fifteenth-century representations of a similar character will be adduced below.

61. A fourteenth-century instance from Paris, Bibl.Nat.,ms.Fr.373, fol.207, with Cupid enthroned and the Three Graces clad in modish garments, is illustrated in A.Warburg, *Bibl.*387, VOL.II, PL.LXIV, *fig.*113 and our *fig.*86 (French, 14th cent.). A later specimen (possibly already influenced by such Italian representations as that in cod. Vat. Reg. 1290, ill. *ibidem, fig.*112 and in H.Liebeschütz, *Bibl.*194, PL.XVIII, *fig.*28) is found in the Flemish manuscript Copenhague, Thott 399, fol.9v. (our *fig.*87) which served as a model for the printed editions of the French version of Berchorius' *Metamorphosis Ovidiana* (cf. M.D.Henkel, *Bibl.*142, 1922); here the Graces are nude, and Cupid hovers in mid-air, but he is still a young man, not a child, and fashionably dressed in spite of his bandage.

62. This is evidenced by a manuscript of Richard de Fournival's *Bestiaire d'Amour* which is preserved in the J.P.Morgan Library and was brought to my attention by Miss Helen

della Francesca's superb figure in S.Francesco at Arezzo (*fig.92*) had to extricate himself from a very strange-looking and, indeed, demoniacal image. This image appears in a group of representations which depict Cupid as a nude, or practically nude, winged boy and thus constitute the earliest returns to the classical type. But they show Cupid not only blindfold, but also with talons as used in images of the Devil and sometimes of Death.[63] By this new stigma Cupid was actually transformed into the *diavolo* to whom Federico dell'Amba had compared him in one of his sonnets.

The best known example of this type appears in the Giottesque allegory of Chastity (now generally dated around 1320/25) in S.Francesco at Assisi (*fig.88*).[64] Here Cupid (inscribed *Amor*) and his nude companion *Ardor* are chased away from the 'Tower of Chastity' by *Mors*—a skeleton with a scythe—, and *Penitentia*—a winged woman attired in monks' garb and holding a scourge; the whole composition is purposely patterned on the lines of an Expulsion from Paradise. Cupid is depicted as a boy of twelve or thirteen, with wings and a crown of roses. His eyes are bandaged and he is entirely nude, except for the string of his quiver, on which are threaded the hearts of his victims like scalps on the belt of an Indian. Instead of human feet he has griffons' claws.

Strange images like this have a way of reappearing sporadically for centuries so that taloned Cupids are not lacking in later periods. They occur in some Quattrocento *tondi* and cassone panels,[65] and a Cupid not only

Franc (M.459, North-Italian, first half of the 14th century). On fol.28, v., where the blindfold Cupid shoots an arrow at the lover, he is nude as is the case with the 'Minne' in our *fig.85* from *Der Wälsche Gast* (cf., on the contrary, our *fig.73* from the *Roman de la Rose*). On the opposite page, fol.29, where he reconciles the lover with his lady, he is shown on horseback and is clad in courtly garments.

63. Cf. especially Francesco Traini's famous fresco in the Camposanto at Pisa, but also such very early instances as the Mors in the Leofric Missal, illustrated in John O.Westwood, *Bibl.*396, PL.33, almost literally identical with London, Brit. Mus., ms. Cott. Tib. c. vi, fol.6v.

64. Good illustration in I.B.Supino, *Bibl.*331, PL.LI.

65. Florentine cassone panel, ill. in Prince d'Essling and E.Müntz, *Bibl.*87, p.1, text p.115. Also a North Italian fresco in the Louvre, ill. in R. van Marle, *Bibl.*210, VOL.II, 1932, *fig.*483, showing Venus and some of her great victims (Samson, Achilles, Paris, Troilus, Tristan and

taloned but also crowned with roses and girded with a string of hearts is seen in a sixteenth-century tapestry illustrating Petrarch's 'Triumph of Love' (*fig.89*).[66] But these later examples are obviously derived from the Assisi figure and thus do not tell us much about the latter's origin.

In the castle of Sabbionara di Avio, however, we find a curious mural (probably executed around 1370) which cannot derive from the fresco in Assisi, but must come from a separate tradition apparently earlier than the Assisi version. For, while the Cupid in Sabbionara, like the Assisi one, is blind (so far as can be inferred from the remains of his head), winged, nude, boyish, and has a bow and arrows and griffons' claws, he lacks the strings of hearts and, surprisingly enough, is shown standing on a galloping horse (*fig.91*).[67]

Thus the taloned Cupid exists in two independent versions: on foot and with the string of hearts, or on horseback without. The inference is that both versions derive from a common source showing the string of hearts and the horse in combination. This common source has come down to us, by a curious chance, not directly but in a deliberate inversion; but the inverted description is so exact and comprehensive that we need only to convert the plus signs into minus, so to speak, to reconstruct the original. This inversion was effected with painstaking effort by a learned, art-loving

Lancelot). Venus is accompanied by two little Cupids with claws instead of feet, and the whole composition resembles the so-called *Planetenkinderbilder*.

66. Prince d'Essling and E.Müntz., *Bibl.*87, p.212, better illustration in E. von Birk, *Bibl.*35, pl.VIII after p.248. A blind Cupid with the chain of hearts, but not with griffons' claws, is also found in a French sixteenth-century tapestry representing Profane Love (Paris, Musée des Arts Décoratifs).

67. The Sabbionara murals were published by A.Morassi, *Bibl.*221 and by J.Weingartner, *Bibl.*393. Our *fig.*91 is reproduced from a photograph kindly supplied by Signor G. Gerola, R. Soprintendente delle Belle Arti per la Venezia Tridentina, to whom I wish to extend my sincere thanks. The head of Cupid is destroyed, but the presence of the fluttering band, as well as the rather pessimistic mood of the whole cycle corroborates Weingartner's assumption that the figure was originally blindfolded. Both Morassi and Weingartner fail to connect this '*pargolo antico trasmutato a metà in fiera dalla torbida coscienza medioevale*' with the Assisi figure and its derivatives on the one hand, and with Francesco Barberino's allegory on the other. A drawing based on the Sabbionara mural (Cupid with human feet!) has been published by J.P.Richter, *Bibl.*280, pl.9, but has been proved to be a forgery (cf. G.B.Cervellini, *Bibl.*64; and H.Beenken, *Bibl.*23).

poet and jurist called Francesco Barberino who, before 1318, composed, wrote, illustrated, and lengthily commented upon, a treatise entitled *Documenti d'Amore.*[68]

The illustrations of this treatise combine in fact the features of the Assisi and Sabbionara versions (*fig.*90). They show the nude, boyish figure of Cupid, the wings, the talons, the roses, the quiver, the string of hearts and the horse—only in a different combination and with a contrary intention. Barberino distinguishes between the Love Divine, the permissible love between humans, and the illicit sensual passions too low to deserve the name of love and beneath the considerations of a serious thinker.[69] He endeavours to glorify the 'Amor Divino,' and in order to do it the more impressively, he comments upon an image devised in the past by what he calls the *saggi.* This image had represented the 'mythographical' or baser Cupid, but Barberino re-interpreted it in such a way that every detail became invested with a new and favourable meaning.

> '*Io non descrivo in altra guisa amore,*' he says,
> '*Che faesser li saggi che tractaro*
> *In dimostrar l'effetto suo in figura . . .*
> *E color che'l vedranno,*
> *Non credan ch'io cio faccia per mutare,*

68. The *Documenti d'Amore*, printed 1640, are preserved in cod. Vat. Barb. XLVI, 18 (now 4076, commonly quoted as A), and cod. Vat. Barb. XLVI, 19 (now 4077, commonly quoted as B). Both were described and partly published by F.Egidi in *Bibl.*81. The complete text was edited by F.Egidi, *Bibl.*20; cf. also A.Thomas, *Bibl.*341. Our *fig.*90 (*Bibl.*81, PL. facing p.8, the corresponding picture in B, ill. *ibidem*, p.8) belongs to the text *Bibl.*20, VOL.III, p.407ss. An almost identical composition serves as a frontispiece in both manuscripts (*Bibl.*81, PL. facing p.4 and p.4. Text *Bibl.*20, VOL.I, p.14ss.). Moreover the same figure of Cupid, but half length and minus the horse, occurs: 1) A, fol.90 (*Bibl.*81, p.83) and B, fol.79 (*ibidem*, p.82), showing Cupid throwing roses to Innocence; 2) A, fol.98, v. and B, fol.87, v. (both *ibidem*, p.86, captions here rectified), showing Cupid above 'Solicitudo,' 'Perseverantia,' 'Veritas' and 'Fortitudo,' and closing a book which even 'Aeternitas' cannot close of her own accord; 3) A, fol.98, v. and B, fol.87, v. (both *ibidem*, p.89): Cupid cut to pieces by Death who has killed the Donna. It would be worth investigating to what extent Barberino, who was widely read even during the Renaissance (cf., e.g., Mario Equicola, I, 5, *Bibl.*84, fol.11, v.ss.; Ripa, s.v. 'Eternità'), influenced Petrarch's *Trionfi.*
69. F.Egidi, *Bibl.*20, VOL.I, p.9ss. Illicit love is defined after Isidorus (p.105, N.31) as '*uno furore inordinato . . .*'

Ma per far novo in altro interpretare.
Che quel che facto e molto da laudare
Secondo lor perfecta intelligença . . .
Et anco amor comandando m'informa
Com'io'l ritragga in una bella forma.
Nudo con ali, ciecho, e fanciul fue
Saviamente ritracto a saettare,
Deritto stante in mobile sostegno.
Or io non muto este facteçe sue,
Ne do ne tolgo, ma vo figurare
Una mia cosa e sol per me la tegno.

Io nol fo ciecho che da ben nel segno,
Ma non si ferma che paia perfetto,
Se no in loco d'ogni vilta netto . . .
Fanciul nol faccio a simile parere
Che parria poca avesse conoscença,
Ma follo quasi nel'adoloscença . . .
Io, si gli o facti i pie suoi di falcone,
A intendimento del forte grenire
Che fa di lor chel sa chel sosterranno . . .
Nudo l'o facto per mostrar com'anno
Le sue vertu spiritual natura . . .
E poi per honestura,
Non per significança; il covre alquanto
Lo dipintor di ghirlanda e non manto . . .
Diedi al cavallo in faretra per pena
Li dardi per mostrar che inamorato
A seco quel dond'egli e poi lanciato . . .'[70]

That is, 'I describe Love in no other shape than did the learned men who dealt in demonstrating his effects in an image . . . And those who will behold my image must not think that I am making it for a change, but to make it new through another interpretation. For what they have devised is very praiseworthy owing to their perfect intelligence . . . And even Love by

70. F.Egidi, *ibidem*, VOL.III, p.409ss. The '*Io nol fo ciecho*' obviously anticipates Petrarch's '*Cieco non già* . . .'. The explanations given in Barberino's Latin commentary upon his frontispiece (*ibidem*, VOL.I, p.9ss.) are even more audacious than those in the Italian poem; the three darts of Cupid symbolize the Trinity, the fact that the horse has to carry the quiver signifies that man has to provide the means by which his heart and works can be united with God (*ibidem*, VOL.I, p.20) etc.

his commands informs me how to portray him in a beautiful fashion. He has
been wisely portrayed as a nude, winged, blind boy in the act of shooting
arrows, standing upright on a mobile support [viz., a horse.] I, now, do not
change these features of his, I neither add nor do I omit. I want to represent
something of my own and keep it only for myself. I do not make him blind
for he hits the target well. But he does not stop in such a way that he seems
perfect, except in a place clean of all impurity . . . I do not make him a
boy for similar reasons, for then he might seem to have little discernment;
I am rendering him nearly as an adolescent . . . If I have given him falcons'
feet it is meant to signify the strong grip with which he holds those whom he
knows will support him . . . I have made him nude in order to show that
his virtues are of a spiritual nature, and the painter covers him somewhat with
a garland, not a mantle, only for the sake of modesty, not in order to convey
a special meaning . . . To the horse I have given the arrows in their quiver
as a load, in order to show that the man in love carries with him that with
which he will later be hit [that is: love does not come but to those poten-
tially prepared for it] . . . '

Except for the fact that Cupid is not blindfold—in this Barberino did not
keep his promise 'neither to add nor to omit'—, the picture explained in this
poem and even more audaciously interpreted in its lengthy Latin commentary can be used to reconstruct the 'traditional' image which was the
prototype of both the Cupid in Assisi and in Sabbionara. This prototype—
depicting, of course, not the 'Amor Divino' as does Barberino's 'reinter-
pretation,' but the less holy type of love—must have been devised well before
Barberino wrote his treatise, though certainly not before the thirteenth
century. It must have contained, like the Sabbionara mural, a horse which
symbolized the lover.[70a] Like the Assisi fresco it must have shown Blind

70a. Professor B.L.Ullman made the attractive suggestion that the curious motif of a nude
boyish Cupid standing sideways on a horse might derive from classical groups showing
Eros on the back of a centaur (see, e.g., Clarac, *Bibl.*66, VOL.II, PL.150, no.181). That this
type was familiar to the Middle Ages is evidenced by such thirteenth-century *aquama-
nilia* as the one illustrated in O. von Falke and E.Meyer, *Bibl.*88 a, PL.120, no.273.

Cupid girt with the string of hearts (which Barberino transferred to the horse) and crowned with roses which originally had stood not for the 'merit to be acquired by observing the commands of Sacred Love,' as Barberino wrote, but for worldly pleasures. Like both versions, finally, the prototype must have shown the talons which Barberino explained as falcons' claws symbolizing the firm hold of 'Amor Divino;' originally they had certainly been griffons' claws as in the image of 'mythographical Cupid' described by Boccaccio, and had denoted a diabolical rather than an angelic kind of 'possession.'

Thus we can easily understand that Boccaccio, while trying to describe Barberino's allegory, confused the learned poet's eulogistic 're-interpretation' with the less flattering original, as reflected in the Assisi fresco, and ended involuntarily by describing the latter: 'In some of his vernacular poems,' he says, 'Francesco Barberino, not a negligible personality, covers Cupid's eyes with a bandage, gives him griffons' feet and girds him with a belt full of hearts.'[71]

From this somewhat entangled situation there emerge two facts: First (as

71. Boccaccio, *Genealogia Deorum*, IX, 4: *'Franciscus de Barbarino non postponendus homo in quibusdam suis poematibus vulgaribus huic* [viz., Cupidini] *oculos fascea velat et griphis pedes attribuit, atque cingulo cordium pleno circundat'* (appropriated by Giov. Paolo Lomazzo, VII,10, *Bibl.*199, p.570). The connection between Boccaccio's description, Barberino's text and the Assisi figure was first observed by H.Thode, *Bibl.*339, p.87, who rightly observed that Barberino's allegory differed from both Boccaccio's paraphrase and the Assisi figure, but inferred the existence of another Barberino invention now lost. Egidi, *Bibl.*81, p.14 erroneously asserts that Barberino's invention had been 'imitated' in the Assisi mural, without mentioning Boccaccio. Thomas, *Bibl.*341, p.74 does not mention the figure in Assisi but points out the discrepancy between Barberino and Boccaccio whom he accuses of having read the former superficially. Supino, *Bibl.*331, p.97ss. takes no definite stand. Our conjecture of an original allegory of unfavourable significance deliberately reversed by Barberino is corroborated by Barberino's own statements, by the mural in Sabbionara which was unknown to the previous writers, and finally by the fact that Boccaccio's own description of Cupid (cf. above) also mentions the griffons' talons. Boccaccio's confusion of Barberino's allegory with the Assisi figure is all the more understandable as the two conceptions have really much in common from a purely visual point of view; moreover Boccaccio's recollection of Barberino's writings seems to have been a somewhat vague one (cf. the passage quoted in this note, and the statement in *Genealogia Deorum*, XV, quoted by A.Thomas, *Bibl.*341, p.35).

could already be inferred from our quotations from Lydgate, Chaucer and Petrarch): that in the fourteenth century the blindness of Cupid had so precise a significance that his image could be changed from a personification of Divine Love to a personification of illicit Sensuality, and vice versa, by simply adding, or removing, the bandage. Second: that the familiar Renaissance type of Cupid, the nude 'blind bow-boy,' came into being as a little monster, created for admonitory purposes.

However, this little monster was so similar to the nude *putti* who around the same time began to invade Trecento art in a purely decorative capacity (a famous instance is found in Traini's Triumph of Death in the Camposanto at Pisa) that a fusion was almost inevitable. The 'Assisi type,' as it may be called, was 'humanized' both in a literal and figurative sense, and through conscious imitation of classical models developed into the typical Renaissance Cupid: nude, boyish or even childlike, winged, armed with bow and arrows (less frequently with a torch), his eyes covered with the *benda* or *fascia*, but his appearance no longer marred by griffons' talons (*fig.92*). The name of these Cupids is Legion, and they entirely supplanted both the diabolical little monster seen in Assisi and the angelic figure of 'Amore' or 'Le Dieu Amour' who had been their mediaeval predecessors.

When this nude and boyish image, traditionally and significantly blindfold, became ubiquitous, the bandage motif frequently ceased to carry a specific meaning. More often than not it was almost as common and insignificant in art as the designations *il fanciul cieco*, 'the blind boy' or *le dieu aveugle* in poetry. A majority of Renaissance artists, the 'vulgo de'moderni pittori,' to speak in the words of Andrea Gesualdo, a humanistic commentator of Petrarch, began to use the Blind Cupid and the Seeing Cupid almost at random.[72] In the illustrations of Petrarch's Triumphs both types appear indiscriminately. The French illuminator who in 1554 made a copy of Oppian's *Cynegetica*, archaeologically faithful in many other respects, auto-

---

72. Petrarch, Bibl.262, fol.184; '*Cieco, com'alcuni il dissero et il vulgo de' moderni pittori il dipinge.*'

matically blindfolded all the Cupids that he was copying from the Byzantine original (*figs*.93, 94). Even the illustrators of Andrea Alciati's *Emblemata*—the first and most famous of the countless collections of illustrated epigrams, or epigrammatic paraphrases of images, so popular in the sixteenth and seventeenth centuries—exhibit, as time goes on, disregard or lack of comprehension for Alciati's meanings and ideas. In the later editions even those Cupids whose blindness is essential for the understanding of the text lose their bandage through negligence on the part of draughtsmen and wood-cutters.[73]

Nevertheless the original distinction between the Blind and the Seeing

73. It is instructive to compare the illustrations of the following Emblemata: cv (*Potentissimus affectus Amor*), cvi (*Potentia Amoris*), cvii (*Vis Amoris*), cx (*Anteros, Amor Virtutis, alium Cupidinem superans*), cxiii (*In statuam Amoris*), cliv (*De Morte et*

	EMBL. CV (blindness optional, but preferable)	EMBL. CVI (blindness optional, but preferable)	EMBL. CVII (blindness optional, but preferable)
Steyner, 1531	fol.A 4, v. Blind.	fol.D 8 Blind.	fol.D 7 Blind.
Wechel, 1534	p.11 Blind.	p.80 Not blind.	p.77 Not blind.
Lyons, 1551	p.115 Not blind.	p.116 Not blind.	p.117 Not blind.
Lyons, 1608 (as all editions after 1574)	p.476 Not blind.	p.481 Not blind.	p.476 Not blind.

74. Cf.,e.g., the specimens adduced in Claude Mignault's commentary upon Alciati, *Emblemata*, cxiii (*Bibl*.5, p.512ss.) and in Natalis Comes (Natale Conti), *Mythologiae*, iv,13 (*Bibl*.67, p.403ss.). Suffice it to adduce two instances which are interesting because of their authors. One is a little poem ascribed to Enea Silvio Piccolomini explaining a German woodcut of the fifteenth century (Heitz, *Bibl*.137, vol.44, 1916, no.13):

'. . . *Pingitur et nudus nullum servare pudorem,*
Et meminit simplex et manifestus amans.
Pingitur et cecus, quia non bene cernit honestum
Nec scit, quo virtus, quo ferat error amans;
Vel quia, que peccet credit secreta latere,
Cuncta nec in sese lumina versa videt . . .'

The other is Helena's description of Love in *Midsummer Night's Dream*, I, 1 the content

BLIND CUPID

Cupid was by no means forgotten. The literati and the more cultivated artists remained conscious of the original meaning of both types. In fact the discussion of Cupid's blindness or non-blindness kept very much alive in Renaissance literature, with this difference however that it was transferred to a definitely humanistic level and thus tended either to degenerate into a mere *jeu d'esprit* or to become associated with the Neoplatonic theories of love which will be discussed in the following chapter.

Sometimes the authors—even Shakespeare in *A Midsummer Night's Dream*, I, 1—exerted their wit by aptly paraphrasing the good old 'moralizations' *à la* Mythographus III or Berchorius,[74] or, inversely, by proving the

Amore), and CLV (*In formosam fato praereptam*). The Emblemata CV, CVI and CVII do not require any explanation, for the content of the others cf. the following paragraphs.

EMBL. CXIII (blindness optional)	EMBL. CX (blindness of Cupid required)	EMBL. CLIV (blindness of both figures required)	EMBL. CLV (blindness of both figures required)
fol.E 7, v. Blind.	fol.E 1, v. Blind.	fol.D 3, v. Both blind.	————
p.102 Not blind.	p.86 Blind.	p.69 Cupid blind, Death not blind.	p.70 Cupid blind, Death not blind.
p.123 Not blind.	p.120 Not blind.	p.167 Both figures not blind.	p.168 Both figures not blind.
p.512 Not blind.	p.499 Not blind.	p.713ss. Both figures not blind (woodcuts belonging to Embl. CLIV and CLV interchanged).	p.713ss. Both figures not blind.

It is characteristic that the indifference toward iconographic correctness sets in with the Lyons edition of 1551 whose woodcuts—generally ascribed to Bernard Salmon—are far superior to the earlier ones in artistic quality.

---

of which is still identical with that of the old 'moralizations,' although its spirit is 'sweetly sad' and emotional instead of depreciating and rationalistic:

> 'Things base and vile, holding no quantity
> Love can transpose to form and dignity.
> Love looks not with the eyes, but with the mind;

inconsistency of the mythographical image; Alciati himself, for instance, remarks on the logical absurdity of the traditional bandage:

> 'If he were blind, what use would be the band
> Hiding the blind boy's eyes? Would he see less?'[75]

Other writers, particularly the emblematists, try to invest the motif of the bandage with a novel and more pointed meaning, as is the case with an amusing engraving by Otho van Veen: it shows Blind Fortune blindfolding Cupid and putting him on her sphere, in order to illustrate the experience that affection changes with luck (*fig.105*).[75a] Still others dwell on the various catastrophes which may be caused by the blindness of Cupid when he hits the wrong person, or chooses by mistake a leaden arrow instead of a gold one.[75b] One version of this theme, a kind of Renaissance variation on the *Danse aux Aveugles*, is truly impressive when illustrated by competent artists: Love and Death set out together on a hunt, with Death obligingly carrying the two quivers and little Cupid the two bows. But blind as they both are they exchange weapons by mistake (or, according to another version, on purpose: Death steals the weapons from Cupid while he sleeps

> And therefore is wing'd Cupid *painted* blind.
> Nor hath love's mind of any judgment taste;
> Wings and no eyes figure unheedy haste:
> And therefore is love said to be a child,
> Because in choice he is so oft beguil'd. . . '

75. Alciati, *Emblemata*, cxiii: '*Si caecus, vittamque gerit, quid taenia caeco*
Utilis est? Ideo num minus ille videt?'

75a. Otho Venius, Bibl.370, p.157. The engraving is based on Ovid's '*Et cum fortuna statque caditque fides*' (*Ex Ponto Epistolae*, II,3,10) and on a pseudo-Ciceronian passage which runs '*Non solum ipsa fortuna caeca est, sed etiam plerumque caecos efficit quos complexa est, adeo ut spernant amores veteres ac indulgent novis.*' The accompanying quatrain, however, runs:

> '*Benda gl'occhi al Amor Fortuna cieca,*
> *E mobile lo tien sul globo tondo,*
> *E miracol non è s'ei cade al fondo,*
> *Poiche l'vn cieco l'altro cieco accieca.*'

75b. Cf., e.g., Achilles Bocchius (Achille Bocchi), Bibl.37, I, symb. xii, p.28s., entitled '*Cupidini caeco puello haud credito.*'

and substitutes his own). Thus the old are doomed to fall in love while the young are doomed to die before they have begun to live (*figs.*102, 104).[76]

As could be expected, the Renaissance spokesmen of Neoplatonic theories refuted the belief that Love was blind as emphatically as the mediaeval champions of poetic Love, and used the figure of Blind Cupid, if at all, as a contrast to set off their own exalted conception.[76a] But it is noteworthy that at times their arguments are founded not only on philosophical but also on antiquarian considerations: 'Greek and Roman antiquity knew nothing of Cupid's blindness,' says Mario Equicola in his famous treatise *Di natura d'Amore*, 'and the proverb has it that love originates from sight. Plato, Alexander of Aphrodisias and Propertius, who distinctly describe the image of Cupid do not give him a veil nor do they make him blind.'[77]

Thus the bandage of blindfold Cupid, despite its indiscriminate use in

76. The first version is treated in Alciati, *Emblemata*, CLIV, the second, *ibidem*, CLV. The woodcut originally belonging to CLIV, but used by mistake for CLV in the later editions, was obviously the inspiration of a lost painting by Matthew Bril transmitted through an anonymous engraving (ill. in Anton Mayer, *Bibl.*212, PL.III, our *fig.*104), the subject of which can therefore be appropriately described by Alciati's distich:
'*Cur puerum, Mors, ausa dolis es carpere Amorem?*
Tela tua ut iaceret, dum propria esse putat.'
It is a fine distinction that in the case of Emblema CLIV, allegedly invented on the occasion of a great plague, the interchange occurs by accident, while in the case of Emblema CLV, lamenting the death of an individual beautiful girl, Death effects the exchange with malice aforethought. According to Claude Mignault the motif as such was borrowed from a poem by 'Johannes Marius Belga' which can be identified with the one reprinted in J.Stecher, *Bibl.*190, VOL.III, 1885, p.39ss. However, this poem, the first of *Trois contes intitulez de Cupido et Atropos*, is in turn translated from an Italian original by Seraphin Ciminelli dall'Aquila, and in both poems the exchange of arrows occurs when Cupid and Death have drunk too much in a tavern. The whole case illustrates the complicated interplay of Northern and Italian, mediaeval and classical ideas in Renaissance art and poetry.
76a. Cf., e.g., Natalis Comes, *Bibl.*67, with a lengthy discussion of 'right' and 'wrong' love, one blind, one clearsighted; Giuseppe Betussi, *Il Raverta*, reprinted in G.Zonta, *Bibl.*413, p.31; or Leo Hebraeus, *Dialoghi d'amore*, *Bibl.*192, p.136, with moralization in the best 'mythographical' style.
77. Mario Equicola, II, 4, *Bibl.*84, fol.67: '*De cecità nulla mentione si fa, et il proverbio è "amore nasce del vedere." Platone, Alessandro Aphrodiseo et Propertio, quali distintamenta della pittura di Amore parlano, velo non gli danno, nè cieco il fanno. Se Vergilio et Catullo cieco amor nominano, intendono latente et occulto. Se Platone nelle leggi afferma l'amante circa la cosa amata inciecarsi, è che li amanti giudicano bello quello gli piace*' (cf. also V.Cartari, *Bibl.*56, p.246).

Renaissance art, tends to retain its specific significance wherever a lower, purely sensual and profane form of love was deliberately contrasted with a higher, more spiritual and sacred one, whether marital, or 'Platonic,' or Christian. What in the Middle Ages had been an alternative between 'poetic Love' and 'mythographical Cupid' now came to be a rivalry between 'Amor sacro' and 'Amor profano.' For instance: when Cupid triumphs over Pan who stands for the simple appetites of nature he is never blind.[78] On the other hand, where he is fettered and punished, his eyes are almost invariably bandaged.[79] This is particularly true of the more conscientious representations of the rivalry between Eros and Anteros which in the Renaissance was often misinterpreted as a struggle between Sensual Love and Virtue. The function of the classical Anteros, who was considered the son either of Venus or Nemesis, had been to assure reciprocity in amorous relations; but while this was clearly understood by scholarly antiquarians (fig.96), moralists and humanists with Platonizing leanings were apt to interpret the preposition ἀντί as 'against' instead of 'in return,' thus turning the God of Mutual Love into a personification of virtuous purity.[79a] One of these

---

78. Instances are very numerous. Suffice it to adduce a drawing ascribed to Correggio, ill. A.Venturi, *Bibl.*372, PL.175; Achilles Bocchius, *Bibl.*37, III, SYMB.LXXV, p.110; Cartari, *Bibl.*56, p.250 (all the more interesting as Cupid triumphing over humans, *ibidem*, p.247, is blind). The subject is a classical one, a nice specimen is found in *Bibl.*151, PL.709.

79. The punishment of Cupid is a favourite motive in Hellenistic art and literature. Cf. O.Jahn, *Bibl.*152, p.153ss. (for epigrams, see *Antholog. Graeca, Bibl.*10, VOL.V, p.272ss., nos.195-199.) But here the punishment is inflicted by way of retaliation, that is by those who had had to suffer from love, e.g. by Psyche, by the artist who had created the image of the fettered Cupid (this is, of course, a joke of the epigrammatists), or by vindictive heroines as is the case with Ausonius' poem *Amor cruciatus*. (Cf. A.Warburg, *Bibl.*387, VOL.I, pp.183-359). It was apparently not until Petrarch employed the motif in his *Triumphus Pudicitiae* (line 94ss.) that the Fettered Cupid became a symbol of Chastity. It must be noted that even Ausonius' poem which was frequently illustrated in the Quattrocento (cf. A.Warburg, *l.c.*) has been interpreted by Boccaccio in the following way (*Genealogia Deorum*, IX,4): 'Eum [i.e. Cupidinem] *cruci affixum si sapimus, documentum est quod quidem sequimur, quotiens animo in vires revocato laudabili exercitio mollitiem superamus nostram et apertis oculis perspectamus quo trahebamur ignavia.*'

79a. Cf. E.Panofsky, *Bibl.*242, Renaissance and Baroque illustrations of Anteros in the genuine classical sense, viz., as a personification of Mutual Love, are found, for instance, in V.Cartari, *Bibl.*56, p.242; in Annibale Carracci's corner pictures in the Galleria Farnese, *Bibl.*242, fig.2; and in Otho van Veen's *Amorum Emblemata, Bibl.*370, p.11 (cf. also

humanists, Petrus Haedus, or Hoedus (*recte* Cavretto), entitled his invectives against love *Anterici*; another, by the name of J.B.Fulgosus (*recte* da Campo Fregoso), published a didactic treatise in a similar vein under the title *Anteros*; and the frontispiece of this book shows blindfold Cupid tied to a tree whose branches symbolize the antidotes against sensual passion, namely Marriage, Prayer, Business and Abstinence; his broken weapons are scattered on the ground, and his evil effects are personified by Mockery, Poverty, etc., while the Devil (*Mors Aeterna*) is depicted running off with a love=stricken soul (*fig.95*).[80] More frequently Anteros is rendered as a handsome, bright-eyed youth tying the defeated Eros (Cupid) to a tree and burning his weapons; and unless the illustrator belonged to the careless kind, Cupid is blindfold (*fig.100*).

The Counter-Reformation transferred this antithesis between 'pure' and 'sensual' Love to a devotional plane and often interpreted it in a spirit of sweetish pietism. Remarkable among the many pretty pictures which came to be invented for this purpose is a little engraving which harks back to the

p.9, 15, 17). As a personification of Virtue conquering sensual love he occurs in Guido Reni's painting in Pisa (*Bibl*.242, *figs*.4 and 5) and in the woodcuts illustrating Alciati's Emblema cx; for these see p.122, N.73 and *fig*.100. The actual duel between Eros and Anteros (*Psychomachia* type), with Eros not blindfold, is found in a fresco in the Palazzo Zuccari at Rome (W.Körte, *Bibl*.171, p.245. and PL.27, 18A) and in several Baroque paintings (e.g., Giov.Baglione, ill. in H.Voss, *Bibl*.384, p.127). In classical art the rivalry of Eros and Anteros was, as it seems, not only rendered as a wrestling match (*Bibl*.242. *fig*.1) or as a torch-race, but also in other ways such as: two Cupids supervising a cock-fight (e.g., red-figured Pyxis, illustrated in C.E.Morgan, *Bibl*.224a; sarcophagus in the Louvre, our *fig*.98; Phaethon sarcophagus, C.Robert, *Bibl*.287, VOL.III, 3, PL.CXV, *fig*.350 b); two Cupids playing the *astragaloi* game (e.g. C.Robert, *ibidem*, *fig*.350 a); two Cupids in an angling contest (e.g. *Museo Borbonico*, XI, 1835, PL.LVI, listed by W.Helbig, *Bibl*.140, no.820, our *fig*.97). A newly discovered mosaic from Antioch (R.Stillwell, *Bibl*.326a, PL.48, no.64, p.189, our *fig*.99) shows a whole collection of these motifs combined with others in a purely decorative fashion: two Cupids supervising a cock-fight, one Cupid (being a combination of the two seen in *Helbig*, no.820) angling, one Cupid standing, one Cupid sleeping, and an old man putting a Cupid into a bird-cage which already contains another, a fairly literal copy of *Helbig*, no.825 (ill. in P.Herrmann, *Bibl*.144, PL.199, and Daremberg-Saglio, *Bibl*.70, VOL.I,2, p.1608). For the famous Pompeian mural known as the Punishment of Cupid, see p.166.

80. G.B.Fulgosus, *Bibl*.108 (cf. M.Equicola, I, 12, *Bibl*.84, fol.26ss.). A French translation (Paris, 1581) is entitled *Contramours*. For Petrus Hoedus who in his *Anterici* (*Bibl*.131) likens Anteros to Hippolytus and Joseph, see M.Equicola, I, 15, fol.31s.

early Christian idea of the Fisher of Men,[81] but at the same time adopts the
Hellenistic type of two *putti* engaged in an angling competition. The result
is: a blindfold Cupid (*L'Amour mondain*) fishing for human hearts in
rivalry with a clearsighted, nimbed, but equally childlike *Saint Amour*, the
caption reading: 'Mittam vobis piscatores multos' (*Jerem.*, XVI, 16) (*fig.*103,
cf. *fig.*97).[82]

Occasionally the victorious adversary of Blind Cupid is explicitly identified with Platonic Love, as in an engraving where *Amor Platonicus* drives
away his blindfold foe by brandishing two torches (*fig.*101).[83] But a much
more ingenious allegory of this kind was devised by Lucas Cranach the Elder
(*fig.*106). A picture of his, preserved in the Pennsylvania Museum of Art,
shows a little Cupid removing the bandage from his eyes with his own hand
and thus transforming himself into a personification of 'seeing' love. To do
this he bases himself most literally on Plato, for he stands on an imposing
volume inscribed *Platonis opera* from which he seems to be 'taking off' for
more elevated spheres.[84]

81. Cf. recently L.Strauch, *Bibl.*327. For angling Cupids in Hellenistic art, see above.
82. Un Père Capuchin, *Bibl.*257, fol.5, v. 6. The picture is further explained by the couplet:
> 'O sainct Amour, pesche mon coeur,
> L'Amour mondain n'est qu'un mocqueur
as well as by three stanzas to the effect that Profane Love fishes for the most 'effeminate'
hearts while Sacred Love '*choisit les nobles et mieux naiz*' (cf. also *ibidem*, p.59s., where
the *Victoire d'Amour* is illustrated on the model of the combat of Eros and Anteros, as
described above: Sacred Love has conquered Blind Cupid who lies on the ground with
broken weapons, and shakes hands with a little girl personifying the soul). The emblems
contained in this little volume are mostly copied from Otho Venius or Vaenius (van
Veen), *Amoris Divini Emblemata, Bibl.*371, and Hermannus Hugo, *Pia Desideria, Bibl.*150,
but the angling contest is not found in either. Another characteristic publication of the
same kind is Benedictus Hafftenius, *Schola Cordis, Bibl.*132.
83. Achilles Bocchius, *Bibl.*37, I, SYMB.XX, p.44, entitled *Platonico Cupidini.* Other blindfold Cupids, always bearing unfavourable implications, occur in Bocchius, *ibidem*, I,
SYMB.VII, p.18; III, SYMB.I.XX, p.150; III, SYMB.I.XXXIX.
84. The picture is listed, but not illustrated in J.G.Johnson, *Bibl.*156, VOL.III, 1913, no.738, and in
M.I.Friedländer und J.Rosenberg, *Bibl.*104, p.68, no.204 q.

PLATE XLI

69

70

PLATE XLII

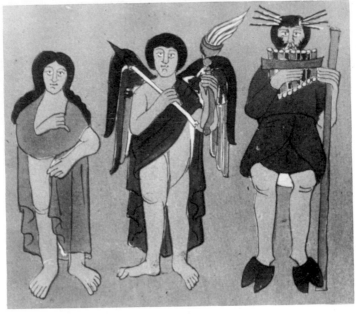

71

72

PLATE XLIII

73

lu en son gentil corps deffenir

msi longuement sans doubtance

75

74

PLATE XLIV

76

77

78

79

PLATE XLV

PLATE XLVI

PLATE XLVII

85

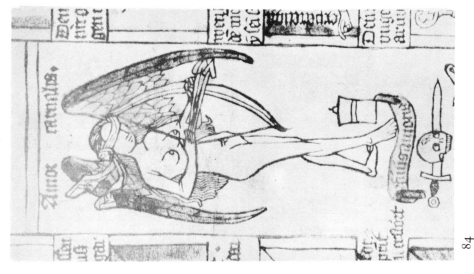

84

83

PLATE XLVIII

86

87

PLATE XLIX

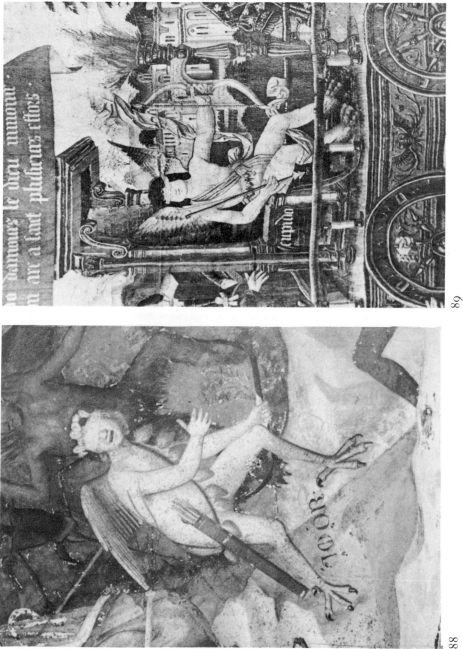

89

88

PLATE L

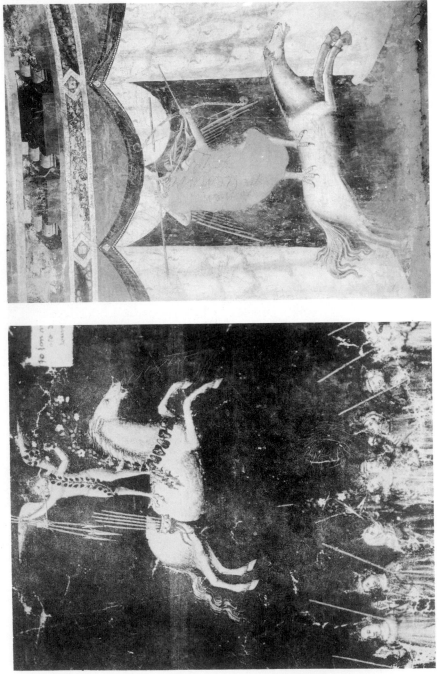

PLATE LI

PLATE LII

ὁ ἔρως

93

94

PLATE LIII

95

96

97

PLATE LIV

98

99

PLATE LV

100

101

102

103

Mittam vobis piscatores multos
O sainct Amour pesche mon cœur,
L'Amour mondain n'est q'un mocqueur.

PLATE LVI

104

105

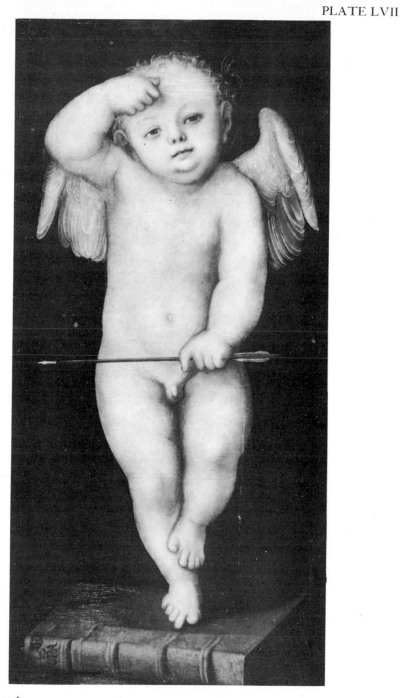

PLATE LVII

V. THE NEOPLATONIC MOVEMENT IN FLORENCE AND NORTH ITALY

(BANDINELLI AND TITIAN)

THAT a provincial German painter like Lucas Cranach should have represented a Cupid 'de-blinding' himself on the strength of Platonic teachings, is eloquent proof of the popularity which the 'Platonic' theory of love had attained during the first quarter of the sixteenth century. In Cranach's time this theory had already been vulgarized through many handsome little books and had become an inevitable subject of modish conversation.

Originally, however, and in undiluted form, it had been part of a philosophical system which must be reckoned among the boldest intellectual structures ever erected by the human mind.

This system had its origin in the 'Platonic Academy' of Florence, a select group of men held together by mutual friendship, a common taste for conviviality and human culture, an almost religious worship of Plato, and a loving admiration for one kindly, delicate little scholar: Marsilio Ficino (1433-1499).

This 'Philosophus Platonicus, Theologus and Medicus,' who half seriously, half playfully patterned his life after that of Plato, and whose modestly comfortable villa at Careggi (a gift of Cosimo de'Medici) purported to be the Academe *redivivus*, was not only the life and soul but also the constructive mind of an informal 'society' which was a combination of club, research seminar and sect, rather than an Academy in the modern sense. It included, among many others: Christoforo Landino, the famous commentator of Virgil, Horace and Dante and author of the well-known *Quaestiones Camaldulenses*; Lorenzo the Magnificent; Pico della Mirandola, who widened the intellectual horizons of the 'Platonica familia' by introducing the study of oriental sources, and generally maintained a comparatively independent attitude towards Ficino; Francesco Cattani di Diacceto (of whom the opposite is true); and Angelo Poliziano.[1]

The task which Ficino had shouldered was threefold. First: to make accessible by translations into Latin—with epitomes and commentaries—the original documents of Platonism, including not only Plato but also the 'Platonici,' viz., Plotinus and such later writers as Proclus, Porphyrius, Jamblichus, Dionysius Pseudo-Areopagita, 'Hermes Trismegistos' and 'Orpheus.'[2] Second: to co-ordinate this enormous mass of information into a coherent and living system capable of instilling a new meaning into the entire cultural heritage of the period, into Virgil and Cicero, as well as into St. Augustine and Dante, into classical mythology as well as into physics, astrology

1. For Florentine Neoplatonism cf. particularly Arnaldo della Torre, *Bibl.*360, and, recently, N.A.Robb, *Bibl.*286 (with useful bibliography). For Ficino in particular cf. G.Saitta, *Bibl.*293, and recently, H.J.Hak, *Bibl.*133; furthermore E.Cassirer, *Bibl.*59, passim.
2. The Renaissance still had to approach Plato through the writings of his followers, and it was not before Leibniz that a fundamental distinction between Platonic and Neoplatonic elements was made or even postulated; cf. R.Klibansky, *Bibl.*165. It is interesting to note that Ficino at twenty-two had already digested Jamblichus, Proclus, Dionysius Pseudo-Areopagita and 'Hermes Trismegistos' while Plato only '*winkte hem van verre*' (H.J.Hak, *Bibl.*133, p.18).

and medicine. Third: to harmonize this system with the Christian religion.

True, Philo of Alexandria had tried to subject Judaism (or rather an alloy of Judaism and Hellenistic mystery-cults)[3] to a Platonic interpretation, and it had been a basic problem for Christian thinkers to incorporate an ever increasing amount of classical ideas into the framework of their thought. But never before had an attempt been made to fuse Christian theology, fully developed as it was, with a great pagan philosophy, without impairing the individuality and completeness of either. The very title of Ficino's proudest work, *Theologia Platonica*, announces his ambition both to re-integrate the 'Platonic' system and to prove its 'full consonance' with Christianity.[4]

Ficino's system[5] holds, roughly speaking, an intermediary position between the scholastic conception according to which God is outside of the finite universe, and the later pantheistic theories according to which the universe is infinite, and God identical with it. Ficino conceives of God much in the same way as Plotinus had conceived of the Ἕν, the ineffable One. But of the two methods used by poor mortals in an endeavour to define the ineffable—i.e., the negation of all predicates (Plotinus), and the characterization in terms of apparent contradictions (Cusanus' *coincidentia oppositorum*)—Ficino adopts both: his God is *uniformis* and *omniformis*, *actus* but not *motus*. God created the world by 'thinking His own self,' for in Him 'being, thinking and willing' are the same thing; and while He is not in the universe, which is limitless but not properly infinite, the universe is in Him: God 'fills it without being filled, pervades it without being pervaded, and includes it without being included.'[6]

---

3. Cf. E.R.Goodenough, *Bibl.*120.
4. Cf. Ficino's letter to the Archbishop Giovanni Niccolini, quoted by H.J.Hak, *Bibl.*133, p.63.
5. The following superficial summary of the Ficinian system is, of course, only meant to bring out those concepts which will prove important for the purpose of this study.
6. Ficino, *Dialogus inter Deum et animam theologus*, *Bibl.*90, p.610 (translated in E.Cassirer, *Bibl.*59, p.201): 'Coelum et terram ego impleo et penetro et contineo. Impleo, non impleor, quia ipsa sum plenitudo. Penetro, non penetror, quia ipsa sum penetrandi potestas. Contineo, non contineor, quia ipsa sum continendi facultas.'

This universe, so strangely distinguished yet not separated from the Supreme Being, unfolds itself in four hierarchies of gradually decreasing perfection: (1) The Cosmic Mind (Greek: Νοῦς, Latin: *mens mundana, intellectus divinus sive angelicus*), which is a purely intelligible and super-celestial realm; like God it is incorruptible and stable, but unlike him it is multiple, containing as it does the ideas and intelligences (angels) which are the prototypes of whatever exists in the lower zones. (2) The Cosmic Soul (Greek: Ψυχή, Latin: *anima mundana*), which is still incorruptible, but no longer stable; it moves with a self-induced motion (*per se mobilis*) and is no longer a realm of pure forms but a realm of pure causes; it is therefore identical with the celestial or translunary world divided into the familiar nine spheres or heavens; the empyrean, the sphere of the fixed stars and the seven spheres of the planets. (3) The Realm of Nature, that is: the sub-lunary or terrestial world, which is corruptible because it is a compound of form and matter and can therefore disintegrate when these components are parted; it moves not *per se* but by and with the celestial world with which it is connected by a somewhat vaguely defined medium called *spiritus mundanus*, also *nodus* or *vinculum*. (4) The Realm of Matter which is formless and lifeless; it is endowed with shape, movement and even existence only in so far as it ceases to be itself and enters a union with form, so as to contribute to the Realm of Nature.

This whole universe is a *divinum animal*; it is enlivened and its various hierarchies are interconnected with each other by a 'divine influence emanating from God, penetrating the heavens, descending through the elements, and coming to an end in matter.'[7] An uninterrupted current of supernatural energy flows from above to below and reverts from below to above, thus forming a *circuitus spiritualis*, to quote Ficino's favourite expression.[8] The Cosmic Mind continually contemplates and loves God, while at the same

---

7. Ficino, *Theolog. Platon.*,x,7, *Bibl.*90, p.234: '. . . *divinus influxus, ex Deo manans, per coelos penetrans, descendens per elementa, in inferiorem materiam desinens* . . .'
8. Ficino, *ibidem*, IX, 4, p.211 (quoted by E.Cassirer, *Bibl.*59, p.141).

time caring for the Cosmic Soul beneath it. The Cosmic Soul in turn converts the static ideas and intelligences comprised in the Cosmic Mind into dynamic causes moving and fertilizing the sublunary world, and thus stimulates nature to produce visible things—the relationship of the Cosmic Mind to God on the one hand and to the Cosmic Soul on the other being comparable to that of Saturn to his father Uranus and to his son Jupiter.[9]

With all its corruptibility the sublunary world participates in the eternal life and beauty of God imparted to it by the 'divine influence.' But on its way through the celestial realm the 'splendour of divine goodness,' as beauty is defined by the Neoplatonists,[10] has been broken up into as many rays as there are spheres or heavens. There is therefore no perfect beauty on earth. Every human being, beast, plant or mineral is 'influenced' (hence this now trivial expression which is originally a cosmological term) by one or more of the celestial bodies. It is the influence of Mars which distinguishes a wolf from a lion (the latter being a solar animal); it is the stored-up effect of the sun and Jupiter which accounts for the medicinal properties of the spearmint. Every natural object or phenomenon is charged, as it were, with celestial energy.[11]

9. For the connection of Saturn with *mens* and contemplation, and of Jupiter with *anima-ratio* and the active life, see E.Panofsky and F.Saxl, *Bibl.*253. One of the most succinct and clearest accounts of this doctrine is found in Pico della Mirandola's commentary on Benivieni *Bibl.*267, 1,7, fol.10 and 11,17, fol.30, v. Even the castration of Uranus by Saturn could be interpreted as a symbolical expression of the fact that the One (God), after having produced the Cosmic Mind, ceased to procreate, whereas the castration of Saturn by Jupiter had to be eliminated: Jupiter only ties him, which means that the *mens* is stable (contemplative), the *anima-ratio*, however, *mobilis per se* (active). For further information about Pico's Commentary on Benivieni see N.A.Robb, *Bibl.*286, pp.60s., 297, 305s.

10. Ficino, *In Convivium Platonis Commentarium* (henceforth to be quoted as *Conv.*) 11, 3, *Bibl.*90, p.1324. From this definition it follows that orthodox Neoplatonism had to endorse Plotinus' objections to the customary, purely phenomenal definition of beauty as a harmonious proportion of the parts in relation to the whole and to each other, combined with agreeable colour; cf., e.g., Ficino, *Conv.* v,3, *Bibl.*90, p.1335, or his Commentary on Plotinus, *Ennead.* 1,6, *Bibl.*90, p.1574, where also the superiority of visual to acoustic beauty is emphasized: '*pulchritudo est gratia quaedam quae magis est in his, quae videntur, quam quae audiuntur, magis etiam, quae cogitantur, neque est proportio.*' For the conflict of the Neoplatonic with the 'phenomenal' definition of beauty in the art-theories of the sixteenth century see E.Panofsky, *Bibl.*244, pp.27ss., 55ss., 122ss. For the evaluation of visual and acoustic beauty see p.148, N.69.

11. From this point of view the borderline between science and magic becomes as fluid as

The Neoplatonic universe has no room for a thing like Hell. Pico calls the realm of matter *Il mondo sotterraneo*;[12] but even matter with its purely negative character[13] cannot be counted as an evil, all the less so as without matter, nature could not exist.[14] Yet, owing to this negative character matter can, in fact, must, cause evil,[15] for its 'nothingness' acts as a passive resistance to the *summum bonum*: matter tends to remain shapeless and is apt to cast off the forms which have been forced upon it.[16] This accounts for the imperfection of the sublunary world: celestial forms are not only incorruptible but also 'pure, complete, effective, free from passions and peaceful;' sublunary things, polluted as they are by matter, are not only perishable but also 'crippled, ineffective, subject to countless passions and, when active, impelled to fight each other to the finish.'[17]

Thus the Realm of Nature, so full of vigour and beauty as a manifestation of the 'divine influence,' when contrasted with the shapelessness and lifelessness of sheer matter, is, at the same time, a place of unending struggle, ugliness and distress, when contrasted with the celestial, let alone the supercelestial world. With a Florentine Neoplatonist it is not inconsistent but

that between the delight in terrestrial beauty and the worship of divine goodness. For Ficino a purposeful use of astral powers, even the making of astrological talismans, is essentially identical with the use of plants in medicine, because these, too, owe their properties to the celestial bodies.

12. Pico, I, 9, *Bibl.*267, fol.12ss., and passim.

13. Ficino, Commentary on Plotinus, *Ennead.*, II,4, *Bibl.*90, p.1642ss., particularly chapters 7, 11,13,16. Ficino's Commentaries on Plotinus are reprinted in the Oxford edition of Plotinus by G.F.Creuzer, 1835.

14. Ficino, Commentary on Dionys. Areopag., *Bibl.*90, p.1084: '*Materia neque malum est, neque proprium bonum, sed aliquid necessarium.*'

15. Ficino, Commentary on Plotinus, *Ennead.* I,8, *Bibl.*90, p.1581ss., particularly chapters 8 ('*Quomodo materia est causa mali*'), and 10.

16. Ficino, Commentary on Plotinus, *Ennead.* II,4, chapter 16, *Bibl.*90, p.1654. Matter is '*non simpliciter quasi nihilum, sed extrema ad primum ens oppositio . . . Proinde, cum acceptis bonis, id est formis, adhuc restet informis . . . , formarumque iacturae sit prona, merito adhuc dicitur esse malum.*'

17. Ficino, Commentary on Plotinus, *Ennead.* I,8, chapter 8, *Bibl.*90, p.1587: '*Formae quidem sub coelo a coelestibus longe degenerant. Illinc* [should read: *Illic*] *enim purae sunt et integrae et efficaces, passionis expertes, neque pugnaces. Hi* [should read: *Hic*] *autem commixtione aliqua inquinatae mancae, inefficaces, innumeris subditae passionibus, et, siquid agunt, ad perniciem inter se pugnantes.*'

inevitable to revel in the 'presence of the spiritual in the material,'[18] and yet to complain of the terrestrial world as a 'prison' where the pure forms or ideas are 'drowned,' 'submerged,' 'perturbed' and 'disfigured beyond recognition.' As a reflex of the *splendor divinae bonitatis* life on earth participates in the blissful purity of a supercelestial realm—as a form of existence inextricably tied up with matter it shares the gloom and grief of what the Greeks had called Hades or Tartaros, the latter name supposedly derived from Greek ταράττειν, meaning: to perturb.[19]

Metaphors like these are mostly applied to that pure form or idea which, even during its material incarnation, remains conscious of its supercelestial origin: the human soul in its relation to the body, in which it lives as *apud inferos*.

Ficino and his followers shared the age-old belief in a structural analogy between the Macrocosmus and the Microcosmus. But they interpreted this

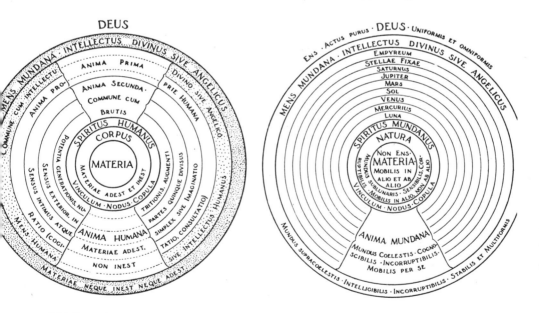

18. N.A.Robb, *Bibl.*286, p.66.
19. Cristoforo Landino, *Bibl.*179, fol.L3, v. For further pertinent passages see below.

analogy in a peculiar manner which I shall try to make somewhat clearer by a diagram (p.135).[20] As the universe is composed of the material world (nature) and the immaterial realm beyond the orbit of the moon, man is composed of body and soul, the body being a form inherent in matter, the soul a form only adherent to it. And as the *spiritus mundanus* interconnects the sublunary world with the translunary, a *spiritus humanus* interconnects the body with the soul. The soul, now, consists of five faculties grouped under the headings of *anima prima* and *anima secunda*.

The *anima secunda*, or Lower Soul, lives in close contact with the body, and consists of those three faculties which both direct and depend on physiological functions: the faculty of propagation, nourishment and growth (*potentia generationis, nutritionis, augmenti*); external perception, i.e. the five senses which receive and transmit the signals from the outer world (*sensus exterior, in partes quinque divisus*); and interior perception or imagination which unifies these scattered signals into coherent psychological images (*sensus intimus atque simplex, imaginatio*). The Lower Soul is, therefore, not free, but determined by 'fate.'[21]

The *anima prima*, or Higher Soul, comprises only two faculties: Reason (*ratio*) and Mind (*mens, intellectus humanus sive angelicus*). Reason is closer to the Lower Soul: it coordinates the images supplied by the imagination according to the rules of logic. The Mind, however, can grasp the truth by directly contemplating the supercelestial ideas. Where Reason is discursive and reflective the Mind is intuitive and creative. Reason becomes involved with the experiences, desires and needs of the body as transmitted by the senses and the imagination. The Mind, on the contrary, communicates with, or even participates in, the *intellectus divinus*, proof of which is found in the fact that human thought would not be able to conceive the

20. The terms used in this diagram are chiefly taken from Ficino, Commentary on Plotinus, *Ennead.* i,i, *Bibl.*90, p.1549ss., and *De vita triplici*, iii,22, *Bibl.*90, p.564.
21. Ficino, Commentary on Plotinus, *Ennead.* iii, 2, *Bibl.*90, p.1619: '*Quomodo anima rationalis non subest fato, irrationalis verso subest.*' Cf. also p.1673ss.

notions of eternity and infinity if it did not share in an eternal and infinite essence.[22]

In contrast with the Lower Soul, Reason is free, that is: it can either allow itself to be carried away by the lower sensations and emotions, or overcome them. This means struggle; and although the Mind does not take sides in this struggle it is indirectly affected by it in so far as it has to illuminate Reason during the fight. For Reason can conquer the claims of man's lower nature only by turning to a higher authority for enlightenment, and thus the Mind is frequently forced to look down at a disturbance beneath it, instead of looking up, as is its proper business, to the supercelestial realm above it.

All this accounts for the unique position of man in the Neoplatonic system. He shares the faculties of his Lower Soul with the dumb animals; he shares his Mind with the *intellectus divinus*; and he shares his Reason with nothing in the universe: his Reason is exclusively human, a faculty unattainable to animals, inferior to the pure intelligence of God and the Angels, yet capable of turning in either direction. This is the meaning of Ficino's definition of man as 'a rational soul participating in the divine mind, employing a body,'[23] which definition says no more nor less than that man is the 'connecting link between God and the world,'[24] or the 'centre of the universe' as Pico della Mirandola puts it:[25] 'Man ascends to the higher realms without discarding the lower world, and can descend to the lower world without forsaking the higher.'[26]

This position of man is both exalted and problematic. With his sensual

---

22. Ficino, *Theolog. Platon.*, VIII, 16, *Bibl.*90, p.200, quoted by E.Cassirer, *Bibl.*59, p.74.
23. Ficino, *In Platonis Alcibiadem Epitome*, *Bibl.*90, p.133: '*Est autem homo anima rationalis, mentis particeps, corpore utens.*'
24. Ficino, *Theolog. Platon.*, III, 2, *Bibl.*90, p.119, where the human soul is called '*essentia tertia et media.*'
25. Cf. N.A.Robb, *Bibl.*286, p.67ss.; H.J.Hak, *Bibl.*133, p.93ss.; E.Cassirer, *Bibl.*59, p.68ss. On Pico's famous '*Oratio de hominis dignitate*' where this concept is gloriously developed, see particularly E.Cassirer, *ibidem*, p.90.
26. Ficino, *Theolog. Platon.*, II, 2.

impulses vacillating between submission and revolt, his Reason facing alternate failure and success, and even his unimperiled Mind often diverted from its proper task, man's 'immortal soul is always miserable in the body;'[27] it 'sleeps, dreams, raves and ails' in it,[28] and is filled with an unending nostalgia ultimately to be satisfied only when it 'returns whence it came.'

Nevertheless: when man's soul recovers from its downfall and begins to remember, however dimly, its pre-existential experiences,[29] the Mind can detach itself from all the indirect disturbances which normally impede its activity; then man can attain, even during his life on earth, a temporal beatitude which at the same time guarantees his redemption in the life hereafter.[29a] This temporal beatitude is twofold: man's Reason, illuminated by his Mind, can be applied to the task of perfecting human life and destiny on earth; and his Mind can directly penetrate the realm of eternal truth and beauty. In the first case he practises the moral virtues comprised under the heading of *iustitia*, and distinguishes himself in the active life; in doing this he emulates the Biblical characters of Leah and Martha and cosmologically, attaches himself to Jupiter. In the second case he adds the theological virtues (*religio*) to the moral ones and devotes himself to a contemplative life, in which case he follows the example of Rachel and the Magdalen and subjects himself to the tutelage of Saturn.

27. Ficino, *Quaestiones quinque de mente, Bibl.*90, p.680.
28. Ficino, Letter quoted p.197, N.76.
29. See, e.g., Landino, *Bibl.*179, fol.A5,v/A6. The human soul, precipitated into '*hanc ultimam faecem*,' remains stunned from its fall until it recovers a memory of its previous state, 'however dim.' This reminiscence causes its '*ardor divinarum rerum*,' which it tries to satisfy within the limits of its corporeal existence, but it is only after death that this nostalgia can end '*At vero cum iam omni mortalitate exuti fuerint animi nostri, et in simplicem quandam naturam reversi, tum demum diuturnam sitim dei cognoscendi non modo sedare, sed penitus extinguere licebit.*'
29a. For the Florentine Neoplatonists it was a matter of course to connect the Platonic idea of pre-existence and reincarnation with the dogma of resurrection in the Christian sense. C.Tolnay, *Bibl.*355 adduces (p.306,n.1) a passage from Ficino's Commentary on Plato's *Phaedo*: '*ubi videtur* [viz., Plato] *mortuorum resurrectionem vaticinari;*' in the Princeton copy of Landino's *Quaestiones Camaldulenses*, IV, fol.L6, v. (where Alberti expounds the Platonic theory of reincarnation) an early sixteenth-century hand has added *in margine*: '*Opinio Platonis de resurrectione.*'

As to the merit of these two possibilities, there was some difference of opinion within the 'Platonic Academy.' Landino, in his famous dialogue on the Active and Contemplative Life, endeavours to be impartial. He compares *iustitia* and *religio*, the principles of action and contemplation, to two wings both of which 'carry the soul to higher spheres;'[30] he quotes Virgil as a witness to the belief that not only pious sages and scholars, but also just and upright men of action are worthy of praise and salvation;[31] and he finally tries to reach a compromise to the effect that Martha and Mary had been sisters living under the same roof, and that both had been agreeable to God. But even so he concludes with the statement: 'Let us keep to Martha so as not to desert our duties to humanity, but much more let us associate with Mary so that our mind might feed on nectar and ambrosia.'[32]

30. Landino, *Bibl.*179, fol.A5,v./A6. When the soul has recovered that 'dim memory' of its pre-existence *'iustitiaque ac religione, veluti duabus alis suffulta, se in altum erigit, atque dei lucem, quoad animi acies contagione corporis hebetata patitur, non sine summa voluptate intuetur'* (cf. also *ibidem*, fol.K2,v./3, with an instructive explanation of the *'duae alae:'* totidem virtutum genera, et aes, quae vitae actiones emendant, quas uno nomine iustitiam nuncupat, et eas, quibus in veri cognitionem ducimur, quas iure optimo religionem nominant' . . .). For the Platonic origin of the interpretation of Justice, not as a 'particular virtue juxtaposed to Prudence, Fortitude and Temperance,' but as 'that fundamental power in the soul which assigns to each of them their particular function,' and for the importance of this conception for the program of the 'Stanza della Segnatura,' see E.Wind, *Bibl.*405.
31. Landino, *Bibl.*179, fol.A5, v.: 'Laudat igitur [viz., Virgil] eos qui diuturna investigatione varias disciplinas atque scientias excogitarunt . . . Sed ut ne alterum vitae genus inhonoratum relinqueret, et rectas actiones sic persequitur:
    "Hic manus ob patriam pugnando vulnera passi,
    Quique sacerdotes casti, dum vita manebat,
    Quique pii vates et Phoebo digna locuti." '
A similar commentary on the same passage (*Aen.* VI, 66oss.) is found in the fourth dialogue, fol.L5.
32. Landino, *Bibl.*179, fol.C2: 'Sorores enim sunt, sub eodem tecto habitant Maria atque Martha, amboe deo placent, Martha ut pascat, Maria ut pascatur . . . Quapropter haerebimus Marthae, ne humanitatis officium deseramus; multo tamen magis Mariae coniungemur, ut mens nostra Ambrosia Nectareque alatur.' In essence this reconciliatory statement sustains the plea in favour of the *vita contemplativa*, fol.B2: 'Vides igitur minime contemnendam esse vitam, quae in agendo versatur. Maxime enim naturam humanam contingit suaque industria suisque laboribus mortalium genus inter sese suavi vinculo colligat et, ut iustitiam et religionem colat, efficit. Verum, cum mens nostra (qua sola homines sumus) non mortali actione sed immortali cognitione perficiatur . . . : Quis non viderit speculationem esse longe anteponendam?'

Ficino was much more radical in espousing the cause of the *vita con-templativa*. With him, the intuitive apprehension, not the rational actualization of the eternal values is practically the only road to temporal beatitude. This road is open to every one who 'seriously devotes his Mind to the pursuit of the true, the good and the beautiful;' but consummate happiness comes only in those exquisite moments when contemplation rises to ecstasy. Then the Mind, 'seeing with an incorporeal eye,'[33] 'calls itself away not only from the body but also from the senses and the imagination,' and thus transforms itself into a 'tool of the divine.'[34] This ineffable bliss, experienced by the Sibyls, the Hebrew Prophets and the Christian visionaries—the favourite instances being Moses and St. Paul[35] —is, of course, what Plato describes as the θεία μανία or *furor divinus*: the 'fine frenzy' of the poet (let it be borne in mind that the utterly non-mediaeval concept of genius, as reflected in this phrase, originated in Ficino's philosophy); the ravishment of the diviner; the raptures of the mystic; and the ecstasy of the lover.[36] Of these four forms of inspired madness, however, the *furor amatorius*, a 'voluntary death,'[37] to use Ficino's words, is the most powerful and sublime.

A thinker who considered Plato as a 'Moses talking Attic Greek'[38] and quoted the ecstasies of St. Paul along with the *amor Socraticus* could not see any essential difference between the Platonic ἔρως and the Christian *caritas*.[39] When Ficino presented a friend with a copy of his Commentary

33. Pico, II, 7, *Bibl.*267, fol.23.
34. Ficino, *De vita triplici*, I, 6, *Bibl.*90, p.498.
35. Cf. e.g., Pico, *ibidem:* 'Con questo viso vidde Moyse vidde Paolo, viddono molti altri eletti la faccia de Dio, et questo e quello che nostri Theologi [viz., the Neoplatonists] chiamano la cognitione intellettuale, cognitione intuitiva.'
36. Ficino, *Conv.*,VII,14 and 15, *Bibl.*90, p.1361ss; cf. Commentary on Plato, *Phaedrus*,IV,ss., *ibidem*, p.1365ss. and several other passages.
37. Ficino, *Conv.*, II,8, *Bibl.*90, p.1327; cf.B.Castiglione, *Il Cortigiano*, where love is called 'vital morte' (quoted in N.A.Robb, *Bibl.*286, p.193).
38. Ficino, *De Christian. Relig.*, XV, *Bibl.*90, p.29 and *Concordia Mosis et Platonis*, ibid., p.866ss.
39. For the Neoplatonic theory of love see particularly E.Cassirer, *Bibl.*59, p.138ss.; H.J. Hak, *Bibl.*133, p.93ss.; N.A.Robb, *Bibl.*286, p.75ss. (on Ficino's Commentary on the Symposium) and p.112ss. (on Benivieni and Pico).

on Plato's *Symposium*, as well as with a copy of his treatise *De Christiana Religione*, he wrote by way of explanation: 'Herewith I send you the *Amor* as I promised; but I also send the *Religio*, to make you see that my love is religious, and my religion amatory.'[40]

The idea of love is, in fact, the very axis of Ficino's philosophical system. Love is the motive power which causes God—or rather by which God causes Himself—to effuse His essence into the world, and which, inversely, causes His creatures to seek a reunion with Him. According to Ficino, *amor* is only another name for that self-reverting current (*circuitus spiritualis*) from God to the world and from the world to God.[41] The loving individual inserts himself into this mystical circuit.

Love is always a desire (*desiderio*), but not every desire is love. When unrelated to the cognitive powers, the desire remains a mere natural urge like the blind force which causes the plant to grow or the stone to fall.[42] Only when the desire, directed by the *virtù cognitive*, becomes conscious of an ultimate goal does it deserve the name of love. This ultimate goal being that divine goodness which manifests itself in beauty, love has to be defined as 'a desire for the fruition of beauty,'[43] or, simply, *desiderio di bellezza*.[44] This beauty, we remember, is spread throughout the

---

40. Ficino, letter to Filippo (not Luca) Controni, *Bibl*.90, p.632 (cf. E.Cassirer, *Bibl*.59, p.139): '*Mitto ad te amorem, quem promiseram. Mitto etiam religionem, ut agnoscas et amorem meum religiosum esse, et religionem amatoriam.*'
41. Ficino, *Conv.*, II, 2, *Bibl*.90, p.1324: '*Quoniam si Deus ad se rapit mundum mundusque rapitur, unus quidem continuus attractus est a Deo incipiens, transiens in mundum, in Deum denique desinens, qui quasi circulo quodam in idem, unde manabit, iterum remeat. Circulus itaque unus et idem a Deo in mundum, a mundo in Deum, tribus nominibus nuncupatur: prout in Deo incipit et allicit, pulchritudo; prout in mundum transiens ipsum rapit, amor; prout in autorem remeans ipsi suum opus coniungit, voluptas.*' The verb *allicit* suggests the old etymological derivation of χάλλος (beauty) from χαλεῖν (to call) which was very popular with the Neoplatonists.
42. Pico, II, 2, *Bibl*.267, fol.19, quoted p.227.
43. Ficino, *Conv.*, I,4, *Bibl*.90, p.1322: '*Amor sit fruendae pulchritudinis desiderium.*' The Italian translation of this definition ('*Amore è desiderio di fruire la bellezza*') is endlessly repeated in all the later treatises and dialogues on love.
44. Pico, II, 2, *Bibl*.267, fol.18, v.

universe; but it exists chiefly in two forms which are symbolized by the 'Two Venuses' (or 'Twin Venuses,' as they are often called by the Neo-platonists)[45] discussed in Plato's Symposium: Ἀφροδίτη Οὐρανία and Ἀφροδίτη Πάνδημος.

Ἀφροδίτη Οὐρανία or Venus Coelestis, that is, the celestial Venus, is the daughter of Uranus and has no mother, which means that she belongs in an entirely immaterial sphere, for the word *mater* (mother) was associated with the word *materia* (matter). She dwells in the highest, supercelestial zone of the universe, i.e., in the zone of the Cosmic Mind, and the beauty symbolized by her is the primary and universal splendour of divinity. She can thus be compared to 'Caritas,' the mediatrix between the human mind and God.[46]

The other Venus, Ἀφροδίτη Πάνδημος or Venus Vulgaris, is the daughter of Zeus-Jupiter and Dione-Juno. Her dwelling-place is the zone between the Cosmic Mind and the sublunary world, that is, the realm of the Cosmic Soul (it is, in fact, not quite correct to translate her name by 'terrestrial Venus;' she should rather be called 'natural Venus').[47] The beauty symbolized by her is therefore a particularized image of the primary beauty, no longer divorced from, but realized in the corporeal world. While the celestial Venus is a pure *intelligentia*, the other Venus is a *vis generandi* which, like Lucretius' Venus Genetrix, gives life and shape to the things in nature and thereby makes the intelligible beauty accessible to our perception and imagination.

Either Venus is accompanied by a congenial Eros or Amor who is rightly considered her son because each form of beauty begets a corresponding form of love. The celestial love or *amor divinus* possesses itself of the highest

45. Ficino, *Conv.*, II,7, Bibl.90, p.1326 ('*De duobus amoris generibus ac de Duplici Venere*'), the *locus classicus* for the doctrine summarized in the following paragraphs. Cf. also Commentary on Plotinus, *Ennead.* III,5, p.1713ss. especially chapters 2 and 3 ('*Geminae Veneres*'), and Commentary on Plotinus, *Ennead.* I,6, p.1574ss., particularly chapter 4: '*Duplex pulchritudo est . . .*'
46. Ficino, *Comm. in Enn.* I, 6, p. 1574.
47. For Pico's non-Ficinian interpretation of the two Venuses see p.144, N.51.

faculty in man, i.e. the Mind or intellect, and impels it to contemplate the intelligible splendour of divine beauty. The son of the other Venus, the *amor vulgaris*, takes hold of the intermediary faculties in man, i.e., imagination and sensual perception, and impels him to procreate a likeness of divine beauty in the physical world.

With Ficino, both Venuses, and both loves, are 'honourable and praiseworthy,' for both pursue the creation of beauty, though each in her own way.[48] However, there is a difference in value between a 'contemplative' form of love which rises from the visible and particular to the intelligible and universal,[49] and an 'active' form of love which finds satisfaction within the visual sphere; and no value whatever can be attached to mere lust which sinks from the sphere of vision to that of touch and should not be given the name of love by self-respecting Platonists. Only he whose visual experience is but the first step, however unavoidable, towards the intelligible and universal beauty reaches the stage of that 'divine love' which makes him an equal of the Saints and Prophets. He who is satisfied with visible beauty remains within the domain of 'human love.' And he who is insusceptible even to visible beauty, or stoops to debauchery, or, even worse, abandons for sensual pleasures a contemplative state already attained, falls prey to a

---

48. Ficino, *Conv.*, ii, 7, Bibl.90, p.1327. Cf. *ibid.*, vi, 7, p.1344: '*Sint igitur duae in anima Veneres: prima coelestis, secunda vero vulgaris. Amorem habeant ambae, coelestis ad divinam pulchritudinem cogitandam, vulgaris ad eandem in mundi materia generandam . . . immo vero utraque fertur ad pulchritudinem generandam, sed suo utraque modo.*'

49. A detailed description of the stages by which this goal can be reached, compared to the rungs of Jacob's ladder, is found in Pico, iii,10, Bibl.267, fol.64ss.: (1) Delight in the visible beauty of an individual (Senses). (2) Idealization of this particular visible beauty (Imagination). (3) Interpretation of it as a mere specimen of visible beauty in general (Reason, applied to visual experience). (4) Interpretation of visible beauty as an expression of moral values ('*Conversione dell'anima in se,*' Reason turning away from visual experience). (5) Interpretation of these moral values as reflexes of metaphysical ones (Reason abdicating, so to speak, in favour of the Mind). (6) Interpretation of the metaphysical values as functions of one universal and intelligible beauty (the Human Mind uniting itself with the Cosmic Mind). It will be noted that in this system (which caught the imagination of metaphysical poets for many centuries) the rise from grade 4 to grade 6 repeats, in an immaterial sphere, that from grade 1 to grade 3, so that the mere love for the 'interior beauty' of any individual, let alone for its moral virtues, does not yet amount to the consummation of Platonic love; cf. Pico, ii, 10, Bibl.267, fol.24, v.

'bestial love' (*amor ferinus*)[50] which, according to Ficino, is a disease rather than a vice: it is a form of insanity caused by the retention of harmful humours in the heart.[51]

Personally, Ficino led a chaste and abstemious life as, he thought, befitted the dignity and preserved the health of the scholar. But his Commentary on the *Symposium* is not a code of morals. It defies moral classifications in the same way as his whole philosophy defies such alternatives as optimism *vs.* pessimism, immanence *vs.* transcendence, sensualism *vs.* conceptualism.

We can easily see how this philosophy was bound to stimulate the imagination of all those who, in a period of growing psychological tensions, longed for new forms of expression for the frightening yet fruitful conflicts of the age: conflicts between freedom and coercion, faith and thought, illimited desires and finite consummations. At the same time, however, the praise of a sublime love divorced from 'base impulses,' yet allowing of an intense delight in visible and tangible beauty, was bound to appeal to the taste of a refined, or would-be refined, society.

50. Ficino, *Conv.*, IV, 8, *Bibl.*90, p.1345: '*Amor . . . omnis incipit ab aspectu. Sed contemplativi hominis amor ab aspectu ascendit in mentem. Voluptuosi ab aspectu descendit in tactum. Activi remanet in aspectu . . . Contemplativi hominis amor divinus, activi humanus, voluptuosi ferinus cognominatur.*' Cf. ibid., II,7, p.1327: '*Siquis generationis avidior contemplationem deserat, aut generationem praeter modum cum feminis, vel contra naturae ordinem cum masculis prosequatur, aut formam corporis pulchritudini animae praeferat, is utique dignitate amoris abutitur.*'
51. Ficino, *Conv.*, VII, 3, *Bibl.*90, p.1357. Ficino the physician was of course familiar with the medical theory that uncontrollable love was a form of madness called *hereos* (cf. J.L. Lowes, *Bibl.*202). The distinction between divine, human, and bestial love is also found in Pico, II,5, *Bibl.*267, fol.20,v./21 and, very circumstantially, II,24 and 25, fol.36,v.ss. There is, however, the following difference: Ficino can handle his three kinds of love without increasing the number of Venuses discussed by Plato and Plotinus, because he disposes of the *amor ferinus* by simply calling it a kind of insanity which has nothing to do with either Venus, or with the faculties of the human soul. Pico, less orthodox a Platonist and less inclined to look upon moral problems from a medical point of view, wished to connect the three forms of love with the three psychological faculties. Consequently he needed three Venuses corresponding to these faculties and introduced a 'Second Celestial Venus' who, according to him, is a daughter of Saturn and thus holds an intermediary position between Plato's Ἀφροδίτη Οὐρανία (daughter of Uranos) and Ἀφροδίτη Πάνδημος (daughter of Zeus and Dione). The latter thus ceases to be an 'honourable and praiseworthy' figure. Some justification of this could be found in the fact the mythographers were not in agreement as to whether the sea from which the motherless Venus had emerged had been

Thus the standard works expounding the Neoplatonic theory of love, i.e., Ficino's Commentary on Plato's *Symposium*, later on generally quoted as 'Ficino's *Convito*,' and Pico della Mirandola's Commentary on a long poem by Girolamo Benivieni which is in turn a versification of Ficino's doctrine—had but a scanty following, as far as strictly philosophical books are concerned;[52] Leone Ebreo's *Dialoghi d'Amore* is the only treatise of the sixteenth century that can be considered the work of a constructive thinker.[53] They exerted, however, a tremendous influence, both directly and indirectly, on artists, poets, and what might be called 'poetical thinkers'

fertilized by the genitals of Uranus or Saturn (cf., e.g. Mythographus III, 1, 7, *Bibl.*38, p.155). In a synoptical table the difference between Pico and Ficino would show as follows:

	FICINO		PICO	
Kinds of love	*Correspond-ing faculty of human soul*	*Corres-ponding Venus*	*Correspond-ing faculty of human soul*	*Corres-ponding Venus*
Amor divinus (Amore divino)	Mens (in-tellectus)	Venus Coe-lestis, daughter of Uranus	Intelletto	Venere Celeste I, daughter of Uranus
Amor humanus (Amore humano)	All other faculties of human soul	Venus Vulgaris, daughter of Zeus and Dione	Ragione	Venere Celeste II, daughter of Saturn
Amor ferinus (Amore best-iale)	———— (Insanity)	———— (Insanity)	Senso	Venere Volgare, daughter of Zeus and Dione

52. A treatise by Ficino's most faithful pupil Francesco Cattani di Diacceto, *Bibl.*62, is only a 'textbook' of the orthodox Florentine theory.
53. Cf. N.A.Robb, *Bibl.*286, p.197ss., and, more specifically, H.Pflaum, *Bibl.*265, throughout.

from Michelangelo to Giordano Bruno, Tasso, Spenser, Donne and even Shaftesbury.[54] On the other hand they occasioned an avalanche of 'Dialogues on Love' mostly of North-Italian origin, and these latter seem to have played a role in Cinquecento society not unlike that of semi-popular books on psychoanalysis in our day. What had been an esoteric philosophy became a kind of social game so that 'finally the courtiers thought it an indispensable part of their job to know how many and what kinds of love there were,' to quote the caustic remark of a sixteenth-century philologist.[55]

The prototypes of these dialogues are the *Asolani* by Pietro Bembo[56] and the *Cortigiano* by the count Baldassar Castiglione (a native of Mantua) who pays his debt to Bembo by making him the spokesman of the 'Platonic' doctrine.[57] In real understanding for Ficino's philosophy, penmanship and power of vision the *Asolani* and, in a slightly lesser degree, the *Cortigiano* are far superior to all the other specimens of their kind, some of which show, however, a greater pretension to profundity and learning.[58] Yet Bembo and Castiglione were by no means constructive thinkers. They wished to enthrall their readers—Bembo with purely poetical intentions, Castiglione with mildly educational aims—by the lure of a rarefied social atmosphere and beautiful

54. For Bruno, cf. E.Cassirer, *Bibl*.59, passim; for the influence of the Florentine 'Neoplatonism' in England, *idem*, *Bibl*.60.
55. Tomitano, *Bibl*.358, quoted by G.Toffanin, *Bibl*.344, p.137. For the 'Dialogues on Love' in general see H.Pflaum, *Bibl*.265; N.A.Robb, *Bibl*.286, p.176ss. (with further references). In addition see G.Toffanin, *l.c.*; G.G.Ferrero, Bibl.89.
56. First edition Venice, 1505, second Venice, 1515. Cf. N.A.Robb, *Bibl*.286, p.184ss., with further references.
57. Cf. N.A.Robb, *ibidem*, p.190ss., with further references.
58. Most of this learning is borrowed from Mario Equicola, *Bibl*.84 (cf. above). For him, see N.A.Robb, *Bibl*.286, p.187ss., where, however, the edition of 1554 is erroneously called the second, and J.Cartwright, *Bibl*.58, passim. Equicola's treatise, begun in Latin as early as 1494, stands in a class by itself. It is neither a philosophical treatise nor a work of art, but a kind of Encyclopaedia, and is of especial interest for its historical attitude which is unique at the time. In the first book the author surveys not only Renaissance literature on love from Ficino to Giovanni Jacopo Calandra (his colleague at the court of Isabella d'Este) whose treatise *Aura* apparently never appeared in print, but also summarizes the opinions of Guittone d'Arezzo, Guido Cavalcanti, Dante, Petrarch, Francesco Barberino, Boccaccio, and even 'Joan de Meun' (as author of the *Roman de la Rose*) and the Troubadours.

diction. It has rightly been said that their response to the Neoplatonic philosophy was 'essentially aesthetic.'[59]

As a result the Florentine gospels were spread in an often attractive,[60] but always diluted and, what is more important, 'socialized' and feminized form.

The setting of Ficino's *Convito* is a stately room in the Villa Medici at Careggi where nine members of the 'Platonic family' have gathered to celebrate the 7th of November (allegedly the date of Plato's birth and death) by a solemn re-enactment of the original Symposium.[61] The scene of the typical 'Dialogue on Love' is laid in the fragrant gardens of distinguished ladies[62] or even in the boudoirs of erudite courtesans, one of whom, Tullia d'Aragona, went to the trouble of writing herself a dialogue 'On the infinity of love.'[63] When the Florentines refer to concrete examples of physical and moral beauty they still quote Phaidros and Alcibiades. The authors of the 'Dialoghi' define, describe and praise the beauty and virtue of woman,[64] and frequently show great interest in questions of etiquette pertaining to the relationship between the sexes.[65] Small wonder that here the very distinction between 'celestial' and 'ordinary' love appears at times in a somewhat distorted form. Some writers reduce it to a mere difference between

---

59. N.A.Robb, *Bibl.*286, p.192.
60. We can readily understand that Spenser was inspired by Castiglione's *Cortigiano*, rather than by the esoteric treatises of the Florentine Fathers; cf. the excellent article by R.W. Lee, *Bibl.*186.
61. Ficino, *Bibl.*90, p.1320. The Platonic circle actually used to celebrate this date by a *Convivium*.
62. Bembo's *Asolani* are staged in the gardens of Caterina Cornaro, Ex-Queen of Cyprus, where the marriage of her favourite Lady-in-Waiting is preceded by three days of merriment and fine conversation on the merit of love. In the first book love is decried, in the second praised, and in the third the problem is settled by the 'Platonic' theory of the two kinds of love. Another dialogue staged in a park is G.Betussi's *Leonora*, reprinted in G.Zonta, *Bibl.*413.
63. Reprinted in G.Zonta, *ibidem*. Betussi's dialogue *Raverta* is staged in the boudoir of the Venitian poetess Franceschina Baffa, or Beffa.
64. Occasionally beauty is even defined in terms of mathematical proportions—which is very unorthodox from the Neoplatonic point of view (cf. p.133, N.10).
65. For the Platonizing metaphysics of kissing, see, e.g., N.A.Robb *Bibl.*286, p.191 and G. Toffanin, *Bibl.*344.

'honest' and 'dishonest' affection,[66] others widen the gap between the 'Two Venuses' to such an extent that the rise from the 'Venere Volgare' to the 'Venere Celeste' appears impracticable.[67] In short: what this type of literature really teaches, is a mixture of Petrarch and Emily Post, couched in Neoplatonic language.[68]

The difference between Ficino and Pico on the one hand and Bembo and Castiglione on the other, is indicative of the difference between Florence and Venice. Where Florentine art is based on design, plastic firmness and tectonic structure, Venetian art is based on colour and atmosphere, pictorial succulence and musical harmony.[69] The Florentine ideal of beauty has found its exemplary expression in statues of proudly erect Davids, the Venetian in paintings of recumbent Venuses.

This contrast is significantly illustrated by two compositions, one Florentine, and one Venetian, both of which translate into images the Neoplatonic

66. Cf., e.g., M.Equicola, *Bibl.*84, Book v, or V.Cartari, *Bibl.*56, p.454, where the difference between '*amore dishonesto e brutto*' and '*amore bello e honesto*' boils down to the application of our soul to '*quello che è rio*' and '*le cose buone.*' This conception reverts to that of Remigius as quoted by the Mythographus III, 11,18, *Bibl.*38, p.239, '*Duae autem secundum Remigium sunt Veneres; una casta et pudica, quam honestis praeesse amoribus quamque Vulcani dicit uxorem; dicitur altera voluptaria, libidinum dea, cuius Hermaphroditum dicit filium esse. Itidemque amores duo, alter bonus et pudicus, quo sapientia et virtutes amantur; alter impudicus et malus, quo ad vitia inclinamur*' (the Remigius passage quoted in H.Liebeschütz, *Bibl.*194, p.45).

67. This is especially true of G.Betussi, *Raverta*, where the 'Venere Volgare' is characterized according to Pico instead of according to Ficino, regardless of the fact that Pico had introduced a second 'Venere Celeste' as an intermediary.

68. For this recrudescence of Petrarchism within the framework of the Platonizing philosophy see particularly G.Toffanin, *Bibl.*344, p.134ss. and G.G.Ferrero, *Bibl.*89. Benedetto Varchi, the chief 'Platonist' of the middle of the sixteenth century, quotes Petrarch almost on every page (*Bibl.*365, p.271-457). Consequently, Pietro Aretino not only ridiculed the Neoplatonic parlance (*Il Filosofo*, especially V, 4), but also the frequent quotations from Dante and Petrarch which he introduces, in his *Raggionamenti*, into a dialogue far from sublime (*Bibl.*12 and 13).

69. Parallels have often been drawn between the great Venetian painters and the two Gabrielis (while Florence had practically no important music at that time), and attention has been called to the enormous role of music in the paintings by Giovanni Bellini, Giorgione, Titian and Veronese. In this connection it is interesting to note that Bembo and Betussi consider the ear, not the eye, as the vehicle of spiritual beauty and love (Bembo, *Asolani*, III, *Bibl.*26, p.217; Betussi, *Raverta*, *Bibl.*413). This is a crime from the orthodox point of view.

theory of love; and their mutual relationship is comparable to that between an orthodox Florentine treatise on love and Pietro Bembo's *Asolani*.

One of these compositions is an engraving after Baccio Bandinelli described by Vasari as 'The fray of Cupid and Apollo, with all the Gods present (*fig.*107).'[70] It shows two groups of classical divinities entrenched on either bank of a deep gorge. The group on the left includes Saturn, Mercury, Diana and Hercules (that is: the divinities of deep thought, acuteness, chastity and manly virtue) and is led by Jupiter and Apollo; the latter has just shot his arrow at his opponents. The other group, chiefly consisting of Vulcan with his helpers and various anonymous nudes of either sex, is led by Venus and a satyr-like Cupid who, on her instigation, points his arrow at Jupiter. Above the Apollo group the sky is clearing up while the other half of the scene, with the temple of Venus and burning ruins in the background, is obscured by dark smoke streaming from a huge trumpet. On the clouds in the centre is poised a beautiful woman, her left arm raised in a gesture of distress; her lowered glance is directed on the Venus group, but in her outstretched right she holds over the adherents of Apollo a vase from which bursts forth a smokeless flame.

The significance of this engraving is explained by the following distichs: 'Here divine Reason and troublesome human Lust fight each other, with thee, generous Mind, as umpire. Thou, however, here throwest light on honourable deeds, and there coverest profane ones with clouds. If Reason wins she will shine on the firmament together with the sun. If Venus wins her glory on earth will be a mere smoke. Learn, ye mortals, that the stars stand as high above the clouds as sacred Reason stands above foul appetites.'[71]

70. Vasari, *Bibl.*366, VOL.V, p.427: '*La zuffa di Cupido e d'Apollo, presenti tutti gli Dei.*' Vasari ascribes the engraving—dated 1545, one year after the publication of Ficino's *Convito* in Italian—to Enea Vico, but general opinion seems to agree with Bartsch's attribution to Nicolas Beatrizet. (*Le Peintre Graveur*, VOL.XV, p.262, no.44.)

71.   '*En Ratio dia, en hominum aerumnosa Cupido*
          Arbitrio pugnant, Mens generosa, tuo.

        Tu vero hinc lucem factis praetendis honestis,
        Illinc obscura nube profana tegis.

This explanation will bewilder rather than enlighten those not conversant with the system and terminology of orthodox Florentine Neoplatonism. Diligent readers of Ficino and Pico, however, will grasp at once that this battle waged by Cupid, Venus and Vulcan (who figures here as their armourer) against the sun-god Apollo with his following of wiser and more virtuous divinities illustrates, on the one hand the strained relations between the Lower Soul and Reason, on the other the peculiar position of the Mind. It will be remembered that in the struggle between Reason and the baser impulses *mens*, the Mind, takes no part, nor does it directly influence the outcome (hence the expression '*arbitrio tuo*'). *Mens*, however, cannot completely ignore the disturbance beneath it (hence the downward glance and annoyed gesture of the figure of 'Mens') and has to illuminate Reason by the flame of divine wisdom.[72]

It is interesting to study, with this engraving in mind, Titian's 'Sacred and Profane Love,' in the Borghese Gallery,[73] executed not later than around 1515 when the influence of Bembo's *Asolani* was at its height (*fig.*108). Though these two compositions could hardly differ more, both in style and mood, nevertheless they have some points in common. In both cases a vase full of heavenly fire is seen in the hand of the most prominent figure; in both cases a contrast is expressed between a sublime and a less lofty principle; and in both cases this contrast is symbolized by the familiar expedient of the bipartite '*paysage moralisé*:'[74] the background of Titian's painting, also, is divided into two halves, a dimly lighted scenery with a fortified town and two hares or rabbits (symbols of animal love and fertility),[75] and a

Si vincat Ratio, cum sole micabit in astris;
Si Venus, in terris gloria fumus erit.
Discite, mortales, tam praestant nubibus astra,
Quam ratio ignavis sancta cupidinibus.'

72. See p.137.
73. Cf. E.Panofsky, *Bibl.*243, p.173ss. with references to previous interpretations. The now familiar title (*Amore celeste e mondano*) which is, relatively, quite correct seems to appear for the first time in D.Montelatici, *Bibl.*219.
74. See p.64.
75. Cf., e.g., Ripa, s.v. 'Fecondità.'

more rustic and less luxurious, but brighter landscape with a flock of sheep and a country church.

The two women in Titian's picture bear a close resemblance to a pair of personifications described and explained by Cesare Ripa under the heading 'Felicità Eterna' (Eternal Bliss) and 'Felicità Breve' (Brief or Transient Bliss). 'Felicità Eterna' is a resplendently beautiful, blonde young woman, whose nudity denotes her contempt for perishable earthly things; a flame in her right hand symbolizes the love of God. 'Felicità Breve' is a 'Lady' whose dress of yellow and white signifies 'satisfaction.' She is adorned with precious stones and holding a vessel full of gold and gems, symbols of vain and shortlived happiness.

From this description we learn that at the end of the sixteenth century the juxtaposition of a nude woman bearing a flame (the attribute of the 'Mens' in the Bandinelli engraving and also of the Christian Faith and 'Caritas') with a richly attired lady was still understood as an antithesis between eternal and temporal values. Yet Ripa's terms would not adequately define the content of Titian's painting. 'Felicità Eterna' and 'Felicità Breve' constitute a moral or even theological contrast as irreconcilable as that depicted in two French tapestries in the Musée des Arts Décoratifs, where a gentleman strengthened by toil, self-mortification, faith and hope, and saved by the grace of God, forms the counterpart of a lady who remains engaged in worldly pursuits and associates herself with Blind Cupid (*figs.*116, 117).[76] Titian's picture, however, is not a document of neo-mediaeval moralism but of Neoplatonic humanism. His figures do not express a contrast between good and evil, but symbolize one principle in two modes of existence and two

76. See R. van Marle, *Bibl.*210, VOL.II, 1932, p.462. The motif of the trap is explained by Psalm xxv,15 (Vulgate): *'Oculi mei semper ad dominum, quoniam ipse evellet de laqueo pedes meos.'* In addition the 'Amour sacré' tapestry shows the phoenix (*'figura resurrectionis'*) and the pelican (*'figura passionis'*), and quotes the following Psalm verses (all numbers garbled by the weaver): xcvii, 11; xvii, 15; xxx, 1; xvi, 10; cii, 6. The companion piece shows a couple of fashionable lovers in the background and is inscribed with numerous invectives against Cupid from Ovid, Tibullus, Seneca, Propertius and St. Ambrose. Blind Cupid still wears the string of hearts around his waist.

grades of perfection. The lofty-minded nude does not despise the worldly creature whose seat she condescends to share, but with a gently persuasive glance seems to impart to her the secrets of a higher realm; and no one can overlook the more than sisterly resemblance between the two figures.

In fact the title of Titian's composition should read: *Geminae Veneres.* It represents the 'Twin Venuses' in the Ficinian sense and with all the Ficinian implications. The nude figure is the 'Venere Celeste' symbolizing the principle of universal and eternal but purely intelligible beauty. The other is the 'Venere Volgare,' symbolizing the 'generative force' that creates the perishable but visible and tangible images of Beauty on earth: humans and animals, flowers and trees, gold and gems and works contrived by art or skill. Both are therefore, as Ficino expressed it, 'honourable and praiseworthy in their own way.'[77]

That Cupid is placed between the two Venuses, though somewhat closer to the 'terrestrial' or 'natural' one, and that he stirs the water in the fountain may express the Neoplatonic belief that love, a principle of cosmic 'mixture,' acts as an intermediary between heaven and earth;[78] and the very fact that Titian's fountain is an ancient sarcophagus,[79] originally destined to hold a corpse but now converted into a spring of life, cannot but emphasize the idea of what Ficino had called the *vis generandi.*

Titian had no need to explain his 'Sacred and Profane Love' by a learned Latin poem. Even those ignorant of the correct title *Geminae Veneres* can understand the picture, and it is the scholar, rather than the 'naïve beholder' who finds it difficult to interpret. Where Bandinelli is complicated and severely linear, Titian is simple and sensuously colouristic. Where Bandinelli is obscure and dialectical, Titian is clear and poetic. And where Bandinelli

77. See p.143.
78. Cf. p.141ss. Furthermore cf. Ficino, *Conv.,* 1, 2, 3, *Bibl.*90, p.1321 ('Amor' originating from 'Chaos'), and particularly *ibid.,* VI,3, p.1341: '*Atque ita amorém ex huiusmodi mixtione medium quendam effectum esse volumus inter pulchrum et non pulchrum, utriusque participem.*' The symbolical significance of the action of Titian's Cupid was brought to my attention by Dr. Otto Brendel.
79. The reliefs on the sarcophagus, invented by Titian in the classical style, have not yet been explained.

shows 'Reson and Sensuallyte' in a bitter and undecided struggle, Titian depicts a wonderful harmony between intelligible and visible beauty. In short: In the one case we have Neoplatonism interpreted by a Florentine Mannerist, in the other by a representative of the Venetian High Renaissance.

With all its originality Titian's picture is not unrelated to earlier traditions, both in iconography and composition.

The Renaissance was well acquainted with the fact that Praxiteles had made two famous statues of Venus, one draped, the other nude, and that the nude one, after having been refused by the inhabitants of Kos, had become the glory of the Isle of Knidos.[80] It was probably on the strength of this information that Mantegna was advised to include 'two Venuses, one nude, the other draped' (*'doi Veneri, una vestida, laltra nuda'*),[81] in his 'Realm of Comus,' an assembly of classical divinities enjoying the music of Orpheus after the ejection of undesirable elements. That these *doi Veneri* were already intended to represent the celestial and 'terrestrial' or 'natural' Venus cannot be proved, but seems very probable, for some of the learned friends of Isabella d'Este for whom the Comus picture was executed were great authorities on 'Platonic' love,[82] and Lucian had referred to the nude of Knidos as Ἀφροδίτη Οὐρανία.[83] At any rate the juxtaposition of a nude Venus with a draped one was demonstrably familiar to a group of humanists and artists closely connected with Titian's own circle.

80. Pliny, *Nat.Hist.*, xxxvi, 20 (J.A.Overbeck, *Bibl.*236, no.1227). The passage is quoted by L.G.Gyraldus, *Bibl.*127, vol.i, col.395 and M.Equicola, ii,3, *Bibl.*84, fol.60, v.
81. For this picture, which was left unfinished by Mantegna and was completed by Lorenzo Costa (now Louvre), see R.Förster, *Bibl.*96, pp.78,154,173; also J.Cartwright, *Bibl.*58, vol.i, p.365ss.
82. Equicola was Isabella's private secretary, and Bembo and Calandra were even directly concerned with the 'Comus' picture for which several artists had been considered before Mantegna accepted the commission: Bembo was asked to approach Giovanni Bellini and to supply him with the *invenzione* in case he should accept, and Calandra carried on the negotiations with Mantegna and furnished the description from which the *doi Venere* passage was quoted. The definitive program is said to have been worked out by one Paride da Ceresara (cf. J.Cartwright, *Bibl.*58, p.372).
83. Lucian, *De Imaginibus*, 23 (Overbeck, *Bibl.*236, no.1232).

153

The scheme of composition, however, derives from a very early type for which the term 'debating-picture' would be a good label: a representation of two allegorical figures symbolizing and advocating two divergent moral or theological principles. It is interesting to note that such debates or συγκρίσεις were frequent in classical literature, whereas classical art had confined itself to the more dramatic representation of actual contests such as those between Apollo and Marsyas, or between the Muses and the Sirens: it took the Christian emphasis on the 'word' to bring about a 'dialogue' type[84] which could be adapted to the disputes of abstract personifications. Where the debating partners stand for such notions as 'Nature' and 'Reason' (fig.111), or 'Nature' and 'Grace' ('Nature' often identified with Eve, 'Reason' or 'Grace' with the Virgin Mary, that is: the 'New Eve'), one of them is frequently nude while the other is draped; and it is quite possible that the reverse of the French medal of Constantine (around 1400) where 'Nature' and 'Grace' are shown on either side of the Fountain of Life (fig.110), was as well known to Titian as was its obverse to the sculptors of the Certosa di Pavia.[85]

In all these instances, as well as in an amusing Byzantine miniature where St. Basilius is shown between 'Wordly Happiness' and 'Heavenly Life' (fig.109),[86] the draped woman stands for the loftier principle and vice versa,

84. See F.Saxl, Bibl.297; also W.Artelt, Bibl.14.
85. Cf. E.Panofsky, Bibl.243, p.176 and PL.LXIII, figs.110 and 111. The influence of the medal of Constantine was first conjectured by G. von Bezold, Bibl.34; for the reliefs of the Certosa di Pavia see J. von Schlosser, Bibl.303, PL.XXII and fig.14. For the derivation of the type which here appears in a slightly secularized form, see the miniature from Verdun, Bibl. de la Ville, ms.119 (our fig.79), where the Church and the Synagogue (the latter half-nude) are placed on either side of a circular fountain-like object from which emerges a small cross.
86. Paris, Bibl. Nat., ms. Grec 923, fol.272. The explanation of this miniature brought to my attention by Dr. Kurt Weitzmann is found in Basilius, Homilia dicta tempore famis et siccitatis, Migne, Patrol. Graec., vol.31, col.325: worldly happiness and heavenly life are compared to two daughters, one prurient, the other chaste and betrothed to Christ. The father is warned not to deprive the chaste daughter 'who, owing to her innate virtue is endowed with the quality and title of a bride' in favour of her sister, and is advised to provide her with 'decent raiment, lest she be refused by her bridegroom when she appears before him.'

whereas in Titian's *Geminae Veneres* the roles are reversed. This is not surprising in view of the ambivalence of nudity as an iconographical motif. Not only in the Bible but also in Roman literature actual nudity was often thought objectionable, because it indicated either poverty, or shamelessness.[87] In a figurative sense, however, it was mostly identified with simplicity, sincerity and the true essence of a thing as opposed to circumlocution, deceit and external appearances. All things are 'naked and opened unto the eyes' of God.[88] A γυμνὸς λόγος is a straightforward, honest speech. *Nuda virtus* is the real virtue appreciated in the good old days when wealth and social distinction did not count,[89] and Horace speaks already of *nuda Veritas*,[90] though the Greek writers, characteristically enough, rather imagined Truth as dressed in simple garments.[91]

When, at the end of the classical period, actual nudity had become so unusual in public life that it had to be 'explained' like any other 'iconographical' feature, the explanation could thus be both damaging and favourable. The same writers who were profuse in disparaging the nakedness of Cupid and Venus, interpreted the nudity of the Graces as a sign of unspoilt loveliness and sincerity.[92] In the Middle Ages the Horse-Tamers on Monte Cavallo were believed to represent two young philosophers named Phidias and Praxiteles who wished to be portrayed in the nude because they did not need

---

87. Characteristic passages from the Bible (setting aside *Genes.*, iii, 7 and ix, 21ss.) are: *Apoc.*, iii, 18 and xvi, 15; *Jerem.*, xiii, 26 and *Nahum*, iii, 5. As to Roman literature see, e.g., Cicero, *Tuscul.*, iv, 33 (70/71) with quotation from Ennius: '*Flagiti principium est nudare inter cives corpora.*'
88. *Hebr.*, iv, 13: '*Omnia autem nuda et aperta sunt oculis eius.*'
89. Petronius, *Sat.*, 88: '*Priscis temporibus cum adhuc nuda virtus placeret.*' Cf. Seneca, *De Beneficiis*, iii, 18: '*Virtus . . . non eligit domum nec censum, nudo homine contenta est.*'
90. Horace, *Carmina*, 1.24,7.
91. Philostratus, *Imagines*, 1,27 (Amphiaraos).
92. Cf., e.g., Fulgentius, *Mitologiae*, ii,1, p.40 Helm: '*Ideo nudae sunt Carites, quia omnis gratia nescit subtilem ornatum;*' Servius, *Comm. in Aen.* 1, 720: '*Ideo autem nudae sunt, quod gratiae sine fuco esse debent;*' Mythographus III, 11, 2, *Bibl.*38, p.229: '*Nudae pinguntur, quia gratia sine fuco, id est non simulata et ficta, sed pura et sincera esse debet.*' This positive interpretation of the nude Graces was to survive in Renaissance poetry in the same way as the negative interpretation of nude Cupid.

earthly possessions, and because everything was 'naked and open unto their eyes.'[93]

Mediaeval moral theology distinguished four symbolical meanings of nudity: *nuditas naturalis*, the natural state of man conducive to humility; *nuditas temporalis*, the lack of earthly goods which can be voluntary (as in the Apostles or monks) or necessitated by poverty; *nuditas virtualis*, a symbol of innocence (preferably innocence acquired through confession); and *nuditas criminalis*, a sign of lust, vanity and the absence of all virtues.[94] Artistic practice, however, had practically excluded the last of these four species,[95] and wherever mediaeval art established a deliberate contrast between a nude figure and a draped one the lack of clothes designates the inferior principle. A good instance of *nuditas naturalis* is furnished by the above mentioned dialogues between 'Nature' and 'Grace,' or 'Nature' and 'Reason.'

It took the Proto-Renaissance spirit to interpret the nudity of Cupid as a symbol of love's 'spiritual nature' (Francesco Barberino), or to employ an entirely naked figure for the representation of a Virtue; yet even then a man appeared at first less shocking than a woman. Nicolo Pisano could use a nude Hercules as a personification of Fortitude as early as around 1260 (pulpit in the Baptistry of Pisa),[96] but it was not before 1302/1310 that his

93. *Mirabilia Urbis Romae*, II,2, *Bibl.*217. It should be noted that the phrase here used ('*Omnia nuda et aperta*') is a quotation from *Hebr.* IV, 13.

94. See P.Berchorius, *Bibl.*27, s.v. 'Nudus, Nuditas.'

95. *Nuditas naturalis* is found in scenes from *Genesis*, Last Judgments, souls leaving their bodies, savages, and, of course, martyr scenes and scientific illustrations; *nuditas criminalis* in representations of pagan divinities, devils, vices, and sinful humans. Cf., to quote a few characteristic instances, the 'mythographical' images of nude Love (in addition to those mentioned above, see, e.g., P.Kristeller, *Bibl.*174, PL.C); pictures such as the 'love-spell' in the Städtisches Museum at Leipzig; and the majority of profane representations of the Gothic period particularly frequent in the minor arts (cf. R. van Marle, *Bibl.*210; H.Kohlhaussen, *Bibl.*172; W.Bode and W.F.Volbach, *Bibl.*39). Two striking instances are found in *Der Wälsche Gast*: The 'Sinful Soul' chained by the Vices (A. von Oechelhäuser, *Bibl.*232, p.56, no.80), and the 'Untugend' with her adherents (Oechelhäuser, *ibid.*, p.59, no.84; in some manuscripts the 'Untugend,' as in our *fig.*83, is erroneously inscribed '*Dugende*').

96. G.Swarzenski, *Bibl.*332, PL.27.

son Giovanni dared to include in the group of Virtues which in his pulpit in the Pisa Cathedral supports the regal figure of *Maria-Sponsa-Ecclesia*, a Temperance or Chastity fashioned after a classical 'Venus Pudica' (*fig.*113).[97]

Iconographically these naked personifications of virtues are still of a strictly ecclesiastical character, and this is also true of the earliest renderings of 'nude Truth' who appears at first (around 1350) in the company of a draped *Misericordia*, to illustrate the verse in Psalm lxxxiv: 'Mercy and Truth are met together; Righteousness and Peace have kissed each other' (*figs.*112, 114).[98] In the Italian Quattrocento, however, the concept of

97. See P.Bacci, *Bibl.*19, *figs.*26,27; A.Venturi, *Bibl.*373, PL.101,102; for the connection with classical statuary see J. von Schlosser, *Bibl.*306, p.141ss. In spite of Bacci's illuminating remarks (p.63ss.), there is still some confusion as to the iconography of the pulpit (cf., e.g., W.R.Valentiner, *Bibl.*363, p.76ss.). As Bacci has shown, the nude figure represents not Prudence, but Temperance or Chastity, while the figure wreathed with ivy and carrying a compass and a cornucopia (Bacci, PL.23) is not Temperance, but Prudence; Bacci correctly refers to St. Ambrose, *De Paradiso*, where, by the way, the source of the very cornucopia—symbol of riches—can be found in the phrase: '*Non enim angusta, sed dives utilitatum prudentia* est' (Migne, *Patrol. lat.*, VOL.14, col.297). Similarly the figure supported by the four cardinal Virtues, a crowned woman nursing two babies (Bacci, *figs.* 22, 29) is not an allegory of the Earth, or even of Pisa, but has been correctly identified by Bacci with the Church. This interpretation can be corroborated by the following passage from the most authoritative commentary on *Solomon's Song*: '*Ecclesiae huius ubera sunt duo testamenta, de quibus rudes animae lac doctrinae sumunt, sicut parvuli lac de uberibus matrum sugunt*' (Honorius Augustudun., *Expositio in Cantic. Cantic.*, I, I, Migne, *Patrol. lat.*, VOL.172, col.361; cf. also P.Berchorius, *Bibl.*27, s.v. 'Ubera'). The only figure still needing explanation is the Hercules (Bacci, *fig.*21) who, unlike the Hercules in Nicolo Pisano's pulpit, cannot stand for Fortitude because this virtue is already represented among the four figures supporting the Maria-Sponsa-Ecclesia. He may symbolize the concept of *virtus generalis* as opposed to the seven (or more) special virtues. This concept was a definitely 'modern' one: in the third quarter of the 15th century Antonio Filarete still considered the representation of virtue '*in una sola figura*' as a new problem (cf. E.Panofsky, *Bibl.*243, p.151ss., 187ss.); but he had a forerunner in the person of Francesco Barberino (cf. p.117ss.) who, at exactly the same time at which Giovanni Pisano's pulpit was made, had tried to refute the belief that 'virtue in general' was not depictable and had proposed to represent it by a Samson-or-Hercules-like figure rending a lion (F.Egidi, *Bibl.*81, p.92 and *fig.* p.89).

98. *Ps.*, lxxxv, 10 (lxxxiv, 11). The earliest instance known to the writer is still a miniature in cod. Pal. lat. 1993, of 1350/51, our *fig.*114; cf. now R.Salomon, *Bibl.*294, p.29, PL.XXXII. Usually this scene is illustrated by two draped women meeting as in a Visitation, and this is also true of the Utrecht Psalter and its derivatives. But in this group of manuscripts the following verse ('Truth shall spring out of the earth, and righteousness shall look down from heaven') is illustrated by a group which seemingly includes a nude Truth:

'nude Truth' came to be transferred to a secular plane. Chiefly responsible for this was Leone Battista Alberti who in his 'Treatise on Painting' (first Latin version 1436) called the attention of modern-minded painters to the 'Calumny of Apelles' as described by Lucian: the conviction and punishment of an innocent victim belatedly vindicated by Repentance and Truth.[99] In his description of this allegory Alberti followed Guarino da Verona's faithful translation of the Greek text. But while Lucian, silent as to the appearance of Truth, had described Repentance as 'weeping and full of shame,' Alberti reversed the situation by saying: 'after Repentance, there appeared a young girl, shamefaced and bashful, named Truth' ('*una fanciulletta vergogniosa et pudica, chiamata: la Verita*').[100] This shift of the

Truth is represented as a practically naked child lifted by a woman who stands for Earth; cf. E.T.DeWald, *Bibl.*74, p.38, PL.LXXVIII, and M.R.James, *Bibl.*154, p.31, fol.150, v., our *fig.*112 (incorrectly identifying the woman with Truth instead of Earth). However, DeWald is absolutely right in pointing out that, from the view-point of representational traditions, this group is nothing but a Virgin Mary with the Infant Jesus, Christ being *Veritas*, according to St. John, xiv, 6.

99. Cf. R.Förster, *Bibl.*98, and R.Altrocchi, *Bibl.*6.

100. Cf. R.Förster, *Bibl.*98, p.33s., where the other versions are also reprinted and R.Altrocchi, *Bibl.*6, p.459 for the date of Guarini's translation; and p.487 for the *Triompho della Calummia* by Bernardo Ruccellai. The phrase in question reads as follows in the various redactions:

Lucian, *Calumn.*, 5	Guarino Guarini of Verona (1408)	L.B.Alberti (Latin version, 1436)	Anonymous translation of 1472 (Berlin, Staatsbibl., cod. Hamilton 416)	Bernardo Ruccellai, *Triompho della Calummia* (around 1493)
ἐπεστρέφετο γοῦν [viz., Μετάνοια] εἰς τοὐπίσω δακρύουσα καὶ μετ' αἰδοῦς πάνυ τὴν Ἀλήθειαν προσιοῦσαν ὑπέβλεπεν.	'obortis igitur lacrimis hec [viz., *Penitentia*] retrovertitur, ut propius accedentem Veritatem *pudibunda* suscipiat.'	'Poenitentia, proxime sequente *pudica* et verecunda *Veritate*.'	'lacrimando si volta indietro La *verita*, che ne viene *vergognosa* et *timida* raghuardando.'	'La tarda penitentia in negro amanto Sguarda la *verità*, ch'è *nuda e pura*.'

epithet *pudica* or *pudibunda* from Repentance to Truth—so small a change
that it has escaped notice thus far—is yet significant. For, while repentance
implies a feeling of guilt akin to shame, Truth could not conceivably be
'shamefaced and bashful,'—were it not for her nudity: it is evident that
Alberti already imagined Truth as a naked figure of the 'Venus Pudica'
type, as she appears in Botticelli's Uffizi panel and many other paraphrases
and representations of the Calumny theme (*fig.*115).

Thus the figure of *nuda Veritas* became one of the most popular personifications in Renaissance and Baroque art; we have already encountered
her in the numerous representations of 'Truth unveiled by Time.' And
nudity as such, especially when contrasted with its opposite, came to be
understood as a symbol of truth in a general philosophical sense. It was
interpreted as an expression of inherent beauty (φυσικὸν κάλλος, *pulchritudo innata*) as opposed to mere accessory charms (ἐπείσακτον κάλλος,
ornamentum);[101] and, with the rise of the Neoplatonic movement, it came to
signify the ideal and intelligible as opposed to the physical and sensible, the
simple and 'true' essence as opposed to its varied and changeable 'images.'[102]
Thus we can easily see how the first author who alludes to Titian's 'Sacred
and Profane Love,' a poet by the name of S. Francucci (1613), came to interpret the nude figure as *Beltà disornata* and to sing her praise at the expense of her overdressed companion: 'She knows that the noble heart loves
and reveres unadorned beauty while the barbarous heart delights in barbarous pomp similar to itself. And when Beauty, rich in native graces, is poor

101. Cf. E. Panofsky, *Bibl.*243, p.174 with quotation of a passage from Alberti (*De re aedifi-
cat.*, VI, 2) and its classical source (Cicero, *De Nat. Deor.*, I, 79). Cf. also Propertius,
Eleg. I, 2, brought to my attention by Professor Godolphin: '*Quid iuvat ornato procedere,
vita, capillo Et tenues Coa veste movere sinus? . . .*'
102. Instructive instances of iconographical nudity in Ripa's *Iconologia*—setting aside the
'Felicità Eterna' already discussed—are: 'Amicizia,' 'Anima,' 'Bellezza,' 'Chiarezza,'
'Ingegno,' 'Sapienza,' 'Verità,' 'Virtù heroica.' In the Venice edition of 1645 (*Bibl.*284)
a personification of 'Idea' is added: she, too, is nude to connote her as a '*sostanza sem-
plicissima*' (according to Ficino) but she wears a transparent white veil to signify her
purity; like the 'Felicità Eterna' and Titian's 'Venere Celeste' she also has a flame.

in gold, it [the barbarous heart] looks down on her, as though the sun in heaven would adorn himself with anything but his own rays.'[102a]

'Sacred and Profane Love' seems to be the only composition in which Titian paid a conscious tribute to the Neoplatonic philosophy. However, the idea of Two Venuses, one symbolizing the ethical, the other a merely natural principle, is not absent from his later work. While compositions such as the numerous variations of the Recumbent Venus, of the Toilet of Venus,[103] of the Feast of Venus according to Philostratus,[104] of Venus and Adonis, etc. glorify the goddess as a divinity of animal beauty and sensual love, others idealize her as a divinity of matrimonial happiness.

It is in this role that Venus appears in two of Titian's most famous 'symbolical' pictures: the so-called 'Allegory of the Marquis Alfonso d'Avalos' in the Louvre, and the so-called 'Education of Cupid' in the Borghese Gallery.

The 'Allegory of the Marquis d'Avalos'—which in reality has nothing to do with this worthy general[105]—shows a distinguished, solemn-looking gentleman in armour, affectionately yet respectfully touching the breast of a young woman who pensively holds on her lap a large glass globe (*fig.* 118). She is greeted by three figures approaching from the right: winged

---

102a. The passage in Francucci's *La Galleria del Illustrissimo Signore Scipione Cardinal Borghese* which for a time seemed to defy verification (cf. E.Panofsky, *Bibl.*243, p.174) has been identified by Dr. Hanns Swarzenski in the Vatican Library, Fondo Borghese, S.IV, TOM.102, fol.55s. The stanza 166, translated in the text, reads:

'Sapea Costei che quanto s'ama e apprezza
Disornata beltà da cor gentile,
Tanto barbaro cor prende vaghezza
Di barbarica pompa a lui simile.
E se pouera è d'or ricca bellezza
Di natie gratie, ei la si prende a uile:
Quasi che d'altro s'adornasse mai
Nel Cielo il sol che de'suoi proprii rai.'

103. Cf.S.Poglayen-Neuwall, *Bibl.*271.
104. Cf.F.Wickhoff, *Bibl.*399.
105. See the conclusive article by K.Wilczek, *Bibl.*400.Wilczek tentatively dates the picture, not in 1533, as had been generally assumed, but in the fifth decade of the century, which seems to go a little too far in the opposite direction.

Cupid, carrying on his shoulder a bundle of sticks, a girl wreathed with myrtle whose expression and gesture reveals intense devotion, and a third figure raising a wide basket full of roses and glancing heavenward with joyful excitement.

The subject of this composition is not the leave-taking of a *condottiere* going to war, as was believed when the male figure was held to be identifiable as the Marquis d'Avalos, but, on the contrary, the Happy Union of a betrothed or newly married couple. The gesture of the gentleman is found in such representations as the Betrothal of Jacob and Rachel[106] or, in even more hieratic form, Rembrandt's 'Jewish Bride;' and the three additional figures are none others than Love, Faith and Hope, provided with special attributes suitable for the occasion.

Cupid stands for Love by definition; but the bundle which he carries instead of his customary weapons is a well-known symbol of unity.[107] The impassioned girl behind him is characterized as Faith by her expression and gesture;[108] but thanks to her wreath of myrtle she qualifies for the special office of a 'Fede Maritale;' for the myrtle, the perennial plant of Venus, and thus a symbol of everlasting love, was called *myrtus coniugalis* in classical literature.[109] The third figure, finally, is identified as Hope by her ecstatic

---

106. Painting by Dirk Zandvoort, Berlin, Private Collection, brought to my attention by Dr. Jacob Rosenberg.

107. Ripa, s.v. 'Concordia.' The *fascio* signifies '*la moltitudine de gl' animi uniti insieme col vincolo della carità et della sincerità.*' Furthermore s.v. 'Unione Civile.' In art, the bundle as a symbol of unity is found, e.g., in Paolo Veronese's 'Virtù Coniugali' in the Villa Barbaro-Giacomelli at Maser (ill. in G.Fiocco, *Bibl.*91, PL.XXXVIII), and even in Rembrandt's 'Eendracht van het Land' in the Boymans Museum at Rotterdam.

108. Cf. Ripa, s.v. 'Fede Cattolica' ('*Donna . . . che si tenga la destra mano sopra il petto*'), and countless representations of Faiths, praying saints etc. In Veronese's 'Fedeltà' or 'Happy Union' (Brit. Mus., no.1326, ill. in G.Fiocco, *Bibl.*91, PL.LXXXIX, 2) the loyal lady is almost copied from the figure in Titian's Louvre painting; a dog, the proverbial symbol of Fidelity (e.g., Ripa, s.v. 'Fedeltà') is chained to her girdle, while a Cupid tries to unleash him (cf. for this motif a picture of Sebastiano Ricci showing Cupid dragging away a dog from Venus, entitled 'Amour jaloux de la Fidélité,' Bordeaux, Musée, no.56).

109. Pliny, Nat. Hist., xv,122. For the myrtle as the plant of Venus see Pauly-Wissowa, *Bibl.*256, VOL.XVI,V,s.v. 'Myrtos,' especially col. 1182. For the later period see, e.g., Mythographus III, 11, 1, *Bibl.*38, p.229; Boccaccio, *Geneal. Deor.*, III, 22, etc.

161

glance (*occhi alzati*, as Ripa puts it),[110] and by the basket of flowers which are the attribute of Hope because 'Hope is the anticipation of fruits;'[111] but that the flowers are roses conveys a parallel meaning to the substitution of a bundle for Cupid's quiver, for the rose denotes 'the pleasures of permanent congeniality.'[112]

The significance of the globe on the lady's lap is less easily explained, the sphere being one of the most variable quantities in iconographical equations. Dr. Otto Brendel, who is preparing a monograph on the subject, suggests the interpretation of 'harmony,' one of the commonest meanings of the sphere as 'the most perfect form,'[113] and this works in well with the symbolism of Cupid's bundle and Hope's roses. But that the sphere is made of glass designates this harmony as easily broken, because glass 'signifies by its fragility the vanity of all things on earth.'[114] And this is perhaps the finest point of the whole allegory. The man, while solemnly taking possession of his bride, consecrates to her his love, faith and hope; she, in accepting both his sway and his devotion, finds herself responsible for a thing as perfect as it is delicate: their common happiness.

Titian's painting is, however, not only an allegorical but also a mythological portrait. The affectionate relationship between a beautiful woman and a man in armour, combined with the presence of Cupid, suggests Mars and Venus. In fact: while some of Titian's followers and imitators attempted to vary (not very successfully) the allegorical elements of the 'd'Avalos' composition,[115] others employed it as a model for double portraits of elegant

110. Ripa, s.v. 'Speranza divina e certa.'
111. Ripa, s.v. 'Speranza,' II: '*La ghirlanda di fiori . . . significa Speranza, sperandosi i frutti all'apparire, che fanno i fiori.*'
112. Ripa, s.v. 'Amicizia,' II: '*La Rosa significa la piaccevolezza quale sempre deve essere tra gli amici, essendo fra loro continua unione di volontà.*'
113. Cf. e.g., Ripa, s.v. 'Scienza:' '*La palla dimostra che la scienza non ha contrarietà d'opinioni, come l'orbe non ha contrarietà di moto.*'
114. Ripa, s.v. 'Miseria Mondana' (a woman with her head in a ball of transparent glass): '*Il vetro . . . mostra la vanità delle cose mondane per la fragilità sua.*'
115. Two of these variations ill. in O.Fischel, *Bibl.*94, p.212. So popular was the 'D'Avalos' composition that it was even copied in faience (Rome, Palazzo Venezia, with the glass ball replaced by a water melon).

couples masquerading as Mars and Venus. This is the case, for instance: with a painting of the school of Paolo Veronese;[116] with two paintings by Paris Bordone, one of which, at least, is demonstrably a marriage picture, for the lady is shown picking, not a lemon but a quince, the wedding fruit *par excellence* (fig.121);[117] and with a picture by Rubens.[118]

It may seem peculiar indeed to portray respectable couples and even newly-weds under the guise of Mars and Venus whose relationship was not of the most legal. Yet this device was not without precedent and justification. A union between beauty and valour seems, in a way, more natural than a union between beauty and craftsmanship; in fact there is evidence in Hesiod and Pausanias that Mars had been the legitimate husband of Venus long before Homer had married her off to Vulcan,[119] and that they had a daughter by the name of Ἀρμονία, that is: Harmony. This old tradition was never quite obliterated by the Homeric version. It lingered on, in somewhat distorted form, in late-antique and mediaeval mythography,[120] and in the more erudite writings of the Renaissance;[121] it was taken for granted by a Byzantine poet named Maximos Planudes who describes the wedding feast of Mars and Venus as though she had never been married to Vulcan;[122] and, what is more im-

116. Frankfurt, Städelsches Kunstinstitut, no.893. As in the picture by Sebastiano Ricci, Cupid is involved in a fight with a dog who in this case is the aggressor.

117. Vienna, Kunsthistorisches Museum, no.233. I wish to thank Mrs. Eleanor C.Marquand for having identified the 'lemon' in this picture as a quince and for having called my attention to a great number of texts testifying to the old custom, allegedly sanctioned by a Solonian law, of presenting couples with a dish of quinces on their wedding day; cf., e.g.,Ripa, s.v. 'Matrimonio,' and H.N.Ellacombe, *Bibl.*83, p.234s. The other Bordone picture (Vienna, no.246) shows Mars disarming Cupid while Venus holds a bunch of myrtle in her bosom, and a young woman is busy with more myrtle twigs.

118. Dulwich Gallery, illustrated in R.Oldenbourg, *Bibl.*234, p.330.

119. Cf. Roscher, *Bibl.*290, s.v. 'Ares,' especially col.646, and 'Harmonia.' Professor Godolphin has called my attention to the ancient tradition according to which Hephaistos, in turn, was married, not to Aphrodite, but to Charis (Homer, *Il.*xviii, 382) or Aglaïa (Hesiod, *Theogon.*, 945).

120. Cf.e.g., Mythographus I, 150.151 and Mythographus II, 78, where Harmonia is mis-named Hermione (as is almost a general rule in mediaeval literature) and in addition called 'ex Martis et Veneris adulterio nata.'

121. See e.g.,Natalis Comes, *Bibl.*67, ix, 14, p.1007ss. Natale Conti gives the correct name, but sticks to the *adulterio nata*, although he quotes the Hesiod passage.

122. The fine little poem was published by C.R.von Holtzinger, *Bibl.*147. For Planudes, the

portant, it always remained the basis of cosmological and, later on, astrological speculations. With Lucretius, who, we remember, interpreted Venus as the great generative force in nature, she alone is capable of neutralizing the destructive principle symbolized by Mars;[123] in Nonnos' *Dionysiaca* and Statius' *Thebais* the idea that only love and beauty can temper strife and hatred, and that their union results in universal harmony became so important that Harmonia, the daughter of Venus and Mars, is almost omnipresent in both poems;[124] in every astrological treatise we find the axiom that Venus by her mildness tempers the ferocity of Mars while he, her 'suitor,' is never strong enough to shatter her gentle power. The Florentine Neoplatonists furnished profound metaphysical explanations for this doctrine.[125]

Thus, in identifying a distinguished couple with Mars and Venus, Titian compared their union, not to the furtive passion of the Homeric lovers but to the auspicious fusion of two cosmic forces begetting harmony. He thereby reinstated a type already familiar to the Antonine period of Roman art, when allegorical myth-interpretation and mythological portraiture were equally *en vogue*. Titian may well have been acquainted with the much repeated marble group of Commodus and Crispina which shows the imperial couple as 'Mars and Venus in conjunction,' so to speak,[126] and the composition of which is not unlike that of the 'd'Avalos' picture, except for the fact that 'Venus,' not 'Mars,' plays the more active role (*text ill.* p.129).

well known compiler of the *Anthologia Graeca*, translator of many Latin works into Greek, and, for a time, Byzantine envoy to Venice, see K.Krumbacher, *Bibl*.175, p.543ss.

123. Cf. p.63, N.77.

124. Statius, *Thebais*, III, 295ss. is quoted by V.Cartari, *Bibl*.56, p.266, in conclusion of his chapter on Venus.

125. Cf., e.g., Pico,II,6, *Bibl*.267, fol.22, or Ficino, *Conv.*,v,8, *Bibl*.90, p.1339: 'Diis aliis, id est planetis aliis, Mars fortitudine praestat . . . Venus hunc domat . . . Martis, ut ita dicamus, compescit malignitatem . . . Mars autem Venerem nunquam domat . . . Mars iterum sequitur Venerem, Venus Martem non sequitur, quoniam audacia amoris pedissequa est, non amor audaciae.'

126. See H.Stuart Jones, *Bibl*.157, PL.73 and S.Reinach, *Bibl*.277, VOL.I, p.346 (mentioned in J.J.Bernouilli, *Bibl*.32, VOL.II,2,1891, p.249). Cf. also S.Reinach, *ibidem*, VOL.I, p.165 and VOL.III, p.257. I wish to thank Professor Margarete Bieber for having called my attention to these groups.

It is an accepted fact that the so-called 'Allegory of the Marquis d'Avalos' anticipates in several respects one of Titian's latest masterpieces: the 'Education of Cupid' in the Borghese Gallery (*fig.*119).[127] In it a beautiful young woman with a little crown in her hair—her sleeve retained above the elbow by a kind of bracelet as in the Louvre picture—blindfolds a little Cupid snuggling in her lap, while a second Cupid, his eyes not bandaged, leans on her shoulder and diverts her attention to himself. Two maidens approach from the right with the weapons of love. One of them proffers the bow, the other, somewhat closer to the main group, carries the quiver.

The general meaning of the composition is not obscure. Since no other Blind Cupid appears in Titian's works we are justified in interpreting the contrast between the two little love-gods as deliberate. The motif of the crowned young woman looking over her shoulder at Cupid is derived from a classical formula expressing what might be called 'Supernatural persuasion.' This formula is used, for instance, in Hellenistic representations of Polyphemus or Paris yielding to the incitement of Eros (*fig.*120);[128] with Eros transformed into an angel, its influence on Renaissance art is manifested in Michelangelo's Isaiah. The heroine of our picture, however, is subject to dissuasion rather than to persuasion. She is bandaging the eyes of the Cupid in her lap, and in the normal course of events the bow and arrows brought in by the two maidens would be given to him, so that he might go out into the world to 'do his worst.'

To this the other Cupid emphatically objects: clear-sighted as he is he foresees trouble if the dangerous weapons should be handed over to a blind little fellow who shoots his arrows at random so as to cause short-lived and disillusioning passions. Whether he suggests the removal of the bandage

127. There is, however, a difference between a great master reverting to and transfiguring his own inventions, and mediocre imitators concocting such *pasticcios* as the 'Education of Cupid' published by W.R.Valentiner, *Bibl.*364, vol.i,1930; pl.25 (now Chicago Art Institute) and its relatives in Genoa and Munich (Alte Pinakothek, no.484, formerly 1116, rightly characterized by Morelli as 'not even a school-picture;' cf. G.Morelli, *Bibl.*223, p.61).

128. Th.Schreiber, *Bibl.*308, pl.ix, xxviii, and lxv; C.Robert, *Bibl.*287, vol.ii *fig.* p.17.

from the eyes of his rival,[129] or claims the bow and arrows for himself, is a matter of surmise, though the latter interpretation seems more probable in view of the fact that there is only one set of weapons available, and that the maiden in the foreground, anxiously scrutinizing the face of her mistress, withholds the quiver as though not knowing what to do with it. One thing, however, is certain: the heroine will adopt the course suggested by the little adviser at her shoulder; Blind Cupid will not be permitted to cause mischief with his bow and arrows. She has already stopped blindfolding him and lends her ear to his rival with the thoughtful and slightly sullen expression of one who 'listens to reason.' Moreover the maiden with the quiver bears a family likeness to the figure of Marital Faith in the 'D'Avalos Allegory;' however, being more alluringly dressed, she might be more appropriately dubbed Marital Affection. Her vigorous and serious companion, clad in a hunting-suit with shoulder-strap is obviously meant to suggest the idea of Diana, the goddess of chastity.

Thus Titian's 'Education of Cupid,' too, has all the necessary ingredients of a marriage picture. The heroine is no less individualized than in the 'Allegory of the Marquis d'Avalos;' and what subject could be more appropriate than The Choice of Beauty between Blind Cupid and Clearsighted Love— or, to quote the favourite expressions of the period, between Eros and 'Anteros, Amor Virtutis,'[130] especially as Marital Affection and Chastity are present to guarantee a wise decision?

129. This interpretation, or one very much like it, has already been suggested in the Catalogue of the *Mostra di Tiziano, Bibl.*369, no.84: '. . . *si vede Venere che benda Amore a prima di lasciarli andare, forse per quello che dietro le spalle le susurra Imene, dubita se stringer la benda.*' All other interpretations of the picture, as far as known to the writer, are rather beside the point. Even L.Venturi's attractive hypothesis according to which the subject was taken from Apuleius, *Metam.*, V, 29 (*Bibl.*374 a) is not convincing. Apuleius' narrative presupposes an adolescent Cupid, not a small child, and it does not account for the blindfolding motif. Moreover, Venus' threats to 'bear another son, better than you' or to 'adopt one of my little servants, to whom I shall hand over the wings, flames, bow and arrows which I gave you to make a better use of them' are not carried out.

130. There is a certain similarity between Titian's Borghese picture and the well-known Pompeian mural, called the 'Punishment of Cupid' (our *fig.*122) where one Cupid looks over the shoulder of Venus, while another, sentenced to work as a *fossor*, is dragged

There remains, however, the problem of finding an adequate name for the main figure. As a concrete human being she is, of course, a handsome bride bidding farewell to the blind god of playful adventures.[131] But who is she as a 'symbolical personality?'

Francucci, again our earliest witness, identifies her with Venus and calls the two maidens 'two nymphs hostile to Love,' bent on defeating the 'perfidious Cupid of the bandaged eyes.' He even knows them by name: one is 'Dori, Ninfa pudica e bella,' and the other, 'girt for shooting,' is 'Armilla, gloria dell' honestate.'[131a] This interpretation was accepted by Jacopo Manilli (1650) who briefly lists the picture as 'una Venere con due Ninfe,'[132] whereas Carlo Ridolfi (1648) describes the subject as 'le Gratie con Cupidine et alcune pastorelle.'[133] Ridolfi's interpretation—inaccurate even from a purely factual point of view, for there are no more than three figures in the picture—has been dismissed by modern art historians who have more or less agreed upon Manilli's *Venere*. The identification of the main figure with Venus is, in fact, unexceptionable, particularly if this Venus—turning from Eros to Anteros—is interpreted as Ἀφροδίτη Ἀποστροφία or 'Venus

away by a severe woman variously interpreted as Venus, again, Peitho, or Nemesis (P.Hermann, *Bibl.*144, additional plate and p.5ss.; R.Curtius, *Bibl.*69, p.280ss., fig.165-166; O.Jahn, *Bibl.*152, especially p.166). Another version (P.Hermann, *ibidem*, TEXT VOL., fig.7) shows Venus alone with the two Cupids. In my opinion this composition represents the punishment of Eros following a complaint of Anteros who, we remember, had to prevent or to prosecute unfairness in love-affairs. This would bear out Curtius' identification of the second woman with Nemesis who was considered to be the mother of Anteros and, like her son, was particularly interested in meting out justice to lovers (cf. Pausanias, *Periegesis*, 1,33,6).

131. For the conception of marriage as a 'farewell to Cupid' (the idea being that the bride could have any number of lovers if she wanted to, but preferred to concentrate on one worthy husband), see E.Panofsky, *Bibl.*242, p.199, Note 3.

131a. S.Francucci, *l.c.*, fol.111ss. The description is very long (more than twenty stanzas), because Francucci uses his Armilla to release the indispensable description of ideal female beauty. The '*perfido Amor bendato*' occurs in stanza 400, and in stanza 401 the author says of Armilla: '. . . *non è Amor mai cieco, qual'hor apre i begli occhi, o, ch'egli è teco.*'

132. Jacopo Manilli, *Bibl.*208, p.64.

133. Carlo Ridolfi, *Bibl.*283, VOL.I, p.197. G.P.Lomazzo, VII,10, *Bibl.*199, p.570, seems to confuse the Borghese picture with other representations of Venus when he writes: '*Fu dipinto* [*viz.*, Cupid] *dal nostro Ticiano appoggiato sopra la spalla di Venere con le altre stagioni, la primavera ornata di verde, co'l specchio in mano, li colombi à piedi di Cupido.*'

Verticordia,' who was considered as the 'Third Venus besides the Celestial and Terrestrial' and was worshipped because she 'opposes and removes from the soul immodest desires and turns the mind of maidens and wives from carnal love to purity.'[134]

Yet Ridolfi's surprising statement, though perhaps due to a mere misunderstanding of Francucci's repeated references to the Three Graces,[134a] may reflect an earlier interpretation which, when considered in the light of Renaissance ideas, is quite compatible with the Venus theory. For, while the current mythographical sources depict the Three Graces as something like Venus' handmaidens or 'Ladies-in-waiting' (*pedissequae*), Platonizing humanists of the Renaissance had come to interpret their relationship to Venus in a more philosophical way. The Three Graces were thought of as qualifications of the entity that was Venus, so much so that they were termed a 'Trinity' of which Venus was the 'Unity:' they were held to embody the threefold aspect of Venus, i.e., supreme Beauty, in much the same way as God the Father, the Son and the Holy Ghost are considered the threefold aspect of the Deity. It was thus possible to replace their traditional names

134. See Roscher, *Bibl.*290, s.v. 'Verticordia.' The *loci classici* known to the Renaissance (cf.,e.g.,L.G.Gyraldus, *Bibl.*127, VOL.I, col.390, and V.Cartari, *Bibl.*56, p.260) are: Pausanias, *Periegesis*, IX, 16, 2: Valerius Maximus, *Fact. et Dict.*, VIII, 15 and Ovid, *Fasti*, IV, 157ss. Cartari's account reads as follows: '*E come che da Venere venghino non meno gli honesti pensieri che le lascive voglie, le votarono già i Romani . . . un tempio, acchioch' ella rivoltasse gli animi delle donne loro . . . à più honeste voglie, et la chiamarono Verticordia . . . Et era questa Venere de'Romani simile a quella che da' Greci fu chiamata Apostrofia . . . perchè era contraria a' dishonesti desiderii, et rimoveva dalle menti humane le libidinose voglie . . . Apresso di costoro* [viz., Thebani] *fù anco una Venere celeste, dalla quale veniva quel puro e sincero Amore, che in tutto è alieno dal congiungimento de i corpi, et un'altra ve ne fù, detta popolare et commune, che faceva l'Amore, d'onde viene la generatione humana.*' It is interesting to note that the classical type of Venus with a Cupid resting on her shoulder has been identified, rightly or wrongly, with this Venus Verticordia (cf. Roscher, *Bibl.*290; O.Jahn, *Bibl.*152; and E.Babelon, *Bibl.*18, VOL.I, p.383).

134a. Francucci, *l.c.*, stanza 382, describes the two 'nymphs' as follows:
'*Ambe son belle, ambe leggiadre, e altere,*
E di gratia celeste ambe fornite,
Si che ceder potrian di numer solo
De le tre Gratie all'amoroso stuolo.'
In stanza 396 he says that the Three Graces 'encircle with their arms the beautiful neck of Armilla.'

(Aglaïa, Euphrosyne, Thalia) by others directly indicative of their co-essentiality with Venus. They were called, for instance, *Pulchritudo, Amor, Voluptas,* or *Pulchritudo, Amor, Castitas* (both these inscriptions are found on medals by Niccolò Fiorentino, *fig.*124),[135] and this not in spite but because of the fact that it was normally a privilege of Venus herself to be identified with *pulchritudo.* From this point of view there is but little difference between the two interpretations of Titian's 'Education of Cupid.' In both cases the lady making her choice between Blind Cupid and Clearsighted Love would be a personification of Beauty, whether the three main figures be identified—as, I think, is the most appropriate way of putting it—with Venus Verticordia, accompanied by two *ninfe* standing for Marital Affection and Chastity, or with the 'Grace *Pulchritudo,*' accompanied by her 'sisters' *Voluptas* and *Castitas.*[136]

135. Cf. particularly A.Warburg, *Bibl.*387, VOL.I, PL.VII, *fig.*11 and pp.29 and 327, with quotation of a passage from Pico where he says: '*Qui* [viz., Orpheus] *profunde et intellectualiter divisionem* unitatis *Venereae in* trinitatem *Gratiarum intellexerit.*' Cf. also Ficino, *Conv.*, v,2, *Bibl.*90, p.1335, or the letter, *ibidem*, p.816. In the Commentary on Plotinus, *Ennead.*, 1,3 Ficino says that the three qualities of the Divine Mind, which is the primary beauty, '*quasi Gratiae tres se invicem complectentes ad integram pulchritudinem plenamque gratiam aeque conducunt.*'

136. A slightly later painter, Francesco Vanni (1565-1609), has connected the classical group of the Three Graces with the conception of Eros and Anteros by adding to it a blindfold Cupid asleep, and a clear-sighted one merrily fluttering about and shooting his arrows (Rome, Borghese Gallery, our *fig.*123). Achilles Bocchius, *Bibl.*37, SYMB.LXXX, p.170s., even entrusts Eros and Anteros to the Three Graces for education.

PLATE LVIII

107

PLATE LIX

PLATE LX

109

110

III

PLATE LXI

112

113

114

115

PLATE LXII

PLATE LXIII

117

PLATE LXIV

PLATE LXV

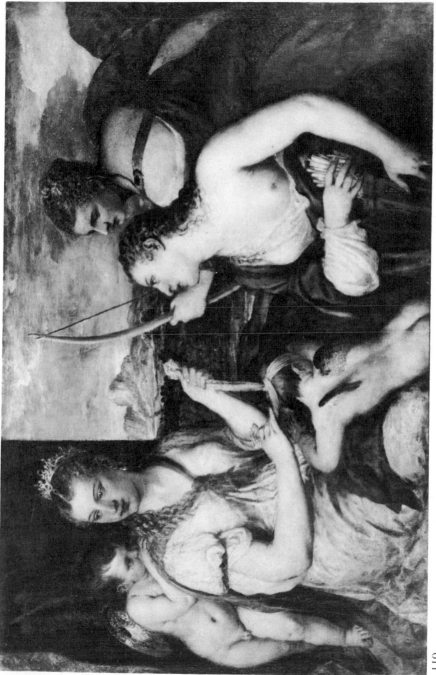

PLATE LXVI

PLATE LXVII

PLATE LXVIII

123

124

VI. THE NEOPLATONIC MOVEMENT
AND MICHELANGELO

MICHELANGELO was a man of tenacious and profound memory,' Vasari says, 'so that, on seeing the works of others only once, he remembered them perfectly and could avail himself of them in such a manner that scarcely anyone has ever noticed it.'[1]

That 'scarcely anyone has ever noticed it,' is easy to understand. For, Michelangelo, when exploiting the 'works of others,' classical or modern, subjected them to a transformation so radical, that the results appear no less

'Michelangelesque' than his independent creations. In fact a comparison between Michelangelo's 'borrowings' and their prototypes makes us particularly aware of certain compositional principles which are entirely his own and remained essentially unaltered until his style underwent the fundamental change discernible in his very latest works.[2]

We may take as an instance the motives inspired by Piero di Cosimo; we may compare the *Ignudo* on the left of Jeremiah or the statue of Giuliano de' Medici to the torso Belvedere; the Erythrean Sibyl to the central figure in Signorelli's youth of Moses; the group of fighters in the drawing Fr.157

1. Vasari, *Bibl.*366, vol..vii, p.277; K.Frey, *Bibl.*103, p.251.
2. See p.229.·

to a scene from Signorelli's 'Inferno;' the Madonna at the Stairs to neo-Attic funeral reliefs; or the twisted figure in the drawing Fr.103 (*fig.126*) to the burning Creusa seen in the Medea Sarcophagi (*fig.125*);[3] we can almost invariably observe the following changes:

(1) Through closing hollows and eliminating projections, the units, figures or groups, are condensed into a compact mass which strictly isolates itself from the surrounding space. Michelangelo's alleged statement that a good sculpture could be rolled down a hill without breaking, apocryphal though it is, is a rather good description of his artistic ideal.

(2) Whether we concentrate upon the two-dimensional pattern, viz., upon the aspect directly offered to the eye by a painting, by a relief, or by a statue when considered from one fixed point of view, or focus our attention on the three-dimensional volume: in both cases Michelangelo's figures differ from their prototypes by a sharp accentuation of what might be called the 'basic directions of space.' Oblique lines tend to be replaced by either horizontals or verticals; and foreshortened volumes tend

3. Drawings by or connected with Michelangelo are quoted as 'Fr.,' as far as illustrated in Karl Frey, *Die Handzeichnungen Michelagniolos Buonarroti*, (*Bibl.*102), and as 'Th.,' as far as not illustrated in this publication, but listed in H.Thode, *Michelangelo, Kritische Untersuchungen über seine Werke*, (*Bibl.*340), VOL.III, 1913. For Michelangelo in general see E.Steinmann und R.Wittkower, *Bibl.*323 (with supplement in E.Steinmann, *Bibl.*324) and the excellent article *Michelangelo* by K.Tolnay in Thieme-Becker's *Allgemeines Künstlerlexikon*, *Bibl.*349. For the influence of classical art on Michelangelo cf. particularly F.Wickoff, *Bibl.*397; A.Grünwald, *Bibl.*125 and *Bibl.*126; J.Wilde, *Bibl.*402; K.Tolnay, *Bibl.*351, especially p.103ss.; A.Hekler, *Bibl.*138 (cf., however, E.Panofsky, *Bibl.*246). For the instances adduced in the text cf. below and above (Piero di Cosimo); K.Tolnay, *Bibl.*351, p.112 (Madonna at the Stairs; a striking parallel is found in a *stele* from Syra, illustrated, e.g., in Springer-Michaelis, *Bibl.*320, *fig.*655); and E.Panofsky, *Bibl.*246. The motif of the drawing Fr.103, which was of course made from a living model posing in the attitude of the Creusa, was not only used in the Battle of Cascina but also, in a more developed form, in the fresco of the Deluge and the Libyan Sibyl. The influence of the Medea sarcophagi (C.Robert, *Bibl.*287, VOL.II, PL.LXII-LXIV) is also evident in the marble *tondo* in the Royal Academy at London (*fig.*127), the posture of the Infant Jesus being derived from the little boy stepping over the fragment of a column. It should also be noted that a lamenting figure by Bandinelli allegedly patterned after a dancing maenad and not very convincingly described as 'petrified in the act of running' (F.Antal, *Bibl.*8, p.71 and PL.9D) is in reality another adaptation of the Creusa, with only the right arm remodelled after a second prototype which may or may not have been a maenad.

to be either frontalized or orthogonalized (that is: made to meet the frontal plane at an angle of 90 degrees). Further emphasis is lent to the horizontal and vertical lines, as well as to the frontal and orthogonal planes by the fact that they frequently serve as *loci* for two or more significant points of the figure. As a result the whole arrangement, both in the picture-plane and in three-dimensional space, seems to be determined by an internal system of coordinates.

(3) The rigidity of this rectangular system operates, however, not as a static but as a dynamic principle. While some oblique motifs are eliminated, others are retained and gain emphasis by sharply contrasting with the basic directions. In addition symmetry often gives way to an antithesis between two halves, one 'closed' and rigid, the other 'open' and movable; and angles of 45 degrees are very frequent. Moreover the straight lines and plane surfaces are counteracted, as it were, by bulging convexities.

In drawings and unfinished sculptures these contrasts are further sharpened by the fact that the internal modelling is not effected by the prolonged curvilinear strokes which in a drawing by Dürer or Raphael seem to follow the swelling movement of the organic forms, but by short, straight cross-hatchings which contradict the roundness they are meant to indicate.

It is interesting, as a control, to compare the transformation of Michelangelo's works at the hands of his followers or copyists with the transformation of prototypes at the hands of Michelangelo. It appears that the imitators consistently eliminate precisely those features which we considered specifically Michelangelesque, thus bearing witness to the fact that Michelangelo's style is neither High Renaissance nor 'Manneristic,'[4] let alone Baroque.[5]

4. For the definition of Mannerism, which in Wölfflin's *Die Klassische Kunst* is still described as '*der Verfall*,' see W.Friedländer, *Bibl.*105 and 106; furthermore F.Antal, *Bibl.*9.
5. The number of instances is infinite. It is instructive to compare Raphael's well-known borrowings from Michelangelo, such as the drawings O.Fischel, *Bibl.*93, PL.81 (Battle of Cascina), 82 and 85 (David), 172 (St. Matthew), the crouching woman in the Deposition in the Borghese Gallery (Madonna Doni), the figures of children deriving from the Infant Jesus in the same picture (G.Gronau, *Bibl.*123) or the Fortitude in the Camera della Segnatura (combining the Ezekiel with the Isaiah) with their respective originals (*figs.*128, 129, 130).

High Renaissance figures are, as a rule, built up around a central axis which serves as a pivot for a free, yet balanced movement of the head, shoulders, pelvis, and extremities. Their freedom is, however, disciplined according to what Adolf Hildebrand has called the principle of *Reliefanschauung* which he mistook for a general law of art while it is merely a special rule applying to classical and classicizing styles: the volume is cleansed of its 'torturing quality'[6] so that the beholder, even when confronted with a statue worked in the round, might be spared the feeling of being 'driven around a three-dimensional object.' This is achieved by perfecting what I have called the 'two-dimensional pattern.' It is organized: first, so as to offer an harmonious aspect in itself (approximate symmetry; preference for moderate angles as opposed to rigid horizontals, verticals and diagonals; and emphasis of undulating contours which were always held to be particularly 'harmonious'); second, so as to clarify the structure of the three-dimensional bodies; the beholder is not expected to make up for 'deficiencies' by using his own imagination, but is presented with a picture free from excessive foreshortenings, obstructive overlappings, etc. Aesthetically, therefore, a High Renaissance statue is a relief rather than a 'round' object, and we can understand that Leonardo da Vinci denied the very idea of three-dimensional sculpture by stating that a statue was really nothing but a combination of two reliefs, one showing the figure from the front, the other from the back.[7]

The Manneristic *figura serpentinata*,[8] on the contrary, not only does not avoid but actually revels in what Hildebrand has called *das Quälende des Kubischen* ('the torturing quality of the three-dimensional'). The contor-

6. Adolf Hildebrand, *Bibl.*145, p.71 (and passim).
7. Leonardo da Vinci, *Bibl.*376, VOL.I, p.95: '*dice lo scultore che non può fare una figura, che non faccia infinite, per l'infiniti termini, che hanno le quantità continue. Rispondesi che l'infiniti termini di tal figura si riducono in due mezze figure, cioè una mezza del mezzo indietro, e l'altra mezza del mezzo inanti, le quali sendo ben proportionate, compongono una figura tonda.*'
8. The expression, allegedly coined by Michelangelo himself, is found in G.P.Lomazzo, VI, 4, *Bibl.*199, p.296.

tions and foreshortenings of Manneristic figures would be unaccountable if not supplemented by the imagination of the spectator. Consequently a Manneristic statue, far from allowing the beholder's eye to rest upon one predominant and satisfactory view, 'seems gradually to turn round so as to display, not one view but a hundred or more,' to quote Benvenuto Cellini, one of the chief representatives of this style.[9] Each of these views being just as interesting and, on the other hand, just as 'incomplete' as the other, the beholder feels indeed compelled to circulate around the statue, and it is not by accident that the Manneristic period abounds in free-standing statuary such as fountains and monuments, whereas High Renaissance statues were preferably placed in niches or set out against the wall.

In contrast with the Manneristic principle of 'multi-view,' or as I should like to call it, 'revolving-view' sculpture,[10] Baroque art tends to reinstate the one-view-principle, but on a basis entirely different from the *Reliefan-schauûng* prevalent in the High Renaissance. The Baroque abandons the Manneristic taste for entangled composition and contorted postures, not in favour of classic discipline and equilibrium, but in favour of seemingly un-limited freedom in arrangement, lighting and expression; and Baroque statues no longer drive us around themselves, not because the plastic units are flattened, as if to conform to an actual relief-plane, but because they are fused with the surrounding space into a coherent visual picture which is two-dimensional only in the same sense, and to the same extent, as the image on our retina. Thus the composition is *flächenhaft* only in so far as it con-forms to our subjective visual experience; it is not *flächenhaft* as an objec-tive design. Its aspect is comparable to that of the stage of a theatre, rather

9. Benvenuto Cellini, *Bibl*.63, p.231: '*La scultura si comincia ancora ella per una sol veduta, di poi s'incommincia a volgere poco a poco . . . e cosi gli vien fatto questa grandissima fatica con cento vedute o più, alle quali egli è necessitato a levare di quel bellissimo modo, in che ella si dimostrava per quella prima veduta.*' In his letter to Benedetto Varchi, Cellini somewhat more modestly claims '*otto vedute*' of equal perfection for every work of sculpture (G.G.Bottari and S.Ticozzi, *Bibl*.47, VOL.I, 1822, p.37).

10. Manneristic reliefs accordingly show sharp contrasts between a *relievo schiacciato* treat-ment and violently projecting motifs. Cellini's Deliverance of Andromeda is illustrated in A.Hildebrand, *Bibl*.145, *fig*.12 as a warning example.

than to that of a relief. Even free-standing monuments such as Bernini's Fountain of the Four Rivers on the Piazza Navona, or the innumerable garden statues of the seventeenth century, offer a plurality of one-view-aspects (each of them appearing 'satisfactory' in relation to the architectonic or quasi-architectonic environment) rather than an infinity of revolving-view aspects, as is the case with Manneristic works of a similar kind.

The mature style of Michelangelo, who was averse to free-standing statuary, differs from Mannerism, in that his figures, with a few well-justified exceptions,[11] force the beholder to concentrate upon one predominant view which strikes him as complete and final.[12] It differs from the Baroque, in that this predominant view is not based on subjective visual experience but on objective frontalization. And it differs from the High Renaissance in that the aesthetical and psychological effect of this frontalization is diametrically opposite to that obtained by the application of Hildebrand's relief principle. Michelangelo refuses to sacrifice the power of volume to the harmony of the two-dimensional pattern; in certain cases the depth of his figures even surpasses their width. He 'tortures' the beholder, not by driving him around the figure, but, much more effectively, by arresting him in front of volumes which seem to be chained to a wall, or half imprisoned in a shallow niche, and whose forms express a mute and deadly struggle of forces forever interlocked with each other.

The *figura serpentinata* of the Mannerists, presenting what I have called a 'revolving view,' seems to consist of a soft substance which can be stretched to any length and twisted in any direction. It conveys the impression of an insecure, unstable situation, which however could be transformed into classic equilibrium if the aimless versatility of the figures were directed by a stabilizing and controlling force. With Michelangelo such a controlling force is not absent. On the contrary, each of his figures is subjected, as we have seen, to a volumetric system of almost Egyptian rigidity. But the fact that this volu-

---

11. See, for instance, p.188, N.56 and p.233.
12. Cf. recently C.Aru, *Bibl.*15.

metric system has been forced upon organisms of entirely un-Egyptian vitality, creates the impression of an interminable interior conflict. And it is this interior conflict, and not a lack of outward direction and discipline, which is expressed by the 'brutal distortions, incongruous proportions and discordant composition' of Michelangelo's figures.[13] Their unhappiness is essential and inevitable, where that of their Manneristic parallels is accidental and conditional.

Undoubtedly, there was in the air at this time a cultural *malaise* caused by the recent realization of the incompatibility of mediaeval Christianity and classicism. But it is not only this discomfort of a transient historical situation which is reflected in Michelangelo's figures: they suffer from human experience itself. Inexorably shackled, they cannot escape from a bondage both invisible and inescapable.[14] Their revolt increases as the conflict sharpens; at times a breaking point is reached, so that their vital energies collapse. Even where no actual physical impediments are shown, as in the Slaves or the soldiers in the Battle of Cascina, their movements seem to be stifled from the start or paralysed before being completed, and their most terrific contortions and muscular tensions never seem to result in effective action, let alone locomotion. Consummate repose, on the other hand, is as absent from Michelangelo's world as achieved action. While the triumphal movement of the youthful conqueror in the Victory group (*fig.*173), and even the condemning gesture of Christ in the Last Judgment seem to be checked by reflective sadness, attitudes of repose do not connote peaceful tranquility but absolute exhaustion, deadly torpor, or fitful drowsiness.

Thus Michelangelo's figures are not conceived in relation to an organic axis but in relation to the surfaces of a rectangular block, the forms emerging

13. C.R.Morey, *Bibl.*224, p.62. Morey's sentences deserve to be quoted in full: 'Michelangelo's powerful inhibited figures reflect the disparity between Christian emotion and the antique ideal, free human will and the will of God: the rational forms of classic sculpture were not made for the ecstasy of a Christian mystic, they writhe in the possession of an unfamiliar spirit and betray by brutal distortion, incongruous proportions and discordant composition the force of the collision of mediaeval Christianity with the Renaissance.'
14. See p.196s.

from the stone as from the water in a slowly drained vessel.[15] They are modelled by the characteristic cross-hatchings which, even in a drawing, look like chisel-marks; they are confined to the limits of their plastic volume instead of merging with space; and their energies consume themselves in an internal conflict of forces mutually stimulating and paralysing one another. All these stylistic principles and technical habits have a more-than-formal significance: they are symptomatic of the very essence of Michelangelo's personality.

They reveal the almost totemistic feeling of the natural-born stone-carver who refused the title of sculpture to any work produced *'per via di porre'* (modelling in clay or wax) instead of *'per forza di levare'* (cutting directly in the 'hard, alpine stone'),[16] and was heart-broken when a carved piece of marble had met or was threatened with destruction.[17] They lend visual expression to the isolation of a man who shrank from contacts with his fellow-beings, and whose inclination for persons of his own sex was strong enough to inactivate, yet not strong enough to replace the ordinary forms of love.[18] And they reflect the convictions of a Platonic.

That Michelangelo's poetry is full of 'Platonic' conceptions was already observed by his contemporaries,[19] and is almost unanimously acknowledged

---

15. See Vasari's famous description of the 'Boboli' Slaves, *Bibl.*366, VOL.VII, p.272ss. (Frey, *Bibl.*103, p.247). It should be borne in mind that Vasari speaks of a 'model lying in a tub of water' only by way of a metaphor, meant to bring out the all-important fact that the forms 'emerge' from a plane surface, whether frontal or orthogonal.

16. For the distinction between sculpture *'per forza di levare'* and *'per via di porre'* see Michelangelo's letter to Benedetto Varchi, G.Milanesi, *Bibl.*216, p.522 (cf. also E.Löwy, *Bibl.*198, and K.Borinski, *Bibl.*44, VOL.II, p.169s. The phrase *'pietra alpestra e dura'* recurs persistently in Michelangelo's poetry; see, e.g., K.Frey, *Bibl.*101), no.LXXXIV; CIX, 50; CIX, 92.

17. Cf. Condivi's account of Michelangelo's rage about Bramante's careless treatment of the columns of Old St. Peter's (Frey, *Bibl.*103, p.110ss.), or his deep concern about the *'imbasamento'* in his long-forgotten vestibule of the Medicean Library at Florence (E. Panofsky, *Bibl.*249, especially p.272).

18. In connection with the 'movement without locomotion' so characteristic of Michelangelo's style it may be noted that, according to the psychoanalysts, an emotional situation of the above-mentioned kind may lead, in ordinary persons, to agoraphobia, because every impulse to move in a certain direction is checked by a reaction in the opposite sense.

19. See Francesco Berni, quoted, e.g., in Frey, *Bibl.*101, no.CLXXII, and Condivi, Frey, *Bibl.*103, p.204.

in modern scholarship.[20] True, even he, a Florentine whose worship and scholarly knowledge of Dante was a byword,[21] and whose writings fairly bristle with reminiscences of Petrarch,[22] could not prevent his thought and language from being tinged with pre-Ficinian elements. But this admixture is negligible in comparison with the importance of genuine Neoplatonism with which the pupil of Poliziano had come in contact as a boy. And just his serious study of Dante's *Divina Commedia* could not fail to deepen his interest in the doctrines of the 'Platonic Academy.' Nobody read Dante without a commentary. And of the ten or eleven editions of Dante printed before 1500 nine are provided with the Commentary by Cristoforo Landino in which every line of the poet is interpreted on Neoplatonic grounds, and is connected with the theories set forth in Landino's other writings. We know that Michelangelo was no less familiar with this commentary than with the Dante text itself;[23] and it is more than probable that he was also acquainted if not with Ficino's Latin works, with Pico's Italian Commentary on the *Canzona d'Amore* by Benivieni.[24]

20. Cf. particularly K.Borinski, *Bibl.*46; furthermore: L.von Scheffler, *Bibl.*301; V.Kaiser, *Bibl.* 161; J.Oeri, *Bibl.*233; E.Panofsky, *Bibl.*244, p.64 (with some emphasis on Aristotelian elements in Michelangelo's art-theory). Recently: G.G.Ferrero, *Bibl.*89; C.Tolnay, *Bibl.* 357; idem, *Bibl.*355; O.G. von Simson, *Bibl.*319, p.106ss.
21. See particularly, K.Borinski, Bibl.46, p.2ss. and passim.
22. See particularly G.G.Ferrero, *Bibl.*89, and K.Borinski, *Bibl.*46, p.19ss. It is interesting that quotations from Petrarch occur even among the casual notes found on some of Michelangelo's drawings, such as the '*Rott*' *è l'alta colonna*' on Fr.27, or the '*La morte el fin d'una prigione scura*' on a sketch-leaf in the Casa Buonarroti discovered and identified as *Trionfo della Morte*, II, 33 by C.Tolnay, *Bibl.*347, p.424. But it is even more interesting, because it shows Michelangelo's familiarity with Petrarch's Latin writings, that the '*etwas zweideutige*' line '*Valle lochus chlausa toto michi nullus in orbe*' on the drawing Fr.54, too, is a quotation from Petrarch: it is the first line of a short elegy on Vaucluse found in a letter to Philippe de Cabassoles, Bishop of Cavaillon:
> '*Valle locus clausa toto mihi nullus in orbe*
> *Gratior aut studiis aptior ora meis*'
(Petrarch, *Bibl.*264, VOL.II, 1934, p.330).
23. Cf. the passage from Donato Giannotti's *Dialoghi*, quoted in K.Borinski, *Bibl.*46, p.3.
24. There is a similarity between Michelangelo's vocabulary and that of Benivieni which can hardly be accidental. Suffice it to quote a few lines from Benivieni's *Canzona* (Pico, *Bibl.* 267, p.41v.) which may be compared to Michelangelo's Sonnet Frey, *Bibl.*101, XCI:
> ' . . . *quanto ellume*
> *Del suo uiuo splendor fia al cor mio scorta*' (st.1).

All this is not exceptional. With an Italian artist of the sixteenth century the presence of Neoplatonic influences is easier to account for than would be their absence. But among all his contemporaries Michelangelo was the only one who adopted Neoplatonism not in certain aspects but in its entirety, and not as a convincing philosophical system, let alone as the fashion of the day, but as a metaphysical justification of his own self. His own emotional experiences, reaching their first climax in his love for Tommaso Cavalieri, and their second in his friendship with Vittoria Colonna, approached the idea of Platonic love in its unadulterated sense. While the Neoplatonic belief in the 'presence of the spiritual in the material' lent a philosophical background to his aesthetic and amorous enthusiasm for beauty, the opposite aspect of Neoplatonism, the interpretation of human life as an unreal, derivative and tormenting form of existence comparable to a life in Hades, was in harmony with that unfathomable dissatisfaction with himself and the universe which is the very signature of Michelangelo's genius. As Piero di Cosimo might be called the only genuine Epicurean among the many artists influenced by Lucretius, Michelangelo might be called the only genuine Platonic among the many artists influenced by Neoplatonism.

Thus Michelangelo's verses, which strike the sensitive Italian ear as harsh and jagged, differ from the more euphonious productions of his contemporaries in that they have the ring of truth. In them the familiar Neoplatonic notions express the same psychological realities which are manifested in his works of art.

His stubborn preference for the laborious *'scoltura per forza di levare'*

> 'Ma perche al pigro ingegno amor quell'ale
> Promesso ha . . .' (st.1).

> 'Rafrena el uan disio . . .' (st.9).

> '. . . . . . quinc'eleuando
> Di grado in grado se nell'increato
> Sol torna, ond'e formato' (st.7).

> 'Quest'al ciel uolga, et quello ad terra hor pieghi' (st.2).

> 'Quel lume in noi, che sopr'aciel ci tira' (st.4).

and his preoccupation with the block-form gives a psychological meaning
to—and at the same time receives a philosophical meaning from—the poems
in which he reinstates Plotinus' allegorical interpretation of the process by
which the form of a statue is extricated from the recalcitrant stone.[25] The
preter-individual or even preter-natural beauty of his figures, not qualified by
conscious thoughts or distinct emotions,[26] but either dimmed as in a trance
or glowing with the excitement of a '*furor divinus*,' reflects—and is reflected
by—his Neoplatonic belief that what the enraptured mind admires in the
'mirror' of individual forms and spiritual qualities[27] is but a reflex of the one,
ineffable splendour of the light divine in which the soul has revelled before its
descent to the earth,[28] which it longingly remembers ever after,[29] and which
it can temporarily regain '*della carne ancor vestita.*'[30] And when Michelangelo speaks, as so many others had done and continued to do, of the
human body as of the '*carcer terreno*,' the 'earthly prison' of the immortal
soul,[31] he carried out this much-used metaphor in tortured attitudes of
struggle or defeat. His figures symbolize the fight waged by the soul to
escape from the bondage of matter. But their plastic isolation denotes the
impenetrability of their prison.

25. See Frey, *Bibl.*101, LXXXIII, LXXXIV, CI, CXXXIV; cf. above and E.Panofsky, *Bibl.*244, p.65 and
   Notes 59,157,281ss. with further references.
26. In this respect Michelangelo's idea of 'expression' is diametrically opposite to the
   classicistic conception according to which a figure is expressive only if the beholder can
   distinctly perceive not only what the person 'is' but also what he or she 'thinks' (H.Jouin,
   *Bibl.*158, p.56, lecture by Charles le Brun). Small wonder that, in Roger de Piles' '*Balance
   des Peintres*' Michelangelo rates only 8 for '*expression*' as against Raphael's 18 and Le Brun's
   16 (cf.J.Schlosser, *Bibl.*305, p.605).
27. See, e.g.Frey, *Bibl.*101, CIX, 99,104,105.
28. See, e.g., Frey, *ibidem*, CIX, 96,105.
29. See, e.g., Frey, *ibidem*, LXXV.
30. Frey, *ibidem*, LXIV.
31. Frey, *ibidem*, CIX, 103,105. For the Platonic sources of the much repeated comparison of
   the human body with a prison see W.Scott's notes to the treatise *Hermes de castigatione
   animae* (*Bibl.*313, VOL.IV,1936, p.277ss, especially p.335). In Plato's *Phaedo*, 62,B the word
   used is φρουρά; in *Axiochus* 377,D εἰρκτή. The *Corpus Hermeticum* has ἡ ἐν τῷ σώματι
   ἐγκεκλεισμένη ψυχή. For the expression '*salma*' (recurring in Frey, *Bibl.*101, CLII) cf. e.g.
   Marcus Aurelius' definition of man as a ψυχάριον βαστάζων νεκρόν, 'a little soul carrying a
   corpse.'

It is significant that Leonardo da Vinci, Michelangelo's adversary both in life and art, professed a philosophy diametrically the opposite of Neoplatonism. With Leonardo, whose figures are as free from restraint as Michelangelo's figures are 'inhibited,'[32] and whose *sfumato* principle reconciles plastic volume with space, the soul is not held in bondage by the body, but the body—or, to speak more precisely, the 'quintessence' of its material elements—is held in bondage by the soul. To Leonardo death does not mean the deliverance and repatriation of the soul which, according to the Neoplatonic belief, may return whence it came when the body has ceased to imprison it; it means, on the contrary, the deliverance and repatriation of the elements which are set free when the soul has ceased to bind them together: 'Behold,' says Leonardo, 'the hope and the desire for repatriation and for the return to our first state is similar to the urge which drives the moths into the light. Man who with continual longing and full of joy looks always forward to the new spring, always to the new summer, always to new months and new years—he does not realize that he wishes for his own destruction. But this wish is the quintessence, the very spirit of the elements, which finds itself imprisoned by the soul, and always longs to return from the human body to Him who has sent it forth.'[33]

Michelangelo's works reflect this Neoplatonic attitude not only in form and motifs but also in iconography and content, although we cannot expect them to be mere illustrations of the Ficinian system like Bandinelli's Combat between Reason and Sensuality (*fig.*107).[34] Where Bandinelli invents personifications to interpret the finer points of the Neoplatonic theory, Michelangelo resorts to Neoplatonism in his search for visual symbols of human life and destiny, as he experienced it.

32. C.R.Morey, *Bibl.*224, *l.c.*

33. J.P.Richter, *Bibl.*281, VOL.II, no.1162. '*Or vedi la speranza e'l desiderio del ripatriarsi e ritornare nel primo caso fa a similitudine della farfalla al lume, e'uomo che con continui desideri sempre con festa aspetta la nuova primavera, sempre la nuova state, sempre e nuovi mesi e nuovi anni . . . : E'non s'avede che desidera la sua disfazione; ma questo desiderio è la quintessenza, spirito degli elementi, che, trovandosi rinchiusa per l'anima, dallo umano corpo desidera sempre ritornare al suo mandatorio.*'

34. Cf. p.148s.

This Neoplatonic symbolism is particularly evident in the Tomb of Julius II and in the Medici Chapel.[35] For, from the earliest times of human history funerary art has manifested the metaphysical beliefs of man more directly and unequivocally than any other form of artistic expression.[36]

The ancient Egyptians wished to provide for the future of the dead rather than to glorify their past life. Funerary statues and reliefs, hidden from any human eye, were intended to supply the deceased with the necessities of after life: with plenty of food and drink, with slaves, with the pleasures of hunting and fishing, and, above all, with an indestructible body. The Kā, the roving spirit of the dead, would enter the burial chamber by a sham door, would slip into the funerary statue and use it, as the souls of living men employ their bodies, while the images on the walls would come to life in a magical way to serve the wishes of their master. The very immobility of Egyptian statues bears witness to the fact that they are not meant to portray a human being endowed with actual life, but to reconstruct a human body forever waiting to be enlivened by a magical power.

The Greeks, concerned with the life on earth rather than with the life in the Beyond and apt to burn their dead instead of mummifying them, reversed this outlook. The Greek expression for tomb is μνῆμα, that is: memorial; and classical sepulchral art became, accordingly, *retrospective* and *representational* where Egyptian sepulchral art had been *prospective* and *magical*. Attic *stelai* show heroes conquering the enemy, warriors dying in battle, wives taking leave of their husbands while preparing for the last voyage, and a Roman statesman or merchant could re-enact the stages of his career in the reliefs of his sarcophagus.[37]

With the decline of classical civilization and the concomitant invasion of oriental creeds an interesting reaction can be observed. Funerary art came again to be focussed on the future instead of on the past. But the future was

35. For Neoplatonic symbolism in the Sistine Ceiling see C.Tolnay, *Bibl.*357. For the drawings executed for Tommaso Cavalieri and related subjects see p.216ss.
36. Cf. A.della Seta, *Bibl.*316.
37. See K.Lehmann-Hartleben, *Bibl.*188, pp.231-237.

now conceived as a transition to an altogether different plane of existence, and not as a mere continuation of earthly life declared in permanence. While Egyptian funerary art had been a magical device to supply the dead with their physical abilities and material possessions, late-antique and Early Christian funerary art produced symbols anticipating their spiritual salvation. Eternal life was assured by faith and hope instead of by magic, and was thought of, not as a perpetuation of the concrete personality but as an ascension of the immortal soul.

In pagan instances this idea was directly expressed in such monuments as the *sarcophagi clipeati* where the images of the dead, encircled by a roundel or shell, are carried upward by Victories, and it was indirectly suggested by the representation of Bacchic scenes, or of suitable myths such as those of Ganymede, Endymion, Meleagros or Prometheus. Early Christian art could easily adopt both these devices with the only difference that Angels were substituted for the Victories and that Christian scenes and symbols took the place of pagan ones. Even the full-length portraits found in African *stelai* anticipate the future instead of commemorating the past: the deceased are shown as *orantes* frequently flanked by such symbols of salvation as birds, fishes, lambs or candlesticks.

For several centuries Christian funerary art refrained from depicting the past life of the dead, excepting of course the deeds of saints whose graves were shrines rather than tombs, and symbolical allusions to qualities and actions memorable from a strictly ecclesiastical point of view. Donors would be represented on their tombs with a tiny model of the church which they had built;[38] virtuous bishops would be portrayed piercing with their crozier a symbol of Vice or Infidelity.[39] To represent a charitable priest mourned by the

38. It is characteristic of the high social standing of French thirteenth-century architects that the donor's privilege of holding the model of a church was occasionally extended to the *magister operis* (cf. the tomb of Hugues Libergier, the builder of St. Nicaise at Reims, illustrated in E.Moreau-Nélation, *Bibl.*222, p.33).

39. The best known instance is the tomb-slab of Friedrich von Wettin in the Cathedral of Magdeburg, who with his crozier pierces a tiny image of the Spinario. In the thirteenth century prominent persons were also made to stand upon the lion and the dragon (according to Ps. xci), a type originally reserved to Christ, but already transferred to the Virgin

beggars whom he had supported during his life (*fig.*134) was about the maximum of permissible glorification according to the standards of around 1200.

The modest tomb-slab of this Presbyter Bruno, '*qui sua pauperibus tribuit*' (died 1194)[40] shows most of the features characteristic of the monumental Gothic wall tombs commonly known as *enfeus*.[41] These *enfeus*, ultimately derived from the niche-tombs equally frequent in pagan and Early Christian times, were intended to give visible form to the theory of salvation elaborated by High Mediaeval theology. The sarcophagus placed in an arched recess of the wall, serves as a *lit de parade* on which reposes the recumbent effigy of the deceased (*gîsant*), mourned by *pleureurs*, and flanked by priests performing the rites of the funeral service. This earthly scene is surmounted by the protective image of the Virgin Mary frequently accompanied by special saints, while the top of the archevault encircling the recess shows the ascension of the soul in the shape of a tiny human figure carried upwards by angels. The whole structure is crowned by the image of Christ or God the Father.

When the Gothic wave swept over Italy, this *enfeu*-scheme was widely adopted, Giovanni Pisano pointing the path towards its further development. The Angels, for instance, frequently draw curtains from the recumbent effigy instead of lifting the image of the soul, and thereby supplanted the officiating priests, while the *pleureurs* and the crowning image of Christ or God the Father are often dispensed with in later instances.[42] The general

in the twelfth century. The archbishop Philipp von Heinsberg (1164-1191; his tomb in Cologne Cathedral erected almost two hundred years after his death) pierces a lion with his crozier, and the slab is surrounded by a crenellated wall reminiscent of the city-wall which he had built.

40. Hildesheim, Cloister of the Cathedral, ill. e.g., in H.Beenken, *Bibl.*22, p.247. Cf. also the tomb of Martin Fernández in the Cloister of the Cathedral of Leon, with an elaborate charity scene on the sarcophagus, ill. in F.B.Deknatel, *Bibl.*71, *figs.*91-93. The coronation of German kings on the tombs of two Archbishops of Mayence (Siegfried von Eppstein and Peter Aspelt or Aichspalt) announces a somewhat contested privilege of their office, rather than illustrates their individual deeds.

41. Cf. L.Pillion, *Bibl.*268; and D.Jalabert, *Bibl.*153.

42. *Pleureurs* are still present in Tino da Camaino's tombs in S.Chiara at Naples; cf. W.R. Valentiner, *Bibl.*363, *fig.*4 and PL.60, 67, 70, 71.

arrangement, however, remained very much the same, even when the Gothic forms were replaced by classicizing ones, and is still recognizable in the representative wall-tombs of the early and high Renaissance.

The only fundamental change indicative of a new 'humanistic' feeling was the gradual intrusion of the biographical and eulogistic element which can be observed during the fourteenth century. Full-sized statues portraying the deceased as a living personality were placed above his recumbent image or even substituted for it.[43] Virtues and, later on, Liberal Arts were added in order to glorify his character and his accomplishments. In the reliefs adorning the sarcophagi princes were seen enthroned between their spiritual and secular councillors,[44] and even before the princes had thus been honoured, the Bolognese Professors had insisted on continuing their lectures, in effigy at least, beyond the grave.[45]

It was, however, not before the second or third decade of the fourteenth century that allegorical images and typified representations of a symbolical character were complemented by renderings of individual episodes or incidents, such as the scenes from the life of the Bishop Simone Saltarelli on his tomb in S. Caterina at Pisa (fig.133),[46] or the warlike exploits of the Scaligeri on their tombs in Verona.[47]

On the whole this revival of a retrospective attitude, frequently confined to mere additions to the time-honoured *enfeu*-arrangement, kept well within the limits of Christian traditions. Cases like the overbearing monuments of the Scaligeri or the Colleoni, whose equestrian statues surmount both secular

43. Cf. W.R.Valentiner, *ibidem*, passim. In Tino da Camaino's tomb of Bishop Antonio degli Orsi (Valentiner, p.63, PL.27,34) we find an interesting compromise: the bishop is represented seated, but with the closed eyes and crossed hands of a *gisant*.
44. See W.R.Valentiner, *ibidem*, PL.60,62,63,72ss.
45. See Corrado Ricci, Bibl.278. Sporadically the *scuola* scene is also found outside of Bologna, as in the tomb of Cino de' Sinibaldi in Pistoia, now attributed to Agnolo di Ventura, cf. W.R.Valentiner, Bibl.363, p.84 and p.11, *fig.1*.
46. See M.Weinberger, Bibl.392. In this beautiful tomb the motifs of angels drawing curtains and carrying the image of the soul appear in combination.
47. The tomb of Can Grande della Scala (died 1329) shows the personifications of the cities of Belluno, Feltre, Padua and Vicenza, as well as incidents from their conquest. For triumphal symbolism on Renaissance tombs see W.Weisbach, Bibl.394, p.98ss.

and religious scenes, are comparatively rare; and still rarer are such instances of positive paganism as Andrea Riccio's reliefs on the tomb of the great anatomist Marcantonio della Torre where no Christian symbol can be discovered, and the whole life of the scientist, including the performance of a genuine *Suovetaurilia* sacrifice, is re-enacted in purely classical costume and setting.[48]

The Quattrocento, particularly in Florence, even tended to restrict the complex iconography of the more sumptuous fourteenth-century tombs in favour of dignified simplicity and purity of design, a climax being reached in Bernardo Rossellino's Tomb of Leonardo Bruni (1444);[49] and it is not until the last third of the fifteenth century that classical subjects, chosen so as to permit a Christian interpretation, began to creep in, at first in rather inconspicuous places.[50] About the same time, the tombs of secular personalities showed the first symptoms of vaingloriousness. The figure of Fame however did not make its appearance in funerary art before the very end of the High Renaissance.[51] In fact the most distinguished monuments of the 'best period,' such as Andrea Sansovino's Rovere tombs in S. Maria del Popolo (1505-07) are intended to impress the beholder by their reticence rather than by their ostentation, at least as far as the iconography is concerned.

To determine the place of Michelangelo's Tomb of Julius II within the course of this development, we have to consider the initial projects—'surpassing every ancient imperial tomb in beauty and pride, richness of ornamentation and abundance of statuary'—[52] rather than the dismal structure ultimately erected in S.Pietro in Vincoli.[53]

48. See L.Planiscig, *Bibl.*269, p.371ss.; the *Suovetaurilia* scene illustrated in *fig.*487.
49. Here, as in Desiderio da Settignano's tomb of Carlo Marzuppini in the same church, the position and achievements of the deceased are only emphasized by the books in their laps.
50. Cf. A.Warburg, *Bibl.*387, vol.i, p.154ss. and F.Saxl, *Bibl.*298, p.108ss.
51. The figure of Fame in Michelangelo's project for the tomb of the *Magnifici* in the Medici Chapel (Fr.9a, our *fig.*150, see p.200) seems to be one of the earliest instances; but the idea was already abandoned in the following project Fr.9b, our *fig.*151.
52. Vasari, *Bibl.*366, vol.vii, p.164; Frey, *Bibl.*103, p.63.
53. For the history of the tomb, excellently surveyed by C.Tolnay, *Bibl.*349, see Thode,

According to the first project (1505) the Tomb was a free-standing monument of impressive dimensions (12 x 18 cubits, or 7.20 m x 10.80 m), with an oval burial chamber inside. The lower storey of the exterior was adorned with a continuous sequence of niches, each housing a Victory group and flanked by two herms to which were tied Slaves (*prigioni*) in varied attitudes. On the corners of the platform were four big statues, namely Moses and—according to Vasari—St. Paul, the *Vita Activa* and the *Vita Contemplativa*. A stepped pyramid rose to a second platform which served as a base for two Angels carrying what is variously termed an *arca* (coffin) or a *bara* (either bier or litter), and possibly was a *sella gestatoria* with the seated image of the Pope.[54] One of the Angels smiled 'as though he were glad that the soul of the Pope had been received among the blessed spirits,' the other wept 'as though he were grieved that the world had been deprived of such a man.'[55] In addition to the 'more than forty' statues of marble (their actual number was probably forty-seven) the Tomb was adorned with many decorative sculptures and several (probably six) bronze reliefs representing 'the deeds of so great a Pontiff' (*figs.*131,132).

In 1513, after the death of the Pope, it was decided to transform the monument into a curious hybrid between a mausoleum and a wall-tomb, projecting into space by 7.70 m. The iconographic program became even more complex. While the lower zone remained practically unaltered except for the change in proportions and its consequences, the number of the statues on the platform was increased to six, now placed at right angles to each other instead of diagonally.[56] On a large catafalque was seen the effigy

Bibl.340, VOL.I, p.127ss.; Tolnay, Bibl.347, 348, 353; J.Wilde, Bibl.401 and 403; E.Panofsky, Bibl.250.

54. Cf. E.Panofsky, *ibidem*.

55. Vasari therefore calls the first figure 'Cielo,' the god of heaven, and the second 'Cibale' (recte Cybele), the goddess of the earth. In doing this he may have had in mind Michelangelo's project for the Medici Chapel (cf. p.202).

56. This arrangement was very much in harmony with Michelangelo's stylistic principles. The Moses statue, being a corner-figure interlocked with its neighbour, had of course to have more than one acceptable view; yet the front view is definitely predominant. The same is true of the Rebellious Slave in the Louvre and two of the 'Boboli' Slaves (Thode, Bibl.340, VOL.I, p.213ss., no.I and IV), where the profile view is the predominant one.

of the Pope supported by four angels, two at his head and two at his feet, and this group was surmounted by a high apse (*capelletta*) projecting from the wall. It sheltered five very large statues, namely a Madonna and, probably, four Saints. The number of reliefs, on the other hand, was reduced to three, one in the centre of each front. In connection with this second plan the Moses (destined for the right front-corner of the platform) and the two Slaves in the Louvre (destined for the left-front corner of the lower storey) were executed during the following years, and the architectural parts still forming the lower storey of the Tomb in S.Pietro in Vincoli were completed by a skillful stone-mason (*figs.*135,136,137).

The year 1516 marks the beginning of a distressing process of reduction. What had been a three-dimensional structure now approached the form of a wall-tomb projecting by less than 3 m. The lower zone of the front remained, of course, unchanged, but the complicated upper structure planned in 1513 was given up in favour of a second storey flush with the lower one. Its central element was a niche with the Pope carried by angels, but their number was again reduced to two; its lateral parts had smaller niches with seated statues surmounted by square reliefs.

In 1526 this intermediary project shrank to a wall-tomb pure and simple, and in a contract of 1532 the parties agreed upon an arrangement similar to that envisaged in 1516, but no longer projecting from the wall and apparently not very different from the present structure. Setting aside the effigy of the Pope now reclining on his sarcophagus, the number of statues to be executed by Michelangelo was reduced to six: a Sibyl, a Prophet, a Madonna, the Moses—now transferred to the centre of the lower zone—and the two Louvre Slaves. The inclusion of these was an obvious *pis-aller*; they were included only because they happened to be ready, and because there was nothing else to fill the niches on either side of the Moses. But they no longer fitted into the program, and we can readily understand that, ten years later, Michelangelo himself proposed to withdraw them altogether and to replace them by the figures of Rachel and Leah personifying the contemplative and the active life. It was in this form that the Tomb was constructed in the years between 1542 and 1545.

However, just when the reduction to a simple wall-tomb had proved inevitable, that is around 1532, Michelangelo made one last desperate effort to compensate by plastic power the loss in architectural magnificence. He decided to discard the architecture completed in 1513-14 altogether so as to make room for four considerably bigger Slaves which in violence of movement and in power of volume (their depth is greater than their width) have never been equalled by any other sculpture classical or modern, and for new Victory groups of similar size. This plan was as sublimely unreasonable as Michelangelo's late projects for S.Giovanni dei Fiorentini where he also considered to discard everything already done in favour of a Utopian vision.[57] It was bound to fail. Only the four unfinished 'Boboli' Slaves, now preserved in the Accademia at Florence, and the Victory group in the Palazzo Vecchio (fig.173) bear witness to the most heroic episode in what Condivi calls *la tragedia della Sepoltura*.[58]

If the Tomb of Julius II, as described by Vasari and Condivi, had been carried out according to the project of 1505 (figs.131,132), the Pope would have entered the Beyond like a *triumphator*, heralded by Joy and followed by Lament. The reliefs would have immortalized his deeds; the slaves would have personified either the 'provinces subjugated by that Pontiff and made obedient to the Apostolic Church,'[59] or the Liberal and Technical Arts such as Painting, Sculpture and Architecture (in order to indicate that 'all the virtues were prisoners of death together with Pope Julius, because they

57. Cf. E.Panofsky, *Bibl*.237; C.Tolnay, *Bibl*.346, with further references.
58. Frey, *Bibl*.103, p.152. The fact that the dimensions of the 'Boboli' Slaves and of the Victory group are irreconcilable with the architecture executed in 1513-14 and extant in S.Pietro in Vincoli, as well as the late date of these works (C.Tolnay, *Bibl*.349, even dates them between 1532 and 1534) was proved by J.Wilde, *Bibl*.403. Wilde's brilliant hypothesis concerning the clay model in the Casa Buonarroti (Thode, *Bibl*.340, VOL.III, no.582, our fig.172), which according to him would have been destined for the companion-piece of the Victory group, is, however, not equally conclusive, and will be discussed in the appendix, p.231ss.
59. Vasari, First edition (1550); Frey, *Bibl*.103, p.66.

would never find a man to favour and nourish them as he had done')[60] or, eventually, both;[61] and the groups in the niches would have been Victories in the literal, not in a figurative sense.

Yet it would be a mistake to interpret the Tomb, even in this first version, as a mere triumphal monument *all' antica.*[62] True, the very idea of an actual mausoleum with an accessible burial chamber inside has something 'pagan' about it. The plastic decoration may have been influenced by the Arches of Constantine and Septimius Severus and by such fantastically classicizing structures as that in Filippino Lippi's fresco of St. Philip exorcizing the Dragon, which had just been finished when Michelangelo left Florence for Rome; and the contradictory and hesitating statements of the biographers may well reflect the popular opinion of their period.

Nevertheless, that the Tomb of Julius II can never have been meant to be a monument of mere human pride and glory, is evidenced: first, by the angels conveying the dead Pope to his eternal destination, an obvious development of a motif constantly found in the funerary art of the Middle Ages; and second, by the four statues on the platform which represented Moses and, probably, St. Paul with the personifications of the Active and the Contemplative Life.[63] These motifs are most certainly intended to open up

60. Condivi, (1553); Frey, *ibidem.*

61. Vasari, Second edition (1568), *Bibl.*366, VOL.VII, p.164; Frey, *ibidem.*

62. This interpretation has been championed by C.Justi, *Bibl.*160, and W.Weisbach, *Bibl.*394, p.109ss. Weisbach goes so far as to deny the connection of the Victory group with the Tomb of Julius II, because its iconography is not quite compatible with a triumphal symbolism in the narrower sense of the term.

63. Vasari, Second edition. Vasari's identification of the second male figure with St. Paul is unexceptionable, as a juxtaposition of Moses and St. Paul conforms to tradition, both from a biblical and a Neoplatonic point of view. His interpretation of the two female figures as *Vita Activa* and *Vita Contemplativa* may be open to question, as there is no documentary proof for the inclusion of these figures before 1542 when the figures of Rachel and Leah were introduced as substitutes for the discarded Louvre Slaves, whereas we know that the program of 1532 already included a Sibyl and a Prophet. Thus it would be theoretically possible that the two female figures planned in 1505 were Sibyls, not personifications of the Active and the Contemplative Life, and that the six seated figures planned in 1513, consisting in all probability of male and female figures in alternation, represented Moses, St. Paul, one Prophet and three Sibyls instead of Moses, St. Paul, one Sibyl, one prophet and the two personifications. On the other hand there is no positive reason to prefer this, or any other, conjecture to the statement of Vasari.

191

the vision of a realm beyond mere political and military struggles and triumphs. But this realm is not quite identical with the Christian Paradise hopefully depicted in the sepulchral monuments of an earlier period.

In these a sharp contrast is shown between the terrestrial and the celestial sphere, so much so that in the mediaeval *enfeus* and even in such Trecento monuments as the tomb of Bishop Saltarelli (*fig.133*) the effigy portraying the deceased as a physical being used to be distinguished from the little image of his soul. In the Tomb of Julius, however, heaven and earth are no longer separated from each other. The four gigantic figures on the platform, placed as they are between the lower zone with the Slaves and Victories and the crowning group of the two Angels carrying the *bara* with the Pope, serve as an intermediary between the terrestrial and the celestial spheres. Thanks to them, the apotheosis of the Pope appears, not as a sudden and miraculous transformation, but as a gradual and almost natural rise; in other words, not as a resurrection in the sense of the orthodox Christian dogma, but as an ascension in the sense of the Neoplatonic philosophy.[64]

According to the doctrine of the Florentine Academy as formulated by Landino the *vita activa* as well as the *vita contemplativa* are, we remember, the two roads to God, although active righteousness is only the prerequisite of contemplative illumination. And when Landino compares *iustitia* and *religio* to the 'two wings on which the soul soars up to heaven' this metaphor may well be applied to the two Angels, one deploring the end of a just and fruitful life of action the other rejoicing over the beginning of a life devoted to the everlasting contemplation of the Deity.

Moses and St. Paul were constantly grouped together by the Florentine Neoplatonists as the greatest examples of those who through a perfect synthesis of action and vision attained spiritual immortality even during their lives on earth. For, though Moses lives in the memory of mankind as a law-

64. See particularly K.Borinski, *Bibl.*46, p.96ss. and O.G. von Simson, *Bibl.*319, generally following Borinski, but with a fine comparison between the Tomb of Julius II and the earlier monuments which do not show an intermediary or transitional zone between the terrestrial and the celestial spheres (pp.48, 108).

giver and ruler rather than as a visionary, he, too, 'saw with the inner eye,'[65] and it is in the capacity of both a leader and an inspired prophet that he has been portrayed by Michelangelo. Given the fact that in the sixteenth century the word 'contemplative' had come to be used as a Neoplatonic term, Condivi's naïve description of the Moses as 'the captain and leader of the Hebrews, shown in the attitude of a contemplative thinker, his face full of light and the Holy Spirit, who inspires the beholder both with love and fear'[66] does infinitely more justice to Michelangelo's most famous sculpture than the still popular conception that Moses, after having sat down for unaccountable reasons, was angered by the dance around the Golden Calf, and was just on the verge of jumping up and shattering the tablets—an interpretation which would never have been invented had not the statue been banished from its predestined place. Michelangelo's Moses sees nothing but what the Neoplatonists called the 'splendour of the light divine.' Like the Sibyls and Prophets on the Sistine ceiling and the mediaeval Evangelists who are the ancestors of both,[67] he reveals by his suddenly arrested movement and awesome expression, not angry surprise but that supernatural excitement which, to quote Ficino, 'petrifies and almost kills the body while it enraptures the soul.'[68]

65. See p.140.
66. Condivi, Frey, *Bibl.*103, p.66.
67. The motifs of the Prophets and Sibyls are in part derived from the earlier Italian tradition (the Erythrean Sibyl from Signorelli, as mentioned above; the Delphian from Quercia—Fonte Gaia—and Giovanni Pisano; the Jeremiah from Ghiberti's St. John on the earlier door of the Baptistry, at Florence)—in part from classical art as is the case with the Isaiah and the Libyan Sibyl. The Zechariah and the Persian Sibyl are, however, connected with the Evangelists' type mostly used for St. Matthew, and the Joel bears a striking similarity with the Evangelist's type represented, for instance, by the St. John in the Reims Gospels, Morgan, M. 728, fol.141, illustrated in *Bibl.*228, PL.3. For the possible influence of mediaeval Evangelists' portraits on great Renaissance artists cf. H.Kauffmann, *Bibl.*162, p.89, PL.19.
68. The erroneous interpretation of the action of the Moses seems to have originated in the late Baroque period, when popular interest was focussed on the dramatic, and the Neoplatonic tradition had fallen into oblivion (cf. the sonnet by G.B.Zappi, 1706, published in Thode, *Bibl.*340,VOL.I, p.197); it has already been corrected by Borinski, *Bibl.*46, p.122ss. C.Tolnay has rightly pointed out that the Moses statue is a '*Weiterbildung der Propheten der Sixtinischen Decke*' (*Bibl.*349).

Thus the four figures on the platform symbolize the powers which assure immortality by acting as intermediaries between the terrestrial and the translunary world. Consequently the decoration of the lower storey, while glorifying the personal achievements of the Pope, symbolizes at the same time Life on Earth as such.

The significance of Victories and Prisoners was by no means confined to a triumphal symbolism in the narrower sense, unless they were destined to lend colour to a definitely pagan environment as is the case in the fresco by Filippino Lippi already mentioned. To a beholder of the sixteenth century, familiar with the tradition of the *Psychomachia*, if not with Neoplatonic ideas, a 'Victory' group would primarily suggest a moral struggle between good and evil, rather than a warlike triumph. Michelangelo's later Victory group was in fact always interpreted in a symbolical sense: Vincenzo Danti used it for a representation of Honour conquering Dishonesty; Giovanni Bologna transformed it into a Combat between Virtue and Vice; and Caravaggio, with an ironical twist characteristic of Michelangelo's most reluctant admirer, turned it into an illustration of the adage *Amor vincit omnia*.

Fettered Slaves, too, were familiar to the Renaissance as moral allegories. They were used as symbols of the unregenerated human soul held in bondage by its natural desires. It is most probably in this capacity that they appear in Antonio Federighi's Holy Water Basin in the Cathedral of Siena, which was well known to Michelangelo and has been rightly considered as a modest forerunner of the Julius Tomb (*fig.*138).[69] Not unlike mediaeval candlesticks,[70] it symbolizes a Christian universe, which, founded upon the four corners of the world and resting on the earth (the turtles), rises to the state of grace (the Holy Water) through the state of nature (the Slaves) and paganism (the *bucrania*). Furthermore in an engraving by Cristoforo Robetta (B.17) (*fig.*139) a contrast is shown between the free human mind

69. P.Schubring, *Bibl.*311, p.66, PL.11.
70. See Adolph Goldschmidt, *Bibl.*115, passim.

194

and enslaved human nature: the former is represented by a poised youth sublimely unsusceptible to the seductive powers of '*Wein, Weib und Gesang*' as personified by a satyr lifting a drinking horn, by a nude girl playing the harp, and by another nude girl offering her breast; the latter is fettered and writhes with agony.

Michelangelo's Slaves convey, however, a more specific meaning. It has been known for a long time that the 'Dying Slave' in the Louvre is accompanied by the image of an ape, emerging from the shapeless mass of stone, and it has been thought that this ape might be an attribute designating this Slave as a personification of Painting.[71] This explanation would agree with iconographic traditions, as well as with Condivi's assertion that the Slaves personified the Arts; but it is not compatible with the fact that an ape, more slightly but no less unmistakably sketched, is also connected with the Rebellious Slave: its round skull, low squarish forehead and protruding muzzle are clearly recognizable behind the Slave's left knee (*fig.*140). The ape can therefore not be interpreted as a specific symbol intended to distinguish one individual Slave from the other, but must be a generic symbol, meant to illustrate the meaning of the Slaves as a class.

Now the most common significance of the ape—far more common than its association with painting, let alone with the other arts and crafts—was a moral one: more closely akin to man in appearance and behaviour than any other beast, yet devoid of reason and proverbially prurient (*turpissima bestia, simillima nostri*) the ape was used as a symbol of everything subhuman in man, of lust, greed, gluttony and shamelessness in the widest possible sense.[72] Thus the 'common denominator' of the Slaves as indicated by

71. Thode, *Bibl.*340, VOL.I, p.181ss. Thode refers to the fact that the painter was frequently called '*scimmia della natura*' (for the history of this metaphor see E.Panofsky, *Bibl.*244, p.89, Note 95); but he could also have quoted Cesare Ripa, s.v. 'Pittura.'

72. Cf.e.g.Ripa, s.v. 'Sensi' (Gula) and 'Sfacciataggine;' furthermore E.Mâle, *Bibl.*207, p.334s. In mediaeval art the *fettered* ape or monkey thus symbolizes frequently the state of the world before the New Revelation (Annunciation in Aix, Ste. Madeleine; Lucas Moser's altarpiece at Tiefenbronn, where a fettered monkey and a broken statue, denoting paganism, serve to support the statue of the Virgin; Hubert van Eyck, Annunciation in the Metropolitan Museum of New York). In Renaissance art, this motif was often used to

the ape would be: animal nature. And this recalls to mind the fact that the Neoplatonists had termed the 'Lower Soul' *commune cum brutis*: that which man has in common with the dumb beasts. From this point of view the apes, designating the Lower Soul, are perfectly logical attributes of fettered prisoners. Tied as they are to the herms in which matter itself shows its face, as it were, the Slaves symbolize the human soul in so far as it is devoid of freedom. We may remember both the age-old similes of the *carcer terreno* and the *prigion oscura*,[73] and the Neoplatonic expression for the principle which binds the incorporeal soul to the material body: it was called *vinculum* which means both 'connecting link' and 'fetter.'[74] Some sentences in which Ficino describes the unhappy condition of the soul after its descent into the material world might serve as a paraphrase of Michelangelo's Slaves who were originally intended to be twenty in number, in countless attitudes of revolt and exhaustion[75] (needless to say that the 'Dying Slave' in the Louvre is not really dying): 'If a little vapour' (Ficino speaks of the effects of the *humor melancholicus* on mental health) 'can do that much to us, how much more must the celestial soul change from its original state when it falls, at the beginning of our lives, from the purity with which it was created, and is imprisoned in the jail of a dark, earthly and mortal body? . . . The Pythagoreans and Platonics say that our mind, as long as our sublime soul is doomed to operate in a base body, is thrown up and down with permanent dis-

designate the subjugation of base emotions in general, as is the case with Dürer's engraving B.42 (*fig*.143) or with the amusing illustration in Jacobus Typotius, *Bibl*.361, p.55s., with the *motto* '*Exacuerunt dentes suos*' meaning the suppression of the '*genius Luxuriae*' (*fig*.142). If Peter Breughel's Fettered Monkeys in the Berlin Museum (*fig*.141) are rightly interpreted as images of the blind and unhappy human soul (see C.Tolnay, *Bibl*.345, p.45), this interpretation would fit in with the idea expressed by Michelangelo.

73. See p.181.

74. Cf. p.136ss. Pico, *Heptaplus*, IV, I, *Bibl*.266, fol.5v., has the following definition: '*Verum inter terrenum corpus et coelestem animi substantiam opus fuit medio vinculo, quod tam distantes naturas invicem copularet. Hinc munere delegatum tenue illud et spiritale corpusculum quod et medici et philosophi spiritum vocant.*'

75. In addition to the two Slaves in the Louvre and the four 'Boboli' Slaves we have the six Slaves shown in the drawing Th.5 (the lower storey retaining the plan of 1505), the six Slaves in the drawing Fr.3 (1513), and various drawings and copy-drawings of single Slaves (cf. C.Tolnay, *Bibl*.353).

196

quietude, and that it *often slumbers* and is *always insane*; so that our movements, actions and passions are nothing but the *vertigos of ailing people*, the
dreams of sleepers and the *ravings of madmen*.'[76]

If the Slaves personify the human soul as enslaved by matter, and therefore comparable to the soul of dumb animals, the Victory groups personify
the *anima proprie humana*, that is: the human soul in its state of freedom,
capable of conquering the base emotions by reason. The Slaves and Victories
complement each other so as to give an image of human life on earth with its
defeats and Pyrrhic victories.

For, the mere victories of reason, worthy though they are of being praised
and glorified in the scenic reliefs with the 'deeds' of the Pope, are not sufficient to assure immortality. Terrestrial life, however meritorious, remains, we remember, a life in Hades. The lasting victory can only be
achieved through that highest power in the human soul which does not
participate in the terrestrial struggles and illuminates rather than conquers:
the *mens* or *intellectus angelicus*, whose two-fold aspect is symbolized by
the figures of the Active and the Contemplative Life and is personified by
Moses and St. Paul.

Thus the content of the Tomb of Julius II is a triumph not so much in a
political and military sense as in a spiritual one.[77] The Pope is 'immortalized'

76. Ficino, Letter to Locterius Neronius, *Bibl.*90, p.837, referred to p.138. The letter is
    inscribed '*Anima in corpore dormit, somniat, delirat, aegrotat.*' The passage here trans-
    lated reads: '*Si fumus quidam exiguus tantam in nobis vim habet,—. . . quanto magis cen-
    sendum est coelestem immortalemquem animum, quando ab initio ab ea puritate, qua
    creatur, delabitur, id est, quando obscuri terreni moribundique corporis carcere includitur,
    tunc, ut est apud Platonicos, e suo illo statu mutari? . . . Quamobrem totum id tempus,
    quod sublimis animus in infimo agit corpore, mentem nostram velut aegram perpetua
    quadam inquietudine hac et illac sursum deorsumve iactari necnon dormitare sem-
    perque delirare Pythagorici et Platonici arbitrantur, singulasque mortalium motiones,
    actiones, passiones nihil esse aliud quam vertigines aegrotantium, dormientium somnia,
    insanorum deliramenta.*'
77. This may also be true of the infrequent triumphal representations on other Renaissance
    tombs collected by W.Weisbach, *Bibl.*394, p.102ss. As K.Lehmann-Hartleben has shown,
    even in Roman times the representation of triumphal rites had already been transferred to
    funerary art and had been connected with the idea of an apotheosis in a religious sense
    (*Bibl.*189).

197

not only by temporal fame but also by eternal salvation,[78] and not only as an individual but also as a representative of humanity. In the true spirit of a philosophy which invested every visible thing with a transcendent meaning, scenic representations, allegories and personifications have been made subservient to a program which might be called an artistic parallel of Ficino's *Theologia Platonica* and *Consonantia Mosis et Platonis*; it defies the old alternative between the glorification of the life on earth and the anticipation of a life hereafter.

Significantly enough, this perfect balance of the pagan and the Christian was already considered somewhat unorthodox when the Pope had died. In the project of 1513 (*figs.*135,136,137) the Christian element was enormously strengthened by the addition of the *capelletta* with the Madonna and Saints, an obvious reversion to the *enfeu* type. In 1542, when Slaves and Victories alike had been discarded, the symbolization of the terrestrial sphere was eliminated altogether. The final result bears witness not only to an individual frustration of the artist, but symbolizes also the failure of the Neoplatonic system to achieve a lasting harmony between the divergent ten-

78. The classical prototype for the lower storey of the Tomb of Julius II, a sarcophagus in the Vatican (illustrated in E.Panofsky, *Bibl.*250, with further references), seems to convey comparatively similar ideas as to the life on earth and immortality: according to Prof.K. Lehmann-Hartleben the representation of husband and wife led to the door of Death, which is adorned with representations of the Four Seasons (symbols of time) and is flanked by nude *genii* surmounted by Victories, would announce the reunion after death and the bestowing of the 'crown of life.'

dencies in post-mediaeval culture: a monument to the 'consonance of Moses and Plato' had developed into a monument to the Counter-Reformation.

Michelangelo's second great project in the field of funerary art, the Medici Chapel,[79] did not fully materialize either. But in this case the present monument, left unfinished in 1534 when Michelangelo departed from Florence forever, is an incomplete, yet not a distorted document of his ultimate intentions. The definitive program, already established towards the end of 1520,[80] can be called a more elaborate restatement of the ideas embodied in the second project for the Tomb of Julius II, where the 'Platonic' element had been subordinated, but not sacrificed to the Christian one. Yet Michelangelo did not directly pursue these ideas, but rather reverted to them after several tentative steps in other directions.

When Lorenzo de' Medici the Younger had died in 1519, it was decided to use the New Sacristy of S.Lorenzo as a memorial chapel for the younger generation of the family in the same way as the Old Sacristy had been used for the older one. It had to house the tombs of the two *Magnifici*, Lorenzo the Magnificent (died 1492) and Giuliano (killed by the Pazzi in 1478), and of the two *Duchi*, Lorenzo the Younger, Duke of Urbino, and Giuliano the Younger, Duke of Nemours (died 1516).[81]

Originally Michelangelo had planned to unite these four tombs in a free-standing structure, either conceived as one massive piece of masonry, (drawing Fr.48, *fig.*146) or as a so-called Janus Arch (*arcus quadrifrons*).[82]

79. For the history of the Medici Chapel cf. particularly Thode, *Bibl.*340, vol.I, p.429ss.; A.E.Popp, *Bibl.*273; C.Tolnay, *Bibl.*354.
80. Cf. C.Tolnay, *ibidem*, p.22.
81. The idea of adding to these four tombs those of the two Medici Popes Leo X and Clement VII turned up too late to affect the general scheme (May 23, 1524). The only solution Michelangelo could think of would have been to place the papal tombs in the small annexes (*lavamani*), but the whole idea was soon discarded.
82. According to this plan—brought to light by C.Tolnay, *Bibl.*354—the four sarcophagi would have been placed on top of the four arches while the tomb of the Cardinal Giulio Medici (later on Pope Clement VII) would have found its place beneath the crossing.

This project[83] was renounced in favour of two double tombs on either side-wall, one for the *Duchi*, the other for the *Magnifici*, while the entrance wall opposite the altar would have been adorned with a Madonna flanked by statues of the Medicean family-Saints, Cosmas and Damian (drawing Fr.47, *fig.*147; developed by simply doubling the front shown in Fr.48).

The ultimate solution was found by allotting the side-walls to the *Duchi* alone, while the 'Sacra Conversazione' on the entrance wall was merged with the tombs of the *Magnifici* into a unified composition. Original studies for this curious combination of double wall-tomb and altarpiece are the drawings Fr.9a and 9b. In Fr.9a (*fig.*150) the structure is not yet axialized and includes no effigies, but in the centre of a zone inserted between the sarcophagi and the 'Sacra Conversazione' is seen the figure of Fame which 'holds in place' the memorial tablets.[84] In Fr.9b (*fig.*151) the composition is more rigidly co-ordinated, and seated statues of the deceased are placed in the intermediary zone the centre of which remains empty. A plan more closely approaching the definitive arrangement is transmitted through a great number of copies which tend to show that ultimately the intermediary zone was abandoned altogether while smaller statues in round-topped niches were placed above the two Saints (*fig.*152).[85]

As for the single tombs of the *Duchi*, only one unquestionable sketch,

83. See the drawings Fr.48,125a,267b,39,70(C.Tolnay, *Bibl.*354, *fig.*8-12). Another sketch on Fr.70 (Tolnay, *fig.*16) might also refer to the free-standing monument; that the projection of the sarcophagi on the receding sides is not shown would not militate against this assumption because the same omission can be observed in Fr.48. The identification of the sketch Fr.39 centre (Tolnay, *fig.*10) with the Janus Arch project seems somewhat doubtful in view of the fact that the big arches are bridged by a horizontal architrave which would seem to presuppose a massive structure as in Fr.125a (Tolnay, *fig.*9).

84. The inclusion of this figure which is very slightly sketched, seems to be a kind of after-thought. The explanation '*La Fama tiene gli epitaffi a giacere*' should be translated: 'Fame holds the epitaphs in position.' The word *epitaffi* cannot mean recumbent effigies, but only the tablets; this agrees with the position of the figure in the drawing and with the fact that the project included no effigies.

85. Drawing Th.531a (A.E.Popp, *Bibl.*273, PL.28); cf. Th.246b,386a,424,459b,462,531b. A.E.Popp, p.131, has shown that the effigies seen in these copies were hardly ever planned by Michelangelo. For the drawing Th.241 (Popp, PL.30a and K.Borinski, *Bibl.*46, *fig.* facing p.136), see Popp, p.129s.

Fr.55, has come down to us (*fig.*148; cf. also *fig.*149),[86] and even here the tomb seems to be a single one by appearance, rather than in iconography and destination. On the whole the drawing Fr.55 is much closer than any other study to the architecture, statues, and models actually executed.[87] But the space in the centre, being an exact square, would not be suitable for a portrait statue, whereas the seated figures which flank the sarcophagus and are not paralleled in the actual arrangement give the impression of portrait statues rather than of allegorical figures, let alone saints.[88] Thus it seems more probable that the drawing Fr.55, although it shows only one sarcophagus, was originally intended for the double tombs (Verrocchio's famous sarcophagus in the Old Sacristy also houses the bodies of two persons, Giovanni and Piero dei Medici). Subsequently the composition was adopted for the single tombs as executed, whereby, of course, the two seated statues on either side of the sarcophagus had to be eliminated.[89]

This material, incomplete though it is, enables us to observe the growth of the iconographical program. The free-standing monument sketched in Fr. 48 included only reliefs—four of which probably represented the Four Seasons and thereby symbolized the idea of time in an as yet traditional form—[89a] and eight statues of mourners. The Madonna with Saints, the effigies of the deceased and River-Gods reclining beneath the sarcophagi were planned in connection with the double-tomb project (Fr.47), and the idea of substituting the Times of Day for the Four Seasons seems to appear still somewhat later (Fr.55 and marginal sketch on Fr.47).

86. Whether the drawing Fr.39, right upper sketch (C.Tolnay, *Bibl.*354, *fig.*13) refers to the single wall-tombs, or renders one side of the free-standing monument is a matter of surmise.

87. Except for the drawing Th.511 a (A.E.Popp, *Bibl.*273, PL.29), which is a free variation on the basis of both preliminary studies and the tombs as executed, cf. A.E.Popp, p.134.

88. Cf. the drawing Fr.9b.

89. This interpretation, generally not accepted in recent literature, has been proposed by B.Berenson, *Bibl.*28, no.1497. The close connection of Fr.55 with the double wall-tomb phase is also evidenced by the fact that one of the reclining figures seen in Fr.55 is sketched on Fr.47.

89a. Cf. A.E.Popp, *Bibl.*273, p.130 and 165ss.

The definitive program included the following features:

(1) The double tomb of the *Magnifici* facing the altar ('*la sepoltura in testa*,' as Michelangelo calls it), *fig.153*. Above the imageless sarcophagi it would have shown the 'Medici Madonna' flanked by the statues of Saints Cosmas and Damian as extant in S.Lorenzo; and, above these, smaller statues one of which has been identified with the David in the Bargello.[90]

(2) The tombs of Giuliano and Lorenzo de' Medici (*figs.144,145*). In addition to the figures extant in S.Lorenzo, viz., the seated statues of the Dukes and the four Times of Day, they would have shown:

(a) Two River-Gods reclining on the base of either tomb (the model for one of them preserved in the Accademia at Florence). (b) Statues of the grieving Earth and the smiling Heaven in the niches flanking the statue of Giuliano,[91] the figure of Earth of course above the Night, the figure of Heaven above the Day.[92] The subject of the corresponding statues in the tomb of Lorenzo is a matter of surmise; possibly they were to be either Truth and Justice according to Psalm lxxxiv, 12: 'Truth shall spring out of earth, and righteousness shall look down from heaven,' or something like Landino's *Iustitia* and *Religio*.[93] (c) An elaborate plastic decoration of the entablature already shown in the drawing Fr.55: it consisted of empty thrones on top of the coupled pilasters, which can still be seen in the Medici Chapel, though they have been deprived of their richly ornamented backs;[94] of trophies in the centre;

90. This identification was made by A.E.Popp, *ibidem*, p.141s.
91. Note on Fr.162; cf. Vasari, *Bibl.*366, VOL.VI, p.65; Frey, *Bibl.*103, p.360.
92. Cf. the drawing Th.511a, where, however, right and left has been reversed. In this drawing Day is characterized as Sol and Night as Luna.
93. Cf. p.138s. That the two statues on either side of Lorenzo de' Medici should have represented the elements Fire and Water (A.E.Popp, *Bibl.*273, p.164) is not very probable because the figures of 'Cielo' and 'Terra,' the former smiling, the latter grieving, personify heaven and earth in a metaphysical sense, and not in the sense of the elements Air and Earth. The four elements are properly symbolized by the River-Gods in the lowest zone of the composition (cf.below).
94. The reasons for this curtailment are as yet not fully elucidated. A careful study for the empty thrones is preserved in the drawing Fr.266.

and of two pairs of crouching children, one of whom has been identified with the Crouching Boy in Leningrad,[95] above the lateral niches.

In addition it was planned to adorn the large lunettes surmounting the three tombs with frescoes. In the lunette above the tomb of the *Magnifici* would have been depicted the Resurrection of Christ (drawings Fr.19 and 59), while the lunette above the Tombs of the *Duchi* would have shown the Brazen Serpent on the one hand (drawing Fr.51) and, possibly, the story of Judith on the other.[96]

It has been observed that both the statues of Giuliano and Lorenzo de' Medici are turned towards the Madonna.[97] It is, indeed, to the *sepoltura in testa* that they have to turn in order to behold the mediators of salvation, the Virgin Mary and the saints, and the great testimony of immortality in the strictly Christian sense, the Resurrection of Christ.

At the same time each of the ducal tombs depicts an apotheosis as conceived by Ficino and his circle: the ascension of the soul through the hierarchies of the Neoplatonic universe.[98]

As will be remembered, the Florentine Neoplatonists called the realm of matter *il mondo sotterraneo* and compared the existence of the human soul, while it is 'imprisoned' in the body, to a life *apud inferos*.[99] It is therefore

95. This identification, too, is due to A.E.Popp, *Bibl.*273, p.142.
96. That the drawings Fr.19,59 and 51 were probably destined for the decoration of the lunettes in the Medici Chapel was first realized by A.E.Popp, *l.c.*,p.158ss. That the Judith scene (prefiguration of the Virgin's Victory over the Devil) might have been envisaged as a counterpart of the Brazen Serpent (prefiguration of the passion of Christ) is suggested by the Sistine Ceiling and the apocryphal drawing Fr.306 which seems to reflect a Michelangelesque composition of the third decade, not unsuitable for the space to be filled.
97. C.Tolnay, *Bibl.*355.
98. The 'Platonic' interpretation of the Medici Chapel was suggested by V.Kaiser, *Bibl.*161 and J.Oeri, *Bibl.*233; it was elaborated by K.Borinski, *Bibl.*46, p.97ss., whose opinions were accepted by O.G.von Simson, *Bibl.*319, p.106ss., and was definitely established by C.Tolnay, *Bibl.*355. In spite of Borinski's uncritical attitude toward the material and his numerous factual errors, he deserves to be given credit for having realized that an interpretation of Michelangelo's works ought to be based on the Florentine Neoplatonists rather than on Plato himself, and for having called attention to the sources in question. The following analysis is greatly indebted to both Borinski and Tolnay.
99. See p.134.

not hazardous to indentify the River-Gods, placed as they are at the very
bottom of the monuments, with the four rivers of Hades: Acheron, Styx,
Phlegethon and Cocytus. These rivers played an important role in Plato's
Phaedo[100] as well as in Dante's *Inferno*; but the Florentine Neoplatonists
interpreted them in a very different fashion. With Plato as well as with
Dante they signify the four stages of expiatory punishment awaiting the
human soul after death. With Landino and Pico they signify the fourfold
aspect of matter enslaving the human soul at the moment of birth. As soon as
it has left its supercelestial home, and has passed the river Lethe which makes
it forget the happiness of its former existence, it finds itself 'deprived of joy'
(Acheron, supposedly derived from Greek ἀ and χαίρειν, to rejoice): it
is stricken by sorrow (Styx); it falls prey to 'burning passions such as mad
wrath or fury' (Phlegethon, from Greek φλόξ, flame); and it remains sub-
mersed in the swamp of everlasting tearful grief (Cocytus, from Greek
κώκυμα, lament, or, to quote Landino, *il pianto che significa confermato
dolore*).[101] Thus the four rivers of Hades stand for 'all those evils which
spring from one single source: matter,'[102] and which destroy the happiness
of the soul: 'The deep gorge of the senses is always shaken by the floods of
Acheron, Styx, Cocytus and Phlegethon,' as Marsilio Ficino puts it.[103] And
so popular was this Neoplatonic interpretation of the four subterranean
rivers that it even turns up in Vincenzo Cartari's *Imagini*.[104]

100. Cf. J.Oeri, *Bibl.*233; K.Borinski, *Bibl.*46, p.130ss.; O.G. von Simson, *Bibl.*319, p.107; C.Tol-
nay, *Bibl.*355, p.305.
101. Landino, Commentary on Dante, *Inferno*, xiv, 116, *Bibl.*180, fol.LXXI,v. (cf. also *ibidem*,
on *Inferno*, iii, 78, fol.xxi; furthermore Landino, *Bibl.*179, fol.K2ss.)
102. Landino, *Bibl.*179, fol.K2ss. 'Ex Hyle igitur unico flumine mala haec omnia eveniunt.'
103. Ficino, Letter to Andrea Cambino, *Bibl.*90, p.671.
104. V.Cartari, *Bibl.*56, p.145: '*Circonda questa Palude l'Inferno, perchè altrove non si trova
mestitia maggiore, et perciò vi fu anco il fiume Lete, Acheronte, Flegetonte, Cocito, et altri
fiumi, che siginificano pianto, dolore, tristezza, ramarico et altre simili passioni, che sen-
tono del continuo i dannati. Le quali i Platonici vogliono intendere, che siano in questo
mondo, dicendo che l'anima allhora va in Inferno, quando discende nel corpo mortale,
ove trova il fiume Lete, che induce oblivione, da questo passa all'Acheronte che vuol dire
privatione di allegrezza, perchè scordatasi l'anima le cose del Cielo . . . , et è perciò cir-
condata dalla Palude Stigia, et se ramarica sovente, et ne piange, che viene a fare il fiume
Cocito, le cui acque sono tutte di lagrime et di pianto, si come Flegetonte le hà di fuoco*

If, then, Michelangelo's River-Gods stand for what Pico calls the *mondo sotterraneo*, that is: the realm of sheer matter, the Times of Day occupying the next higher zone of the ducal monuments stand for the terrestrial world, that is: the Realm of Nature, built up of matter and form. This realm which includes the life of man on earth is in fact the only sphere subject to time. Sheer matter is no less eternal and indestructible than pure form, and the celestial spheres produce time without being subject to it. It is only the transient union of matter and form in nature which is bound to begin and to come to an end.

That the figures of Dawn, Day, Evening and Night are primarily intended to designate the destructive power of time is evidenced by Michelangelo's own words 'Day and Night speak; and they say: with our fast course we have led to death the Duke Giuliano,'[105] as well as by Condivi's statement that Day and Night together were intended to symbolize *il Tempo che consuma il tutto*; according to him Michelangelo had even planned to add a mouse to these two figures, 'because this little animal continually gnaws and consumes like all-devouring time.'[106]

et di fiamme, che mostrano l'ardore dell'ira et de gli altri affetti, che ci tormentano mentre che siamo nell' inferno di questo corpo.'

105. '*Il Dì e la Notte parlano, e dicono: Noi abbiamo col nostro veloce corso condotto alla morte il duca Giuliano*' (Fr.162 and Frey, *Bibl.*101, XVII). Parallels are found in the earlier tradition, e.g. in a German woodcut of around 1470 (F.M.Haberditzl, *Bibl.*129, I, p.168 and PL.CVIII, also illustrated in E.Panofsky, *Bibl.*243, PL.LXVIII, *fig.*102), where Day and Night, symbolized by the sun and the moon, speak the following lines:
'wir tag und nacht dich ersleichen
des kanstu n(it ent)weichen.'
That the rest of Michelangelo's text refers to the Neoplatonic doctrine of immortality (C.Tolnay, *Bibl.*355, p.302), is however hardly provable. For the interpretation of the line: '*Che avrebbe di noi dunque fatto, mentre vivea?*' ('What would he have done with us when alive?') as 'What would his *soul* have done with us if he *had lived* longer?' (that is: 'if his soul would exercise an even greater power owing to his longer life on earth?') is not borne out by the text. The introduction of Fame into the project Fr.9a would seem to show that Michelangelo, before his plans had ripened, was not absolutely opposed to elaborate, allegorical eulogies.
106. Condivi, Frey, *Bibl.*103, p.136: '*. . . significandosi per queste il Giorno et la Notte o per ambi duo il Tempo, che consuma il tutto. . . . Et per la significatione del tempo voleua fare un topo . . . percioche tale animaluccio di continuo rode et consuma, non altrimenti chel tempo ogni cosa diuora.'* For the motif of the mouse, see p.81, N.42.

However, in the Medici Chapel this idea has taken shape, not in conventional allegories or personifications of time such as the Four Seasons as originally planned, but in four figures which, unprecedented in earlier iconography, convey the impression of intense and incurable pain. Not unlike the Slaves in the Tomb of Julius II they seem to 'dream, to sleep, to ail and to rage:' The 'Aurora' awakening with deep disgust at life in general, the 'Giorno' convulsed with causeless and ineffective wrath, the 'Crepuscolo' exhausted with ineffable fatigue, and even the 'Notte,' with her eyes not fully closed, not finding real rest.

Thus, while the four River-Gods depict the fourfold aspect of matter as a source of potential evil, the four Times of Day depict the fourfold aspect of life on earth as a state of actual suffering; and it is easy to see the intrinsic connection between the two sets of figures. For a Renaissance thinker it was self-evident that the four forms of matter symbolized by the four rivers of Hades could only be the four elements, Acheron standing for air, Phlegethon for fire, Styx for earth, and Cocytus for water.[107] On the other hand these same four elements were unanimously held to be coessential with the four humours which constitute the human body and determine human psychology. And these four humours were in turn associated, among other things, with the four seasons, and with the four times of day: air was associated with the sanguine temperament, with spring and with morning; fire with the choleric temperament, with summer and with midday; earth with

---

107. See Pico, 1,9, *Bibl.*267 fol.12ss., and Ficino, *Argumentum in Phaedonem, Bibl.*90, p.1394: '*Acheron . . . respondet quoque aeri partique mundi meridianae. Phlegethon igni respondet atque orienti . . . Styx Cocytusque respondet terrae atque occasui*' (cf. also *Theol. Plat.*,XVIII,10, *Bibl.*90, p.421). However, Ficino's philological conscience prevented him from whole-heartedly accepting the interpretation of the rivers in Hades as symbols of the material elements and their qualities, for he realized that Plato speaks of them in a purely eschatological sense: '*quae* [viz., flumina] *quisquis secundum nostri corporis humores animique perturbationes* in hac vita *nos affligentes exponit, nonnihil adducit simile vero, veruntamen veritatem integram non assequitur. Plato enim et hic et in Republica significat praemia virtutum et supplicia vitiorum* ad alteram vitam *potissimum pertinere.*' (*Argum. in Phaed., l.c.*; roman is mine.)

the melancholy temperament, with autumn and with dusk; and water with the phlegmatic temperament, with winter and with night.[108]

According to this cosmological scheme which has already been mentioned in connection with Bronzino's so-called 'Flora' tapestry and has preserved its poetic appeal throughout the centuries, Michelangelo's Times of Day comprise indeed the whole life of nature, based as it is on the four elements,[109] and can thus be connected with the four River-Gods in a perfectly consistent way. Acheron, the 'Joyless,' would have had his place beneath the Aurora, for both Acheron and dawn were held to correspond to the element of air and to the sanguine humour; Phlegethon, the 'Flaming,' beneath the Giorno, for both Phlegethon and midday were held to correspond to the element of fire and to the choleric humour; Styx, the 'Mournful,' beneath the Crepuscolo, for both Styx and evening were held to correspond to the element of earth and to the *humor melancholicus*; and Cocytus, the 'Swamp of tears,' beneath the Notte, for both Cocytus and night were held to correspond to the element of water and to phlegm.

Michelangelo's Times of Day do not 'personify,' of course, the Four Temperaments. They illustrate, however, the various disturbing and depressing influences to which the human soul is subjected as long as it lives in a body composed of four 'material' principles. With the Neoplatonists, and especially with Michelangelo who was emotionally incapable of producing a really joyful or a really restful figure, the 'sanguine' and the 'phlegmatic' conditions differ from the 'choleric' and the 'melancholy,' but they are by no means happier ones. A contemporary beholder conversant with the

108. See Ficino's expression '*corporis humores animique perturbationes*' in the passage quoted in the preceding note. For the identification of Night with water cf. also the phrase '*nox umida*' in Virgil, *Aen.*,v,738 and 835.
109. E.Steinmann was quite right in assuming that the Times of Day imply, in a way, the action of the elements and the humours (*Bibl.*322). He committed, however, the mistake, first, of basing himself almost exclusively on a carnival song ('*man stutzt von vorn herein,*' says Thode), which is but a feeble reflex of a great cosmological tradition; second, of disregarding the program in its entirety; third, of connecting the four figures with the four elements, etc. at random, instead of on the basis of the established tradition.

theory that melancholy distress can be caused by each of the four humours, including the sanguine, might have interpreted the four Times of Day as paradigms of the *melancholia ex sanguine*, the *melancholia ex phlegmate*, the *melancholia ex cholera rubra* and the *melancholia ex cholera nigra*.[110]

From the inert realm of matter and from the tortured, time-ruled realm of nature there emerge the images of Giuliano and Lorenzo, the latter known as the 'Pensieroso,' or 'Pensoso,' from the sixteenth century.[111] These images, so impersonal in character as to astonish Michelangelo's contemporaries and flanked by figures announcing the transition from a lower form of existence to a higher one, are neither portraits of living individuals nor personifications of abstract ideas. It has rightly been said that they portray the immortalized souls of the deceased rather than their empirical personality, and that their compositional relationship with the Times of Day beneath them is reminiscent of those Roman sarcophagi where the image of the dead is carried beyond the sphere of earthly life symbolized by the reclining figures of Ocean and Earth (*text ill.* p.171).[112]

Yet, however transfigured, the images of Giuliano and Lorenzo de' Medici denote a definite contrast which is expressed not only by their postures and expressions, but also by distinctive attributes; and this contrast cannot be described more adequately than in terms of the ancient antithesis between active and contemplative life.[113]

From the Neoplatonic point of view there is no contradiction between the fact that the two Dukes are represented as immortalized souls, and the fact that Giuliano is characterized as the *vir activus* while Lorenzo is characterized as the *vir contemplativus*.[114] On the contrary, these characteriza-

110. For this wide-spread theory see *Bibl.*252 and 253.
111. Vasari, *Bibl.*366, VOL.VII, p.196, Frey, *Bibl.*103, p.133.
112. C.Tolnay, *Bibl.*355, p.289, 292 and *fig.*10.
113. It seems that this interpretation was first proposed by J.Richardson, *Bibl.*279, VOL.III, p.136ss. It was however Borinski who first considered it in connection with the contemporary Neoplatonic sources.
114. Thus it is quite possible to accept C.Tolnay's interpretation of the ducal portraits as '*immagini delle anime trapassate, divinizzate alla maniera antica*' (*Bibl.*355, p.289),

tions account for their apotheosis. For, as we know, it is only by leading a truly active and a truly contemplative life, ruled either by *iustitia* or *religio*, that men can escape from the vicious circle of mere natural existence and can attain both temporal beatitude and eternal immortality.

Now, how can the ideal *vir contemplativus* and the ideal *vir activus* be portrayed according to Neoplatonic standards? Only by designating the former as the perfect votary of Saturn, and the latter as the perfect votary of Jupiter. Plotinus, we remember, had already interpreted Saturn as Νοῦς, the Cosmic Mind, and Jupiter as Ψυχή, the Cosmic Soul. Consequently the human soul was believed to be endowed, on her descent to the earth, with the 'power of discernment and thought' by Saturn, and with the 'power to act' by Jupiter.[114a] And for the Florentine Neoplatonists it was a matter of course that the 'children' of Saturn—the most unfortunate of mortals in ordinary judicial astrology—were in reality predestined for a life of intellectual contemplation, whereas the children of Jupiter were predestined for a life of rational action.

It is not possible here to discuss the more universal aspects of this doctrine which, in combination with a 'rediscovery' of the Aristotelian theory that all great men were melancholics, was to lead to the modern concept of genius, nor is it necessary to illustrate it by a selection of texts. Suffice it to adduce one characteristic passage from Pico della Mirandola's Commentary on Benivieni: 'Saturn signifies the intellectual nature which is only devoted to and intent on understanding and contemplating. Jupiter signifies the active life which consists of superintending, administering and keeping in motion by its rules the things subjected to it. These two properties are found in the two planets called by the same names, viz., Saturn and Jupiter. For, as

without denying that their obvious contrast brings out the antithesis between the active and the contemplative life, both of them justifying a claim to immortality.

114a. The *locus classicus* for this doctrine, unforgotten even during the Middle Ages, but attaining a new importance in the Renaissance, is Macrobius, *Comm. in Somnium Scipionis*, I, 12-14: '*In Saturni* [viz., *sphaera producit anima*] *ratiocinationem et intelligentiam, quod* λογιστικόν et θεωρητικόν *vocant; in Jovis vim agendi, quod* πρακτικόν *dicitur.*'

they say, Saturn produces contemplative men, while Jupiter gives them principalities, government, and the administration of peoples.'[115]

In the sources to which this passage implicitly refers, that is in the textual and pictorial documents of astrology, the characters of the Saturnian and the Jovial bear an unmistakable resemblance with what modern psychologists call the 'introvert' and the 'extrovert' type; the ancient astrologers even anticipated the notion that differences as basic as these are also reflected in such peculiarities as the attitude towards money. The contemplative Saturnian is 'closed to the world;' he is morose, taciturn, entirely concentrated upon his own self, a friend of solitude and darkness, and avaricious or at least parsimonious. The active Jovial is 'open to the world;' he is alert, eloquent, companionable, interested in his fellow-beings, and unlimitedly generous.[116]

In the Medici Chapel this antithesis is indicated, in a general way, by the contrast between the 'open' composition of the Giuliano statue (*fig.155*) and the 'closed' composition of the 'Penseroso' (*fig.154*), as well as by the two pairs of personifications with which the two statues are grouped together: the Giuliano is placed above the virile Giorno and the fertile Nòtte, the Μήτηρ Νύξ or *Mater Nox* of classical poetry,[117] Lorenzo above the virgin Aurora (note her 'zone') and the elderly Crepuscolo, his age and mood possibly alluding to the myth of Aurora and her husband Tithonus who had been granted eternal life but not eternal youth.[117a] But the Saturnian and Jovial connotations of the two portraits are emphasized by more specific features. Like the face of Dürer's *Melencolia*, the face of the

---

115. Pico, I, 7, *Bibl.*267, fol.10: 'Saturno è significatiuo della natura intellettuale, laquale solo attende et è uolta allo intendere et contemplare. Gioue è significatiuo della uita attiua, laquale consiste nel reggere, administrare et muouere con lo imperio suo le cose à se soggiette et inferiori. Queste dua proprietà si truouano ne pianeti da e medesimi nomi significati, cioè Saturno e Giuoe; perchè come lore dicono, Saturno fa li huomini contemplatiui, Giuoe dà loro principati, gouerni, et administratione di popoli.'
116. See, instead of all other instances, the inscriptions on the Florentine engravings representing the Children of Jupiter (F.Lippmann, *Bibl.*195, PL. A II, B II).
117. Cf. J.B.Carter, *Bibl.*57, s.v. 'Nox,' and C.F.M.Bruchmann, *Bibl.*51, s.v. Νύξ.
117a. K.Borinski, *Bibl.*46, p.157ss.

'Penseroso' is darkened by a heavy shadow suggesting the *facies nigra* of the Saturnian melancholic. The index finger of his left hand covers his mouth with the gesture of Saturnian silence.[118] His elbow rests on a closed cash-box, a typical symbol of Saturnian parsimony;[119] and, to make the symbolism still more explicit, the front of this cash-box is adorned with the head of a bat, the emblematic animal of Dürer's engraving *Melencolia* I.[120]

Giuliano, on the other hand, holds a princely sceptre and with his open left he offers two coins. Both these motifs, symbolically contrasting him who 'spends' himself in outward action with him who 'shuts himself off' in self-centred contemplation, are described by Ripa under the heading 'Magnanimità,' and this is just as much a Jovial trait as parsimony is a Saturnian one: *'Iupiter dat magnanimitatem animi,'* to quote one of the most popular astrological texts.[121] Small wonder that in the Florentine engravings illustrating the Children of Jupiter we encounter a prince holding his sceptre and bestowing favours upon his subjects (*fig.*156).[122] It has been thought that the general composition of the Giuliano statue may have been suggested by two Byzantine reliefs at the façade of St. Mark's representing St. George and St. Demetrius (*fig.*157);[123] if this conjecture—not altogether improbable in view of the fact that Michelangelo had revisited Venice shortly before commencing the Giuliano statue—be true, it would be all the more significant

---

118. Cf.Ripa,s.v. 'Silentio:' *'il dito indice alla bocca;' 'un dito alle labbre della bocca;' 'col dito alla bocca.'* Ripa's 'Malanconico' (s.v. 'Complessioni') has even his mouth covered with a bandage which *'significa il silentio.'*

119. In cod. Vat. lat.1398, fol.11, Saturn is shown holding the keys to a closed strong-box. In cod. Tubingensis M.d.2 the melancholic sets out to bury a strong-box filled with money and the attributes of a purse and/or a table covered with coins is ubiquitous in representations both of Saturn and the melancholic (see the illustrations in *Melancholia, Bibl.*253); in Leonardo Dati's *Sfera* the qualities of thoughtfulness and avarice are mentioned in the same breath: *'Disposti* [viz., the melancholics] *a tucte larti davaritia, et a molti pensieri sempre hanno il core.'*

120. That Lorenzo holds a crumpled handkerchief in his left hand may express a similar idea as the involved crewel in Ripa's 'Pensiero.'

121. According to the redaction of the above-mentioned passage from Macrobius found in the 'Kyeser' manuscripts, reprinted in A.Hauber, *Bibl.*135, p.54.

122. F.Lippmann, *Bibl.*195, PL. A II, B II.

123. E.Steinmann, *Bibl.*322, p.110s., fig.27-28.

that he replaced the attribute of those saints, the sword, by the symbols of Jovial magnanimity.

Both the contemplative thinker and the magnanimous doer are entitled to a Neoplatonic apotheosis. Its consummation is symbolized by the motifs adorning the fourth and highest zone of the ducal tombs. This zone might be interpreted as the supercelestial sphere above the celestial. The trophies in the centre connote the ultimate triumph over the lower forms of existence; the children crouching down with grief and fear stand probably for unborn souls doomed to descend into the lower spheres;[124] and the empty throne is one of the oldest and most widely used symbols for the invisible presence of an immortal. The preparation of empty thrones for the Last Judgment, the so-called Hetoimasia, is probably based on Daniel, vii,9. But its renderings in art[125] are patterned after pagan representations, which have come down to us in large numbers. In ancient Rome empty thrones figured in expiatory ceremonies for certain goddesses and, more important, on the occasion of the *ludi scaenici*, when they were solemnly carried to the theatre and placed at the disposal of the gods. After the death of Caesar this privilege was granted to him and, later on, to other deified emperors.[126] If Michelangelo had lived under Hadrian he could not have chosen a more eloquent symbol to crown the monument of a *Divus Caesar*. But in the Medici Chapel the empty thrones would have been surmounted by those stories from the Old Testament which would have subordinated the whole content of the ducal tombs to the Christian idea of salvation translated into images in the *sepoltura in testa*.

For the cupola, too, a fresco had been intended. Sebastiano del Piombo refers to this plan in a letter of July 7, 1533, where he says: 'As to the

---

124. K.Borinski, *Bibl*.46, p.135.
125. See P.Durand, *Bibl*.80; J.Wilpert, *Bibl*.404, vol.i, p.58ss. It is characteristic that St. Maura in her vision (quoted by Wilpert, *l.c.*) sees the throne 'draped' as it appears in all the pagan representations; cf. *text ill*. p.198.
126. See L.R.Taylor, *Bibl*.335; also A.L.Abaecherli, *Bibl*.1.

painting in the vault of the lantern, Our Lord [viz., Pope Clement VII] leaves it to you to do what you like. I think the Ganymede would look nice there, you could give him a halo so that he would appear as St. John of the Apocalypse carried to Heaven.'[127] No one who understands the spirit of mockery so characteristic of Sebastiano's epistolary style and particularly ubiquitous in his letters to his 'compare' Michelangelo can fail to see that this suggestion is a joke.[128] But it is a very good joke. For, whether or not Sebastiano remembered it, in the *Moralized Ovid* Ganymede had in fact been interpreted as a prefiguration of St. John the Evangelist, the Eagle standing for Christ, or else for the sublime Clarity which enabled St. John to reveal the secrets of Heaven;[129] and this interpretation was still referred to in the sixteenth century.[130]

Moralizations of this kind were still familiar to the Renaissance; the humanists did not even scruple to quote the verses *Sinite parvuli ad me veniant* and *Nisi efficiamur sicut parvuli* . . . in connection with Jupiter's love for a handsome boy;[131] and it is easy to see that such well-meant christianizations of pagan myths seemed more objectionable to the Church than their treatment in genuine classical poetry.[132] Yet they are but one chapter in the history of the interpretations to which the myth of Ganymede, the only favourite of Zeus ever admitted to Olympus, had been subjected in the course of the centuries.

In the fourth century B.C. we find already two opposite conceptions:

127. G.Milanesi, *Bibl.*215, p.104.
128. The passage has been taken seriously only by K.Borinski, *Bibl.*46, p.142, and, on his authority, by O.G.von Simson, *Bibl.*319, p.109. Even in business transactions Sebastiano can hardly manage to be quite serious; cf., e.g., his amusing proposition to the Duke Ferrante Gonzaga (P.D'Acchiardi, *Bibl.*2, p.276).
129. 'Thomas Walleys,' *Bibl.*386, fol.lxxxii.
130. See for instance Claudius Minos' Commentary on Alciati, EMBLEMATA, IV, *Bibl.*5, p.61ss. The eagle (the word *aquila* supposedly deriving from *acumen*) would be the attribute of St. John, '*ut eius in divinis rebus acumen longe perspicax et oculatum, ut ita dicam, ostenderent.*' Minos concludes the passage with the sentence: '*Sed hic me cohibeo, quod id esse videam Theologorum pensum.*'
131. Claudius Minos, *ibidem.*
132. See p.70, N.2.

while Plato believed the myth of Ganymede to have been invented by the Cretans in order to justify amorous relations between men and boys or adolescents,[133] Xenophon explained it as a moral allegory denoting the superiority of the mind in comparison with the body; according to him the very name of Ganymede, supposedly derived from Greek γάνυσθαι (to enjoy) and μήδεα (intelligence), would bear witness to the fact that intellectual, not physical advantages win the affection of the gods and assure immortality.[134]

The more realistic version of the Ganymede theme (later on, of course, exploited by the Christian Fathers in their invectives against paganism)[135] was either developed in a Euhemeristic spirit,[136] or interpreted as an astral myth.[137] The idealistic version, on the other hand, was transferred from a moral plane to a metaphysical or even mystical one. In one of the Roman sarcophagi which depict the rise of the soul beyond the terrestrial realm of Earth and Ocean the group of Ganymede and the Eagle is placed in the centre of the composition (*text ill.* p.171).[138]

The High Middle Ages were either satisfied with the Euhemeristic and astronomical interpretations,[139] or, when the time had come for a specifically Christian moralization, indulged in drawing such parallels as the one between Ganymede and St. John the Evangelist. For the Renaissance, however, it was a matter of course to prefer an interpretation which connected the myth of Ganymede with the Neoplatonic doctrine of the *furor divinus*.

In his commentary on Dante, *Purgatorio*, IX, 19 ss., Landino explicitly draws the line between the Neoplatonic interpretation and the Christian one

---

133. Plato, *Leges*, I, 636c.
134. Xenophon, *Symposium*, VIII,30.
135. Cf., e.g., Augustinus, *De Civ. Dei*, VII,26 and XVIII,13, probably on the basis of Cicero, *Tuscul.*, IV,33 (70,71). In *Tuscul.*, I,26 (65) Cicero adheres, however, to the Xenophontian interpretation.
136. See, e.g., Fulgentius, *Mitol.*, I,25, taken over by Mythographus II,198.
137. See Hyginus, *De Astronomia*, II,29, taken over by Mythographus III,3,5, *Bibl.*38, p.162.
138. Clarac, *Bibl.*66, VOL.II, PL.181, no.28.
139. This line of tradition is summarized in Boccaccio, *Geneal. Deor.*, VI,4.

as championed by his old-fashioned predecessors. He quotes Francesco da Buti (1324-85) according to whom the Eagle would signify *la divina charità*, while the locale of Ganymede's abduction, the forest of mount Ida, would call to mind the fact that hermits, doing penitence in the woods, are more likely to be saved than other mortals; and he says that this interpretation was 'pietosa et accomodata alla christiana religione.' But he prefers to think that Ganymede designates the Mind (*mens*), as opposed to the lower faculties of the human soul, and that his abduction denotes the rise of the Mind to a state of enraptured contemplation: 'Ganymede, then, would signify the *mens humana*, beloved by Jupiter, that is: the Supreme Being. His companions would stand for the other faculties of the soul, to wit the vegetal and sensorial. Jupiter, realizing that the Mind is in the forest—that is, remote from mortal things, transports it to heaven by means of the eagle. Thus it leaves behind its companions—that is, the vegetative and sensitive soul; and being removed, or, as Plato says, divorced from the body, and forgetting corporeal things, it concentrates entirely on contemplating the secrets of Heaven.'[140] This Neoplatonic interpretation, corroborated as it seemed to be by the Xenophontian etymology, was almost unanimously accepted by the humanists such as Alciati (whose Emblema IV bears the double title γάνυσθαι μήδεσι and *In Deo laetandum*),[141] Achille Bocchi,[142] and Natale Conti;[143]

140. Landino, Commentary on Dante, *Bibl.*180, fol.CLVI, v.:'*Sia adunque Ganimede l'humana mente la quale Gioue, idest el sommo Idio ama. Sieno e suoi compagni l'altre potentie dell'anima come e vegetatiua et sensitiua* [the latter here obviously comprising both the *sensus exterior* and the *sensus interior* or imagination]. *Apposto adunque Gioue, che essa sia nella selua, idest remota delle cose mortali, et con l'aquila già detta la inalza al cielo. Onde essa abbandona e compagni, idest la vegetatiua et sensitiua; et abstratta et quasi, come dice Platone, rimossa dal corpo, è tutta posta nella contemplatione de' secreti del cielo.*'

141. Claudius Minos' commentary on this Emblema (see p.213, N.131) is almost a monograph on Ganymede.

142. A.Bocchius, *Bibl.*37, SYMB.LXXVIII ('*Vera in cognitione dei cultuque voluptas;*' Oὐχ ἡδὺ σώματος ὀνομασθείς, ἀλλὰ ἡδὺ γνώμων) and LXXIX ('*Pacati emblema hoc corporis atque animi est;*' Γάνυσθαι μήδεσι). For the illustrations of these two *concetti* see below.

143. Natalis Comes, *Bibl.*67, IX,13, also very learned and comprehensive, ultimately decides in favour of an idealistic interpretation: '*Nam quid aliud per hanc fabulam demonstrabant sapientes, quam prudentem virum a Deo amari, et illum solum proxime accedere ad divinam naturam?*'

and it throws light on the object of Sebastiano del Piombo's joke: '*the*' Ganymede mentioned in his letter to Michelangelo is obviously the one in the drawing which Michelangelo had made for his young friend Tommaso Cavalieri about half a year before that letter was written, and which had become very famous in the meantime (*fig.*158).[144] It shows Ganymede in a state of trance without a will or a thought of his own, reduced to passive immobility by the iron grip of the gigantic eagle, the posture of his arms suggesting the attitude of an unconscious person or a corpse,[145] and his soul really *rimossa dal corpo*, to use Landino's words.

Thus it cannot be questioned that this drawing symbolizes the *furor divinus*,[146] or, to be more precise, the *furor amatorius*, and this not in an abstract and general way but as an expression of the truly Platonic, all-pervasive and all-effacing passion which had shaken Michelangelo's life when he had met Tommaso Cavalieri.

We happen to know that the Ganymede drawing, given to Cavalieri towards the end of 1532, was accompanied by another, and that the owner considered these two as belonging together: the Tityus (Fr.6, *fig.*159).[147] Tityus is one of the four great sinners tortured in Hades, the others being Tantalus, Ixion and Sisyphus. He was punished for having attacked Latona, the mother of Apollo and Diana, and his punishment was similar to that of

144. The best replica of the lost original is the drawing Fr.18. For other copies, engravings etc. see Thode, *Bibl.*349, vol.II, p.350ss. It is interesting to note that the illustrations of Bocchi's SYMB.LXVIII and LXIX, quoted in note 142, are also borrowed from Michelangelo's composition. The second, however, shows Ganymede draped instead of nude (with reference to Pliny's statement as to the classical sculptor Leochares, *Nat. Hist.*, XXXIV,8), in order to illustrate a perfect harmony of soul and body, Ganymede not being hurt by the eagle's talons.

145. A classical prototype, very much restored and known only through the engraving in Clarac, *Bibl.*66 III, PL.407, no.696, has been proposed by H.Hekler, *Bibl.*138, p.220. A similar type is transmitted through a mosaic in Sousse (*Bibl.*151, PL.136). But no representation prior to Michelangelo shows the Ganymede so firmly held in the grip of the eagle.

146. Cf. K.Borinski, *Bibl.*46, p.142 with quotation of Landino. F.Wickhoff, *Bibl.*397, p.433 quotes as poetic parallels the line: '*Volo con le vostr'ale e senza piume*' from Frey, *Bibl.*101, CIX,19, and the second stanza of the sonnet Frey, *ibidem*, XLIV.

147. See Thode, *Bibl.*340, vol.II, p.350 and 356ss., with further references. The reproduction in Frey is reversed; a correct reproduction is found in B.Berenson, *Bibl.*28, PL.CXLXXX.

Prometheus, only that his 'immortal liver'[148] was devoured by a vulture instead of by an eagle.[149] The liver supposedly producing the blood and therefore being the seat of physical passions (Petrarch, like many others, considered it the aim of Cupid's arrows),[150] it is easy to see how the punishment inflicted upon the unfortunate lover of Latona came to be interpreted as an allegory of the 'tortures caused by immoderate love:'

> 'Sed Tityos nobis hic est, in amore iacentem
> Quem volucres lacerant, atque exest anxius angor
> Aut aliae quaevis scindunt cuppedine curae,'[151]

as Lucretius puts it. 'The misery of the lover,' according to Bembo, 'grows because he feeds his tortures with his own self. This is Tityus who with his liver feeds the vulture,'[152] and Ripa's allegory of the 'Tortures of Love' consists of 'a sad man . . . with his breast open and lacerated by a vulture.'[153]

---

148. Virgil, Aen., VI,497.
149. The Homeric version according to which Tityus was tortured by two vultures (Odyss., XI,576ss.) fell into oblivion until the sixteenth century. Since Ovid, Met.,IV,456ss. the combination of the four above-mentioned characters is a standard feature of descriptions and representations of Hades, or the 'Realm of the Furies,' as Hades is often called on the basis of Ovid, Met., IV, 453, where the 'three sisters' are referred to as the janitors of Hades, so to speak. The formal similarity between Tityus and Prometheus has led to much confusion in modern writing. Even Michelangelo's Tityus is occasionally misquoted (F.Wickhoff, Bibl.397, p.434; the drawing was in fact used for a Prometheus by Rubens, R.Oldenbourg, Bibl.234, p.74 fig.161), and Titian's Tityus in the Prado is still constantly referred to and reproduced as Prometheus. That this picture (fig.160) represents Tityus is evidenced, not only by the snake which is indicative of the subterranean world, but also by the fact that it belongs to a series which comprised Sisyphus (still extant), Tantalus and Ixion (the latter two pictures mentioned in the inventory of Queen Mary of Hungary; R.Beer, Bibl.24, P.clxiv, no.86). The four pictures were united in one room called 'la pieza de las Furias,' which simply means the Hades Room, and are correctly described by V.Carducho, Bibl.55, p.349. The confusion seems to have been caused by Vasari who mentions an otherwise unknown Prometheus along with the Tityus, but explicitly adds that the Prometheus picture had never reached Spain (Bibl.366, VOL.VII, p.451, repeated by G.P.Lomazzo, VII, 32, Bibl.199, p.676 in the chapter 'Della forma delle tre furie infernali').
150. Petrarch, Africa, Bibl.263, referred to above, p.109, N.46.
151. Lucretius, De Rer. Nat., III, 982ss.
152. P.Bembo, Asolani, I, Bibl.26, p.85.
153. Ripa, s.v. 'Tormento d'Amore.'

Thus the two drawings were in fact 'counterparts' in content, though not in a technical sense. The Ganymede, ascending to Heaven on the wings of an eagle, symbolizes the ecstasy of Platonic love, powerful to the point of annihilation, but freeing the soul from its physical bondages and carrying it to a sphere of Olympian bliss. Tityus, tortured in Hades by a vulture, symbolizes the agonies of sensual passion, enslaving the soul and debasing it even beneath its normal terrestrial state. Taken together, the two drawings might be called the Michelangelesque version of the theme: '*Amor Sacro e Profano.*' In both compositions the traditional allegorical interpretation of a mythological subject was accepted, but it was invested with the deeper meaning of a personal confession, so that both forms of love were conceived as the two aspects of one essentially tragic experience.[154] If the 'Boboli' Slaves and the Victory in the Palazzo Vecchio (*fig.*173) were in fact executed as late as 1532-34, it would be possible to think that these five sculptures too, though unquestionably destined for the Tomb of Julius II, nevertheless reflect Michelangelo's passion for Cavalieri. The substitution of a wingless Victor, saddened by his own triumph, for the rejoicing winged Victories, and the tragic contrast between youth and old age (Michelangelo was fifty-seven in 1532) inevitably recalls the line: '*Resto prigion d'un Cavalier armato.*'[155]

A similarly subjective interpretation of a mythological 'morality' can be observed in a third composition which Michelangelo had made for Tommaso Cavalieri: the Fall of Phaethon.[156] It exists in three versions (Fr.57, 75, 58,*figs.*162,163,164), the last of which (Fr.58) was received by Cavalieri early in September 1533, while the first one (Fr.57) seems to have been exe-

154. Cf. e.g., the letter to Bartolommeo Angiolini, Milanesi, *Bibl.*216, p.469.
155. Frey, *Bibl.*101, LXXXVI. From this point of view the interpretation of the Victory group as a kind of spiritual self-portrait with Platonic connotations is quite defensible in spite of the fact that it was destined for the Tomb of Julius II.
156. Thode, *Bibl.*340, VOL.II, p.358ss. For classical sources cf. the articles quoted p.172, N.3.

cuted some time before that date,[157] perhaps even before the drawings of Ganymede and Tityus.

Setting aside the inevitable Euhemeristic and naturalistic interpretations,[158] there is only one allegorical explanation of the myth of Phaethon: the fate of the daring mortal who had tried to defy human limitations was held to symbolize the fate of every *temerarius*, presumptuous enough to overstep the bounds of his allotted 'state and situation.'[159]

With this in mind, the Phaethon composition, given to Cavalieri by Michelangelo at the very beginning of their friendship, is understandable as an expression of the feeling of utter inferiority manifested in Michelangelo's first letters to the young nobleman: 'Very inconsiderately I have ventured to write to you, and I was *presumptuous* enough to make the first move where I should properly have waited for one of yours to answer it,' Michelangelo writes on January 1, 1533, and: 'you, the light of our century unique in the world, cannot be satisfied with the work of any other man, having nobody to equal or to resemble you.'[160] Even later he says: 'although

157. The sequence given in Thode (Fr.57, 75, 58) is almost generally accepted (A.E.Brinckmann, *Bibl*.49, p.45ss. suggests however the sequence Fr.57, 58, 75) and evidently correct. In Fr.57 Michelangelo keeps comparatively closely to classical models, with a strong asymmetry owing to the vertical arrangement of motifs which were originally aligned in a horizontal space. Fr.75 is rigidly axialized and almost emphatically non-classical, with the horses divided into symmetrical groups, and Phaethon falling head over heels in the centre of the composition (cf. the illustrations of Alciati's Emblema LVI, our *fig*.170). Fr.58 gives the ultimate solution in that the principles followed in the two other compositions are synthesized.

158. See, e.g., Lucretius, *De Rer. Nat.*, v,396ss.; Mythographus III, 8,15, *Bibl*.38, p.208. A whole collection of Euhemeristic and naturalistic interpretations is found in Boccaccio, *Geneal. Deor.*, vii,41, and in Natalis Comes, *Bibl*.67, vi,1, p.552.

159. See e.g., the French *Moralized Ovid*, C.de Boer, *Bibl*.40, vol.i, p.186ss. (Phaethon as an arrogant philosopher, also as Ante-Christ while Sol stands for Christ); 'Thomas Walleys,' *Bibl*.386, fol.xxvi, v. (Phaethon denoting bad judges and prelates); Gaguin, *De Sodoma* (the fate of Phaethon as a parallel to that of Sodom, thus illustrated in a group of *Cité de Dieu* manuscripts, although he is not mentioned in the text, cf. V.de Laborde, *Bibl*.178, vol.ii, p.410 and pl.xl.vii, cx); Landino, Commentary on Dante, *Inferno*, xvii, 106, *Bibl*. 180, fol.lxxix (Phaethon and Icarus standing for '*tutti quelli e quali mossi da troppa presumptione di se medesimi et da temerità ardiscono a fare imprese sopra le forze e le facultà loro*'); Alciati, *Emblemata*, LVI *In temerarios* (our *fig*.170).

160. G.Milanesi, *Bibl*.216, p.462-464 (note the use of the word '*prosuntuoso*,' reminiscent of Landino's '*presumptione*').

I speak most *presumptuously*, being very inferior to you, I do not think that anything can stand in the way of our friendship.'[161]

This feeling of abject humility is almost incomprehensible from a rational point of view, so that Michelangelo's letters were believed to have been destined for Vittoria Colonna, with Cavalieri only serving as an intermediary;[162] it is, however, inevitably associated with a transcendental form of love. The Platonic lover, identifying as he does the concrete object of his passion with a metaphysical idea, endows it with an almost religious sublimity and feels himself unworthy of a god whom he himself has created: 'he would worship his friend with actual sacrifices were he not afraid of being considered a madman.'[163]

Thus we can understand how Michelangelo could compare his imaginary 'presumptuousness' with the temerity of Phaethon and, at the same time, could liken the deadly fire of his passion to the flaming thunderbolts by which Phaethon had perished. That such a subjectively erotic interpretation of the Phaethon myth was possible in the sixteenth century, can be inferred, not only from Michelangelo's own poetry,[164] but also from a sonnet written about the same time by Francesco Maria Molza, a poet who moved in Michelangelo's circles and was certainly acquainted with the Cavalieri compositions.

'Altero fiume, che a Fetonte involto
Nel fumo già de le saette ardenti
Il grembo de' tuoi rivi almi e lucenti
Apristi di pietà turbato il volto:

E le caste sorelle, a cui l'accolto
Dolor formò così dogliosi accenti,
Ch'en selve se n'andar meste e dolenti,
Pasci ancor su le sponde e pregi molto:

161. Letter of July 28, 1533, *ibidem*, p.468.
162. See Milanesi's note to the letter of July 28, 1533.
163. Plato, *Phaedrus*, 251a.
164. See particularly Frey, *Bibl.*101, CIV, adduced by K.Borinski, *Bibl.*46, p.35.

A me, che'ndarno il pianto e la voce ergo,
Cinto di fuoco alla mia fiamma viva,
Pietoso dal tuo verde antro rispondi:

E se pur neghi entro'l gran letto albergo
Al duro incendio, almen su questa riva
Verdeggi anch'io con pure e nove frondi.'[165]

The last of the compositions demonstrably executed for Cavalieri is the Children's Bacchanal, preserved in the copy Fr.187 (*fig.165*).[166] In the centre it shows seven *putti* carrying a dead deer.[167] In the upper zone a group of children make preparations for the boiling of a young pig, while another group, with unmistakable signs of intoxication, frolics around a vat of wine. In the lower left corner an aged she-Pan nurses a human baby with another infant playing on her lap, and in the lower right corner four children make fun of a drunken man who may or may not be meant to be Silenus.[168]

More than any other work of Michelangelo's this composition seems to be pervaded by a pagan spirit. In a general way it is related to the reliefs on the base of Donatello's Judith[169] and to Titian's Feast of Venus and Andrii which Michelangelo had probably seen when visiting with the Duke Alfonso of Ferrara in 1529.[170] Several motifs are borrowed from Roman sarcophagi,[171] while other figures such as the boy protecting himself against the

---

165. F.M.Molza, *Bibl.*218, no.LVI, p.145; cf. E.Panofsky, *Bibl.*246, col.50. A sonnet by Molza addressed to Michelangelo reprinted *ibidem*; Michelangelo's *rilievo* style is employed for an elaborate allegory in the sonnet, no.CXXVII, p.416. With a short interruption, Molza lived from 1529 to 1535 with the Cardinal Ippolito Farnese who was particularly interested in the Cavalieri drawings (cf. Thode, *Bibl.*340,VOL.II, p.351).
166. According to C.Tolnay, *Bibl.*349. For other replicas, engravings etc. see Thode, *Bibl.*340, VOL.II, p.363ss.
167. Curiously enough this evidently cloven-footed animal is constantly referred to as a donkey; K.Borinski, *Bibl.*46, p.69 has even built an iconographical explanation on this assumption.
168. There is a relatively 'idealistic' Silenus type in Renaissance art.
169. K.Frey, *Bibl.*102, text to Fr.187.
170. It is interesting to note that the urinating boy in Titian's 'Bacchanal' (*recte* Andrii) is borrowed from the same sarcophagus type (*Bibl.*66, VOL.II, PL.132, no.38) which was one of the main sources of Michelangelo's Children's Bacchanal.
171. Cf. Thode, *Bibl.*340, VOL.II, p.363ss.; for classical sources cf. the articles listed p.172, N.3.

221

smoke might be termed self-parodies;[172] and a definite connection exists between Michelangelo's Children's Bacchanal and Piero di Cosimo's Vespucci panels, not only in the general scheme of composition, but also in individual motifs: the she-Pan nursing a baby seen in the lower left hand corner of Michelangelo's composition is obviously derived from the charming group analogously placed in Piero's Discovery of Honey (fig.31).[173] Right and left are reversed within the borrowed unit, but the formal similarity is unmistakable. It extends even to such details as the motif of the mother's arm crossed diagonally over her body.

However, the *contrapposto* which in Piero's painting reveals a comical conflict between maternal duty and naïve curiosity was used by Michelangelo to express hopeless dejection and lethargy. He sensed an undercurrent of sorrow and humiliation in what Vasari had termed *una letizia al vivo*. There is, in fact, little hilarity in the entire scene. The group around the beautiful dead animal—patterned after the same classical type of composition which had been employed by Mantegna and Raphael for the Deposition of Christ—strikes us as pathetic rather than funny; few of the children look really happy; and the 'Silenus' forming the counterpart of the tired old she-Pan offers an aspect of deadly torpor—so much so that Michelangelo could use a similar motif in the dead Christ in the much later Pietà for Vittoria Colonna.[174]

The symbolical content of the strange composition—if there is any—is hard to explain. Conventionally, orgiastic bacchanalian scenes were associated with Luxury,[175] but this interpretation would be too moralistic for

172. This figure is a diminutive edition of the young woman in the Sacrifice of Noah which in turn is patterned after a classical model (cf. E.Gombrich, *Bibl*.119). The figure of the boy carrying a bundle of logs is developed from the correspondent figure in the same fresco, and the 'Silenus' group is generally patterned after the Shame of Noah.
173. See p.59ss.
174. Cf.Thode, *Bibl*.340, VOL.II, p.492ss.
175. Cf. E.Wind, *Bibl*.406. It is characteristic that F.G.Bonsignori's translation of Ovid, *Bibl*.42, circumscribes the lines *Met*. XII,219ss. as follows: '*Uno degli centauri ardea di duplicata* luxuria: *cioè damore e per ebrieza di vino*' (quoted in C.Tolnay, *Bibl*.351, p.106, Note 2).

Michelangelo's general attitude. For want of a better solution, we may re-member Landino's exposition of the myth of Ganymede. On its flight to the higher spheres, he had said, the Mind leaves behind the lower faculties of the soul, namely: the 'sensorial' and the 'vegetal,' the former comprising the five senses and the imagination, the latter taking care of nothing but 'pro-pagation, nourishment and growth' (*'vis generationis, nutritionis, augmenti'* as Ficino puts it).[176] Now, it is within the compass of these most primitive natural functions that the scenes in the Children's Bacchanal unfold: eating, drinking (and the opposite of both), nursing of babies and drunken sleep, all this enacted by beings either too young, or too little distinguished from animals, or too much deprived of their consciousness and dignity, to be fully human. If the flight of Ganymede symbolizes the enraptured ascension of the Mind, and if again the punishment of Tityus and the fall of Phaethon exemplify the fate of those who are incapable of controlling their sensuality and imagination, the Children's Bacchanal, which is entirely devoid of amorous tension, might thus be the image of a still lower sphere: the sphere of a purely vegetative life which is as much beneath specifically human digni-ty as the Mind is above specifically human limitations.

The further compositions of the same period should be considered at this point though we do not know whether they were also intended for Tom-maso Cavalieri. Be that as it may, they are closely allied by their expressional qualities as to the four drawings just discussed.

While in these traditional mythological subjects are invested with a sym-bolical meaning, the two compositions now to be examined are free inven-tions of a purely imaginary character: they represent scenes enacted, not by concrete persons transubstantiated by Michelangelo's interpretation, but by abstract personifications enlivened by Michelangelo's power of vision.

One of these compositions, the often copied Dream or 'Sogno' (drawing Th.520, of somewhat doubtful authenticity, *fig.*167)[177] shows a youth re-

176. See p.136.
177. For further references see Thode, *Bibl.*340, vol.ii, p.375ss.; cf. also A.E.Brinckmann, *Bibl.*49, no.59, and T.Borenius and R.Wittkower, *Bibl.*43, p.39.

clining on a box filled with masks of all descriptions, the upper part of his body supported by the terrestrial globe marked by the equator; in most of the copies the continents are entered in addition. He is surrounded by a semi-circular halo of smaller figures and groups sketched in an unreal, vaporous manner and thus easily recognizable as dream-visions; they represent unquestionably the seven Capital Sins, namely (from left to right): Gluttony, Lechery, Avarice, Luxury, Wrath, Envy and Sloth. But a winged genius or angel, descending from heaven, awakes the youth by the sounding of a trumpet.

The meaning of this composition was already adequately explained by Hieronymus Tetius, who in his description of the Palazzo Barberini printed in 1642 describes a painted copy of the 'Sogno' and interprets it as follows: 'In my opinion this youth denotes nothing but the human Mind called back to Virtue from the Vices, as though it were repatriated after a long journey.'[178]

This interpretation speaks for itself and can be further corroborated by the well-known significance of the masks as symbols of fallacy and deceit,[179] and, more especially, by what Ripa says about the figure of 'Emulation, contest and stimulus of glory,' whom he describes as holding a trumpet: 'The trumpet of fame awakes the mind of the virtuous, rouses them from the slumber of laziness, and makes them stay awake in permanent vigil.'[180] In fact, Michelangelo's 'Sogno,' exploiting a representational type rather frequent in moralistic iconography, might be called a counterblast to Dürer's engraving commonly known as the 'Dream of the Doctor' (B.76, *fig.168*),

178. Hieronymus Tetius, *Bibl.337*, p.158: '*Mundi globo Juvenis innixus, nudo corpore, eodem-que singulis membris affabre compaginato, primo se intuentibus offert; quem angelus, tuba ad aures admota, dormientem excitat: hunc non aliud referre crediderim, quam ipsam Hominis mentem a vitiis ad virtutes, longo veluti postliminio, revocatam; ac proinde, remota ab eius oculis longius, vitia circumspicies.*' The passage is referred to in the *Michelangelo-Bibliographie, Bibl.323*, no.1901, but seems to have been disregarded in recent writing.

179. See p.89.

180. Ripa, s.v. 'Emulatione, Contesa e Stimolo di Gloria:' '*La tromba parimente della fama escita gli animi de' virtuosi dal sonno della pigritia et fa che stiano in continue vigilie.*'

which, in reality, is an allegory of laziness. In it a pampered elderly idler is shown asleep beside his gigantic stove, while the devil takes advantage of his sleep to prompt him with a pair of bellows so as to conjure up the tempting vision of *Venus Carnalis*.[181] In Michelangelo's 'Sogno' we have a vigorous youth enveloped by sinful dreams, but roused by the trumpet of a helpful angel. But even this moral allegory is slightly tinged with Neoplatonic metaphysics. That the youth reclines on a sphere, can be accounted for by the fact that the sphere frequently stands for instability; suffice it to recall to mind Giotto's representation of 'Inconstantia,' and the countless images of the fickle goddess Fortuna who was sometimes contrasted with the personification of Virtue with the explanation: *Sedes Fortunae rotunda; sedes Virtutis quadrata*.[182] But this sphere is characterized as a terrestrial globe, and thus connotes the situation of the human Mind, placed as it is between the fallacious and unreal life on earth and the celestial realm whence the awakening inspiration descends to dispel the evil dreams. Tetius clearly alludes to this Neoplatonic flavour of the composition when he speaks of the *longum postliminium*, the 'return of the human Mind to its rightful home after a long journey.'

The second composition, the Archers or, to use Vasari's expression, the *Saettatori*, (drawing Fr.298, an excellent copy *fig.166*) is no less enigmatical than the Children's Bacchanal.[183] It shows nine nude figures, two of them women, shooting arrows at a target suspended before the breast of a herm. But in contrast with the little stucco relief in the Golden House of Nero, which Michelangelo probably used as a model (*fig.171*), the figures do not aim quietly and deliberately: four of the archers run, one kneels down, two

181. Cf. E.Panofsky, *Bibl.*251.
182. Cf.A.Doren, *Bibl.*77, and E.Cassirer, *Bibl.*59, PL.II; also Ripa, s.v. 'Fortuna' and 'Instabilità.'
183. See Thode, *Bibl.*340, VOL.II, p.365ss., also A.E.Brinckmann, *Bibl.*49, no.52. That the drawing Fr.298 is only a copy has been pointed out by A.E.Popp, *Bibl.*274 and 272. The writer has to admit that he was in error when defending its authenticity (*Bibl.*245, p.242). For the interpretation cf. K.Borinski, *Bibl.*46, p.63ss.; R.Förster, *Bibl.*97 (reviewed by E.Panofsky, *Bibl.*246,col.47). For classical models A.Hekler, *Bibl.*138, p.222 (Kairos-type) and F.Weege, *Bibl.*391, p.179.

lie on the ground, and the two women float in the air. Behind them a satyr-like figure clothed in billowing drapery bends a bow; two *putti* mingle with the archers, while two others blow a fire and feed it with logs, apparently in order to harden the arrow-heads by dipping them red-hot into a goblet. Beneath the herm, Cupid is seen asleep on a bundle.

The most puzzling feature is that, while the bow bent by the 'satyr' is meticulously rendered, the archers themselves are not provided with weapons, although arrows are seen sticking in the target. The engravers and painters who copied the composition did not hesitate to correct what they obviously thought was due to the unfinished state of the original. But the resulting maze of bows, strings and arrows is so detrimental to the effect of the composition that the omission might be regarded as deliberate. To judge from the very good copy Fr.298, the original was no less finished than any other drawing of Michelangelo's. Therefore I am tempted to believe that the bows and arrows were omitted on purpose, though not necessarily for aesthetic reasons, for Michelangelo could well have solved the formal problem of arming his figures if he had so wished. It seems possible to assume that the omission of the weapons conveys a definite idea. Some of the figures run, some actually float towards the target, others break down; it is as though they were under the spell of an irresistible power which makes them act as though they were shooting, while in reality they themselves are darts. If we look at the drawing in this light, it would seem that the weapons might have been omitted in order to turn the archers into tools of a force beyond their will and consciousness, and this interpretation would fit in with the other iconographic features of the composition.

In his attempt to clarify the definition of love as *desiderio della bellezza* (desire for beauty), Pico della Mirandola distinguishes, as we remember, between unconscious and conscious desire (*desiderio senza cognitione* and *desiderio con cognitione*). Only the desire which consciously aims at beauty is love. The desire not yet directed by the faculty of cognition is a mere natural urge (*desiderio naturale*), as irresistible as the law of gravitation, and present in all that lives, whereas the conscious desire is restricted to rational beings; it automatically directs the creatures towards a goal which is not beauty but happiness: 'And in order fully to understand the meaning of *desiderio naturale* it must be borne in mind that, since the good is the object of every desire, and every creature has some perfection of its own to participate in the divine goodness . . . , all creatures must have a certain aim (*fine*) in which they find whatever happiness is within the scope of their capacities; and they naturally turn and direct themselves to this aim as every heavy body to its centre. This inclination in creatures not endowed with cognition is called "natural desire," a great testimony to the divine providence by which such creatures are directed toward their aim as the dart of the archer is directed towards its target (*berzaglio*), which target is not known to the dart, but only to him who drives it towards the same with the eye of fore-seeing wisdom.'[184]

Since no entirely convincing explanation of the 'Saettatori' has been suggested thus far,[185] it seems permissible tentatively to connect them with this

184. Pico, II, 2, Bibl.267, fol.18, v.-19, referred to above: '*Et per piena intelligentia che cosa è desiderio naturale, e da intendere che essendolo oggietto del desiderio el bene, et hauendo ogni creatura qualche perfettione à se propria per participatione della bontà diuina . . . bisogna che habbia uno certo fine, nel quale quel grado, di che lei è capace di felicità, rittuoua, et in quello naturalmente si diriza et uolga, come ogni cosa graue al suo centro. Questa inclinatione nelle creature che non hanno cognitione, si chiama desiderio naturale, grande testimonio della prouidentia diuina, dalaquale sono state queste tali creature al suo fine dirizate, come la saetta del saggittario al suo berzaglio, il quale non è dalla saetta conosciuto, ma da colui che con occhio di sapientissima prouidentia uerso quello la muoue.*'

185. Among the previous interpretations only the one championed by R.Förster, Bibl.97, seemed to be acceptable, so much so that the writer adhered to it before he came across the above passage from Pico (Bibl.246,col.47): It was believed that Michelangelo's composition had been inspired by Lucian, Nigrinus,36, where the effect of a well-turned philosophical speech is likened to that of a well-aimed shot. For, this interpretation seemed to be corroborated by the fact that the Homeric phrase βάλλ' οὕτως which is quoted at the end of the Lucian passage, was adopted as a *motto* by the Cardinal Alessandro Farnese and was illustrated by the shielded herm seen in the drawing Fr.298. This seemed to confirm the connection of the *Saettatori* composition with the Lucian passage, all the more so as the *motto* had been suggested by F.M.Molza. However, the sleeping Cupid, the satyr-like figure and the *putti* preparing the weapons, and the impression that the figures do not act of their own accord, are hard to reconcile with the Lucian text (translated in R.Förster, l.c.), while these motifs would perfectly agree with

passage from a book which in all likelihood was known to Michelangelo. When interpreted as a fantasia on the theme '*desiderio naturale*,' the composition could be explained as a bold image illustrating both the inexorable power and the unfailing sureness of the 'natural urge,' whereas the individual creature may fail and fall. The figures driven towards the herm which they intend to hit, and hitting it with arrows which they could not have shot, would translate into one visual symbol the idea of the 'creatures directed towards their aim by a power unknown to them' with the metaphor of the darts 'hitting the target seen only by the archer.' The *putti* and the 'satyr' preparing the weapons and spurring the energies of the archers could be interpreted, in accordance with their customary significance, as personifications of the natural forces by which these creatures are stimulated into action. And the fact that the Cupid sleeps would eloquently illustrate the basic contrast which Pico intended to make clear: the doctrine that the *desiderio naturale*, before it is controlled by cognitive powers, has nothing to do with love, whether terrestrial or celestial. Only when the natural urge became active in creatures endowed with consciousness—only then would the *desiderio naturale* transform itself into the conscious desire for beauty, and the love-god awake.

It is disappointing to conclude these chapters with another '*non liquet*.' But the symbolical creations of geniuses are unfortunately harder to nail down to a definite subject then the allegorical inventions of minor artists.

Looking back upon the iconography of Michelangelo's works in their entirety, we can observe that secular subjects are only found in his early works, and then again in the period between 1525 and his definitive return to Rome in 1534, a climax being reached in the initial stages of his friendship with Cavalieri. 'It is as though harking back to his youth,' it has been said,

the passage from Pico. When Molza saw Michelangelo's drawing, he might have hit upon the idea of using the shielded herm for an illustration of the βάλλ' οὕτως *motto*— which, incidentally, may have been drawn directly from Homer, instead of from Lucian—quite independently of the content of Michelangelo's invention.

'that Michelangelo, under the spell of this passion, reverted to classical antiquity and completed a series of drawings which strike us as one coherent confession.'[186]

With the exception of the bust of Brutus,[187] which is a political document rather than a manifestation of artistic propensities, no secular subject is found among Michelangelo's works produced after 1534. Even his style gradually developed in a direction opposite to classical ideals, and ultimately he abandoned the compositional principles discernible in his previous works. His violent yet inhibited *contrapposti* had expressed a struggle between the natural and the spiritual. In his latest works this struggle subsides because the spiritual has won the battle. In the Last Judgment, which bears all the earmarks of a transitional period preceding the development of a really 'late' style, we still find reminiscences of the Torso Belvedere, the Niobe group and other Hellenistic works. His very latest works, beginning with the Crucifixion of St. Peter in the Paolina Chapel[188] and paralleled by the sonnets in which he deplores his earlier interest in the 'fables of the world' and takes his refuge to Christ,[189] show an incorporeal transparency and a frozen intensity evocative of mediaeval art, and in several instances the actual use of Gothic prototypes can be observed.[190]

Thus in Michelangelo's last works the dualism between the Christian and the classical was solved. But it was a solution by way of surrender. Another solution became possible only when the conflict between these two spheres ceased to be real, and this because the very principle of reality was shifted to the subjective human consciousness. This occurred in the Baroque period

186. F.Wickhoff, *Bibl.*397, p.433.
187. Cf. C.Tolnay, *Bibl.*350.
188. See F.Baumgart and B.Biagetti, *Bibl.*21, p.16ss.
189. Frey, *Bibl.*101, CL.
190. Cf.,e.g., the late Crucifixions which resume the ancient Y-shaped cross (Fr.129), or (Fr.128,130) show the Virgin Mary in a similar posture as such fourteenth-century works as the Mühlhausen altarpiece of 1385 (ill.,e.g., in C.Glaser, *Bibl.*113, p.20); the Pietà Rondanini (cf. C.Tolnay, *Bibl.*352); the Annunciation, Fr.140 which reverts to the type exemplified by Lorenzo Monaco's panel in the Accademia in Florence (this was pointed out by C.Tolnay in a lecture not yet published, so far as I know); and the Pietà in the Cathedral of Florence.

when entirely new forms of artistic expression such as the modern Drama, the modern Opera and the modern Novel, paralleled the Cartesian '*Cogito ergo sum*;' when the awareness of irreconcilable contrasts could find an outlet in the humour of Cervantes or Shakespeare; and when the combined effort of the various arts transformed both churches and palaces into grandiose show-pieces. This was a solution by way of subjective deliverance. But this subjective deliverance naturally tended towards a gradual disintegration both of Christian faith and classical humanity, the results of which are very much in evidence in the world of today.

PLATE LXIX

125

126

127

PLATE LXX

128

129

130

PLATE LXXI

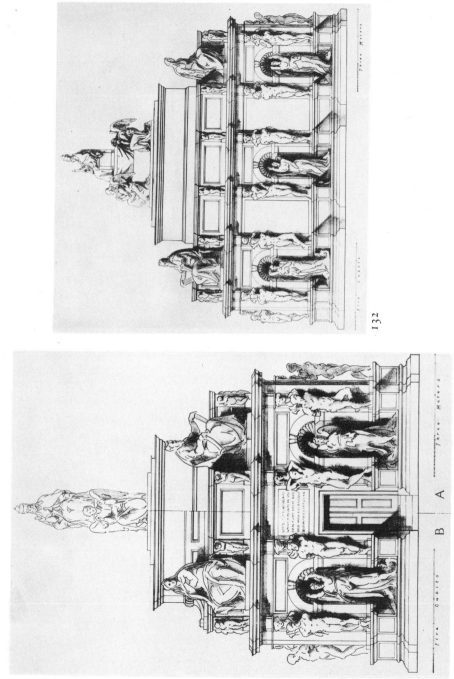

PLATE LXXII

PLATE LXXIII

134

135

PLATE LXXIV

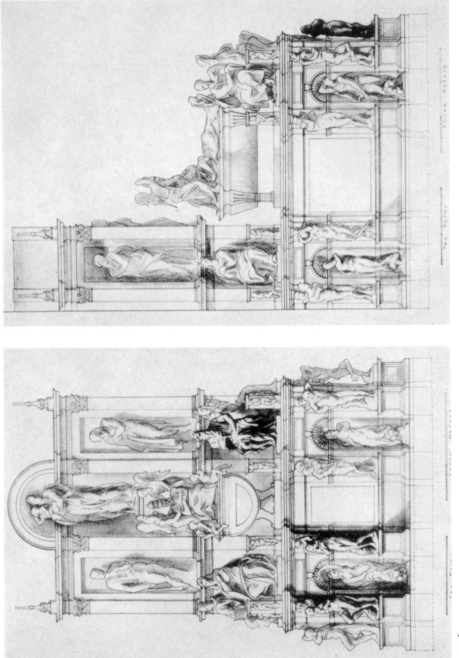

PLATE LXXV

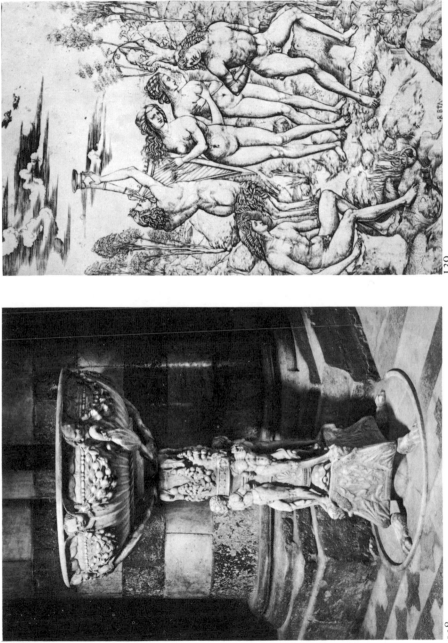

139

138

PLATE LXXVI

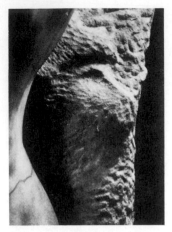

140

141

142

143

PLATE LXXVII

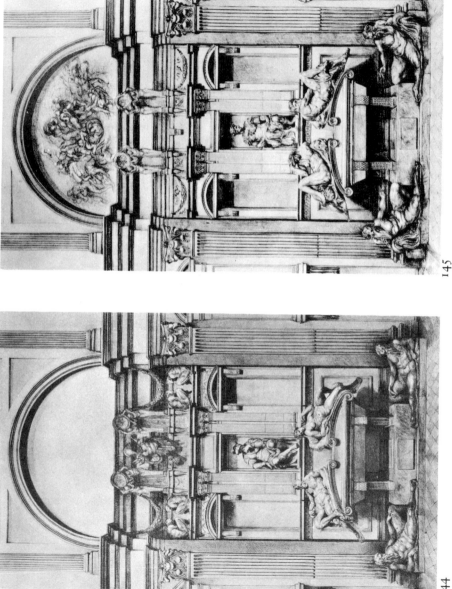

145

144

PLATE LXXVIII

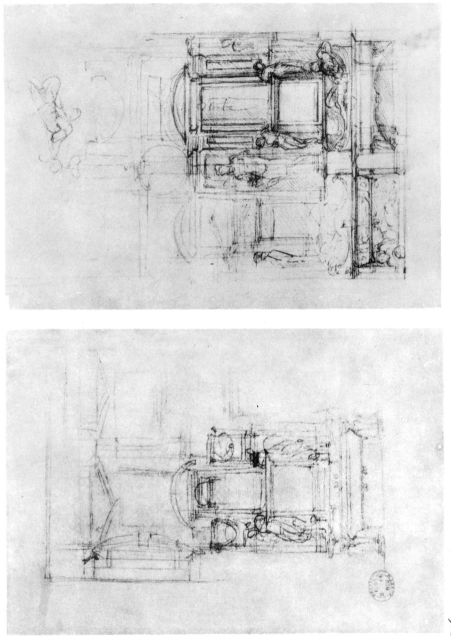

147

146

PLATE LXXIX

149

148

PLATE LXXX

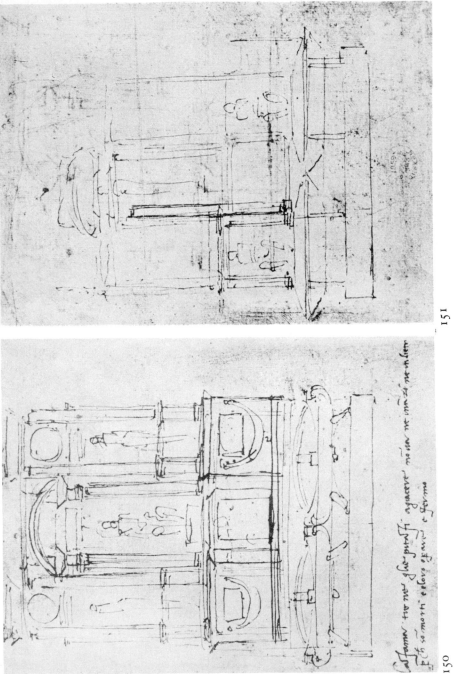

151

150

PLATE LXXXI

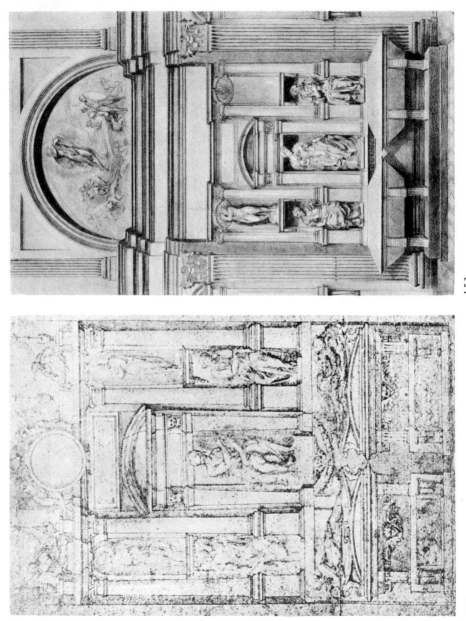

153

152

PLATE LXXXII

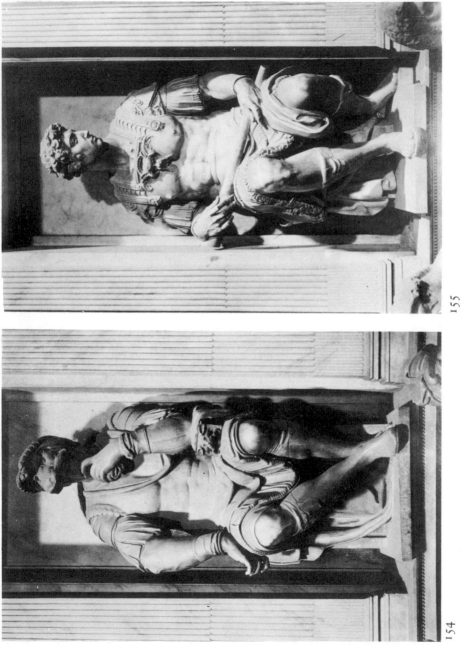

155

154

PLATE LXXXIII

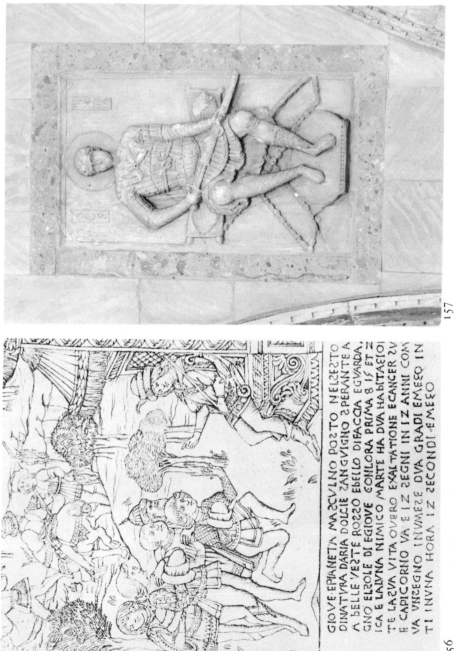

157

156

GIOVE: EPIANETA MASCVLINO POSTO NELCETO
DINATVRA DARIA DOLCIE ZANGVIGNO ZPERANTE A
A BELLE VERTE ROZZO EBELLO DIFACCIA EGVARDA,
GNO ELROLE DI EGIOVE CONLORA PRIMA 8 15 ET 2
ICA E LAIVNA NIMICO MARTE HA DVA HABITATIOI
TE LAZVA VITA OVERO EXALTATIONE ECANCER 2V
E CAPICORNO VA E 12 ZEGNI IN 12 ANNI COM
VA VNZEGNO INVMEZE DVA GRADI EMEZO IN
TI INVNA HORA 12 ZECONDI EMEZO

PLATE LXXXIV

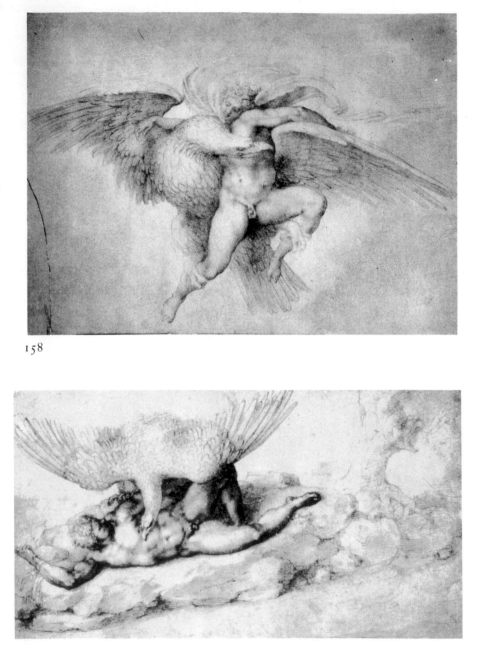

158

159

PLATE LXXXIV

PLATE LXXXVI

PLATE LXXXVII

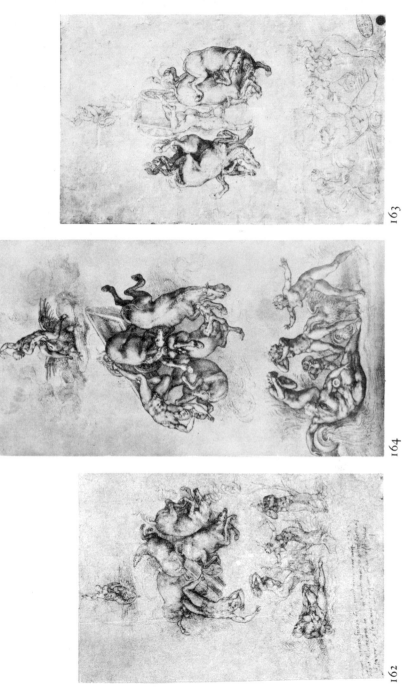

163

164

162

PLATE LXXXVIII

165

166

PLATE LXXXIX

PLATE LXXXX

168

169

170

171

PLATE-LXXXXI

172

PLATE LXXXXII

173

APPENDIX

THE CLAY MODEL IN THE CASA BUONARROTI

I N his article on the Tomb of Julius II,[1] J.Wilde attempts to show that the clay model in the Casa Buonarroti (*fig.172*) which he had successfully reintegrated after having discovered the 'lost' head, had been intended for the companion-piece of the Victory group in the Palazzo Vecchio, and not, as had been generally assumed, for the notorious marble group on the Piazza della Signoria, which had been alternately entrusted to Michelangelo and Bandinelli, and was finally executed by the latter as Hercules conquering Cacus.[2]

It is true that Vasari in his Life of Bandinelli gives the dimensions of the 'bone of contention,' namely a huge block of marble quarried as early as around 1508, but not shipped to Florence until July 20, 1525, as 5 by 9.5 cubits,[3] thus stating its proportions as about 1:2, whereas the proportions of the clay model are about 1:3. However, in a much more authoritative source, namely, the official records of the Community of Florence, the dimensions of the block are given as 2.5 by 8.5 cubits, and as approximately square in ground plan;[4] it was thus even slenderer than 1:3. This is borne out by Bandinelli's Hercules and Cacus group on the Piazza della Signoria which is about 1:3 in front and 1:3.5 in profile.[5] Thus the measurements of the clay model do not militate against its connection with the Piazza project.

1. J.Wilde, *Bibl.*403; *cf. idem, Bibl.*401.
2. See Thode, *Bibl.*340,VOL.II, p.288ss., with references to all the sources here adduced.
3. Vasari, *Bibl.*366, VOL.VI, p.148; Frey, *Bibl.*103, p.365. In the life of Michelangelo, *Bibl.*366, VOL.VII, p.200 (Frey, *Bibl.*103, p.143) the height is even reduced to 9 cubits.
4. Florence, Bibl. Riccardiana, ms. Riccardiano 1854, fol.128, reprinted in G.Gaye, *Bibl.*111, VOL.II, 1840, p.464. I am much indebted to Signore A.Panella for having verified Gaye's reading of the text. Vasari's error might be accounted for by the misprinting of 3 as 5. 3 by 9 cubits, or 3 by 9.5 cubits would be approximately correct.
5. It should be borne in mind that the wide base with the four animals' heads at the corners is not part of the block itself: it consists, as was pointed out to the writer by Mr.H.Arnasson, of a separate piece of marble.

231

As to the iconography, the known facts are these: (1) Around 1508 Michelangelo had intended to use the block for a Hercules and Cacus group.[6] (2) In 1525 he planned, instead, to use it for a group of Hercules and Antaeus.[7] (3) On August 22, 1528, he was formally commissioned to make '*una figura insieme o congiunta con altra, che et come parrà et piacerà a Michelagniolo decto,*'[8] that is: one figure connected with one other, just as he pleased. (4) After this he intended to make a Samson with two Philistines; this composition was known to Vasari and has come down to us in numerous copies, both sculptures and drawings.[9]

Thus, while there is indeed no evidence for Michelangelo's intention to make a Hercules and Cacus group during the years between 1525 and 1530 (when the commission definitely went to Bandinelli), there is no evidence to the contrary either. For, the contract of 1528 gave him *carte blanche* as to the subject; and Vasari's statement that Michelangelo had given up the Hercules and Cacus subject in favour of Samson with two Philistines does not exclude the possibility that he had also made a model of a group with only two figures, not mentioned by Vasari, which either showed Hercules and Cacus, as originally planned, or Samson with only one Philistine.[10] This would even have been more consistent with the official commission of 1528 which not only mentions the fact that the block had been brought to Florence in 1525 '*per farne la Imagine et figura di Cacco,*' but also explicitly stipulates '*una figura insieme o congiunta con* altra,' that is: a group of two figures only.

It is therefore not necessary to abandon the old assumption that the

6. Vasari, *Bibl.*366, VOL.VI, p.148; Frey, *Bibl.*103, p.365.
7. Giovanni Cambi, *Istorie*, reprinted in G.Gaye, *Bibl.*111, *l.c.*, p.464; see the drawings Fr.145 and Fr.31, the proportions of the group being 1:2.5 in Fr.31 and in the left sketch on Fr.145, and 1:2,8 in the right sketch on Fr.145.
8. G.Gaye, *Bibl.*111, *l.c.*, p.98; G.Milanesi, *Bibl.*216, p.700.
9. Vasari, *Bibl.*366, VOL.VI, p.145; Frey, *Bibl.*103, p.368. Cf. *Bibl.*366, VII, p.200; Frey, *Bibl.*103, p.143. The copies of this composition published by A.E.Brinckmann *Bibl.*50 show proportions of about 1:2.5.
10. This interpretation was suggested by K.Frey, *Bibl.*102, text to Fr.157, and is adopted by F.Knapp, *Bibl.*166, p.166.

clay model in the Casa Buonarroti was destined for the Piazza della Signoria, all the less so because this old assumption is corroborated by two facts: (1) The clay model, like the group of Samson with two Philistines, but unlike all the other mature works of Michelangelo's, offers a multitude of satisfactory aspects; the inclination of the chest which, as Wilde points out, impairs the axial symmetry of the group from certain points of view, would have been counterbalanced by the raised right arm with club or jaw-bone. The composition thus seems more suitable for an open square than for one of the niches on the Tomb of Julius II. (2) The head discovered by Wilde is that of a sturdy and even somewhat vulgar-looking fighter, middle-aged and bearded. This type is consistent with the traditional features of both Hercules and Samson, and is in fact almost identical with that of the Samson in the group with two Philistines; but it would hardly have been suitable for a counterpart of the slender adolescent seen in the Victory group.

BIBLIOGRAPHY
OF
REFERENCES CITED[1]

1 ABAECHERLI, A.L., Imperial Symbols on Certain Flavian Coins: *Classical Philology*, xxx, 1935, p.131-140

2 Achiardi, P.d', *Sebastiano del Piombo*, Rome: 1908

3 Alberti, L.B., *De re aedificatoria . . .* , Florence: 1805

4 Alciati, A., *Emblemata . . . denuo ab ipso autore recognita ac, quae desiderabantur, imaginibus locupletata,* Lyons: 1551

5 Alciati, A., *Omnia Andreae Alciati . . . emblemata . . . adjectae novae appendices . . . per C. Minoem.* Paris: 1608
Alciati, A., For the editions by Steyner (1531) and Wechel (1534) *see:* Green.

6 Altrocchi, R., The Calumny of Apelles in the Literature of the Quattrocento: *Publications of the Modern Language Association of America*, xxxvi, 1921, p.454-491

7 Amelli, A.M.(ed.), *Miniature sacre e profane dell'anno* 1023, *illustranti l'enciclopedia med:oevale di Rabano Mauro*, Montecassino: 1896 (Documenti per la storia della miniatura e dell' iconografia)

8 Antal, F., Some Examples of the Role of the Maenad in Florentine Art of the Later Fifteenth and Sixteenth Centuries (The Maenad under the Cross, Part 2): *Journal of the Warburg Institute*, i, 1937, p.71-73

9 Antal, F., Zum Problem des niederländischen Manierismus: *Kritische Berichte zur kunstgeschichtlichen Literatur*, ii, 1928/29, p.207-256

10 *Anthologia graeca*, The Greek Anthology, with an English translation by W.R.Paton . . . , London and New York: 1916-26, 5 vols. (The Loeb Classical Library)

11 *Anthologia latina; sive, poesis latinae supplementum*, F.Buecheler and A.Riese (ed.), Leipzig: 1894-1926, 2 vols. in 5

12 Aretino, P., *Opere*, ordinate ed annotate per M.Fabi, Milan: 1881

13 Aretino, P., *L'oeuvre du divin Aretin* (S.Apollinaire, tr.), Paris: 1909/1910 (Bibliothèque des curieux, 2 vols.)

14 Artelt, W., *Die Quellen der mittelalterlichen Dialogdarstellung*, Berlin: 1934 (Kunstgeschichtliche Studien, Heft 3)

15 Aru, C., La "veduta unica" e il problema del "non finito" in Michelangelo: *L'Arte*, n.s.viii, 1937, p.46-52

16 A(ustin), A.E., Jr., Hylas and the Nymphs, by Piero di Cosimo: *Bulletin of the Wadsworth Atheneum*, x, no.1, January, 1932, p.1-6

17 BABELON, E., *Le Cabinet des antiques . . .* , Paris: 1887-88, 2 vols. (Bibliothèque Nationale; département des médailles et des antiques)

18 Babelon, E., *Description historique et chronologique des monnaies de la République romaine . . .* , Paris: 1885-86, 2 vols.

19 Bacci, P., *La Ricostruzione del pergamo di Giovanni Pisano nel duomo di Pisa*, Milan: 1926

1. Editions listed in the bibliography are editions actually used. Well known authors, such as classical writers and poets like Shakespeare and Chaucer, have been omitted except in cases where a special edition has been used for a special reason.

20 Barberino, F. (F.Egidi, ed.), *I documenti d'amore di Francesco da Barberino*, Rome: 1905-27 (Società filologica romana. Documenti di storia letteraria, 3-6)

21 Baumgart, F., and B.Biagetti, *Die Fresken des Michelangelo, L.Sabbatini und F.Zuccari in der Capella Paolina im Vatikan*, Città del Vaticano: 1934 (Monumenti vaticani di archeologia e d'arte . . . vol.3)

22 Beenken, H., *Romanische Skulptur in Deutschland*, Leipzig: 1924 (Handbücher der Kunstgeschichte)

23 Beenken, H., (Review of J.P.Richter, *Altichiero* . . .): *Zeitschrift für Kunstgeschichte*, v, 1936, p.78-80

24 Beer, R., (ed.), Acten, Registen und Inventare aus dem Archivio General zu Simancas: *Jahrbuch der Kunstsammlungen des Allerhöchsten Kaiserhauses*, xii, 1891

25 Behrendsen, O., *Darstellungen von Planetengottheiten an und in deutschen Bauten*, Strassburg: 1926

26 Bembo, P., *Opere del Cardinale P.Bembo*, vol.i, Milan: 1808 (Società tipografica de' Classici Italiani)

27 Berchorius, Petrus (Pierre Bersuire, Bercheur), *Dictionarii sev repertorii moralis . . . pars prima-tertia*, Venice: 1583
Berchorius, Petrus, see also: Walleys

28 Berenson, B., *The Drawings of Florentine Painters*, New York: 1903

29 Berenson, B., *The Florentine Painters of the Renaissance*, New York: 1909

30 Berenson, B., *Italian Pictures of the Renaissance*, Oxford: 1932

31 Berenson, B., *Pitture Italiane del Rinascimento*, Milan: 1936

32 Bernouilli, J.J., *Römische Ikonographie*, Stuttgart: 1882-91, 2 vols.

33 Bezold, F. von, *Das Fortleben der antiken Götter im mittelalterlichen Humanismus*, Bonn: 1922

34 Bezold, G. von, Tizians himmlische und irdische Liebe: *Mitteilungen aus dem Germanischen Nationalmuseum*, 1903, p.174-177

34a Bing, G., Nugae circa Veritatem: *Journal of the Warburg Institute*, i, 1937, p.304-312

35 Birk, E. von, Inventar der im Besitze des Allerhöchsten Kaiserhauses befindlichen Niederländer Tapeten und Gobelins: *Jahrbuch der Kunstsammlungen des Allerhöchsten Kaiserhauses*, i, 1883, p.213-248 (+13 plates)

36 Boccaccio, G., *Genealogiae Ioannis Boccatii*, etc., Venice: 1511

37 Bocchius(Bocchi), A., *Symbolicarum quaestionum de universo genere . . . libri quinque*, Bologna: 1574

38 Bode, G.H. (ed.), *Scriptores rerum mythicarum latini tres Romae nuper reperti*, Celle: 1834, 2 vols.

39 Bode, W., and W.F.Volbach, Mittelrheinische Ton- und Steinmodel aus der ersten Hälfte des XV Jahrhunderts: *Jahrbuch der Königlich Preussischen Kunstsammlungen*, xxxix, 1918, p.89-134

40 Boer, C.de (ed.), "Ovide Moralisé": *Verhandelingen der koninklijke Akademie van Wetenschapen te Amsterdam*; Afdeeling Letterkunde, vol.i: n.s.xv, 1915; vol.ii: n.s.xxi, 1920; vol.iii: n.s.xxx, 1931/32

41 Boll, F., and C.Bezold, *Sternglaube und Sterndeutung* (3rd ed.), Leipzig and Berlin: 1926

42 Bonsignori, G. (tr.), *Ovidio methamorphoses vulgare*, Venice: 1497

43 Borenius, T., and R.Wittkower, *Catalogue of the Collection of Drawings by the Old Masters, formed by Sir Robert Mond*, London: 1937

44 Borinski, K., *Die Antike in Poetik und Kunsttheorie*, Leipzig: 1914-1924, 2 vols.

45 Borinski, K., Die Deutung der Piero di Cosimo zugeschriebenen Prometheus-Bilder: *Sitzungsberichte der bayrischen Akademie der Wissenschaften*, phil.-hist. Klasse, no.12, 1920

46 Borinski, K., *Die Rätsel Michelangelos*, Munich: 1908

47 Bottari, G.G., and S.Ticozzi, *Raccolta di lettere sulla pittura, scultura, ed architettura*, Milan: 1822-25, 8 vols.

48 Brauer, H., and R.Wittkower, *Die Zeichnungen des Gianlorenzo Bernini*, Berlin: 1931, 2 vols. (Römische Forschungen der Bibliotheca Hertziana, vols.IX-X)

49 Brinckmann, A.E., *Michelangelo, Zeichnungen* . . . , Munich: 1925

50 Brinckmann, A.E., Die Simson-Gruppe des Michelangelo: *Belvedere*, XI, 1927, p.155-159

51 Bruchmann, K.F.H., *Epitheta deorum, quae apud poetas graecos leguntur*, Leipzig: 1893 (Ausführliches Lexikon der griechischen und römischen Mythologie, ed. W.H.Roscher. Supplement, 1893)

52 Byvanck, A.W., Die geïllustreerde Handschriften van Oppianus' Cynegetica: *Mededelingen van het Nederlandsch historisch Instituut te Rome*, v, 1925, p.34-64

53 CAMBI, G., *Istorie*, Florence: 1785-86, 4 vols. (Delizie degli eruditi toscani, vols.XX-XXIII)

54 Camerarius, J., *Symbolorum et emblematum centuriae quattuor*, Nürnberg: 1605

55 Carducho, V., *Dialogos de la Pintura*, Madrid: 1865 (Biblioteca de el arte en España, vol.I)

56 Cartari, V., *Imagini delli dei de gl' antichi* . . . , Venice: 1674

57 Carter, J.G., *Epitheta deorum, quae apud poetas latinos leguntur*, Leipzig: 1902 (Ausführliches Lexikon der griechischen und römischen Mythologie, ed. W.H.Roscher. Supplement, 1902)

58 Cartwright, J., *Isabella d'Este, Marchioness of Mantua, 1474-1539; a Study of the Renaissance*, New York: 1903, 2 vols.

59 Cassirer, E., *Individuum und Kosmos in der Philosophie der Renaissance*, Leipzig: 1927 (Studien der Bibliothek Warburg, 10)

60 Cassirer, E., *Die platonische Renaissance in England und die Schule von Cambridge*, Leipzig: 1932 (Studien der Bibliothek Warburg, 24)

61 Castiglione, B., *Il Cortigiano*, Venice: 1546

62 Cattani di Diacceto, F., *I tre libri d'amore*, Venice: 1561

63 Cellini, B. (C.Milanesi, ed.), *I trattati dell' orificeria e della scultura*, Florence: 1857

64 Cervellini, G.B., La cronaca su Altichiero recentemente pubblicata è falsa: *Atti del R. Istituto Veneto*, xcv, 1936

65 *Christie's Season*, London: 1928-31, 4 vols.

66 Clarac, C.O.F.J.-B. de, *Museé de sculpture antique et moderne* . . . , Paris: Text 1841-1850, Plates 1826-1853

67 Comes, Natalis (Conti, Natale), *Mythologiae, sive explicationis fabularum libri decem* . . . , Frankfurt: 1596
Condivi, A., *see:* Frey, K., *Le Vite.* . . .

68 Cumont, F., *Textes et monuments figurés relatifs aux mystères de Mithra*, Brussels: 1896, 2 vols.

69 Curtius, L., *Die Wandmalerei Pompejis*, Leipzig: 1929

70 DAREMBERG-SAGLIO (ed.), *Dictionnaire des antiquités grecques et romaines*, Paris, 1877-1919, 5 vols.

71 Deknatel, F.B., The Thirteenth Century Sculptures of the Cathedrals of Burgos and Leon: *Art Bulletin*, XVII, 1935, p.242-389

72 Delbrück, R., *Die Consulardiptychen, und verwandte Denkmäler*, Berlin: 1929 (Studien zur spätantiken Kunstgeschichte, 2)

73 Demay, G., *Inventaire des sceaux de Picardie* . . . , Paris: 1877/75 (Inventaire des sceaux de l'Artois et de la Picardie, vol. 2, 1875)

74 DeWald, E.T., *The Illustrations of the Utrecht Psalter*, Princeton: 1932

75 Diehl, C., *La peinture byzantine*, Paris: 1933 (Histoire de l'art byzantin)

76 Diez, F., *Die Poesie der Troubadours*, Leipzig: 1883

77 Doren, A., Fortuna im Mittelalter und in der Renaissance: *Vorträge der*

Bibliothek Warburg, 1922/23, I, p.71-144

78 D(resser), L., The Peaceable Kingdom: *Bulletin of the Worcester Art Museum*, spring, 1934, p.25-30

79 Durand, G., *Monographie de l'église Notre-Dame, Cathédrale d'Amiens*, Paris: 1901-03, 2 vols. (Mémoires de la société des antiquaires de Picardie)

80 Durand, P., *Étude sur l'étimacia, symbole du jugement dernier dans l'iconographie grecque chrétienne*, Chartres: 1868 (Extrait des Mémoires de la société archéologique d'Eure-et-Loire)

81 EGIDI, F., Le miniature dei Codici Barberini dei "Documenti d'Amore": *L'Arte*, v, 1902, p.1-20; 78-95

82 Eisler, R., Orphisch-Dionysische Mysteriengedanken in der christlichen Antike: *Vorträge der Bibliothek Warburg*, 1922/23, II, p.2-end

83 Ellacombe, H.N., *The Plant-lore and Garden-craft of Shakespeare*, London and New York: 1896

84 Equicola, M., *Libro di natura d'amore*, Venice: 1531

85 *Eruditorium Penitentiale*, Paris: 1487

86 Essling, Prince d', *Les livres à figures vénitiens de la fin du XVᵉ siècle et du commencement du XVIᵉ*, Florence and Paris: 1907-14 (Études sur l'art de la gravure sur bois à Venise)

87 Essling, Prince d', and E.Müntz, *Pétrarque; ses études d'art, son influence sur les artistes, ses portraits, et ceux de Laure, l'illustration de ses écrits . . .*, Paris: 1902

88 Eusthatius Makrembolites (L.H. Teucher, ed.), *De Ismeniae et Imenes amoribus libellus, graece et latine*, Leipzig: 1792

88a FALKE, O.von, and Meyer, E., *Bronzegeräte des Mittelalters*, Berlin: 1936

89 Ferrero, G.G., *Il Petrarchismo del Bembo e le rime di Michelangelo*, Torino: 1935 (Estratto da *L'Erma*, VI, 1935)

90 Ficino, M., *Opera, & quae hactenus extetêre, & quae in lucem nunc primum prodiêre omnia . . .*, Basel: 1576, 2 vols.

91 Fiocco, G., *Paolo Veronese, 1528-1588 . . .*, Bologna: c. 1928

92 Fiocco, G., *Venetian painting of the Seicento and the Settecento*, Florence and New York: 1929 (The Pantheon Series)

93 Fischel, O., *Raphaels Zeichnungen*, Berlin: 1913-23

94 Fischel, O., *Tizian* (Klassiker der Kunst, III; 4th ed.), Stuttgart: 1911

95 Förster, R., Laocoon im Mittelalter und in der Renaissance: *Jahrbuch der Königlich Preussischen Kunstsammlungen*, XXVII, 1906, p.149-178

96 Förster, R., Studien zu Mantegna und den Bildern im Studierzimmer der Isabella Gonzaga: *Jahrbuch der Königlich Preussischen Kunstsammlungen*, XXII, 1901, p.78-87; 154-180

97 Förster, R., Tizians himmliche Liebe und Michelangelos Bogenschützen: *Neue Jahrbücher für das klassische Altertum*, XXXV, 1915, p.573-588

98 Förster, R., Die Verleumdung des Apelles in der Renaissance: *Jahrbuch der Königlich Preussischen Kunstsammlungen*, VII, 1887, p.29-56; 89-113

99 Freudenthal, H., *Das Feuer im deutschen Glauben und Brauch*, Berlin: 1931

100 Freund, L., "Amor": *Reallexikon der deutschen Kunstgeschichte*, Stuttgart: 1937, vol.I, col.641-651

101 Frey, K. (ed.), *Die Dichtungen des Michelagniolo Buonarroti*, Berlin: 1897

102 Frey, K., *Die Handzeichnungen Michelagniolos Buonarroti*, Berlin: 1909-11, 3 vols. (vol.3 ed. by F.Knapp)

103 Frey, K. (ed.), *Le Vite di Michelangelo Buonarroti; scritte da Giorgio Vasari e da Ascanio Condivi*, Berlin: 1887 (Sammlung ausgewählter Biographien Vasaris, II)

104 Friedländer, M.I., and J.Rosenberg, *Die*

BIBLIOGRAPHY

Gemälde von Lucas Cranach, Berlin: 1932

105 Friedländer, W., Der antimanieristische Stil um 1590 und sein Verhältnis zum Übersinnlichen: *Vorträge der Bibliothek Warburg*, 1928/29, p.214-243

106 Friedländer, W., Die Enstehung des antiklassischen Stiles in der italienischen Malerei um 1520: *Repertorium für Kunstwissenschaft*, XLVI, 1925, p.49-86

107 Fry, R., Pictures at the Burlington Fine Arts Club: *Burlington Magazine*, XXXVIII, 1921, p.131-137

108 Fulgosus, G.B. (Battista da Campo Fregoso), *Anteros*, Milan: 1496

109 Furtwängler, A., *Die antiken Gemmen; Geschichte der Steinschneidekunst im klassischen Altertum*, Leipzig and Berlin: 1900, 3 vols.

110 GAMBA, C., Piero di Cosimo e i suoi quadri mitologici: *Bolletino d'Arte*, ser.3, XXX, 1936, p.45-57

111 Gaye, G., *Carteggio inedito d'artisti dei secoli XIV, XV, XVI*, Florence: 1839-1840, 3 vols.

112 Giglioli, G.Q., La Calumnia di Apelle: *Rassegna d'arte*, VII, 1920, p.173-182

113 Glaser, C., *Die altdeutsche Malerei*, Munich: 1924

114 Goebel, H., *Wandteppiche*, Leipzig: 1923-34, 3 vols.

115 Goldschmidt, A., *Der Albanipsalter in Hildesheim und seine Beziehung zur symbolischen Kirchenskulptur des XII. Jahrhunderts*, Berlin: 1895

116 Goldschmidt, A., and K.Weitzmann, *Die byzantinischen Elfenbeinskulpturen des X.–XIII. Jahrhunderts*, Berlin: 1930-34, 2 vols.

117 Goldschmidt, A., *Die Elfenbeinskulpturen aus der Zeit der karolingischen und sächsischen Kaiser*, Berlin: 1914, 4 vols. (Denkmäler der deutschen Kunst, II)

118 Goldschmidt, A., *German Illumination* (I. Carolingian period,–II. Ottonian period) Florence and New York: 1928, 2 vols. (The Pantheon Series)

119 Gombrich, E., A Classical Quotation in Michael Angelo's "Sacrifice of Noah": *Journal of the Warburg Institute*, I, 1937, p.69

120 Goodenough, E.R., *By Light, Light; the Mystic Gospel of Hellenistic Judaism*, New Haven and London: 1935

121 Green, H. (ed.), *Andreae Alciati emblematum fontes quattuor*, Manchester: 1870 (The Holbein Society's Fac-simile Reprints, vol.IV)

122 Greifenhagen, A., Zum Saturnglauben der Renaissance: *Die Antike*, XI, 1935, p.67-84

123 Gronau, G., *Aus Raphaels Florentiner Tagen*, Berlin: 1902

124 Grote, L., Carl Wilhelm Kolbe (1758-1835) ein Beitrag zum Sturm und Drang in der Malerei: *Zeitschrift des deutschen Vereins für Kunstwissenschaft*, III, 1936, p.369-389

125 Grünwald, A., Über einige Werke Michelangelos in ihrem Verhältnisse zur Antike: *Jahrbuch der Kunstsammlungen des Allerhöchsten Kaiserhauses*, XXVII, 1907, p.125-153

126 Grünwald, A., Zur Arbeitsweise einiger hervorragender Meister der Renaissance: *Münchner Jahrbuch der bildenden Kunst*, VII, 1912, p.165-177

127 Gyraldus, L.G. (Giraldi), *Opera omnia*, Leyden: 1696

128 HABERDITZL, F.M., Die Lehrer des Rubens: *Jahrbuch der Kunstsammlungen des Allerhöchsten Kaiserhauses*, XXVII, 1907, p.161-235

129 Haberditzl, F.M., *Einblattdrucke des 15. Jahrhunderts in der Hofbibliothek zu Wien*, Vienna: 1920 (Gesellschaft für vervielfältigende Kunst, 1920)

130 Habich, G., Über zwei Prometheus-Bilder angeblich von Piero di Cosimo: *Sitzungsberichte der bayrischen Akademie der Wissenschaften*, phil.-hist. Klasse, 1920, no.2.

131 Haedus (Hoedus), P., *De amoris generibus*, Treviso: 1492

132 Hafftenius (van Haeften), B., *Schola Cordis*, Antwerp: 1635

239

133 Hak, H.J., *Marsilio Ficino*, Amsterdam and Paris: 1934 (Diss. Theol., Utrecht, 1934)

134 Hamann, R., Girl and the Ram: *The Burlington Magazine*, LX, 1932, p.91-97

135 Hauber, A., *Planetenkinderbilder und Sternbilder; zur Geschichte des menschlichen Glaubens und Irrens*, Strassburg: 1916

136 Hawes, Stephen (W.E.Mead, ed.), *The Pastime of Pleasure*, London: 1928 (Early English Text Society, Original Series, vol.173)

137 Heitz, P., *Einblattdrucke des fünfzehnten Jahrhunderts*, Strassburg: 1899-1937, 92 vols.

138 Hekler, A., Michelangelo und die Antike: *Wiener Jahrbuch für Kunstgeschichte*, VII, 1930, p.201-223

139 Helbig, W., *Führer durch die öffentlichen Sammlungen klassischer Altertümer in Rom*, 3rd. ed., Leipzig: 1912/13, 2 vols. (vol.I, Die vatikanischen Sammlungen,)

140 Helbig, W., *Wandgemälde der vom Vesuv verschütteten Städte Campaniens*, Leipzig: 1868

141 Held, J., "Allegorie": *Reallexikon der deutschen Kunstgeschichte*, Stuttgart: 1937, vol.I, col.346-365

142 Henkel, M.D., *De Houtsneden van Mansion's Ovide Moralisé*, Amsterdam: 1922

143 Hermann, H.J., *Die deutschen romanischen Handschriften: Beschreibendes Verzeichnis der illustrierten Handschriften in Oesterreich*, N.F., vol.VIII (Die illuminierten Handschriften und Inkunabeln der Nationalbibliothek in Wien), part II, Leipzig: 1926

144 Hermann, P., *Denkmäler der Malerei des klassischen Altertums*, Munich: 1904-31 (I. Serie)

145 Hildebrand, A., *Das Problem der Form in der bildenden Kunst*, 3rd ed., Strassburg: 1913

146 Hind, A.M., *Catalogue of Early Italian Engravings in the Department of Prints and Drawings in the British Museum*, London: 1910

147 Holtzinger, C.R.von, Ein Idyll des Maximus Planudes: *Zeitschrift für das Oesterreichische Gymnasium*, LXIV, 1893, p.385 ff.

148 Horne, H.P., The Last Communion of St. Jerome by Sandro Botticelli: *The Bulletin of the Metropolitan Museum of Art*, X, 1915, p.52-56; 72-75; 101-105.

149 Houvet, E., *La Cathédrale de Chartres; portail nord*, Chelles: 1919

150 Hugo, P.Hermannus, *Pia desideria, emblematis, elegiis et affectibus SS. patrum illustrata*, Antwerp: 1624

151 *INVENTAIRE des mosaïques de la Gaule et de l'Afrique*, Paris: 1909-25 (Publié sous les auspices de l'Académie des inscriptions et belles-lettres), vol.III

152 JAHN, O., Über einige auf Eros und Psyche bezügliche Kunstwerke: *Berichte der Gesellschaft der Wissenschaften zu Leipzig*, III, 1851, p.153-179

153 Jalabert, D., Le tombeau gothique: *Revue de l'art ancien et moderne*, LXIV, 1933, p.145-166; LXV, 1934, p.11-30

154 (James, M.R.), *The Canterbury Psalter*, London: 1935 (published for the Friends of Canterbury Cathedral)

155 Janson, H., The Putto with the Death's Head: *The Art Bulletin*, XIX, 1937, p.423-449

156 Johnson, J.G., *Catalogue of a collection of paintings and some art objects . . .*, Philadelphia: 1913-14, 3 vols.

157 Jones, H.S., *The Sculptures in the Museo Capitolino (A Catalogue of the Ancient Sculptures preserved in the Municipal Collections of Rome, by Members of the British School at Rome, vol.I)*, Oxford: 1912

158 Jouin, H.A., *Conférences de l'académie royale de peinture et de sculpture*, Paris: 1883

159 Junker, H., Ueber iranische Quellen der hellenistischen Aion-Vorstellung: *Vorträge der Bibliothek Warburg*, 1921/22, p.125-178

160 Justi, C., *Michelangelo; Beiträge zur Erklärung der Werke und des Menschen*, Leipzig: 1900

161 KAISER, V., Der Platonismus Michelangelos: *Zeitschrift für Völkerpsychologie und Sprachwissenschaft*, xv, 1884, p.209-238; xvi, 1886, p.138-187, 209-249

162 Kauffmann, H., *Donatello; eine Einführung in sein Bilden und Denken*, Berlin: 1935

163 Keyser, P. de, i. Het "Vrou Aventure"-Drukkersmerk van Jan van Doesborch; ii. De Houtsnijder van Gerard Leeu's van den Drie Blinde Danssen (Gouda, 1482): *Gentsche Bijdragen tot de Kunstgeschiedenis*, i, 1934, p.45-57; 57-66

164 Kittredge, G.L., To take time by the forelock: *Modern Language Notes*, viii, 1893, p.459-470

165 Klibansky, R., Ein Proklosfund und seine Bedeutung: *Sitzungsberichte des Heidelberger Akademie der Wissenschaften*, phil.-hist. Klasse, xix, 1928/29, no.5

166 Knapp, F., *Michelangelo* (Klassiker der Kunst, vii; 5th ed.), Stuttgart: s.a.

167 Knapp, F., *Piero di Cosimo; ein Uebergangsmeister vom Florentiner Quattrocento zum Cinquecento*, Halle a.S.: 1899

168 Kock, T. (ed.), *Comicorum atticorum fragmenta*, Leipzig: 1880-88, 3 vols.

169 Koechlin, R., Le dieu d'amour et le château d'amour sur les valves de boîtes à miroirs: *Gazette des beaux-arts*, ser.2, lxiii, 1921, p.279-297

170 Koechlin, R., *Les ivoires gothiques français*, Paris: 1924, 3 vols.

171 Körte, W., *Der Palazzo Zuccari in Rom; sein Freskenschmuck und seine Geschichte*, Leipzig: 1935 (Römische Forschungen der Bibliotheca Hertziana, vol.xii)

172 Kohlhaussen, H., *Minnekästchen im Mittelalter*, Berlin: 1928

173 Konrad von Würzburg (A. von Keller, ed.), *Der trojanische Krieg*, Stuttgart: 1858 (Bibliothek des Litterarischens Vereins in Stuttgart, xliv)

174 Kristeller, P., *Holzschnitte im königlichen Kupferstichkabinett zu Berlin*, Berlin: 1915 (Graphische Gesellschaft, xxi)

175 Krumbacher, K., *Geschichte der byzantinischen Literatur, von Justinian bis zum Ende des Oströmischen Reiches*, Munich: 1891 (Handbuch der klassischen Altertumswissenschaft)

176 Kuhn, A., Die Illustration des Rosenromans: *Jahrbuch der Kunstsammlungen des Allerhöchsten Kaiserhauses*, xxxi, 1913/14, p.1-66

177 LABORDE, A. de, *La mort chevauchant un boeuf; origine de cette illustration de l'office des morts dans certains livres d'heures de la fin du XVe siècle*, Paris: 1923

178 Laborde, A. de, *Les manuscrits à peintures de la Cité de Dieu de Saint Augustin*, Paris: 1909, 3 vols. (Société des bibliophiles français)

179 Landino, C., *Christophori Landini libri quattuor*, Strassburg: 1508

180 Landino, C., *Commedia di Danthe Alighieri. . . . . con l'espositione di Cristoforo Landino*, Venice: 1529

181 Landucci, L., (T. del Badia, ed.), *Diario fiorentino dal 1480 al 1516*, Florence: 1883 (Biblioteca di carteggi, diarii, memorie)

182 Lange, K., and F.Fuhse, *Dürers schriftlicher Nachlass auf Grund der Originalhandschriften und theilweise neu entdeckter alter Abschriften*, Halle a.S.: 1893

183 Latini, B., (B.Wiese, ed.), *Der Tesoretto* und *Favolello: Zeitschrift für romanische Philologie*, vii, 1883, p.236-389

184 Latini, B. (P.Chabaille, ed.), *Il tesoro*, Bologna: 1877-83, 4 vols. (Collezione d'opere inedite o rare dei primi tre secoli della lingua)

185 Lazzaroni, M. and A.Muñoz, *Filarete, scultore e architetto del secolo XV*, Rome: 1908

186 Lee, R.W., Castiglione's Influence on Edmund Spenser's Early Hymns:

241

BIBLIOGRAPHY

Philological Quarterly, VII, 1928,
p.65-77

187 Lehmann, P., Fuldaer Studien, neue
Folge: Sitzungsberichte der bayrischen
Akademie der Wissenschaften, phil.-
hist. Klasse, 1927, no.2

188 Lehmann-Hartleben, K., Die antiken
Hafenanlagen des Mittelmeeres;
Beiträge zur Geschichte des Städtebaus
im Altertum, Leipzig: 1923 (Klio,
Beiheft XIV, neue Folge, Heft 1)

189 Lehmann-Hartleben, K., L'arco di
Tito: Bolletino della commissione
archeologica communale, Roma, LXII,
1934, p.89-122

190 Leidinger, G., Das sogenannte Evange-
liar Otto's III (Miniaturen aus Handschriften der königlichen Hof- und
Staatsbibliothek zu München, vol.1),
Munich: 1912-1928

191 Lemaire, Jean (J.Stecher, ed.),
Oeuvres de Jean Lemaire de Belges,
Louvain: 1882

192 Leo Hebraeus, (S.Caramella, ed.), Leo
Hebraeus, . . . dialoghi d'amore, Bari:
1929 (Scrittori d'Italia, 114)

193 Lewis, C.S., The Allegory of Love, a
Study in Mediaeval Tradition, Oxford:
1936

194 Liebeschütz, H., Fulgentius Metaforalis; ein Beitrag zur Geschichte der
antiken Mythologie im Mittelalter,
Leipzig: 1926 (Studien der Bibliothek
Warburg, 4)

195 Lippmann, F., The Seven Planets,
transl. from the German by F.Sim-
monds, London and New York: 1895
(International Chalcographic Society)

196 Lippmann, F., Zeichnungen von
Albrecht Dürer, Berlin: 1883-1929,
7 vols.

197 Lobeck, C.A., Aglaophamus, sive, de
theologiae mysticae graecorum causis
libri tres . . . , Königsberg: 1829,
2 vols.

198 Löwy, E., Stein und Erz in der
statuarischen Kunst: Kunstgeschichtliche Anzeigen, Beiblatt der Mitteilungen des Instituts für oesterreichische

Geschichtsforschung, XXXVI, 1915,
p.5-40

199 Lomazzo, G.P., Trattato dell'arte della
pittura, scoltura, et architettura,
Milan: 1585

200 London. Royal Academy of Arts. A
Commemorative Catalogue of the
Exhibition of Italian Art held in the
Galleries of the Royal Academy,
Burlington House, London, Jan.-Mar.
1930, London: 1931, 2 vols.

201 Lovejoy, A.O., and G.Boas, Primitivism and Related Ideas in Antiquity
(A Documentary History of Primitivism and Related Ideas, vol.1),
Baltimore: 1935

202 Lowes, J.L., The Loveres Maladye of
Hereos: Modern Philology, XI, 1914,
p.491-546

203 Lukomski, G., I maestri della architettura classica Italiana da Vitruvio allo
Scamozzi, Milan: 1933

204 Lydgate, J. (E.Sieper, ed.), Lydgate's
Reson and Sensuallyte, London:
1901-03 (Early English Text Society,
extra series, LXXXIV, LXXXIX)

205 MACHAUT, Guillaume de,
(E.Hoepffner, ed.), Oeuvres de
Guillaume Machaut, Paris: 1908-21
(Société des anciens textes français)

206 Mackeprang, M., V.Madsen, and C.S.
Petersen, Greek and Latin Illuminated
Manuscripts . . . in Danish Collec-
tions, Copenhagen: 1921

207 Mâle, E., L'art religieux de la fin du
moyen âge en France; étude sur l'iconographie du moyen âge et sur ses sources
d'inspiration, Paris: 1925

208 Manilli, J., Villa Borghese fuori di
Porta Pinciana, Rome: 1650

209 Marle, R. van, The Development of the
Italian Schools of Painting, The
Hague: 1923-36, 16 vols.

210 Marle, R. van, Iconographie de l'art
profane au moyen âge et à la renaissance et la décoration des demeures,
The Hague: 1931-32, 2 vols.

211 M(ather), F.J. (Note to W.Rankin,
Cassone-Fronts in American Collec-

242

tions): *The Burlington Magazine*, 1907, X, p.335

212 Mayer, W., *Das Leben und die Werke der Brüder Mattheus und Paul Bril*, Leipzig: 1910 (Kunstgeschichtliche Monographien, XIV)

213 McComb, A., *Agnolo Bronzino; his Life and Works*, Cambridge, Mass.: 1928

214 Migne, J.P., *Patrologiae cursus completus; seu bibliotheca universalis. . . . omnium ss. patrum, doctorum scriptorumque ecclesiasticorum, sive latinorum, sive graecorum*, Paris: 1857 ff.

215 Milanesi, G. (ed.), *Les correspondants de Michelange. 1. Sebastiano del Piombo*, Paris: 1890 (Bibliothèque internationale de l'art)

216 Milanesi, G. (ed.), *Le lettere di Michelangelo Buonarroti*, Florence: 1875

217 *Mirabilia urbis Romae. The Marvels of Rome, or a Picture of the Golden City*, Eng. ed. by F.M.Nichols, London and Rome: 1889

218 Molza, F.M., *Poesie*, Milan: 1808 (Società tipografica de' Classici Italiani)

219 Montelatici, D., *Villa Borghese fuori di Porta Pinciana, con l'ornamenti che si osservano nel di lei palazzo, e con le figure delle statue più singolari*, Rome: 1700

220 *Monumenta Germaniae, Poetarum latinorum medii aevi*, Berlin: 1881-1923, 4 vols.

221 Morassi, A., Una "Camera d'amore" nel Castello di Avio: *Festschrift für Julius Schlosser zum 60. Geburtstage*, Zürich: (1926), p.99-103

222 Moreau-Nélaton, E., *La cathédrale de Reims*, Paris: (1915)

223 Morelli, G., *Italian Painters . . . , The Galleries of Munich and Dresden (Italian Painters . . . , vol.II)*, London: 1893

224 Morey, C.R., *Christian Art*, London and New York: c. 1935

224a Morgan, Charles E.II, A Pyxis by the "Eretria Painter:" *Worcester Museum Annual*, II, 1936/37, p.29-31

225 Mueller, E. von, Die Augenbinde der Justitia: *Zeitschrift für christliche Kunst*, XVIII, 1905, no.4, col.107-122; no.5, col.142-152

226 Müntz, E., La tradition antique au moyen âge: *Journal des savants*, 1888, p.40-50

227 NANNUCCI, V., *Manuale della letteratura del primo secolo della lingua Italiana*, Florence: 1883.

227a New York. The Metropolitan Museum of Art. *Tiepolo and his Contemporaries*, an exhibition held March 14 through April 24, 1938, New York: 1938

228 New York. Pierpont Morgan Library. *Exhibition of illuminated manuscripts held at the New York Public Library*, 1933/34

229 *The New Yorker*, XI, New York: 1936

230 Nordenfalk, C., *Der Kalender vom Jahr 354 und die lateinische Buchmalerei der IV. Jahrhunderts*, Gothenburg: 1936 (Göteborgs K. Vetenskaps-och vitterhets samhälle, Handlinger, 5. foljder, ser.A, bd.5, nr.2, 1936)

231 Nykl, A.R., '*Alī ibn Ahmed telled Ibn Hazm, A Book Containing the Risāla known as The Dove's Neckring*, Paris: 1931

232 OECHELHÄUSER, A. von, *Der Bilderkreis zum Wälschen Gaste des Thomasin von Zerclaere*, Heidelberg: 1890

233 Oeri, J., Hellenisches in der Mediceercapelle: *Basler Nachrichten*, LXI, July 3, 1905

234 Oldenbourg, R., *Rubens* (Klassiker der Kunst, V; 4th ed.), Stuttgart: s.a.

235 Omont, H., *Miniatures des plus anciens manuscrits grecs de la Bibliothèque Nationale du VIe au XIVe siècle*, Paris: 1929

236 Overbeck, J.A., *Die antiken Schriftquellen zur Geschichte der bildenden Künste bei den Griechen*, Leipzig: 1868

237 PANOFSKY, E., Bemerkungen zu Dagobert Frey's Michelangelostudien: *Archiv für Geschichte und Aesthetik der Architektur* (supplement of *Wasmuths Monatshefte für Baukunst und Städtebau*), I, 1920/21, p.35-45

238 Panofsky, E. and F.Saxl, Classical Mythology in Mediaeval Art: *Metropolitan Museum Studies*, IV, 2, 1933, p.228-280

239 Panofsky, E., The Early History of Man in a series of paintings by Piero di Cosimo: *Journal of the Warburg Institute*, I, 1937, p.12-30.

240 Panofsky, E., Das erste Blatt aus dem "Libro" Giorgio Vasaris; eine Studie über die Beurteilung der Gothik in der italienischen Renaissance: *Städel-Jahrbuch*, VI, 1930, p.25-72

241 Panofsky, E., Et in Arcadia ego: *Philosophy and History*, Essays presented to Ernst Cassirer, Oxford: 1936, p.223-254

242 Panofsky, E., Der gefesselte Eros: *Oud Holland*, L, 1933, p.193-217

243 Panofsky, E., *Hercules am Scheidewege, und andere antike Bildstoffe in der neueren Kunst*, Leipzig: 1930 (Studien der Bibliothek Warburg, 18)

244 Panofsky, E., *"Idea"; ein Beitrag zur Begriffsgeschichte der älteren Kunsttheorie*, Leipzig: 1924 (Studien der Bibliothek Warburg, 5)

245 Panofsky, E., Kopie oder Fälschung; ein Beitrag zur Kritik einiger Zeichnungen aus der Werkstatt Michelangelos: *Zeitschrift für bildende Kunst*, LXI, 1927/28, p.221-243

246 Panofsky, E., Die Michelangelo-Literatur seit 1914: *Wiener Jahrbuch für Kunstgeschichte*, I, 1921, Buchbesprechungen, col.1-63

247 Panofsky, E., Piero di Cosimo's "Discovery of Honey" in the Worcester Art Museum: *Worcester Art Museum Annual*, II, 1936/37, p.32-43

248 Panofsky, E., Zum Problem der Beschreibung und Inhaltsdeutung von Werken der bildenden Kunst: *Logos*, XXI, 1932, p.103-119

249 Panofsky, E., Die Treppe der Libreria di S. Lorenzo; Bemerkungen zu einer unveröffentlichten Skizze Michelangelos: *Monatshefte für Kunstwissenschaft*, XV, 1922, p.262-274

250 Panofsky, E., The first two projects of Michelangelo's Tomb of Julius II: *Art Bulletin*, XIX, 1937, p.561-579

251 Panofsky, E., Zwei Dürerprobleme: *Münchner Jahrbuch der bildenden Kunst*, N.F., VIII, 1931, p.1-48

252 Panofsky, E., and F.Saxl, *Dürers "Melencolia I", eine quellen- und typengeschichtliche Untersuchung*, Berlin and Leipzig: 1923 (Studien der Bibliothek Warburg, 2)

253 Panofsky, E., and F.Saxl, *Melancholia*, Second edition of Bibl.252 (*in print*)

254 Patch, H.R., *The Goddess Fortuna in Mediaeval Literature*, Cambridge, Mass.: 1927

255 Patch, H.R., *The Tradition of the Goddess Fortuna in Medieval Philosophy and Literature*, Northampton: 1922 (Smith College Studies in Modern Languages, VOL.III)

256 Pauly-Wissowa, *Realencyclopaedie der Klassischen Altertumswissenschaft*, Stuttgart: 1894-1937

257 Un Père Capucin, *Les emblêmes d'amour divin et humain ensemble*, Paris: 1631

258 Perrier, F., *Segmenta nobilium signorum et statuarum quae temporis dentem inuidium* [sic] *euasere*, Rome: 1638; Dutch ed., *Eigentlyke Afbeeldinge van Hondert der aldervermaerdste Statuen of Antique-Beelden Staande binnen Romen*, Amsterdam: 1702

259 Petrarch, *Petrarcha . . .*, Venice (Johannes Capcasa di Codeca): 1493

260 Petrarch, *Petrarcha con doi commenti sopra li sonetti et canzone*, Trieste (Gregorio de Gregorii): 1508

261 Petrarch, *Il Petrarca con l'espositione d'A. Vellutello*, Venice: 1560

262 Petrarch, *Il Petrarcha con l'espositione de M.G.A. Gesualdo*, Venice: 1581

263 Petrarch (N.Festa, ed.), *Petrarca,*

L'Africa, edizione critica, Florence: 1926 (Edizione nazionale delle opere di Francesco Petrarca, I)

264 Petrarch (V.Rossi, ed.), *Petrarca, Le Familiari*, edizione critica, Florence: 1933, 1937 (Edizione nazionale delle opere di Francesco Petrarca, X,XI)

265 Pflaum, H., *Die Idee der Liebe-Leone Ebreo*, Tübingen: 1926 (Heidelberger Abhandlungen zur Philosophie und ihrer Geschichte, VII)

266 Pico della Mirandola, G., *Ioannis Pici Mirandulani philosophi . . . omnia quae extant opera*, Venice: 1557

267 Pico della Mirandola, *Opere di Giovanni Benivieni Firentino . . . con una canzona dello amor celeste & divino, col commento dello Ill. S. conte Giovanni Pico Mirandolano*, Venice: 1522

268 Pillion, L., Le portail roman de la Cathédrale de Reims: *Gazette des beaux-arts*, XXXII, 1904, p.177-199

269 Planiscig, L., *Andrea Riccio*, Vienna: 1927

270 Poensgen, G., Beiträge zu Baldung und seinem Kreis: *Zeitschrift für Kunstgeschichte*, VI, 1937, p.36-41

271 Poglayen-Neuwall, S., Eine Tizianeske Toilette der Venus aus dem Cranach-Kreis: *Münchner Jahrbuch der bildenden Kunst*, N.F., VI, 1929, p.167-199

272 Popp, A.E., Kopie oder Fälschung, zu dem Aufsatz von Erwin Panofsky: *Zeitschrift für bildende Kunst*, LXII, 1928/29, p.54-67

273 Popp, A.E., *Die Medici-Kapelle Michelangelos*, Munich: 1922

274 Popp, A.E., (Review of A.E.Brinckmann, *Michelangelo Zeichnungen*): *Belvedere*, VIII, 1925, "Forum", p.72-75

275 Porter, A.K., *Romanesque Sculpture of the Pilgrimage Roads*, Boston: 1923, 10 vols.

276 REINACH, S., *Répertoire des reliefs grecs et romains*, Paris: 1909-12, 3 vols.

277 Reinach, S., *Répertoire de la statuaire grecque et romaine*, Paris: 1897-1930, 6 vols.

278 Ricci, C., *Monumenti sepolcrali di lettori dello studio bolognese nei secoli XIII, XIV, XV*, Bologna: 1888

279 Richardson, J., *Traité de la peinture et de la sculpture*, Amsterdam: 1728, 3 vols.

280 Richter, J.P., *Altichiero*, Leipzig: 1935

281 Richter, J.P., *The Literary Works of Leonardo da Vinci*, London: 1883, 2 vols.

282 Richter, J.P., *La Collezione Hertz e gli affreschi di Giulio Romano nel Palazzo Zuccari*, Leipzig: 1928 (Römische Forschungen der Bibliotheca Hertziana, v)

283 Ridolfi, C. (D. von Hadeln, ed.), *Le maraviglie dell'arte, overo le vite de gl'illustri pittori veneti, e dello stato*, Berlin: 1914-24, 2 vols.

284 Ripa, C., *Iconologia . . . , nella quale si descrivono diverse imagini di virtu, vitij, passioni humane . . . .*, Rome: 1613

285 Ripa, C., *Iconologia di Cesare Ripa . . . divisa in tre libri . . .*, Venice: 1645

286 Robb, N.A., *Neoplatonism of the Italian Renaissance*, London: 1935

287 Robert, C., *Die antiken Sarkophag-Reliefs*, Berlin: 1890-1919, 3 vols.

288 Roman de la Rose (E.Langlois, ed.), *Le Roman de la Rose par Guillaume de Lorris et Jean de Meun*, Paris: 1914-24, 5 vols. (Société des anciens textes français)

289 Rome, Vatican Library, *Menologio di Basilio II (Cod. Vaticano Greco 1613)*, Torino: 1907 (Codices Vaticani selecti phototypice expressi consilio et opera curatorum Biliothecae Vaticanae, VIII)

290 Roscher, W.H. (ed.), *Ausführliches Lexicon der griechischen und römischen Mythologie*, Leipzig: 1884-1924, 5 vols.

291 Rousselot, P., *Pour l'histoire du problème de l'amour au moyen âge*, Münster: 1908 (Beiträge zur Geschichte der Philosophie des Mittelalters, VI, 6)

292 Rusconi, G.A., *I dieci libri d'architettura*, Venice: 1660

293 SAITTA, G., *La filosofia di Marsilio Ficino*, Messina: 1923 (Studi filosofici, 15)

294 Salomon, R., *Opicinus de Canistris; Weltbild und Bekenntnisse eines avignonesischen Klerikers des 14. Jahrhunderts*, London: 1936 (Studies of the Warburg Institute, 1 a-b)

295 Saxl, F., Aller Tugenden und Laster Abbildung: *Festschrift für Julius Schlosser zum 60. Geburtstäge*, Zürich: (1926), p.104-121

296 Saxl, F., Beiträge zu einer Geschichte der Planetendarstellungen im Orient und Occident: *Der Islam*, III, 1912, p.151-177

297 Saxl, F., Frühes Christentum und spätes Heidentum in ihren künstlerischen Ausdrucksformen; 1. Der Dialog als Thema der christlichen Kunst: *Wiener Jahrbuch für Kunstgeschichte*, II, 1923, p.63-77

298 Saxl, F., *Mithras; typengeschichtliche Untersuchungen*, Berlin: 1931

299 Saxl, F., Verzeichnis astrologischer und mythologischer illustrierter Handschriften des lateinischen Mittelalters in römischen Bibliotheken: *Sitzungsberichte der Heidelberger Akademie der Wissenschaften*, phil.-hist. Klasse, VI, 1915

300 Saxl, F., Veritas Filia Temporis: *Philosophy and History*, Essays presented to Ernst Cassirer, Oxford: 1936, p.197-222

301 Scheffler, L. von, *Michelangelo; eine Renaissancestudie*, Altenburg: 1892

302 Schering, A., *Geschichte der Musik in Beispielen*, Leipzig: 1931

303 Schlosser, J. von, Die ältesten Medaillen und die Antike: *Jahrbuch der Kunstsammlungen des Allerhöchsten Kaiserhauses*, XVIII, 1897, p.64-108

304 Schlosser, J. von, Giustos Fresken in Padua und die Vorläufer der Stanza della Segnatura: *Jahrbuch der Kunstsammlungen des Allerhöchsten Kaiserhauses*, XVII, 1896, p.13-100

305 Schlosser, J. von, *Die Kunstliteratur; ein Handbuch zur Quellenkunde der neueren Kunstgeschichte*, Vienna: 1924

306 Schlosser, J. von, Über einige Antiken Ghibertis: *Jahrbuch der Kunstsammlungen des Allerhöchsten Kaiserhauses*, XXIV, 1903, p.124-159

307 Schramm, P.E., *Die deutschen Kaiser und Könige in Bildern ihrer Zeit*, Leipzig: 1928 (Leipzig, Universität, Institut für Kultur- und Universalgeschichte; Veröffentlichungen, Die Entwicklung des menschlichen Bildnisses, 1)

308 Schreiber, *Die Hellenistischen Reliefbilder*, Leipzig: 1894, 2 vols.

309 Schubring, P., *Cassoni; Truhen und Truhenbilder der italienischen Frührenaissance*, Leipzig: 1915

310 Schubring, P., *Cassoni, Supplement*, Leipzig: 1923

311 Schubring, P., *Die Plastik Sienas im Quattrocento*, Berlin: 1907

312 Schulze, H., *Die Werke des Angelo Bronzino*, Strassburg: 1911

313 Scott, W., *Hermetica; The Ancient Greek and Latin Writings . . . . . ascribed to Hermes Trismegistus*, Oxford: 1924-36, 4 vols.

314 Servius, *Commentarii in Virgilii opera*, Strassburg edition of about 1473 (Rusch; Hain, *Rep. Bibl.*14704)

315 Servius, *Commentarii in Virgilii opera*, Milan edition of 1475 (Zarotus; Hain, *Rep. Bibl.*14708)

316 Seta, A. della, *Religione e arte figurata*, Rome: 1912; Eng. transl., *Religion and Art*, London: 1914.

317 Shapley, F.R., A Student of Ancient Ceramics, Antonio Pollajuolo: *The Art Bulletin*, II, 1919, p.78-86

318 Sieper, E., *Les échecs amoureux . . .*, Weimar: 1898 (Litterarhistorische Forschungen, ed. by J.Schick and M. von Waldberg, vol.IX)

319 Simson, O.G. von, *Zur Genealogie der weltlichen Apotheose im Barock*, Strassburg: 1936 (Akademische Abhandlungen zur Kulturgeschichte)

320 Springer-Michaelis (ed.), *Handbuch der Kunstgeschichte*, 9th ed., Leipzig: 1911

321 Stark, C.B., *Systematik und Geschichte der Archäologie der Kunst* (Handbuch der Archäologie der Kunst, 1), Leipzig: 1880

322 Steinmann, E., *Das Geheimnis der Medicigräber Michelangelos*, Leipzig: 1907 (Kunstgeschichtliche Monographien, 4)

323 Steinmann, E. and R.Wittkower, *Michelangelo-Bibliographie*, 1510-1926, Leipzig: 1927 (Römische Forschungen der Bibliotheca Hertziana, vol.I)

324 Steinmann, E., *Michelangelo im Spiegel seiner Zeit*, Leipzig: 1930 (Römische Forschungen der Bibliotheca Hertziana, vol.VIII)

325 Stettiner, R., *Die illustrierten Prudentius-Handschriften*, Berlin: 1895, 1905

326 Stevenson, B., *Home Book of Quotations*, New York: 1934

326a Stillwell, R., *Antioch-on-the-Orontes*, II, Princeton, N.J., 1938

327 Strauch, L., "Angler": *Reallexikon der deutschen Kunstgeschichte*, Stuttgart: 1937, vol.I, col.694-698

328 Strzygowski, J., Die Calenderbilder des Chronographen vom Jahre 354: *Jahrbuch des Kaiserlichen, deutschen archaelogischen Instituts*, 1888, Ergänzungsheft 1

329 Strzygowski, J., *Koptische Kunst*, Vienna: 1904 (Catalogue général des antiquités égyptiennes du Musée du Caire)

330 Suidas (A.Adler, ed.), *Suidae lexicon*, Leipzig: 1928-35, 4 vols. (Lexicographi graeci, vol.I)

331 Supino, J.B., *Giotto*, Florence: 1920

332 Swarzenski, G., *Nicolo Pisano*, Frankfurt a.M.: 1926 (Meister der Plastik, 1)

333 Swarzenski, G., *Die Regensburger Buchmalerei des X. und XI. Jahrhunderts*, Leipzig: 1901 (Denkmäler der süddeutschen Malerei des frühen Mittelalters, 1)

334 Swarzenski, G., *Die Salzburger Malerei von den ersten Anfängen bis zur Blütezeit des romanischen Stils*, Leipzig: 1908-13 (Denkmäler der süddeutschen Malerei des frühen Mittelalters, II)

335 TAYLOR, L.R., The "Sellisternium" and the Theatrical "Pompa": *Classical Philology*, XXX, 1935, p.122-130

336 Terret, V., *La sculpture bourguignonne aux XIIe et XIIIe siècles, ses origines et ses sources d'inspiration; Cluny, Autun*, Paris: 1914

337 Tetius, H., *Aedes Barberinae ad Quirinalem*, Rome: 1642

338 Thiele, G., *Antike Himmelsbilder*, Berlin: 1898

339 Thode, H., *Giotto*, Bielefeld and Leipzig: 1899

340 Thode, H., *Michelangelo; Kritische Untersuchungen über seine Werke*, Berlin: 1908-13, 3 vols.

341 Thomas, A., *Francesco da Barberino et la littérature provençale en Italie au moyen âge*, Paris: 1883 (Bibliothèque des écoles françaises d'Athènes et de Rome, 35)

Thomasin von Zerclaere, *see:* von Oechelhäuser

342 Tietze-Conrat, E., Lost Michelangelo Reconstructed: *The Burlington Magazine*, LXVIII, 1936, p.163-70

343 Tinti, M., *Angelo Bronzino*, Florence: 1920 (Piccola collezione d'arte, 10)

344 Toffanin, G., *Il cinquecento* (Storia letteraria d'Italia), Milan: 1929

345 Tolnay (Tolnai), K. (C.), von (de), *Pierre Bruegel l'Ancien*, Brussels: 1935 (Bibliothèque du XVIe siècle)

346 Tolnay, K., Zu den späten architektonischen Projekten Michelangelos: *Jahrbuch der Königlich Preussischen Kunstsammlungen*, LI, 1930, p.1-48 (LIII, 1932, p.231-253)

347 Tolnay, K., Die Handzeichnungen Michelangelos im Archivio Buonarroti: *Münchner Jahrbuch der bildenden Kunst*, N.F., V, 1928, p.377-476

348 Tolnay, K., Die Handzeichnungen Michelangelos im Codex Vaticanus: *Repertorium für Kunstwissenschaft*, XLVIII, 1927, p.157-205

349 Tolnay, K., "Michelangelo": Thieme-Becker, *Allgemeines Künstlerlexikon.*, vol.xxiv, p.515-526

350 Tolnay, K., Michelangelo's Bust of Brutus: *The Burlington Magazine*, LXVII, 1935, p.23-29

351 Tolnay, K., Michelangelostudien; die Jugendwerke: *Jahrbuch der preussischen Kunstsammlungen*, LIV, 1933, p.95-122

352 Tolnay, K., The Rondanini Pietà: *The Burlington Magazine*, LXV, 1935, p.146-157

353 Tolnay, K., Eine Sklavenskizze Michelangelos: *Münchner Jahrbuch der bildenden Kunst*, N.F., v, 1928, p.70-85

354 Tolnay, K., Studi sulla Capella Medicea, I: *L'Arte*, n.s., v, 1934, p.5-44

355 Tolnay, K., Studi sulla Capella Medicea, II: *L'Arte*, n.s., v, 1934, p.281-307

356 Tolnay, K., The Visionary Evangelists of the Reichenau School: *The Burlington Magazine*, LXIX, 1936, p.257-263

357 Tolnay, K., La volta della capella Sistina: *Bolletino d'arte*, ser.3, xxix, 1935/36, p.389-408

358 Tomitano, B., *Quattro libri della lingua Thoscana*, . . . *ove si prova la philosophia esser necessaria al perfetto oratore, & poeta*, Padua: 1570

359 Torr, C., *Ancient Ships*, Cambridge: 1895

360 Torre, A. della, *Storia dell'Accademia Platonica di Firenze*, Florence: 1902 (Pubblicazioni del R. Istituto de' studi superiori . . . in Firenze. Sezione di filosofia e filologia, 28)

361 Typotius (Typoets), J., *Symbola divina et humana pontificum, imperatorum, regum*, Arnheim: 1666

362 ULMANN, H., Piero di Cosimo: *Jahrbuch der Königlich Preussischen Kunstsammlungen*, XVII, 1896, p.120-142

363 VALENTINER, W.R., *Tino di Camaino, a Sienese Sculptor of the Fourteenth Century*, Paris: 1935

364 Valentiner, W.R., *Unknown Masterpieces in Public and Private Collections*,

London: 1930
Valeys, *see*: Walleys

365 Varchi, B., *Lezzioni* . . . *sopra diverse materie, poetiche e filosofiche, raccolte nuovamente*, Florence: 1590

366 Vasari, G. (G.Milanesi, ed.), *Le vite de' più eccellenti pittori, scrittori ed architettori, scritte da Giorgio Vasari, pittore Aretino*, Florence: 1878-1906, 9 vols.

367 Vasari, G. (E.Jaeschke, ed.), *Giorgio Vasari, Die Lebensbeschreibungen der berühmtesten Architekten, Bildhauer und Maler*, vol.II: *Die Florentiner Maler des 15. Jahrhunderts*, Strassburg: 1904

368 Vasari, G., (E.Bianchi, ed.), *Le vite de' più eccellenti pittori, scultori, architetti.* . . . , Florence: 1930
Vasari, *see*: Frey, *Le vite* . . . ,
Veen, Otho van, see: Venius

369 Venice. *Mostra Tiziano, Venezia, 25 apr.–4 nov. 1935, Catalogo delle opere*, Venice: 1935

370 Venius (Vaenius, van Veen), O., *Amorum Emblemata*, Antwerp: 1608; reprint: *Les emblèmes de l'amour humain*, Brussels: 1667

371 Venius (Vaenius, van Veen), O., *Amoris divini emblemata*, Antwerp: 1615

372 Venturi, A., *Correggio* (German edition), Leipzig and Rome: 1926

373 Venturi, A., *Giovanni Pisano; his Life and Work*, Paris: 1928

374 Venturi, A., *Studi dal vero; attraverso le raccolte artistiche d'Europa*, Milan: 1927

374a Venturi, L., Contributi: *L'Arte*, n.s., III, 1932, p.484

375 Venturi, L., *Pitture Italiane in America*, Milan: 1931

376 Vinci, Leonardo da (H.Ludwig, ed.), *Das Buch von der Malerei*, Vienna: 1881 (Quellenschriften zur Kunstgeschichte, 15-18)

377 Viollet-le-Duc, E.E., *Dictionnaire raisonné d'architecture française du XIᵉ au XVIᵉ siècle*, Paris: 1858-68, 10 vols.

BIBLIOGRAPHY

378 *Vitruvius* [Giocondo, Fra.] *M.Vitruvius per Jocundum solito castigatior factus cum figuris et tabula ut jam legi et intelligi possit*, Venice: 1511

379 *Vitruvius* [Cesariano, C.] *Di Lucio Vitruuio Pollione De Architettura. . . . libri dece. . . . , commentato ed affigurato da Cesare Cesariano*, Como: 1521

380 *Vitruvius* [Martin, J.] *M.V.P. Architectura ou art de bien bastir, mis de latin en françois par Jean Martin*, Paris: 1547

381 *Vitruvius* [Poleni, J.] *M.V.P. Architectura . . . cum exercitationibus notisque . . . J.Poleni*, Udine: 1825-30, 4 vols.

382 *Vitruvius* [Ryff] *M.V.P. De Architectura, Vitruvius Teutsch, durch G.H.Rivium*, Nürnberg: 1548

383 Vitry, P., *La cathédrale de Reims; architecture et sculpture*, Paris: 1919, 2 vols.

384 Voss, H., *Die Malerei des Barock in Rom*, Berlin: 1924

385 Vossler, K., *Die philosophischen Grundlagen zum "süssen neuen Stil" des G.Guinicelli, G.Cavalcanti und Dante Alighieri*, Heidelberg: 1904

386 WALLEYS (Walleis, Valeys), T., *Metamorphosis Ovidiana moraliter. . . . explanata*, Paris: 1515

387 Warburg, A., *Gesammelte Schriften*, Leipzig: 1932, 2 vols. (ed. Bibliothek Warburg)

388 Weber, P., *Geistliches Schauspiel und kirchliche Kunst in ihrem Verhältnis erläutert an einer Ikonographie der Kirche und Synagoge*, Stuttgart: 1894

389 Wechssler, E., *Eros und Minne: Vorträge der Bibliothek Warburg*, 1921/22, p.69-93

390 Wechssler, E., *Das Kulturproblem des Minnesangs; Studien zur Vorgeschichte der Renaissance* (vol.1. *Minnesang und Christentum*), Halle a.S.: 1909

391 Weege, F., Das goldene Haus des Nero: *Jahrbuch des Kaiserlichen deutschen archaeologischen Instituts*, XXVIII, 1913, p.127-244

392 Weinberger, M., Nino Pisano: *The Art Bulletin*, XIX, 1937, p.58-91

393 Weingartner, J., Die profane Wandmalerei Tirols im Mittelalter: *Münchner Jahrbuch der bildenden Kunst*, N.F., V, 1928, p.1-63

394 Weisbach, W., *Trionfi*, Berlin: 1919

395 Weitzmann, K., Das Evangelion im Skevophylakion zu Lawra: *Seminarium Kondakovianum*, VIII, 1936, p.83-98

396 Westwood, J.O., *Facsimiles of the Miniatures and Ornaments of Anglo-Saxon and Irish Manuscripts*, London: 1868

397 Wickhoff, F., Die Antike im Bildungsgange Michelangelos: *Mitteilungen des Instituts für oesterreichische Geschichtsforschung*, III, 1882, p.408-435

398 Wickhoff, F., Die Gestalt Amors in der Phantasie des Italienischen Mittelalters: *Jahrbuch der Königlich Preussischen Kunstsammlungen*, XI, 1890, p.41-53

399 Wickhoff, F., Venezianische Bilder: *Jahrbuch der Königlich Preussischen Kunstsammlungen*, XXIII, 1902, p.118-123

400 Wilczek, K., Ein Bildnis des Alfonso Davalos von Tizian: *Zeitschrift für bildende Kunst*, LXIII, 1929/30, p.240-247

401 Wilde, J., Due modelli di Michelangelo ricomposti: *Dedalo*, VIII, 1927/28, p.653-671

402 Wilde, J., Eine Studie Michelangelos nach der Antike: *Mitteilungen des Kunsthistorischen Instituts in Florenz*, IV, 1932, p.41-64

403 Wilde, J., Zwei Modelle Michelangelos für das Julius-Grabmal: *Jahrbuch der kunsthistorischen Sammlungen in Wien*, N.F., II, 1928, p.199-218

404 Wilpert, J., *Die Römischen Mosaiken und Malereien der kirchlichen Bauten vom IV. bis XIII. Jahrhundert*, Freiburg im Breisgau: 1916, 4 vols.

405 Wind, E., Platonic Justice, Designed by Raphael: *Journal of the Warburg Institute*, I, 1937, p.69-70

406 Wind, E., Donatello's Judith: a Symbol of "Sanctimonia": *Journal of the Warburg Institute*, I, 1937, p.62

407 Wind, E., *Das Experiment und die Metaphysik, zur Auflösung der kosmologischen Antinomien*, Tübingen: 1934 (Beiträge zur Philosophie und ihrer Geschichte, 3)

408 Wind, E., Some Points of Contact between History and Science: *Philosophy and History*, Essays presented to Ernst Cassirer, Oxford: 1936, p.255-264

408a Wittkower, R., Chance, Time and Virtue: *Journal of the Warburg Institute*, I, 1937, p.313-321

409 Wölfflin, H., *Die klassische Kunst. Eine Einführung in die italienische Renaissance*, Munich: 1898

410 Wolters, P., Ein Apotropaion aus Baden im Aargau: *Bonner Jahrbücher*, CXVIII, 1909, p.257-274

411 Wolters, P., Faden und Knoten als Amulett: *Archiv für Religionswissenschaft*, VIII, Beiheft, 1905, p.1-22

412 Worcester, Mass. Worcester Art Museum. *"The Dark Ages"*, *Loan Exhibition*, 1937

413 Zonta, G. (ed.), *Trattati d'amore del cinquecento*, Bari: 1912 (Scrittori d'Italia)

INDEX

INDEX

Bernard, St., 107 N.

Berni, Francesco, 178 N.

Bernini, Gianlorenzo, Fountain of the Four Rivers, 176; 'Time' (drawing), 82 N.; 'Time and Death' (clay model), 83 N.; 'Time Revealing Truth' (drawing), 83, *fig*.59; 'Time with Obelisk' (drawing), 82, *fig*.58b; 'Time with Roundel' (drawing), 83 N., *fig*.58a; tomb of Alexander VII, 83

Bersuire, *see* Berchorius

Bettini, Bartolommeo, 90 N.

Betussi, Giuseppe, 125 N., 147 N., 148 N.

Biblia Pauperum, 6 N.

Boccaccio, 23 *s*., 38 *ss*., 42, 43, 45, 49 N., 50, 53, 102 N., 107, 120, 126 N., 146 N., 161 N., 214 N., 219 N.

Bocchius, Achilles, 124 N., 126 N., 169 N., 215, 216 N., illustration: 'Platonic Love Chasing Blind Cupid,' 128, *fig*.101

Bologna, Giovanni, 'Combat of Vice and Virtue,' 194

Bonaventura, Pseudo-, 7

Bonsignori, F.G., 222 N.

Bordone, Paris, 'Mars Disarming Cupid,' 163; 'Matrimonial Allegory,' 163, *fig*.121

Bosch, Jerome, 55

Botticelli, Sandro, 33; 'Calumny of Apelles,' 159, *fig*.115, 'Venus and Mars,' 63 N.

Bracciolini, Poggio, 39 N.

Bramante, Donato, 178 N.

Brant, Sebastian, 110 N.

Breughel, Peter, 'Fettered Monkeys,' 196 N., *fig*.141

Bridget, St., 7

Bril, Matthew, engraving (after a lost picture), 'Death Stealing Weapons of Cupid,' 125, *fig*.104

Bronzino, Angelo, 'Allegory of Luxury,' 86 *ss*., *fig*.66; 'Descent into Limbo,' 84 N.; 'Flora,' 85 *s*., 207; 'Innocence,' 84 *ss*.; Portrait of Andrea Doria, 6 N.; 'Venus and Cupid' (Budapest), 90 N.; *see also* Rost

Brunetto Latini, *see* Latini

Bruni, Leonardo, tomb of, 187

Bruno, Giordano, 146

Bruno, Presbyter, tomb of, 185, *fig*.134

Buti, Francesco da, 215

CABASSOLES, Philippe de, Bishop of Cavaillon, 179 N.

Cacus, 231 *s*.

Caesar, 212

Cain, 40

252

Cairo: Museum, Coptic relief, 'Opportunity,' 72 N.

Calandra, Giovanni Jacopo, 146 N., 153

Callimachus, 99

Cambi, Giovanni, 57, 58 N., 232 N.

Cambino, Andrea, 204 N.

Camerarius, Joachim, 60 N.

Campo Fregoso, *see* Fulgosus

Caraglio, Jacopo, engraving *B.24* (after Rosso Fiorentino), 'Saturn,' 79, *fig*.47

Caravaggio, Michelangelo da, '*Amor vincitore,*' 194

Carducho, Vincenzio, 217 N.

Carracci, Annibale,'Eros and Anteros,' 126 N.

Cartari, Vincenzo, 75 N., 81 N., 85 N., 125 N., 148 N., 164 N., 168 N., 204; illustration: 'Eros and Anteros,' 126, *fig*.96.

Cassirer, Ernst, 8, 16

Castiglione, Baldassare, 140 N., 146 *s*., 148

Catullus, 60 N., 96 N., 125 N.

Cavalcanti, Guido, 101, 103 N., 146 N.

Cavalieri, Tommaso, 180, 183 N., 216 *ss*.

Cavretto, *see* Haedus

Cellini, Benvenuto, 175; 'Deliverance of Andromeda,' 175 N.

Celsus, 63 N.

Ceresara, Paride da, 153 N.

Cesariano, Cesare, 41 N.

Charis, 163 N.

Chartres: Cathedral (north transept), sculptures, 'Blind Night Led by Day,' 111 N., *fig*.80

Chaucer, 103, 121

Chicago: Art Institute, 'Education of Cupid' (imitation of Titian), 165 N.

Christina, Queen of Sweden, 82 N.

Cicero, 96 N., 130, 155 N., 214 N.; (pseudo), 124 N.

Cielo, 188 N.; *see also* Personifications: Heaven

Cima da Conegliano, 'Procession of Silenus,' 55 N.

Ciminelli dall'Aquila, Seraphin, 125 N.

Claudius Minos, *see* Minos

Clement VII, Pope, 199 N., 213

Cleveland: The Cleveland Museum of Art, Byzantine ivory casket, 'Adam and Eve Doing Blacksmith's Work,' 45 N., *fig*.25

Clio, 82 N.

Cluny: Musée Ochier, capital, 'Wind Gods,' 46 N.

Cocytus, 204; *see also* Personifications: River-Gods

Coelus, 20 N.; *see also* Personifications: Heaven

INDEX

INDEX

KĀ, 183
Konrad von Würzburg, *see* Würzburg
Krates, 74 N.
Kronos, 72 N., 73 *ss.*, 81 N.; *see also* Saturn

LANCELOT, 116 N.
Landino, Cristoforo, 130, 135 N., 138 N., 139, 179, 192, 202, 204, 214 *s.*, 216, 219 N., 223
Landucci, Luca, 47 N.
Laocoön, 19
Latini, Brunetto, 22, 49 N., 106
Latona, 216
Laura, 100
Leah, 138; *see also* Michelangelo, Rome: S. Pietro in Vincoli
Le Brun, Charles, 181 N.
Leibniz, 130 N.
Leipzig: Städtisches Museum, 'Love Spell,' 156 N.
Lemaire, Jean de Belge, 125 N.
Leo X, Pope, 199 N.
Leochares, 216 N.
Leo Hebraeus, 125 N., 145
Leon: Cloister of the Cathedral, tomb of Martin Fernandez, 185 N.
Leonardo da Vinci, 174 N., 182; 'Last Supper,' 8
Leyden: University Library, *Cod.Voss., G.G.F.4*, 'Allegory of Sloth,' 88 N., *fig.65; Cod. Voss. lat.79*, 28, 75 N.; *Cod. Voss. lat.* Oct.16, 'Cupid and Jest in Flight,' 98, *fig.72*
Libellus de Imaginibus Deorum, 23, 44 N., 45, 46 N., 106
Liber, *see* Bacchus
Libergier, Hugues, tomb of, 184 N.
Lippi, Filippino, 'St.Philip Exorcizing the Dragon,' 70, 191, 194
Lomazzo, Giovanni Paolo, 120 N., 167 N., 174 N., 217
London: British Museum, Classical relief, 'Apotheosis of Homer,' 72 N.; *Ms. Add.19352*, 98 N.; *Ms. Cott. Galba E. IV*, 'Truth Lifted by Earth,' 157, *fig. 112; Ms. Cott. Tib. C.VI*, 115 N.; *Ms. Sloane 3983*, 77 N.
Victoria and Albert Museum Byzantine ivory casket, 'Abduction of Europa,' 26, 97, *fig.69*
Lorris, Guillaume de, *see* Roman de la Rose
Lucian, 58, 84, 153, 158, 227 N.
Lucretius, 40 *ss.*, 53, 54 N., 55, 63 N., 65, 96 N., 99, 142, 164, 180, 217, 219 N.
Luna, 25, 85 N., 202 N.
Lydgate, John, 102 N., 103, 121

Lyons: Bibliothèque de la Ville, *Ms.742*, 'The Abduction of Europa,' 29 N., *fig.15*
Bibliothèque du Palais des Arts, *Ms.22*, 'Cupid,' 98; illus.p.95
Lysippos, 'Kairos,' 72 N.

MACHAUT, Guillaume de, 101 N.
Macrobius, 74 N., 79 N., 209 N., 211 N.
Maffei, Francesco, 'Judith' (so-called 'Salome'), 12 *s., fig.3*
Magdeburg: Cathedral, tomb of Friedrich von Wettin, 184 N.
Manilli, Jacopo, 167
Mantegna, Andrea, 'Deposition of Christ,' 222; 'Realm of Comus,' 153
Marcus Aurelius, 181 N.
Mars, 49, 56, 63 N., 91, 133, 162 *ss.*
Marsyas, 154
Martha, 138, 139
Martianus Capella, 22, 74 N.
Mary Magdelene, 138, 139
Mary, Queen of Hungary, 217 N.
Marzuppini, Carlo, tomb of, *see* Settignano
Masinissa, 109 N.
Matthew, St., 20 N.
Maura, St., 212 N.
Mayence: Cathedral, tombs of Archbishops Siegfried von Eppstein and Peter Aspelt (Aichspalt), 185 N.
Medea, 21, 172
Medici, de': Cosimo, 91, 130
Giovanni, tomb of, *see* Verrocchio
Giuliano, 199, 205; *see also* Michelangelo, Florence: S.Lorenzo
Giuliano the Younger, Duke of Nemours, 199
Giulio, Cardinal, *see* Clement VII
Lorenzo the Magnificent, 130, 199; *see also* Michelangelo, Florence: S.Lorenzo
Lorenzo the Younger, Duke of Urbino, 57, 199
Piero, tomb of, *see* Verrocchio
Meleagros, 184
Mengs, Raphael, 'Allegory of Time and History,' 82 N.
Mercury, 26, 85 N., 91, 149; *see also* Hermes
Meun, Jean de, *see* Roman de la Rose
Michael Scotus, 26 N., 77 N.
Michault, Pierre, 112 *s.*, 124
Michelangelo, 7, 33, 88 N., 146, 171 *ss.*
Florence:
Accademia, 'Boboli Slaves,' 177, 178 N., 188 N., 190, 218; 'David,' 173 N.; 'River-God' (model), 201, 202; 'St.Matthew,' 173 N.
Casa Buonarroti, 'Battle of Lapiths and

255

INDEX

256

INDEX

INDEX

INDEX